DELINQUENCY AND CITIZENSHIP

Delinquency and Citizenship

Reclaiming the Young Offender, 1914–1948

VICTOR BAILEY

CLARENDON PRESS · OXFORD
1987

Oxford University Press, Walton Street, OX2 6DP
Oxford New York Toronto
Delhi Bombay Calcutta Madras Karachi
Petaling Jaya Singapore Hong Kong Tokyo
Nairobi Dar es Salaam Cape Town
Melbourne Auckland
and associated companies in
Beirut Berlin Ibadan Nicosia

Oxford is a trade mark of Oxford University Press

Published in the United States
by Oxford University Press, New York

British Library Cataloguing in Publication Data
Bailey, Victor
Delinquency and citizenship : reclaiming the young offender.
1. Juvenile corrections — England — History — 20th century
I. Title
364.6 HV9146.A5
ISBN 0-19-822664-0

Library of Congress Cataloging in Publication Data
Bailey, Victor
Delinquency and citizenship.
Bibliography: p.
Includes index.
1. Juvenile corrections — Great Britain — History — 20th century. 2. Juvenile justice, Administration of — Great Britain — History — 20th century. 3. Juvenile delinquency — Great Britain — History — 20th century.
I. Title.
HV9145.A5B35 1987 364.3'6'0941 86-10419
ISBN 0-19-822664-0

Typeset by Burgess & Son (Abingdon) Ltd.
Printed in Great Britain
at the University Printing House, Oxford
by David Stanford
Printer to the University

FOR JENNIFER

Preface

This study is an amended report on the History of Modern Criminal Policy, commissioned by, and originally submitted to the Home Office Research Unit. In this connection I would like to thank Mr John Croft, former head of the Research Unit, who befriended the project at every stage, not least by arranging for considerable financial support; and Sir Leon Radzinowicz and Dr Roger Hood, without whose backing the project would have been stillborn. I was helped inestimably by Dr Jane Morgan, who put aside her own work on the policing of industrial disorders to provide research assistance for two industrious years. I would also like to record my thanks to the Provost and Fellows of Worcester College, Oxford, who provided me with an ideal environment in which to complete this work. Lord Briggs, in particular, gave me essential help and encouragement.

My feel for the criminal justice system of the inter-war period was greatly assisted by conversation and correspondence with the following staff, past and present, of the Home Office and prison service: Alan Bainton, H. E. Crew, Tom Hayes, C. P. Hill, Michael Selby, H. J. Taylor, and L. M. Wiltshire. Lord Fenner Brockway drew on his personal experience of imprisonment as a conscientious objector to help me with the Great War years. I also benefited from a week's voluntary residence, as one of Her Majesty's guests, in Gaynes Hall open Borstal. For the use of documents and private papers I am grateful to K. J. Neale, Revd R. R. Maxwell, Frank Foster, and John Ross. I acknowledge gratefully help from the staffs of the Public Record Office, the Bodleian Library, the Home Office Library, and the libraries of the Social Studies Faculty and the Centre for Criminological Research in Oxford. I am obliged to the Controller of Her Majesty's Stationery Office for permission to make use of Crown Copyright material in the Public Record Office, and to Miss Mary White for permission to consult Home Office and Prison Commission papers.

Many other people have helped me at the various stages of my research. I would particularly like to express my gratitude to Andrew Ashworth, Harry Pitt, and Kenneth O. Morgan, who made many valuable suggestions; to Sarah McCabe who scrutinized the entire book with her customary precision; to Joyce Bellamy and John Saville who made available the rich biographical seams of the *Dictionary of Labour Biography*; to Ivon Asquith who helped in the book's publication; and to Jennifer Donnelly, Hilary Prior, and Terry Sharman for typing and secretarial assistance. It only remains to say that I alone bear the responsibility for the arguments presented in this book.

V.B.

August 1985

Contents

Tables and Figures

TABLES

FIGURES

Abbreviations

The following abbreviations have been used throughout the text:

ACTO	Advisory Council on the Treatment of Offenders
BA	Borstal Association
CDPAS	Central Discharged Prisoners' Aid Society
CETS	Church of England Temperance Society
DNB	*Dictionary of National Biography*
HO	Home Office
JOC	Juvenile Organisations Committee
LSE	London School of Economics
NAPO	National Association of Probation Officers
NUT	National Union of Teachers
P.Com.	Prison Commissioners
PP	Parliamentary Papers
PRO	Public Record Office
TES	*Times Educational Supplement*
YOC	Departmental Committee on the Treatment of Young Offenders (1927)

Note: All references cited were published in London unless otherwise stated.

We want our sons and the sons of the country to be reliable, capable of hard endeavour and of 'sticking it' when things are difficult and disagreeable. We want to be able to trust their word and their sense of honour. We want them to be loyal to each other and to their leaders, playing fair and square all round, and ready to give a helping hand to those who need it. From the civic point of view we want them to have a sense of what Herbert Spencer used to call 'reciprocity', which is the very antithesis of an anti-social or class-conscious attitude. It implies a sturdy independence, a wish to stand on our own feet, and to give back to the community at least as much as we have drawn from it. In fact we want them to develop strongly a sense of citizen duties as well as citizen rights, so that each may function worthily in his own corner of our Great 'Society'.

L. Le Mesurier (Leader of the Women Workers at the Boys' Prison, London), *Boys in Trouble: A Study of Adolescent Crime and its Treatment* (1931), p. 208

Introduction

The departure point for this study is the judgement that historians of the welfare state tend to ignore the strand of social policy to do with crime and punishment. It is rare for either the Children Act of 1908 or the Criminal Justice Act of 1948 to be linked to the changes in health, education, and social security which stamp the first fifty years of this century as an era of collectivist thought and social reconstruction. This study attempts to repair the neglect which modern criminal policy has suffered. It is concerned with the formation, development, and implementation of criminal policy for young offenders, in the general context of the social and welfare activities of the modern state. In the belief that historians should maintain the complexity of historical reality, the study tries to be precise in describing events, aware of distinct and differing views, and even-handed in the estimate of influential groups and individuals. Much less will be found on the testimony of those defined as delinquents than on those whose ideas and actions led to changes in the way delinquency was perceived and prevented. By this is meant the key Home Office administrators in the Children's Branch and the Prison Commission, the spokesmen of the penal reform lobby, and the staffs of the juvenile court, probation service, and Borstal reformatories.

Modern-day interpretations of the history of delinquency commonly emphasize the social-control motives of the advocates and founders of juvenile courts and reformatory institutions. The 'child-savers', according to one historian, invented the pathology of delinquency, and established courts and reformatories as instruments of coercive class control.[1] The aim of the present study, however, is to account for policy change without imputing conspiratorial designs to a ruling élite, yet without reducing change either to *ad hoc* adaptation to crisis and contingency, or to the triumphs of a humanitarian crusade. The first step to this end is to place these men and women reformers in their social and ideological setting.

[1] Anthony Platt, *The Child Savers: The Invention of Delinquency* (Chicago, 1969). See also Robert M. Mennel, 'Attitudes and Policies toward Juvenile Delinquency in the United States: A Historiographical Review', in M. Tonry and N. Morris (eds.), *Crime and Justice* (Chicago, 1983), vol. 4, pp. 191–224.

An effective starting point is the landslide Liberal victory of 1906 and the subsequent introduction of the juvenile court and the probation service (meant especially for young offenders), which consolidated the earlier provisions of child welfare, notably school meals and medical inspection and treatment. These state-sponsored measures of social welfare aimed to alleviate the worst evils of capitalist society (disease, malnutrition, criminality) which both the social enquiries of Booth and Rowntree and the inadequacies of Boer War recruits had graphically uncovered.[2] From this legislative climax, however, we need to return to the social philosophy that lay behind the legislation, to the new liberal theory of society of the 1870s.

In this theory, put briefly, social progress was an inevitable evolutionary process, which the state could assist by acting on behalf of 'the social good' to improve health, housing, and nutrition. Men would, thereby, become morally improved. In a word, state intervention would so 'moralize' capitalism as to assist the attainment of full citizenship by the working class. Citizenship also made demands on the privileged: it obliged them to inform the disadvantaged of their political and social rights and duties, a task earnestly taken up by the young university men who 'crossed the bridges' to reside in the settlement houses of south and east London.[3]

The significance, for present purposes, of the intellectual force represented by the views of new liberals like T. H. Green and Arnold Toynbee, is that it shaped the *idée fixe* of a number of people who figured prominently in the making of criminal policy. None more so than Alec Paterson, the architect of the improved Borstal system of the inter-war years, and leading light of the reforming Prison Commission of that period. Paterson's career as social reformer began in a south London settlement house, on the basis of which he wrote *Across the Bridges* in 1911. In this work Paterson declared that the only antidote to 'systematic socialism' was the raising up of an industrious generation of parents, by way of feeding the present generation of school children. State action of this kind would ultimately help working-class families to help themselves. Paterson also argued for a voluntary ethics, based

[2] See D. Fraser, *The Evolution of the British Welfare State* (1981), ch. 7, *passim*.

[3] See Melvin Richter, *The Politics of Conscience: T. H. Green and his Age* (1964), ch. 11, *passim*; G. Stedman Jones, *Outcast London* (Oxford, 1971), pp. 7–11; P. Clarke, *Liberals and Social Democrats* (Cambridge, 1978), ch. 1, *passim*.

on a mutual knowledge and understanding between masters and men, as an essential preface to compulsory legislation: 'For deliverance [of the underfed and over-worked] will not come from a thousand laws or constitutions, but only by the growth of a race of a thousand parents and employers, good landlords and builders.'[4] These people could help to remove 'the causes which turn lusty boys into weaklings, and sap the country of a hardy rank and file'. As Paterson concluded, in the prevalent language of 'national efficiency', no country 'that has joined the struggle for supremacy' could tolerate the existing waste of human material.[5]

An integral feature of the new liberal outlook was a set of attitudes to crime and punishment associated with the European positivist movement. According to the positivists, criminal behaviour was deeply influenced, some were to say determined, by the offender's innate constitution and environment; punishment was to be adapted to the offender's rehabilitation. Positivists were still concerned with the individual offender; hence, internal constraints upon behaviour were as important as external ones. Paterson's cure for delinquency was 'the distraction afforded by more healthy pursuits and the building of a surer self-control'. Positivists also sought the control of crime essentially through the criminal law and the penal system. But they took account of social conditions, at least as they affected the individual, and they believed, as Leon Radzinowicz stated, 'that penal policy and welfare policy could interact in the prevention and control of crime...' Liberal legislation to diminish poverty could not but have bearing upon the efficacy of the juvenile court, the Borstal system and the probation service. The new penal legislation, moreover, brought out the true 'colonizing' instinct in all social positivists. 'As soon as the growing elasticity and reasonableness of the present system is realized', predicted Paterson, 'employers will with confidence prosecute their office-boys and junior clerks, while mere dismissal will rank as the lazy indifference of a callous and uncharitable man.'[6]

Social positivism gradually permeated the 'leftish intelligentsia' of

[4] A. Paterson, *Across the Bridges, or Life By the South London River-Side* (1911), p. 271. See also pp. 29, 33, and 133.

[5] Ibid., pp. 256–7.

[6] Ibid., pp. 174 and 190; L. Radzinowicz and J. King, *The Growth of Crime* (1977), p. 63. cf. V. Bailey, 'Churchill as Home Secretary: Prison Reform', *History Today*, March 1985, pp. 10–13.

the inter-war years. Whether in official administration, in parliament, or amongst the band of voluntary penal reformers, 'the progressive centre' was instrumental in moulding inter-war views on the explanation of deviance and on the strategies for eliminating delinquency. The influence of these reformers came to a head in the optimistic climate of post-war Britain.[7] From 1945, changes in both criminal and welfare policy derived, in large part, from the promise and expectation of social reconstruction. The commitment to an expanded welfare state brought not only the National Health Service, an enlarged social insurance scheme, and a new Education Act, but also the Criminal Justice Act of 1948, which, like its 1938 predecessor, sought a more humane and effective treatment of young offenders. Significantly, the statute drew heavily on the social positivism of previous decades and particularly on the ideas and actions of Alec Paterson, the 'Beveridge' of the penal system.

The role of the 'liberal progressive' reformers is the central theme of the study. Exactly what views they held, how they got their views incorporated into policy, how they defended their advance positions, are the questions that have been borne in mind at all stages of the work. In answering these questions, other influences on the formation of law and policy between 1914 and 1948 have inevitably come into focus: the incidence of crime, the impact of war, the effect of mass unemployment. At one level, therefore, this book is a historical case-study of both law-making and penal policy-making. At another level, it is a detailed survey of the main developments in policy for young offenders, particularly during the inter-war years. Above all, however, the book is an assessment of the system of beliefs about the causes and correctives of delinquency, beliefs which were first tempered in the heat of voluntary social work amongst school-children and working youths. Thus ideology, not pragmatism, exerted a powerful influence on the policies and procedures of English criminal justice, an ideology that shares, much more than historians have allowed, a similar intellectual heritage with the better-known measures which compose the modern welfare state.

[7] cf. Paul Addison, *The Road to 1945* (1982, first edn. 1975), pp. 183, 277–8, for an account of the triumph in the 1940s of the progressive centre.

PART I

The Young Delinquent: Causes and Correctives

I

Juvenile Delinquency and the Juvenile Court, 1914–1926

The Children Act of 1908, or the 'Children's Charter', as it was popularly known, drew together late-Victorian legislation on the protection of children (concerning employment, begging, parental cruelty, or neglect) and established an age-specific legal apparatus for the consideration of deprived and delinquent juveniles. For delinquents under sixteen years of age, the Act enshrined the principle that offenders should receive special treatment at all stages of the judicial process: while on remand, when before the newly-established juvenile courts, and following the sentence of the court.[1] The Prevention of Crime Act of the same year set the seal of government approval on the system of Borstal training, the main institutional alternative to the supposed evils of imprisonment for offenders aged sixteen to twenty-one.[2] A year earlier, the Probation of Offenders Act had provided for the appointment of probation officers, with the aim of reclaiming young offenders within their home environment through the personal influence of a social worker.[3] But these celebrated changes in penal policy were rather overtaken by events. Magistrates and police court missionaries had barely accustomed themselves to the full implications of the new legislation before the 1914–18 war shifted attention away from the penal system. Within a few years of the outbreak of war, the Home Office was facing a sharp increase in juvenile crime and consequent congestion in the industrial and reformatory schools.[4] Hence, with the end of the Great War, under the stimulus of a zeal for 'reconstruction', penal reformers pressed not only for the full implementation of the pre-war legislation but also for improvements to it. Whilst the pace of penal change remained sluggish, as in most

[1] Jean S. Heywood, *Children in Care* (1959).

[2] R. G. Hood, *Borstal Re-Assessed* (1965), ch. 1.

[3] Dorothy Bochel, *Probation and After-Care. Its Development in England and Wales*, chs. 1–2.

[4] Gordon Rose, *The Struggle for Penal Reform* (1961), pp. 88–91. See Tables 1(a), 1(b), 2 and 3.

areas of social policy in the aftermath of the war, the next two decades were indeed to witness far-reaching administrative and legislative changes in the treatment of young offenders.

The following chapters assess the diverse origins of these inter-war developments, starting in the first six chapters with the young delinquent under the age of sixteen. Inevitably the Children and Young Persons Act 1933, is the focus of these early chapters, a statute which underlay juvenile justice until the end of the 1960s. It took a number of years for this important measure to reach the statute-book, during which time a blend of social, economic and intellectual determinants were at work. Penal reform groups, penal practitioners, government enquiries, and civil servants all played a part in this act of law creation. Their contribution will be assessed in relation to the main strands of the new legislation: juvenile courts, remand homes, probation, certified schools, and corporal punishment. But an essential preface to this study of policy-making is an assessment of the prevailing conception of delinquency. By the 1920s, it will be argued, there existed a widely-held view of the causes and cures of juvenile delinquency, a perspective which borrowed extensively from the insights of practical social work with children, and which guided so many of the policy changes of the inter-war period.

The Social Conception of Delinquency

A discussion of the inter-war conception of delinquency needs to start with the 'discovery' of adolescence in the late nineteenth and early twentieth centuries, and with the response to this 'social problem' in the form of youth movements aiming to improve the leisure time of young working-class adolescents.[5] In part, the 'discovery' of adolescence was related to a new awareness of the emotional and physical changes of puberty, which were deemed to make adolescence a formative, not to say perilous, period. Many adolescents, it was believed, failed during this period to make a proper adjustment to their social surroundings as defined by home, school, and work. The outcome could be the first steps in a criminal calling. As Stanley Hall claimed in his renowned study, 'adolescence is pre-eminently the

[5] See John R. Gillis, *Youth and History* (New York, 1974), ch. 4; id., 'The Evolution of Juvenile Delinquency in England, 1890–1914', *Past and Present*, 67 (1975), pp. 96–126; John Springhall, *Youth, Empire and Society. British Youth Movements 1883–1940* (1977).

criminal age when most first commitments occur and most vicious careers are begun'.[6] In part, also, the 'discovery' of adolescence was associated with the mission, on the part of university settlements and charitable relief societies, to take spiritual and material succour to the inhabitants of the city slums. In the first years of this century the problem of neglected adolescence came under particular scrutiny from unpaid social workers, active in the settlements and the boys' clubs of the big cities.[7] In particular, the investigations of youth and settlement workers disclosed the 'problem of boy labour': the growth of unskilled, 'blind-alley' jobs which damaged the character, discipline and long-term employment prospects of urban youth.[8] Of these studies, none was more popular than Alexander Paterson's *Across the Bridges*, a rather generalized but vivid sketch of the struggles of river-side life in Bermondsey. The author's personal experience as resident of one of the worst tenement buildings in the district, as elementary school teacher, and as warden of the Oxford and Bermondsey Boys' Club, manifestly informed the whole study.[9]

Paterson emphasized the essential decency of the river-side inhabitants and appealed to the better-off to bridge the social and geographical divide which separated them from the likes of the Bermondsey poor. He couched his appeal in terms of both brotherhood and 'national efficiency'. 'No country that has joined the struggle for

[6] G. S. Hall, *Adolescence* (1908, first published 1904), vol. 1, p. 325 and ch. 5; see also Basil Henriques, 'The Causes and Cure of Crime: A Social Worker's Point of View', *Howard Journal*, vol. 3 (1933), p. 65.

[7] See W. McG. Eagar, *Making Men: The History of Boys' Clubs and Related Movements in Great Britain* (1953), ch. 6.

[8] For the most important monographs, see E. J. Urwick (ed.), *Studies of Boy Life in Our Cities* (1904); R. A. Bray, *The Town Child* (1907); Barclay Baron, *The Growing Generation, a Study of Working Boys and Girls in our Cities* (Edinburgh, 1912); and Arnold Freeman, *Boy Life and Labour* (1914).

[9] For the Oxford and Bermondsey Mission, see W. McG. Eagar, op. cit., pp. 230–6; A. Paterson, 'Children and the Child', *Fratres*, vol. VII (Dec. 1907), pp. 5–8; id., 'The Mission and its Work', *Annual Report of the Oxford Medical Mission* (1908), pp. 11–29; Barclay Baron, *The Doctor: the Story of John Stansfeld of Oxford and Bermondsey* (1952); and T. P. Gee and J. H. S. Wild, 'Social Work in London: The Univ. Connection', *University College Record*, vol. VII (1979), pp. 251–9. For Paterson (1884–1947), see Gordon Hawkins, *Alec Paterson. An Appreciation* (printed privately), pp. 5–12; *DNB, 1941–50*, p. 65; *The Times*, 10 Nov. 1947 (obituary); Barclay Baron, 'Across the Bridges. In Memory of Alec Paterson', *Toc H Journal*, vol. XXVI (Jan. 1948), pp. 1 ff. Prior to the Children Act of 1908, Paterson had been asked by Herbert Samuel, Parliamentary Under-Secretary of State at the Home Office, to visit the children's courts which had been established unofficially. Paterson had recommended the general institution of special courts: *Report of the Departmental Committee on the Treatment of Young Offenders*, PP 1927, XII (Cmd. 2831), p. 959, *Minutes of Evidence* (seen by permission of the Home Office), p. 167, q. 1124.

supremacy', he submitted, 'can allow the finest human material to grow stiff or die for lack of help and understanding.'[10] Naturally, Paterson gave an important role to the boys' clubs in training working-class lads for 'good citizenship'. The clubs had the task of shaping manners and morals, of teaching self-control and the lesson of 'playing the game'; performing, in short, the task which the public school discharged for privileged boys. *Across the Bridges* also referred to the lads who dropped out of 'the race of life'.

'The elements of a boyish crime', according to Paterson, 'are a desire for something, the opportunity to obtain it with probable impunity, the lack of self-control to restrain him.'[11] In this view, juvenile crime was a response less to evil instincts and more to poor surroundings and inadequate character training. Accordingly, the treatment of these boys had to be guided by two objects. First, it was necessary to distract the boy's mind from the personal desires which led him astray: 'The boy out of work steals because hunger has obliterated all else in his mind. Another suffers from the brooding desires of immorality, because there is a lack of healthy interests to banish vile thoughts.'[12] A varied programme of distractions was required, including education, hobbies, sports and energetic work. Summer camps were an integral feature of this scheme.[13] The second object was to enlarge the boys' powers of self-control by strengthening character and encouraging habits of restraint. This double-edged approach was the very essence of boys' club work. It was also, as Paterson indicated, the basis of the treatment of juvenile offenders as embodied in the Probation of Offenders Act and the Children Act, not to mention the administration of the Borstal system. In subsequent years the linkage between the spheres of boys' club work and of juvenile justice became much tighter, a relationship symbolized by the appointment in 1913 of Charles Russell as chief inspector of reformatory and industrial schools.

Russell was an energetic contributor to boy-welfare work in Manchester from 1892, when he first helped in a boys' club in Ancoats. Residence in a slum district gave him personal knowledge of the environment in which delinquent and neglected children grew up, and the conviction that to save lost sheep was worth any amount of effort.

[10] Paterson, *Across the Bridges, or Life By the South London River-Side* (1912, new edn.), p. 170.

[11] Ibid., p. 122.

[12] Ibid., pp. 125–6.

[13] cf. Mary Barnett, *Young Delinquents* (1913), p. 9.

On the strength of his voluntary social work and of his writings on delinquency, Russell was appointed to the Departmental Committee on Reformatory and Industrial Schools in 1911. He was an energetic yet tolerant person, very practical-minded, seldom theoretical. The experience he had gained by 1913 proved influential in his new official role.[14]

Largely on Russell's advice, the Home Office responded to the unprecedented increase in juvenile delinquency during the First World War by encouraging magistrates to revive the work of the boys' clubs, many of which had stopped functioning due to the absence of their leaders, and by promoting the appointment of local committees to co-ordinate the work of the existing agencies for juvenile welfare. The aim of this initiative was to strengthen and extend the work of voluntary organizations in the provision of wholesome recreation and physical training for young people by the formation of local juvenile organizations in the larger towns, which were to be affiliated to a central Juvenile Organisations Committee (JOC), appointed by the Home Secretary in December 1916.[15]

Behind this strategy was the belief that the rise in juvenile crime was caused by a weakening of parental control (reflecting the absence of fathers on military service and the multiplication of working mothers), by greater opportunities for misapplied energy (particularly at night in the darkened streets), and by fewer legitimate outlets for a heightened spirit of adventure. The root of the problem, many felt, was that boys had been left too much to their own devices.[16] It was also recognized that the condition of many homes, and the lack of proper upbringing in such homes, forced children to spend their leisure hours in the surrounding streets. As Russell wrote in *The Problem of Juvenile Crime*, behind all 'lies the national disgrace of the slum with its overcrowding and all the concomitant conditions we have allowed to exist like a cancer at the heart of the community'.[17] The work of the youth

[14] Russell was the author of *The Making of the Criminal* (1906), with L. M. Rigby, and of *Young Gaol-Birds* (1910). See McG. Eagar, op. cit., pp. 355–62; Alexander Maxwell, 'Charles Russell', *The Boy*, vol. XXV (Winter, 1952–3), pp. 120–3.

[15] See McG. Eagar, op. cit., pp. 396–9; *The Times*, 19 Feb. 1918, p. 3; Russell, *The Problem of Juvenile Crime* (Oxford, 1917), Barnett House Paper, No. 1, p. 9; PRO, HO45/16515/375684; HO45/10962/349554; PRO, Ed. 24/1231–2; Ed. 24/2110. For the later history of the Juvenile Organisations Committee, see Ed. 24/1235–8.

[16] 'Juvenile Crime and the War', *Justice of the Peace*, vol. 80, 17 June 1916, pp. 261–2; PRO, HO45/10962/349554 (Herbert Samuel's speech to the Conference of representatives of clubs, etc., 23 Oct. 1916); Cecil Leeson, *The Child and the War* (1917), ch. 2.

[17] Russell, op. cit., p. 5.

organizations was to afford counter-attractions to this life of the streets. In addition to this preventive social work, the central JOC launched an enquiry into juvenile delinquency. Published in 1920, the enquiry's report beat out the same message: juvenile crime was in large part a reflection of the lack of opportunities for healthy recreation.[18]

By the start of the inter-war period, then, it is possible to discern a prevailing view that delinquency was intimately bound up with the temporary strains of adolescence and, more importantly, was a way of finding the excitement which could not be found in legitimate directions. Moreover, the most effective preventive and remedy was felt to lie in the adequate provision of voluntary organizations such as clubs, Boys' Brigades, or Scout troops, and of recreational facilities like playing fields. More significantly still, it was a conception of delinquency which continued to guide the thinking of social workers, magistrates, and public servants. Dr Arthur Norris, a former youth worker with Russell in Manchester, and Russell's successor as chief inspector of reformatory and industrial schools, impressed upon the Departmental Committee on the Treatment of Young Offenders in February 1925 that the inmates of the certified schools were 'in the main just the same type of boy and girl as one used to meet with in those lads' clubs and camps, only, to a large extent through no fault of their own, they have got into difficulties and been brought before the Court'.[19]

Yet this conception of delinquency was not a static one. A gradual shift in approach to the explanation of juvenile delinquency took place in the 1920s. The original emphasis on social and economic factors, on the effects of unemployment, and on the material conditions of the home, was slowly replaced by a modified environmental approach in which the psychological conditions obtaining in the home and family were given greater prominence. Whether or not children became law-abiding, it was said, depended largely on the influence of friends, relatives, and parents on the child's mental constitution. By the same token, delinquency was considered to be a natural reaction on the part of the child to an unnatural family situation. This view of crime was

[18] *Report by the Juvenile Organisations Committee of the Board of Education on Juvenile Delinquency* (1920), a copy of which is in PRO, HO45/16515/375684/42.

[19] *Report of Young Offenders Committee,* op. cit., *Evidence*, p. 111, q. 686. A. H. Norris, born in 1875, was appointed chief inspector in November 1917. Previously he had been senior medical officer at the Children's Dispensary in Manchester. He spent much of his spare time in lads' club work. See *The Times*, 24 Feb. 1953, p. 10; J. Carlebach, *Caring for Children in Trouble* (1970), pp. 130–33.

shaped by a number of systematic investigations into the causes of delinquency, the most important of which was Cyril Burt's *The Young Delinquent*. Psychologist to the Education Department of the London County Council, Burt combined case material and clinical insight with new statistical techniques in order to assess the existing theories of delinquency.[20] His huge study deserves more extended discussion in so far as it oiled the wheels of criminological debate for the rest of the inter-war period, and made a distinct impression upon the content of penal policy.

Cyril Burt's early career bears comparison with those of people like Russell and Paterson. His interest in juvenile delinquency was similarly stimulated by residence in a university settlement, one situated on the edge of Liverpool's dockland.[21] From this experience he gained an intimate awareness of the social background of delinquency, reinforced a few years later by his exploration of the social topography of London's East End.[22] Yet Burt's work as an applied psychologist, advising on the psychological difficulties of London children from 1913 onwards, and his membership of the Psychological War Research Committee, inevitably gave him a perspective on juvenile crime not possessed by contemporary social workers.[23] Burt was more than ready to examine material and cultural conditions—poverty, unemployment, uncongenial school and work, bad companions, and inadequate leisure facilities—but he was also insistent that the crucial component in the creation of delinquency was not poor conditions in themselves, but 'the workings of these bad surroundings on the thoughts and feelings of a susceptible mind'.[24] Burt's approach too readily segregated environmental factors from 'inner personal weaknesses' and wrongly conceived of the environment as something substantially external to an individual's personality. None the less, his investigations gave him the evidence to challenge the mono-causal criminology which relied on 'some solitary panacea', whether of congenital or environmental

[20] For the origin, scope, and methods of the enquiry see the earlier article by Burt, 'The Causal Factors of Juvenile Crime', *British Journal of Medical Psychology*, vol. III (1923), pp. 1–33. See also, id., *The Young Delinquent* (1927), pp. 12–13; A. M. Carr-Saunders *et al.*, *Young Offenders. An Enquiry into Juvenile Delinquency* (Cambridge, 1942), pp. 18–23.

[21] See L. S. Hearnshaw, *Cyril Burt. Psychologist* (1979), p. 31; *The Times*, 12 Oct. 1971, p. 12.

[22] Ibid., p. 39.

[23] Ibid., pp. 72 and 104.

[24] Burt, *The Young Delinquent*, p. 188.

origin, and to posit instead the view that delinquency was 'the outcome of a concurrence of subversive factors: it needs many coats of pitch to paint a thing thoroughly black'.[25] At the same time, Burt felt his evidence pointed to the relative importance of environmental conditions within the home—'defective discipline' and 'defective family relationships'[26]—at least as these were mediated through the mind of the child.[27] In short, Burt impressed upon his audience that both soil and seed were important to the germination of delinquency. As he put it, in a sentence which best sums up this modified environmentalism, 'the typical delinquent is a child with a dull, uneducated mind, struggling to control an emotional and impulsive temperament, both housed in a weak, afflicted body, and living with a demoralised family in an impoverished home'.[28]

Through newspaper articles, radio broadcasts, and short pamphlets, Burt's findings and judgements were transmitted to an extremely wide audience.[29] They were given endorsement, too, a year after the publication of *The Young Delinquent*, by William Healy and Augusta Bronner, directors of the Judge Baker Child Guidance Centre in Boston, and pioneers of the casework investigation of delinquency. *Delinquents and Criminals* similarly emphasized the complexity of causative forces and likewise traced the source of the mental conflicts which were found in many persistent offenders to the delinquent's early relationship with his parents.[30] Not surprisingly, therefore, this viewpoint became a commonplace of the English literature on juvenile courts and delinquent youth. Dr R. G. Gordon, psychologist to the Bath Clinic for Difficult Children, stressed the vital relationship between the deficient personality (in respect of the juvenile's power to adjust to his social setting) and the social milieu (of which the broken

[25] Ibid., p. 600.

[26] 'Defective family relationships' included the 'only child' situation as well as the 'broken home'.

[27] Burt, *The Young Delinquent*, pp. 96–7.

[28] Burt, *Psychology of the Young Criminal*, Howard League Pamphlet, No. 4 (1924). For discussion of Burt's *Young Delinquent*, see Gordon Rose, 'Trends in the Development of Criminology in Britain', *British Journal of Sociology*, vol. 9 (1958), pp. 53 ff; L. Radzinowicz, *Ideology and Crime* (1966), p. 77.

[29] See *The Times*, 14 June 1926, p. 11; Burt, 'The Delinquent Child', *Child*, vol. XVI Aug. (1926), pp. 321–32; idem, 'The Psychology of the Bad Child', *Listener*, 6 Feb. (1929) pp. 129–30.

[30] W. Healy and A. T. Bronner, *Delinquents and Criminals. Their Making and Unmaking* (New Jersey, 1969; 1st edn., 1926), pp. 209–10. William Healy's earlier study, *The Individual Delinquent* (1915), had influenced Burt's own work.

home was the most crucial feature).[31] But non-psychologists also incorporated Burt's outlook into their written work. William Clarke Hall, the progressive stipendiary magistrate of the Old Street police court, underlined the role of 'defective discipline', embracing all types of parental neglect, in the genesis of delinquency. 'My own experience', he insisted, 'and that of my probation officers fully bears out this view.'[32]

In some instances, Burt's findings were prey to re-interpretation, illustrating the ease with which they were incorporated into the existing conception of delinquency. Fenner Brockway, in *A New Way With Crime*, was not prepared to discount the contribution of poverty to delinquency, and put forward the plausible suggestion 'that many of the other prime factors he [Burt] cites—defective parental discipline, vicious homes, defective family relationships, bad companionships, and faulty physique, intellect and emotions—have their roots in poverty.'[33]

It was a standard assumption in the 1920s, particularly among those of radical political persuasion, that poverty was the ultimate cause of delinquency.[34] What is significant in the present context is that Burt's exploration of the psychology of juvenile crime, his insistence that crime was a 'mental symptom with a mental origin', was not held to be inconsistent with the belief in the causative role of unemployment and poverty. The explanation for this rests, at least in part, on the enduring importance of environmental considerations to English psychology. Essentially an outgrowth of biology, English psychology always envisaged the mind of the individual child as in constant dynamic interaction with its environment. So, for example, the branch of psychology known as child guidance conceived its task to be that of adjusting the growing individual to its own immediate environment, thereby according a role to the teacher, social worker, and school

[31] R. G. Gordon, *Autolycus or the Future for Miscreant Youth* (1928), pp. 36 and 42. See also L. A. Weatherly, 'Juvenile Psychological Delinquents', *Transactions of the Medico-Legal Society*, vol. XXIII (1928–29), p. 20.

[32] Clarke Hall, *Children's Courts* (1926), p. 32. See also 'The Home Secretary on Young Offenders', *Magistrate*, vol. 1 (July 1928), pp. 241–2; Herbert H. Lou, *Juvenile Courts in the United States* (Oxford, 1927), p. 182.

[33] Fenner Brockway, *A New Way With Crime* (1928), p. 32. Brockway was a prominent member of the Independent Labour Party (ILP), and author, with Stephen Hobhouse, of *English Prisons To-Day* (1922).

[34] See *Annual Report of the Prison Commissioners for 1923–4*, PP 1924–25, XV (Cmd. 2307), p. 397; Hermann Mannheim, *Social Aspects of Crime in England Between the Wars* (1940), pp. 131–3.

medical officer, in addition to the psychologist.[35] Hence, too, such an avid proponent of psychotherapy as M. Hamblin Smith could, in *The Psychology of the Criminal*, still write thus: 'Poverty, overwork, and lack of opportunity for normal modes of expression, are all potent factors in the production of juvenile delinquency. Enforced unemployment may also act in this direction.'[36] There was, therefore, no 'psychiatric deluge', as was the case in America in the 1920s, sufficient to shift the focus of investigation on to the individual, and away from the social matrix in which the individual lived.[37] What developed in England was a conception of delinquency which incorporated the insights of social and educational psychology.

It will become evident in subsequent chapters just how influential this conception of delinquency was to inter-war penal practice and policy. At this stage, suffice it to point to the more obvious impressions made by this viewpoint on the policy for young delinquents. For a start, the viewpoint suggested that juvenile offenders were far from constituting a homogeneous class. As Cyril Burt stated in the preface to *The Young Delinquent*: 'Delinquency I regard as nothing but an outstanding sample—dangerous perhaps and extreme, but none the less typical—of common childish naughtiness.'[38]

The observed overlap between neglect and delinquency reinforced the point. According to the Departmental Committee on Young Offenders, 'the tendency to commit offences is only an outcome of the conditions of neglect, and there is little room for discrimination either in the character of the young person concerned or in the appropriate method of treatment'.[39] Thus it seemed wise to treat neglected and delinquent children along similar lines, abandoning a distinction which had been institutionalized in the mid nineteenth century. It also seemed essential to see the problem of juvenile crime 'as but one inseparable portion of the larger enterprise for child welfare', in Burt's words. Indeed, one of Burt's 'practical deductions' from the mass of evidence in *The Young Delinquent* was as follows:

[35] See Gertrude Keir, 'Symposium on Psychologists and Psychiatrists in the Child Guidance Service. III—A History of Child Guidance', *British Journal of Educational Psychology*, vol. XXII (1952), pp. 6, 11 and 28.

[36] M. Hamblin Smith, *The Psychology of the Criminal* (1922), p. 165.

[37] See S. Clement Brown, 'Looking Backwards. Reminiscences: 1922–1946', *British Journal of Psychiatric Social Work*, vol. 10 (1970), p. 162; Kathleen Woodroofe, *From Charity to Social Work in England and the United States* (1968, first published 1962), pp. 136–9.

[38] Burt, *The Young Delinquent*, p. viii.

[39] *Report of Young Offenders Committee*, op. cit., p. 964.

Crime in children is not a unique, well-marked, or self-contained phenomenon, to be handled solely by the policeman and the children's court. It touches every side of social work. The teacher, the care committee worker, the magistrate, the probation officer... should be working hand in hand, not only with each other, but with all the clubs, societies, and agencies, voluntary as well as public, that seek to better the day-to-day life of the child.[40]

Secondly, the view of the delinquent as 'a unique human being, with a peculiar constitution, peculiar difficulties, and peculiar problems of his own' underpinned the demands, heard throughout the inter-war period, for pre-sentence investigation of the mental and physical condition of each delinquent as well as of his home and wider social environment.[41] Thirdly, the corollary to a detailed investigation of the delinquent was the provision of a variety of forms of treatment to match the needs of each offender. The prevailing view of delinquency also suggested how these forms of treatment might be used. Such was the importance of family relationships, for example, that where they were not hopelessly defective, the child, it was thought, should be kept at home under the guidance of a probation officer. Where the home conditions were deficient, committal to a certified school seemed to be the best course. Lastly, in so far as crime was believed to be largely learned behaviour, a normal response to abnormal surroundings, it was considered important to devise penal treatments which would aim to re-educate delinquents in fresh habits and interests. Success was considered more likely, furthermore, with young offenders; their character was still 'plastic', and more readily moulded by sympathetic treatment.

The Departmental Committee on the Treatment of Young Offenders

In the course of the Great War, juvenile crime increased suddenly and substantially. A pre-war total of 37,500 young persons under sixteen charged before the juvenile courts each year went up to 51,000 cases by 1917. After the war there was an equally rapid fall to 30,000 cases by 1921. The Children's Branch of the Home Office ascribed this reduction to 'the increase in infant welfare centres, school medical

[40] Burt, *The Young Delinquent*, p. 610.

[41] Ibid. Burt's casework approach was probably reinforced by the Quaker emphasis on the individual, 'different from all others in his characteristics and his temptations and his needs': Janet Whitney, *Geraldine S. Cadbury 1865–1941* (1948), p. 133.

inspection, improved elementary education, better education and higher wages of parents, the Probation System and Reformatory and Industrial Schools'.[42] No doubt for some of the same reasons, there was also a decrease in the number of parents proceeded against for cruelty or neglect of children. As Sydney Harris, Assistant Secretary in charge of the Children's Branch, was moved to say of the improved situation, '(s)urely there has never been a time in which greater attention has been given to the welfare of children'.[43] Yet it led to little complacency. In October 1921 the National Council of Women of Great Britain pressed the Home Office to appoint an official committee to consider the treatment of delinquency.[44] Sydney Harris advised against this course of action, pointing out that the Report of the Juvenile Organisations Committee had only recently appeared, the recommendations in which had been communicated to magistrates by way of a circular letter. In 1923 a bill for the protection of children was introduced under the auspices of the Labour party. This measure, according to the Children's Branch, contained some proposals which were too far-reaching, and some provisions which were not extensive enough. In January 1924, when the first Labour government was in office, the bill was again introduced, but still Harris could not accept it as a practicable contribution towards a new Children Act. The head of the Children's Branch advised the Home Secretary that the bill had been drafted without consulting either the Home Office or the NSPCC, and that many of its proposals cried out for more searching investigation before being put before Parliament.[45]

Not that the Home Office were content to rely indefinitely on the Children Act of 1908. By the early 1920s the Children's Branch were considering the desirability of preparing a new Children Bill, and already some of the official staff were collating the notes of points where minor amendments to the Act of 1908 were needed. There had

[42] Quoted in *Howard Journal*, vol. 1 (April 1924), p. 155. See Table 1(a). Between 75 and 80% of all indictable crime committed by persons under sixteen between 1913 and 1927 came under the category: 'simple larceny and offences punishable as simple larceny'. The Children's Branch was formed in 1914, following the Departmental Committee on Industrial and Reformatory Schools, to specialize in the treatment of juveniles.

[43] 14 Feb. 1923, PRO, HO45/18716/385052/14. S. W. Harris, born in 1876, entered the Home Office in 1903. Between 1909 and 1919 he was private secretary to successive home secretaries. Between 1919 and 1934 he was assistant secretary in charge of the Children's Branch. See *Who Was Who*, 1961–70; *The Times*, 27 July 1962, p. 16.

[44] 5 Oct. 1921, PRO, HO45/16515/375684/44.

[45] PRO, HO45/11959/445305/1 and 3.

been regular complaints, for example, about the publication in local newspapers of the names of children charged before the juvenile courts. The press, it seems, did not invariably refrain from including these personal details in its court reports.[46] Another point, which was raised by the Association of Superintendents and Managers of Reformatory and Industrial Schools, was whether offenders who were liable to be sent to reformatory schools should have a conviction recorded against them, as the present law required.[47] Over and above these minor adjustments, however, Harris was clearly looking to a more comprehensive consideration of juvenile policy as a preface to legislation. His minute of 29 February 1924 is worth quoting in full:

> Any proposal for amending the Children Act should be preceded by an inquiry by a Committee or a Royal Commission as it will be essential not only to consider points of detail, but to take stock of the general policy of dealing with juvenile offenders. For instance, Juvenile Courts are playing a considerable part in the administration of justice, and it would be necessary to consider whether the existing machinery is the best that can be devised, or whether it should be given a civil rather than a criminal character as in America and some other countries. The character of certified schools has undergone a considerable change since the Act of 1908 was passed, and we must satisfy ourselves on what lines they ought to be continued vis-à-vis the Probation System and Borstal Institutions.[48]

Harris felt unable to recommend immediate action along the lines set out in his minute, since the energies of the Children's Branch were fully absorbed by the development of the probation system, and by a bout of reorganization which led to the branch assuming responsibility for the work previously performed by the Reformatory and Industrial Schools Department.[49] Even so, an enquiry was foreshadowed by Rhys Davies, the Parliamentary Under-Secretary of State at the Home Department, in his reply to C. G. Ammon, mover of the 1924 bill for the protection of children.[50] During the tenure of the Labour government, however, the Home Office remained fully stretched by the Bill to consolidate the Factory Acts, and it had to be left to the next Home Secretary, Sir William Joynson-Hicks, to appoint the Departmental Committee on the Treatment of Young Offenders. Never one

46 PRO, HO45/13655/180010.

47 19 April 1920, PRO, HO45/10996/173982/28. See also HO45/14714/516360/1A.

48 PRO, HO45/11959/445305/3.

49 See PRO, HO45/18442/455959.

50 PRO, HO45/11959/445305/3 and 4. Ammon was Labour MP for N. Camberwell.

for understatement, Joynson-Hicks told the Ladies Imperial Club of the likely significance of his action—'It will be an important committee and it will be a committee which will really revolutionise the whole position of our dealing with young offenders.'[51] Not surprisingly, the announcement was widely applauded in the legal and penological press.[52]

In asking the Home Secretary to initiate the inquiry, the object of the Children's Branch, according to Harris, was 'to try and co-ordinate the various methods to see what the relations of the schools should be to the probation system and other systems'.[53] Another strong argument for the appointment of the committee, according to Dr A. H. Norris, the chief inspector of certified schools, 'was the feeling that administration had in many directions somewhat overstepped legislative sanction in a desire to secure that the treatment of the young offenders and neglected young people who required protection and training should, as far as possible, be free from all penal taint and carry with it no stigma which should be in after years a handicap to the young person'.[54] One example of the law lagging behind administrative practice was the use of institutional training in voluntary homes as a condition of a probation order. This practice had certainly developed beyond what was probably ever in the mind of parliament. Further, there was a good deal of evidence to suggest that in the early 1920s child welfare workers were becoming reluctant to secure protection and training for neglected and delinquent youth, in so far as this required a 'charge' in the unfitting confines of a criminal court and a conviction which for ever barred the child from employment in some of the armed services and from emigration to the colonies. As Dr Norris stated, a few years after the appointment of the committee:

'Evidence was being frequently brought to the notice of the Inspectors of the Children's Branch of the Home Office of persistent refusal by Magistrates, those responsible for the care and protection of children and by social workers generally, to handicap a child's future by invoking the aid of the Law with such consequences.'[55]

[51] *The Times*, 17 Dec. 1924, p. 11. Joynson-Hicks was Conservative MP for Middlesex (Twickenham); and President of the National Church League from 1921; H. A. Taylor, *Jix: Viscount Brentford* (1933).

[52] See *Justice of the Peace*, vol. 89, 10 Jan. 1925, p. 32; *Howard Journal*, vol. 1 (April 1925), pp. 197–9.

[53] *Report of Young Offenders Committee*, op. cit., *Evidence*, p. 113, q. 698.

[54] 24 Oct. 1927, PRO, HO45/13403/510865/7. See also *Evidence*, p. 113, q. 699.

[55] Ibid.

The committee would, it was hoped, find a way out of these difficulties.

The terms of reference of the committee were extremely wide: to look into the treatment of young offenders under twenty-one years of age and of young people who, as a result of poor surroundings, were in need of 'protection and training', and to report what changes in the existing law or its administration were needed. Such breadth reflected contemporary thinking about the causes of juvenile delinquency and the related advocacy of reclamation or reformation as a main objective in dealing with young offenders. When the thrust of juvenile justice was towards the diagnosis of an offender's needs and the selection of an appropriate treatment, only a wide-ranging enquiry would suffice. The committee was chaired by Sir Thomas Molony, formerly Lord Chief Justice of Ireland.[56] Other committee members included Sydney Harris of the Children's Branch and Maurice Waller of the Prison Commission, MPs from the main political parties, a number of magistrates (including Mrs Barrow Cadbury of the Birmingham juvenile court), a justices' clerk, and a director of education.[57] The committee took evidence for some forty-five days, from nearly one hundred witnesses to whom they put over 24,000 questions. The report, published in 1926, proved to be a major stepping-stone to the Children and Young Persons Act of 1933, and thus warrants extended investigation. The aim is to examine the main sections of the report in the context of the discussions about juvenile justice which took place between 1908 and 1926. This makes it more possible to uncover the diverse streams of opinion which fed into the Young Offenders Committee.

[56] See *Who Was Who*, 1941–50, p. 805. Sir Evelyn Cecil, Conservative MP for the Aston division of Birmingham, was originally appointed chairman, but illness forced him to retire.

[57] Geraldine Cadbury, born in 1865 into a Quaker family, was appointed a juvenile court magistrate for the City of Birmingham in 1920, and made chairman of the Juvenile Court Panel of Justices in 1923. See *The Times*, 31 Jan. 1941, p. 7. The MPs appointed to the committee were Mr (later Sir) Edmund R. Turton, Unionist member for Thirsk and Malton; and Mr Rhys Davies, Labour member for Westhoughton, Lancashire, former farm labourer and miner, active in Manchester municipal affairs, and Parliamentary Under-Secretary of State, Home Office, in 1924. See *The Times*, 2 Nov. 1954, p. 6. The director of education was Mr Spurley Hey of Manchester, author of *Juvenile Crime* (1916). In addition, there was Lady Arabella Lawrence, formerly Labour MP for N. East Ham, a member of the Education Committee of the LCC, and organizer for the National Federation of Women Workers from 1912 to 1921; and Sir Wemyss Grant-Wilson, Director of the Borstal Association, a JP for the County of London and director of a boys' club in Camberwell. See *Who Was Who*, 1951–60, p. 446.

Juvenile Courts

The Children Act 1908 provided that a court of summary jurisdiction, when hearing charges against children, should sit either in a different room or building, or on a different day or at a different time, from the ordinary magistrates' courts. Yet at the start of the inter-war period it was reasonably clear that the working of these juvenile courts was far from uniform.[58] Moreover, it was still rare for a young offender to be confronted by magistrates with a sympathetic and informed insight into the mind of the child, by a courtroom divested of the trappings and personnel of an ordinary police court, and by a simple, informal and elastic procedure. This was particularly brought home to the Children's Branch by the Report on Juvenile Delinquency of the Juvenile Organisations Committee. This report seems to have represented the majority opinion amongst social workers, some of the latter having appeared as witnesses before the committee.[59] The main indictment which the JOC presented was the complete absence of any system in dealing with young offenders on the part of the juvenile courts. Methods of treatment varied considerably in different courts. The justices of one town would rely heavily on corporal punishment; those of another town on certified schools. So, too, the justices of the same court would often try one method of punishment after another on the same boy, 'without any constructive scheme in view'.[60] The upshot, the JOC believed, was a wholly unnecessary amount of recidivism.

In order to surmount the difficulties encountered in the juvenile courts, the report of the JOC looked to the appointment of men and women as magistrates who had experience in dealing with children. Without this, the report stressed, neither legislation nor the administrative work of the Home Office would be of much value:

> The neglect of the opportunities afforded by the Probation of Offenders Act, 1907, for the rehabilitation of juvenile offenders without conviction; the loose procedure in many so-called 'Children's Courts'; the failure to observe the various sections of the Children Act, 1908, relating to the conduct of juvenile

[58] *Report of Indian Jails Committee 1919–20*, PP 1921, X, p. 363, Appendix IX, pp. 840–1.

[59] *Report of the JOC*, op. cit., in PRO, HO45/16515/375684/42. The report referred to the provincial situation more than to that in London, being based on returns from Liverpool, Manchester, Sheffield and West Ham. Evidence was received from, amongst others, Clarke Hall, Judge Lindsay of Colorado, and Mrs Mary Mackintosh, probation worker in the Manchester police courts.

[60] *Report of JOC*, pp. 24–5. See also 'Memo on Women Justices in Children's Courts' by Clarke Hall, 20 Feb. 1920, PRO, LCO 2/463.

courts and the conditions under which children, and particularly girls, are called upon to give evidence; the ignorance of Circulars and Instructions issued from the Home Office to justices and justices' clerks, are all difficulties which would never arise if the magistrate had a sympathetic understanding of child life, and was keen to avail himself of the many facilities for considerate treatment of young people which existing statutes and regulations already place at his disposal.[61]

Additionally, the Juvenile Organisations Committee recommended that juvenile courts should not be held in the same room as that used for sittings of the ordinary court.[62] Dr Norris, one of the two Home Office representatives on the committee, immediately pressed the department to take action, legislative as well as administrative, on these and the other proposals, particularly in view of the unanimously favourable press response to the report. The head of the Children's Branch preferred, rather, to wait until the Juvenile Courts (Metropolis) Bill had become law. This would give effect to the recommendation concerning the selection of magistrates, at least as far as the Metropolitan Police District was concerned.[63] Shortly afterwards, however, the preparation of a circular on juvenile courts was set in motion, timed to appear after the Metropolitan Bill had passed.

The Home Office Circular of April 1921 reproduced, in the main, the previous circulars on the subject of juvenile courts, and reinforced them on the points on which the Juvenile Organisations Committee had made recommendations, notably the practice of holding juvenile courts in separate buildings or rooms, and the assignment to a court of a separate rota of justices with experience of the problems of delinquency. In short, the thrust of the circular was for trial by specialist magistrates in special courts.[64] The same two points had, in effect, been accorded parliamentary sanction by the Juvenile Courts (Metropolis) Act 1920. This statute laid down that children's courts should be held in premises entirely separate from those used for adult offenders, and that the courts should be presided over by a stipendiary

[61] Ibid., p. 36.

[62] PRO, HO45/16515/375684/42; HO45/11152/240518/6; *Times Educational Supplement*, 26 Aug. 1920, p. 467. cf. Scottish National Council of Juvenile Organisations, *Report of an Enquiry into Juvenile Delinquency* (Edinburgh, 1923).

[63] PRO, HO45/11152/240518/6.

[64] For a copy of the circular, see PRO, HO45/16515/375684/43. The State Children's Association sent the circular, with a letter, to all petty sessional courts: HO45/11152/240518/43.

magistrate, assisted by two lay justices, one of whom was to be a woman.[65] The introduction of the original bill owed most to the Lord Chancellor, Birkenhead, who was eager to make full use of the newly-appointed women magistrates in London, following the Sex Disqualification (Removal) Act, especially for cases arising under the Children Act.[66] Unfortunately, the bill became the subject of keen controversy both inside and outside parliament. At one stage in the parliamentary proceedings, indeed, the Home Secretary, Edward Shortt, was provoked into declaring that the bill's proposals 'have been, perhaps, more misrepresented and more misunderstood than almost any Bill that I remember of this description'.[67]

On one side, the stipendiary magistrates were opposed to the appointment of lay justices, whether male or female, to act on equal terms with them. When consulted by the Lord Chancellor, they elected for no change in the existing system. The women probation officers to the London courts also, alas, opposed the employment of inexperienced women magistrates.[68] On the other side, the associations connected with penal reform and child welfare—Howard Association, Penal Reform League, State Children's Association, National Council of Women—along with the Labour party, proposed that a small number of stipendiary magistrates, say four, should do all the work of the metropolitan juvenile courts, with the assistance of selected lay justices, in buildings which were not used as police courts.[69] Using this second body of opinion as shield, the Lord Chancellor brooked no further opposition from the police magistrates. In order to secure general agreement, however, the bill as drafted and enacted left the number of courts and the number of 'selected' stipendiary magistrates to be settled by Orders in Council.[70] Within a few years it seemed hard to credit that the statute had aroused such controversy. A number of police magistrates were soon on record as saying that the presence of

[65] Juvenile Courts (Metropolis) Act, 1920, 10 and 11 Geo. 5, c. 68.

[66] PRO, LCO 2/465; HO45/10970/404139/1.

[67] *Hansard*, vol. 134, 1 Nov. 1920, col. 135. Shortt was Liberal MP for Newcastle upon Tyne, West: *DNB., 1931–40*, p. 810.

[68] *Hansard*, vol. 40 (Lords), 15 June 1920, cols. 591 ff, 24 June 1920, cols. 798 ff; *The Times*, 10 May 1920, p. 13, 25 May 1920, p. 11, 24 June 1920, p. 12; *Justice of the Peace*, vol. 84, 22 May 1920, pp. 223–5.

[69] *The Times*, 12 May 1920, p. 12; PRO, HO45/10970/404139/26a and 30.

[70] *Hansard*, vol. 41 (Lords), 6 Aug. 1920, cols. 920 ff; *Hansard*, vol. 134, 1 Nov. 1920, cols. 133 ff; vol. 135, 29 Nov. 1920, cols. 962 ff; vol. 136, 16 Dec. 1920, cols. 894 ff.

the lay magistrates, male and female, was particularly helpful.[71] The Act was an important victory, even so, for the proponents of separate buildings for children's courts and of specially selected magistrates. Not least importantly, it stirred the penal reform bodies to press for legislation to obtain the same improvements for provincial juvenile courts.

One of the most ardent proponents of reform was William Clarke Hall. Appointed as a metropolitan police magistrate in 1913, Clarke Hall was president of the Toynbee Hall and Islington juvenile courts in the 1920s. He had commenced his legal career as prosecuting counsel for the NSPCC, due doubtless to the fact that his wife was the daughter of Revd Benjamin Waugh, the Society's founder.[72] It meant that in his juvenile court work, Clarke Hall had the advantage of knowing, with some intimacy, the streets and children of the East End. He always strove to provide a sympathetic forum in which to befriend the delinquent and to uncover the information which he considered essential to effective sentencing; he even went to the trouble of convening each week a preliminary court of advice, avoiding thereby the need in some cases for court action. Despite holding magisterial office, Clarke Hall was an outspoken champion of reform in juvenile justice, putting forward his views, particularly on the role of the juvenile courts and on probation, in a series of pamphlets, articles, and books, the most well-known of which was *The State and the Child* (1918), rewritten in 1926 as *Children's Courts*.[73] Moreover, through membership of such bodies as the sub-committee of the JOC, which drafted the Report on Juvenile Delinquency (1920), he became increasingly *persona grata* at the Home Office.

The vision which underlay Clarke Hall's writings on the juvenile court was that a court should not be the forum for 'the dramatic staging of a trial for a crime', but for an examination of the causes of the child's delinquency and for an informed decision as to preventive treatment. He always maintained that, in so far as the courts were there to help, many more children ought to be brought before them than was the case:

[71] Henry T. Waddy, *The Police Court and its Work* (1925), p. 143; William Clarke Hall, *Children's Courts* (1926), p. 254.

[72] See *Who Was Who*, 1929–40, p. 580; *Probation*, vol. 1 (Jan. 1932), pp. 145–6; *The Times*, 29 Oct. 1932, p. 12.

[73] See Clarke Hall, 'The Aims and Work of the Children's Courts', *Child*, vol. XI (April 1921), pp. 198–200; id., 'The Importance of the Juvenile Court', *Magistrate*, vol. 1 (March 1927), pp. 163–4.

The number of children charged bears no real relation to the number of child offenders, and still less relation to the number of children living in undesirable surroundings. Yet these children who have *not* been charged are the real danger to the community. It is they who will in the future replenish the ranks of the criminal classes.[74]

His view represented a faith in the benign value of judicial action which, in turn, owed a good deal to American example where the jurisdiction exercised by the juvenile courts was civil, or chancery, and not criminal in character, and where judges endeavoured to provide children with the guidance which they should have received from their parents.[75] Yet Clarke Hall was not convinced that a purely chancery jurisdiction ought to be introduced in England, remaining of the opinion that punishment had a role to play in some cases.[76] Rather, in a draft bill which appeared as an appendix to *Children's Courts*, he recommended for the provinces the appointment of stipendiary magistrates, who would act in conjunction with the lay justices in juvenile courts. The courts would have the additional power of guardianship, or making delinquent and neglected children wards of the court, in consequence of which no delinquent would be 'convicted'.[77]

Clarke Hall was none too optimistic that his more radical proposals would claim political support. But neither was he a lone figure in the wilderness. Indeed, a wide range of pressure groups, including the Howard League, the People's League of Health, the National Association of Head Teachers, and the State Children's Association, continuously impressed upon successive home secretaries the need to remove children's courts from the precincts of the police courts.[78] Some, like the People's League, urged that juvenile courts be framed on the model of the Chancery courts.[79] Yet in spite of the stimulus provided by progressive magistrates like Clarke Hall, by penal reform and child welfare organizations, as well as by parliamentary discussions and newspaper articles, the work of the provincial juvenile courts still

[74] Clarke Hall, *Children's Courts* (1926), p. 188.

[75] See Mrs J. St. Loe Strachey, ' American Juvenile Courts and Children's Courts in England', *Magistrate*, vol. 1 (March 1926), p. 117. The American Chancery Courts had been described in Cecil Leeson, *The Probation System* (1914), pp. 11–13.

[76] Clarke Hall, *Children's Courts*, pp. 58, 64–5.

[77] Ibid., pp. 261–3, 266. See also L. L. Loewe, *Basil Henriques. A Portrait* (1976), p. 72.

[78] See *Howard Journal*, vol. 1 (Oct. 1921), pp. 39–40; *Hansard*, vol. 173, 15 May 1924, col. 1599; *Daily News*, 31 July 1925. The Howard League, formed in 1921, was an amalgamation of the Howard Association and the Penal Reform League. It sought a critical but not confrontational dialogue with government.

[79] *The Times*, 18 July 1925, p. 9.

left a lot to be desired. This became sharply evident to the Children's Branch in the same year that the Departmental Committee on Young Offenders was appointed.

The Children's Branch had issued a questionnaire to all non-metropolitan courts of summary jurisdiction, asking for information about the present methods of the juvenile court. Over a thousand courts submitted replies, the information from which was summarized in the Third Report of the Children's Branch. It was depressing reading. In over half of the petty sessional divisions under review, the juvenile court was held in the ordinary police court, either on a different day or, more often, prior to or succeeding the adult sittings. Children's cases were generally heard by the ordinary justices, few magistrates specializing in juvenile work. Those justices who did concentrate on children's cases tended to be women, but many divisions still had no women on the bench. There was, finally, a considerable diversity of practice as to the number of magistrates and assorted personnel who were present during sittings of the juvenile court.[80] Quite obviously, then, the whole system was in need of review, and much was expected, in consequence, of the departmental committee, which started taking evidence in February 1925.

There was a good deal of unanimity amongst the witnesses giving evidence to the departmental committee with reference to a number of changes in the constitution and procedure of the juvenile court, all of which were meant to mark a distinction between juvenile and adult courts, and all of which formed part of the committee's recommendations. Thus, juvenile court justices were to be specially qualified and specially selected for dealing with young people; the court was to be held in premises not utilized for the holding of other courts; there were to be more simplified legal procedures; publication of the names of children in the press was to be prohibited; and the use of the terms 'conviction' and 'sentence' was to be abolished in the juvenile court.[81] Views were less unanimous on the age of criminal responsibility and on the age limit for the juvenile court. On the first point the Labour party wanted it to be ten years of age, and some members of the departmental committee, notably Geraldine Cadbury, wanted it to go

[80] Home Office, *Third Report on the Work of the Children's Branch* (1925), pp. 6–11.

[81] See *Report of Young Offenders Committee*, op. cit., *Evidence*, p. 168 (Paterson); pp. 963–4 (Mrs Rackham). On the issue of publishing names in the press, see also *Report of the Departmental Committee on Sexual Offences against Young Persons*, PP 1924–5, XV (Cmd. 2561), pp. 957–8.

to nine or ten years. In fact, the committee recommended that the age of responsibility should rise from seven to eight years of age.[82] Many witnesses also urged the committee to raise the age limit to eighteen and even higher, but, according to Harris, 'they decided to make what they thought was a conservative recommendation', that a young person should mean anyone under seventeen years of age.[83] There was less consensus still on the wisdom of changing the underlying legal principle of the juvenile court.

Miss Grace Abbott of the Children's Bureau, Washington, described to the committee the American pattern of chancery jurisdiction and how the child tried before the juvenile court was judged to be a person in need of the care and protection of the state.[84] Other witnesses looked forward to the English juvenile courts likewise becoming part of the civil administration. One such was Mrs Clara Rackham who presented evidence on behalf of the Magistrates Association.[85] Another influential proponent was Dr Norris, who made it clear, however, that he spoke in a personal, not an official capacity. Norris seemed to have no definite scheme in mind, but was of the view that the fundamental purpose of juvenile court procedure in delinquency cases should not be to determine whether the child had committed an offence for which punishment must be inflicted, but to discover whether he was a fit subject for the protection, care, and guardianship of the community, in the same degree as the neglected or homeless child. In brief, it was less important to prove a child guilty or not guilty than to find whether or not he was in need of training. Moreover, Norris was ready to promote such a change in the character of the court, even if it meant reconsideration of the laws of evidence. Short of a radical change in legal principle, Norris approved of a mere widening of the categories covered by s. 58 of the Children Act. This would have meant that more children could be dealt with on grounds of neglect than on a criminal charge, thus enlarging the civil as opposed to criminal functions of the court.[86] Confusing the issue further was the evidence on behalf of the Trades Union Congress and the Labour party which endorsed Clarke Hall's idea of a court of guardianship. Part of this court's responsibility,

[82] Janet Whitney, op. cit., p. 129.

[83] Harris, 25 July 1927: PRO, HO45/14714/516360/1. See also *Evidence*, p. 167 (Paterson); p. 205 (Clarke Hall).

[84] *Evidence*, p. 1219.

[85] Ibid., pp. 963–4.

[86] Ibid., p. 55, q. 331; p. 66, q. 389.

however, would be to discover whether the child was guilty of the alleged offence.[87] And as if these proposals were not enough, a number of witnesses suggested a form of preliminary action, either by the police or by the education authority, in which trivial offences committed by young first offenders would be dealt with outside the juvenile court altogether, as was the practice already in some regions.[88]

Against any change of legal principle were a number of equally influential voices. It was clear from the questions put to witnesses by Sydney Harris and by the chairman, Sir Thomas Molony, that some scepticism existed within the committee for the idea of ignoring the offence which brought the young offender before the court. Amongst the witnesses, the alternative case was put with greatest effectiveness by Margery Fry, on behalf of the Howard League for Penal Reform. Miss Fry's evidence indicated that the League was deeply committed to treating the delinquent child from the point of view of its needs rather than for what it had done, but that equally it wished to retain the safeguards, such as the laws of evidence, of a court of justice. In a statement which has been echoed in recent years by criminologists eager to bring justice back into the juvenile courts, Fry told the committee: 'I think there is a kind of feeling that a child's matters are small matters, and can be met by kindness and goodwill, and there is a certain danger of not giving the child its rights if you do not maintain those laws.'[89]

It was the unwillingness to divorce the trial of young persons from criminal jurisdiction which informed the approach of the departmental committee. The report emphasized two considerations. First, that the young offender should have the chance to rebut the charge against him. Secondly, that to dispense with court-like procedures could undermine the gravity of the offence and the feeling of respect for the law in the eyes of the offender. Rather than a change of legal principle,

[87] Ibid., p. 2673, q. 23817. See also pp. 195–200 (Clarke Hall).

[88] Ibid., pp. 1395–1401 (Mr. Crawley, Chief Constable of Newcastle upon Tyne); pp. 1545–6 (Capt. Moore, Secretary of Chief Constables' Association); pp. 663 and 700 (Mr I. Ellis, Superintendent of Hayes School for Jewish Boys, representing Society of Headmasters of Certified Schools).

[89] Ibid., p. 402, q. 3211, quoted in E. H. Jones, *Margery Fry* (1966), p. 122. Miss Fry, born in 1874, a Quaker, was Warden of University House, Birmingham until 1914. In 1919 she became the secretary of the Penal Reform League and was instrumental in uniting the League with the Howard Association. She retired the secretaryship in 1926 on becoming Principal of Somerville College. She was one of the first women magistrates to be appointed in 1921: *DNB, 1951–60*, pp. 381–4; *Times Obituaries* 1951–60, pp. 264–5.

therefore, the report recommended only an enlargement of the civil functions of the court. The committee also discountenanced the practice of the police and education authorities in usurping the functions of the juvenile court, although it did accept the continued use of police cautions.[90]

But if the committee's proposals embodied a further shift of the juvenile court from its origin as a criminal court, they did nothing to resolve the dilemma of conflicting principles which had always afflicted the jurisdiction. On one hand, the courts were magistrates' courts, focusing upon a particular criminal act, employing procedures geared to the proof of criminal responsibility. On the other hand, the courts were tribunals of social welfare, concerned with the character and needs of offenders whose delinquency was the product of distinct psychological and social conditions. The report of the departmental committee reflected this dilemma without resolving it. Whilst insisting that the 'main function' of the juvenile court should be 'to consider the welfare of the young persons who come before it and to prescribe appropriate treatment for them', the report also expressed the view that 'there is some danger in adopting any principle which might lead to ignoring the offence on which the action of the juvenile court in dealing with delinquents must be based'.[91] If the committee believed the delinquent to be more sinned against than sinning, they also saw his delinquency as a deliberate, not to say wicked, form of behaviour. Clearly, then, the deterministic features of the social conception of delinquency had failed to triumph in the deliberations of the Molony Committee. There was life yet in the old notion of criminal responsibility. The only resolution of this dilemma which the committee's report implicitly provided, was for the juvenile court to use these differing conceptions of the delinquent child in sequential fashion. That is to say, at the trial stage efforts should be made to determine the guilt of the delinquent child. Once the offence was admitted to or proven, the court should assess the various ways in which the offender could be dealt with, having sole regard at this stage to the welfare of the child.[92]

[90] *Report of YOC*, op. cit., pp. 975–80.

[91] Ibid., p. 992.

[92] cf. *Report of the Committee on Children and Young Persons* (Ingleby), Cmd. 1191 (HMSO, 1960), pp. 22–4; Allison Morris and Mary McIsaac, *Juvenile Justice? The Practice of Social Welfare* (1978), pp. 10–14.

The Psychological Clinic

If the second stage in the sequence was to be effective, it was essential for the juvenile court to have the fullest possible information as to the personal and social antecedents of the offence. Ironically, the Children Act 1908, by excluding the use of prison for remanding children and young persons, had deprived some young offenders of the skilled medical examination and observation which they would have received in prison. By 1920 the Juvenile Organisations Committee was uncovering evidence to the effect that many of the children brought before the courts were physically or mentally defective, sometimes both, without the fact ever being discovered. Accordingly, the Report on Juvenile Delinquency, like the Penal Reform League's *A National Minimum for Youth* three years earlier, pressed for a wider use of pre-sentence enquiries: 'A psychological study of the child would in many cases diagnose the reason for so many of the acts which lead to court proceedings, and would certainly assist the magistrate in deciding the effective method of treating the child.'[93] Particular reference was made by the report of the laudable example of the Birmingham justices who had appointed Dr W. A. Potts and Dr Hamblin Smith to examine offenders referred to them by the courts for 'mental inefficiency'.[94] The full proposal of the JOC was that *every* child charged should be examined; the Children's Branch of the Home Office agreed that in some, if not all cases, a medical examination would be helpful, and could generally be provided for by remanding a child to a 'place of detention' for the purpose.[95] In the Circular of April 1921, therefore, the Home Secretary advised the magistrates that in a large proportion of cases, a medical examination was 'desirable if not essential'.[96] This was reinforced, finally, in the First Report of the Children's Branch (1923) in which magistrates were encouraged to make greater use of the places of detention, and to have at the disposal of their courts the services of a doctor.[97]

In the course of the next few years, the pressure to base the

[93] *Report of JOC*, op. cit., p. 12; Penal Reform League, *A National Minimum for Youth* (1917).

[94] PRO, HO45/18736/438456/7–16; W. A. Potts, 'The Treatment of Delinquents', *Child Study Society Journal*, vol. 1 (1921–2), pp. 32–3.

[95] PRO, HO45/16515/375684/42.

[96] Ibid., 375684/43.

[97] Home Office, *First Report on the Work of the Children's Branch* (1923), p. 66. cf. Burt, *The Young Delinquent*, p. 262.

sentencing decision of the juvenile court on a wide-ranging enquiry into the circumstances of the offence and offender became a good deal more insistent, and centred increasingly on the need for a central remand home or observation centre. The most active proponents of a system of examination of offenders were the leading societies interested in child welfare. The People's League of Health was encouraging physicians in mental diseases, like Sir Robert Armstrong-Jones and Dr Hamilton-Pearson, to attend the court presided over by Clarke Hall to offer much-needed advice on individual cases.[98] As for the Howard League, its role was determined by its secretary, Margery Fry. Miss Fry's first experience as a magistrate of one of the London juvenile courts in 1922 had provoked her to comment to a friend thus: 'It impresses me profoundly with the need for psychological advice. Really we are at an *incredibly* crude stage in matters of human nature!'[99]

A year later, in an address to the Howard League, she was singing the praises of L'Établissement Central d'Observation à Moll-Huttes, following her visit to Belgium. She described a 'psychological laboratory' where boys between the ages of seven and twenty-one remained for between two and four months, during which time a diagnosis was reached as to the particular needs of each offender.[100] By this date, too, Fry had been in touch with Dr Cyril Burt, the psychologist attached to the Education Department of the London County Council. In 1924 she arranged for three articles by Burt on the new psychology and the young offender, first published in the *Daily News,* to be reprinted in the Howard League's pamphlet series.[101] By now, Burt was close to publishing *The Young Delinquent*, a study based partially on his experience of examining the delinquent children referred to him by magistrates, teachers, and care committee visitors. Burt's book did perhaps more than anything else to inform opinion on the issue of pre-sentence investigation in the 1920s.

Interest in the behaviour problems and personality difficulties of children, particularly delinquents, had been developing since well before the First World War. This had been mainly an offshoot of the

[98] See Clarke Hall, *Children's Courts* (1926), p. 97; Edgar A. Hamilton-Pearson, 'The Problem of the Delinquent Child', *Child*, vol. XI (Sep. 1921), pp. 357–61.

[99] Quoted in E. H. Jones, loc. cit.

[100] S. Margery Fry, 'A Belgian Psychological Laboratory', *Howard Journal*, vol. 1 (April 1924), pp. 121–7. Support for Moll was also widespread at a conference between representatives of the certified schools and of the probation system: *Seeking and Saving* (April 1926), p. 126.

[101] Burt, *Psychology of the Young Criminal* (1924).

widespread interest in child study and child guidance, itself epitomized in the establishment in 1893 of the British Child Study Association. It was an influential member of this body, Dr C. W. Kimmins, chief inspector of London schools, who was responsible for drawing up the initial plan which resulted in the appointment in 1913 of a psychologist to the inspectorate of the education department of the London County Council. The post went to Burt, his task to investigate children with special difficulties.[102] Burt's work during the war and beyond was based, like that of William Healy in Chicago, on a case-study approach. Above all, it convinced him that crime was only a symptom, and that before you could start deciding how to remedy the underlying problem you had first to look for the cause in each delinquent—'to study him individually as a unique human being, with a special history, a special constitution, special problems of his own'.[103] For this, in Burt's view, the establishment of psychological clinics for young offenders was essential.

Drawing upon the experience of clinics in the United States and of the small beginnings in Birmingham, Burt devised a plan for the organization, aims, and methods of a psychological clinic. This first appeared in an appendix to *The Young Delinquent*, having started life as part of a larger report on psychological centres, prepared to assist the post-war changes under the impact of the Fisher Education Act.[104] The clinic was to be staffed by social workers, who would investigate home circumstances; by a medical officer, who would look for physical defects; and by a psychologist. The latter's task was to administer mental tests, assess temperamental qualities, and analyse unconscious motives. Burt's scheme included not only a day clinic, but also a residential observation centre, along the lines of the Belgian scheme.

This plan proved to be the required catalyst. It caught the eye of a London magistrate, Mrs St. Loe Strachey, wife of the editor of the *Spectator*. She visited Burt at the London Day Training College, to which Burt had been appointed part-time Professor of Education in 1924, to discuss the possibility of enlisting the support of Harkness, the benefactor of the American Commonwealth Fund.[105] The outcome

[102] Gertrude Keir, op. cit., pp. 10, 14–16; Cyril Burt, 'An Autobiographical Sketch', *Occupational Psychology*, vol. XXIII (Jan. 1949), p. 15.

[103] C. Burt, *Psychology of the Young Criminal* (1924). cf. Healy and Bronner, op. cit., p. 221.

[104] Burt, *The Young Delinquent*, App. II, 'The Psychological Clinic for Juvenile Delinquents', pp. 617–27.

[105] Keir, op. cit., p. 23; L. S. Hearnshaw, op. cit., p. 97; Burt, 'An Autobiographical Sketch', op. cit., p. 19.

was a Child Guidance council which, in time, secured the establishment of the London Child Guidance clinic in Islington in 1928.[106] The initial centre of interest had been in delinquency, as is clear from the support given to the idea of a psychological clinic by individual magistrates, the Magistrates Association, and the Howard League. But it was ultimately agreed that the scope of the service ought to cover all forms of child guidance.[107] This meant that whilst the clinics were available for referring delinquents to, and whilst they provided important training for social workers and psychologists, they were never seen to be the complete answer by those who specialized in the problems of delinquency.

This was made abundantly clear from the summary published in the Third Report of the Children's Branch, which illustrated that the information at the disposal of juvenile courts was still extremely unsatisfactory. Most of the courts which supplied information to the Children's Branch claimed that they obtained reports about offenders' home surroundings from either the police, which was most common, or officers of the local education authority, and probation officers. By no means all courts obtained an account of the young offender's school history, and only a tiny minority required a medical examination. The Third Report also indicated that, although magistrates were increasingly asking for the sort of guidance which could only come from enquiries conducted whilst the offender was under remand, the accommodation provided in the existing 'places of detention' was generally unsuitable for a long remand. In country areas, police stations, private houses (particularly of married constables), and workhouses were all pressed into service. But even in large urban areas like London, where the number of children needing custody was large and constant, remand facilities were poor. It was exceptional, for example, for a medical examination to be made on admission as a regular feature.[108] Still, it seemed, the precise purpose which remand homes were expected to serve remained unclear; the whole question of preliminary examination remained in an experimental stage. The Children's Branch were doubtless hoping for guidance from the Young Offenders Committee.

[106] M. Ashdown and S. Clement Brown, *Social Service and Mental Health* (1953), p. 16. A year earlier, the Jewish Health Organisation had established the East London child guidance clinic under the direction of Dr Emanuel Miller.

[107] S. Clement Brown, 'Looking Backwards', op. cit., p. 162.

[108] *Third Report* (1925), op. cit., pp. 9–10, 37–45. See also *TES*, 2 Oct. 1919; *Second Report on the Work of the Children's Branch* (1924), p. 9.

The witnesses before the departmental committee fully endorsed the previous criticisms of the existing remand homes. The London homes came under particular attack from Clarke Hall and Dr Norris, although the latter acknowledged that the London County Council were considering a scheme for new remand accommodation.[109] In addition, the committee heard some persuasive advocacy on behalf of residential observation centres or central remand homes from Sir Robert Armstrong-Jones, consulting physician in mental diseases at St. Bartholomew's Hospital, who was representing the Magistrates Association, from Dr Hamilton-Pearson of the Tavistock Clinic, and from Burt, Norris, and Margery Fry.[110] The last-mentioned told the Young Offenders Committee of the observation centre at Moll, which, in fact, two members of the committee went to visit.[111] Mr Rhys Davies, Labour MP, and Geraldine Cadbury, chairman of the Birmingham juvenile court panel, returned from Belgium with reservations concerning certain small details, but in general they were impressed by what they had seen.[112] Not surprisingly, in view of the unanimity of evidence and the favourable report on Moll of the two committee members, the report accepted the need for better facilities for the examination and observation of young offenders, a need which had become more emphatic than ever with the recent difficulties posed by the sequelae of *encephalitis lethargica*, or sleeping sickness.[113] The report recommended the state provision of at least three central remand homes, to be available for all offenders under twenty-one years of age.[114] It was an important recommendation, at the very heart of the principle set down by the committee 'that the duty of the court is not so much to punish for the offence as to readjust the offender to the community'. It epitomized the belief, moreover, that the observation and examination of the young delinquent was an essential preliminary to his allocation to the most appropriate form of treatment, be that probation or a certified school.

[109] *Evidence*, p. 210, q. 1422; p. 58, q. 341.

[110] Ibid., p. 34 (Norris); p. 936 (Armstrong-Jones); p. 2397 (Burt); E. A. Hamilton-Pearson, 'Child Delinquency', *Lancet*, 17 Dec. 1927, pp. 1312–3.

[111] *Evidence*, pp. 406–8 (Fry); E. H. Jones, op. cit., p. 160.

[112] Janet Whitney, op. cit., pp. 152–3.

[113] *Report of YOC*, op. cit., p. 1001.

[114] Ibid., pp. 1003–5.

2

Probation and Reformatories

According to Herbert Samuel, Parliamentary Under-Secretary for the Home Department at the time, the Probation of Offenders Act 1907 'attracted very little attention, either in Parliament or outside, and passed through all its stages in both Houses almost without discussion'.[1] Perhaps for this reason, the Act was put into operation by the justices both slowly and unevenly. Fortunately, the Home Secretary, Herbert Gladstone, had planned to review the system after one year's working, and hence the Departmental Committee on the Probation of Offenders Act sat and reported in 1909.[2] The objects of the 1907 Act were fully explained in this report. The offender was to be brought under 'the direct personal influence of a man or woman chosen for excellence of character and for strength of personal influence'. This was exemplified as follows:

> Often without friends of their own, more often with friends only of a degraded type, out of touch with any civilizing influence, the probation officer comes to them from a different level of society, giving a helping hand to lift them out of the groove that leads to serious crime. He assists the man out of work to find employment. He puts the lad into touch with the managers of a boys' club, where he can be brought under healthy influences. He helps to improve the bad homes which are the breeding ground of child-offenders.[3]

Probation was intended, then, as a means of support and encouragement, and considered to be particularly suited to the needs of the first offender. In response to the departmental committee's report, the Home Office pressed the magistrates to use probation more widely, and to take more interest in the work of the probation officers. At this

[1] Herbert Samuel, *Memoirs* (1945), p. 54, cited in *The Results of Probation*, A Report of the Cambridge Dept. of Criminal Science (1958), p. xiii. Samuel was Liberal MP for the North Riding of Yorkshire, 1902–18, Parliamentary Under-Secretary of State, 1905–9, and Home Secretary in Jan.–Dec. 1916 and again in 1931–2: *Who Was Who*, 1961–70, p. 997.

[2] Bochel, op. cit., p. 49.

[3] Cited in *Report of Indian Jails Committee, op. cit.*, pp. 842–3.

stage the officers were generally police court missionaries, generally agents of the Diocesan branches of the Church of England Temperance Society (CETS), and said to be of 'the educated artisan class'. Only in London did the Home Office appoint a small number of special children's officers, all of whom were women. In these early years, finally, the probation system was seen as particularly appropriate for young offenders. This was due, in part, to the historical lineages of probation and in part to the close links between probation and the new children's courts. For this reason it is necessary to merge discussion of probation and the young delinquent with the development of the probation system as a whole.[4]

Before 1920 the pressure to make greater use of the Probation of Offenders Act came from two directions: from groups like the Penal Reform League, the Howard Association, and the State Children's Association; and from the Home Office itself. In response to the wartime increase in the amount of juvenile crime, the home secretary circularized the magistrates to encourage the wider use of probation and the employment of more women as probation officers.[5] The reform organizations pressed for a number of improvements to the present inadequate system. In order to avoid the misuse of probation, they suggested that preliminary inquiries should be made by probation officers into the home circumstances of every case coming before a juvenile court. They recommended the appointment of well-educated and trained persons as social workers, the payment of adequate salaries instead of fees, and the use of unsalaried, volunteer probation officers. The aim which these groups had in mind was described for the Home Office by the Penal Reform League: 'A zealous juvenile court magistrate with competent probation officers would soon become a centre of vigorous social co-operation'.[6] The efforts of the reform societies were enlivened by the publication of Cecil Leeson's *The Probation System* (1914) and *The Child and the War* (1917), and of William Clarke Hall's *The State and the Child* (1918), all of which emphasized the value of probation for the delinquent child. Leeson, a Sheffield Quaker, had been a probation officer in Birmingham before the war, having first taken the Diploma in Social Studies at the University. In

[4] Bochel, op. cit., p. 52. Table 7 illustrates that over 40% of *all* probation orders were given to persons under sixteen years of age, in the selected years 1913, 1920, and 1925.

[5] *Justice of the Peace*, vol. 80, 17 June 1916, p. 262.

[6] 29 Apr. 1912: PRO, HO45/10572/176696/13. See also C. Russell, *The Problem of Juvenile Crime* (Oxford, 1917), p. 15; Clarke Hall, *Children's Courts* (1926), pp. 126–31.

1916 he became secretary of the Howard Association; in 1920 he became secretary also of the Magistrates Association, which he was instrumental in forming. In these capacities he was extremely influential in the development of the probation system.[7] William Clarke Hall, whose work as a stipendiary magistrate has already been mentioned, was particularly interested in two features of the probation system. He wanted a more systematic use of volunteer workers, the latter being responsible for one or two probationers each. To this end he had organized a scheme of voluntary workers acting under official probation officers in his own East End court. Clarke Hall also advocated the abandonment of the system of 'dual control', urging the State to take full command of the probation system at the expense of the voluntary societies like the Church of England Temperance Society.[8] On the first point the Home Office in 1917 encouraged all magistrates to use volunteer workers, and suggested that for this purpose probation officers might link up with the local juvenile organisations committee.[9] On the second issue, the Home Office were less helpful. The department seemed reluctant either to halt the supply of probation officers from the voluntary societies or to assume greater central control of, and financial responsibility for, the probation system.

In the course of the First World War, however, Home Office opinion on the issue of central control seemed to change. This was due most probably to a number of factors. Demands for the abolition of dual control became more insistent as bodies like the National Association of Probation Officers made themselves heard.[10] The Church of England Temperance Society were forced on to the defensive, as a number of courts began to appoint their own probation officers. Moreover, it became evident to the Home Office from the replies of justices' clerks to the circular of 11 January 1919, that the existing system was unsatisfactory. Rarely were probation officers able to give their undivided attention to juvenile cases; the remuneration of officers was often decidedly inadequate. It was these factors which, towards the end of 1919, prompted Alexander Maxwell, who was

[7] Bochel, op. cit., pp. 64–5.

[8] PRO, HO45/16515/375684/10; HO45/10962/349554/66; *Seeking and Saving* (May 1919), p. 140.

[9] PRO, HO45/16515/375684/37. The Manchester City justices linked up with the local juvenile organisations committee in 1918: 375684/11.

[10] Bochel, op. cit., pp. 74–5; Walton, op. cit., p. 96.

charged with the oversight of probation matters within the Home Office, to minute thus: 'What is wanted is a Treasury grant towards Probation work carrying with it some control by the Home Office or a central body over the selection, work and remuneration of P.O.'s.'[11] But first he thought a departmental committee should be appointed to consider the whole question of the training, appointment, and payment of probation officers.

The departmental committee, under the chairmanship of Sir John Baird, Parliamentary Under-Secretary of State at the Home Office,[12] and including Sydney Harris, testified to the important contribution which the probation system was making to the treatment of offenders. Of the 40,473 cases dealt with in the juvenile courts in 1919, 4,188, or over 11 per cent, were put on probation.[13] Yet it was also apparent from the report that the use of probation was extremely variable. The police returns from sixteen towns showed that whilst the average quota of juveniles put on probation in 1919 was 13.8 per cent, the range was from 1.4 to 43.6 per cent. The committee were also disappointed that, fourteen years after the principal Act, 215 courts of summary jurisdiction, out of a total of 1,034, still had not appointed a probation officer.[14] Finally, the report noted, as had the report of the Juvenile Organisations Committee, that many witnesses considered that probation was being used too late in an offender's career, and that it was best to use probation at the child's first or second offence.[15]

The main proposals of the committee, in addition to the recommendation that every court should have the services of a probation officer available to them, can be grouped under four main heads. First, the training of probation officers, the importance of which the Howard

[11] PRO, HO45/10568/175294/91A. Evelyn Ruggles-Brise, Chairman of the Prison Commission, was of the opinion that probation 'ought to be under the direct control and supervision of the state': *The English Prison System* (1921), p. 113. Alexander Maxwell, born in 1880, entered the Home Office in 1904, and was secretary to the Departmental Committee on Reformatory and Industrial Schools in 1911. After Russell's death in April 1917, he acted as chief inspector of reformatory and industrial schools until Norris's appointment in Dec. 1917. In 1928 he became Chairman of the Prison Commission: *Who Was Who*, 1961–70.

[12] Baird was Conservative MP for the Rugby division of Warwickshire.

[13] *Report of the Departmental Committee on the Training, Appointment and Payment of Probation Officers*, PP 1922, X (Cmd. 1601), pp. 424 and 445. This figure did not include those dismissed or released on recognizances without supervision. Over 30% of young offenders found guilty of *indictable* offences in 1920 were sentenced to probation: see Table 4. See also Tables 1(a) and 1(b).

[14] Ibid., pp. 424 and 449.

[15] *Report of JOC*, op. cit., pp. 22, 30–1; PRO, HO45/16515/375684/42.

Association had long emphasized.[16] At this date, training opportunities for probation officers were limited mainly to the courses run by the Police Court Mission (of the CETS) and the Church Army for their own police court missionaries. Disappointingly for the reform groups, the report accepted this state of affairs without comment. With reference to more specialized training, notably the university-based courses of social science, the report came out with the equally dispiriting comment that it was unlikely the probation service would be able to attract university graduates, since the latter would be hoping for 'a professional career'.[17] Secondly, the report recommended a shade more central supervision of the probation system by an extension of advisory services. In particular, it suggested the appointment of a central advisory committee of ten to twelve members, its task to keep the magistrates abreast of developments within probation. Potentially more important for enhancing central supervision was the proposal that a government grant should be provided to cover half the cost of the probation service.[18] The other two main heads were treated more fully by the report of the departmental committee.

The Howard League, in the person of Margery Fry, had pressed the committee to accept that all probation officers should be appointed and paid for by the State. This proposal was an integral part of the League's proposition, embodied in a private member's bill in 1921, that a paid National Probation Commission of three members should supervise the probation system, with the assistance of an inspectorate, and with power to delegate the task of appointing probation officers to local probation authorities.[19] Most witnesses, however, according to the committee's report, had opposed this proposal. The committee itself was equally unprepared to jeopardize what it considered to be the essential co-operation between court and probation officer, a risk which a scheme of central appointment would run. Hence, the report recommended that magistrates should retain 'a direct voice in the selection and control of their officers', whilst also suggesting that the justices should delegate two or three of their number to select probation officers and generally to organize the probation work.[20]

[16] *Howard Journal*, vol. 1 (Oct. 1921), p. 36.

[17] *Report*, pp. 431–2.

[18] Ibid., pp. 436 and 439.

[19] Ibid., p. 435; *Law Times*, 26 Nov. 1921, pp. 341–2; 'A Bill to constitute a Probation Commission . . . ', PP 1921, vol. IV (234), p. 547.

[20] Ibid., pp. 425 and 438.

Finally, the committee had to face the task of spelling out the role within the probation system of the agents of the voluntary societies, a task confounded by the division of opinion amongst the witnesses who gave evidence. A large number of witnesses spoke critically of the identification of probation officers with temperance propaganda, which the Church of England Temperance Society abetted. The committee was clearly persuaded by this body of opinion, requesting in consequence that the CETS reorganize its probation work, commencing with a divorce of its probation and temperance activities. Yet the committee did not wish to diminish what it felt to be the valuable work performed by the missionaries of the various societies. Here again, the evidence which it had taken was influential. Most witnesses had agreed that, of the qualities required of a good probation officer, 'a keen missionary spirit, based on religious conviction, is essential'.[21] And in the report, the committee appealed to the English tradition of voluntary social work, in defence of its view: 'It must be remembered that in this country much of the best social work has been accomplished by voluntary organisations, and probation offers a field in which private enterprise may be looked upon to yield good results.'[22] Local magistrates were left free, therefore, to choose between appointing agents of the voluntary societies or nominating their own officers to carry out probation work. Additionally, however, the report recommended that 'specially qualified children's officers should be attached to every Juvenile Court'.[23]

Such, then, were the lines laid down by the departmental committee for the future development of the probation system. A number of the reforms urged on the Home Office during the previous years, had found a place in the list of recommendations. At the same time, no dramatic shift had been proposed in the contribution of the voluntary societies or in the source, training and control of probation officers. The probation system would, in the committee's scheme of things, remain a permissive service, with the Home Office persuading and cajoling the magistrates from the sidelines. Clearly, the official mind was still imbued more with the missionary than with the professional spirit. The appeal to the traditions of charitable social work, not to mention the parsimonious instincts of government at a time when Geddes was wielding his axe, had won a respite for the voluntary

[21] Ibid., p. 431.
[22] Ibid., pp. 426–8.
[23] Ibid., p. 429.

societies. With the good grace of a body getting a welcome second chance, the CETS set about implementing the recommendations which specifically applied to its work, both in London and in the provinces.[24]

The *Justice of the Peace* was alone in appreciating the unassuming approach of a committee 'not captured by the idea of organisation, standardisation and state control'.[25] Other groups were less impressed by the departmental committee's performance. Inevitably, the Howard League was critical of the committee's failure to overcome the weakness in the central organization of probation. The League remained convinced that this weakness was part cause of the fragmentary nature of the probation system at the local level. Not that the League was too surprised at the committee's poor showing. It was always unlikely, they complained, that a departmental committee would feel justified in passing comment on the department's poor record with regard to central co-ordination.[26] The League was joined by the newly-formed Magistrates Association, which criticized the reluctance of the government to make available immediately a grant to cover some of the cost of the probation service.[27] These two organizations continued to agitate in the next few years for an end to dual control, for less local divergence in the use of probation, and for an exchequer grant towards the cost of the service. They were accompanied by the Incorporated Society of Justices' Clerks, the National Association of Probation Officers, and the Parliamentary Penal Reform Group.[28] In the shadow of Geddes, however, few departments were allowed to sanction new expenditure.

The Home Office's initial response to the report of the departmental committee was predictable and two-fold. In July 1922, the report was sent to every bench of magistrates, accompanied by a circular letter in which the Home Secretary spelt out the need for every court to have the services of a probation officer, for a small number of magistrates in

[24] Bochel, op. cit., pp. 89, 92–3. For Geddes, see *Second Interim Report of Committee on National Expenditure*, PP 1922, IX (Cmd. 1582), pp. 251–60.

[25] *Justice of the Peace*, vol. LXXXVI, 1 April 1922, p. 150.

[26] *Howard Journal*, vol. 1 (1922) , pp. 36–45.

[27] *Magistrate*, vol. 1 (1921), p. 11.

[28] *Magistrate*, vol. 1 (May 1923), p. 3; vol. 1 (Jan. 1924), p. 1; PRO, HO45/16943/399376. The Parliamentary Penal Reform Group, formed in 1922, was under the presidency of Lord Henry Cavendish-Bentinck, Conservative MP for Nottingham S., and Chairman of the Howard League. For the Group's activities, see *Hansard*, vol. 166, 19 July 1923, cols. 2476–9; *The Times*, 31 July 1924, p. 14.

each district to have responsibility for the progress of probation, and for courts to review the methods and scale of remuneration of their probation officers.[29] The Home Secretary also appointed an Advisory Committee on Probation to which were appointed Harris, Geraldine Cadbury, Clarke Hall, Alexander Paterson (recently appointed to the Prison Commission), and the Revd Harry Pearson (Secretary of the London Police Court Mission). The advisory committee's first task was to revise the probation rules in order to obtain annual returns from the criminal courts and, thereby, fuller information about the local workings of the probation system.[30]

This information made it possible for the Children's Branch to monitor the response of the provincial courts to the recommendations of the Baird Committee and to the Home Office circular. It was clear that the number and proportion of offenders being put on probation was increasing. In 1910, 10.6 per cent (3,568) of all young persons tried in the juvenile courts had been put on probation; in 1923, 18.9 per cent (5,448) were so dealt with. But still there were courts without a probation officer. Nor had magistrates always set about reviewing the remuneration of officers. And the Children's Branch also uncovered the first signs of a worrying development which would claim more attention in years to come. It concerned a provision of the Criminal Justice Administration Act 1914, which enabled a court to insert in the probation order, conditions regarding residence. Gradually it had become a not uncommon practice to require a probationer to live in a home during the whole or part of the period of probation. Yet these homes were not liable to inspection, many were far from satisfactory, and in some cases probationers, notably young women, were being sent to them for periods of two or three years. This was an institutional sentence by the back door.[31]

The evidence which went into the reports of the Children's Branch was clearly influential in persuading the Home Office that the time had come for them to take a more authoritative role, without which a truly national probation system would never develop. The first step, taken just before the first Labour government took office, was to get the Treasury to set aside a sum of £22,250 to cover half the cost incurred by the local authorities. Owing to the unsettled political situation, this

[29] Home Office, *First Report on the Work of the Children's Branch* (1923), pp. 61–3.

[30] Ibid., p. 63; PRO, HO45/16204/465471/1.

[31] Ibid., pp. 57–61; *Second Report on the Work of the Children's Branch* (1924), pp. 12–16. See also *Report on Sexual Offences*, op. cit., p. 983.

grant-in-aid was distributed to the local authorities without waiting for the passage of the Criminal Justice Bill.[32] The other step in the creation of a national probation system was the Criminal Justice Bill itself. The parliamentary progress of this measure had been impeded by the general elections of 1923 and 1924.[33] In 1925, with the return of a Conservative government and a Home Secretary, Sir William Joynson-Hicks, who had long supported the probation system, the measure succeeded in reaching the statute-book.[34] Drawing largely upon the proposals of the Baird Committee, the Act required that a probation officer be appointed for every probation area, that the appointment and payment of probation officers be entrusted to a probation committee of magistrates, and that the cost of probation be shared between the local authorities and the Exchequer.[35] There had been little opposition to the bill. As to the fears of the voluntary societies that the appointment of probation officers by a committee of magistrates might lead to an abridgment of the work of their agents, these had been allayed by the Home Secretary, a long-standing protagonist on behalf of the CETS, who secured the position of the societies by way of an amendment to the bill.[36]

Nearly one-third of all probation officers were still attached to a voluntary, generally religious, organization.[37] The financial contribution which the voluntary societies thereby made to the probation service was bound to influence government, notably Treasury, thinking on the issue of dual control. Added to this was a determination on the part of Joynson-Hicks to preserve the spirit of missionary zeal within an improved probation system. To this end he urged the magistrates to select probation officers 'because they want to rescue the perishing, because they want to raise up the fallen, because they want to take a human soul and bring it back to God'. By the same token, Joynson-Hicks warned the annual conference of the National Association of Probation Officers, following the implementation of the Criminal Justice Act, against an introspective professionalism. 'You might become a caste,' he cautioned, 'a section of the community with

[32] *Hansard*, vol. 173, 15 May 1924, col. 1606.

[33] PRO, HO45/11934/427105/103; *Law Journal*, vol. 60, 14 Mar. 1925, p. 252.

[34] *Justice of the Peace*, 7 Feb. 1925, p. 89; H. A. Taylor, *Jix*, op. cit., p. 189.

[35] Criminal Justice Act, 15 and 16 Geo. V, c. 86.

[36] *Hansard*, vol. 183, 11 May 1925, cols. 1594–5; vol. 188, 16 Nov. 1925, cols. 128–9. For Joynson-Hicks' relationship with the CETS, see Bochel, op. cit., p. 67.

[37] *Hansard*, vol. 180, 17 Feb. 1925, col. 921; Elizabeth Macadam, *The Equipment of the Social Worker* (1925), p. 139.

crystallized ideas of your own in regard to the work of the police court mission.'[38] Harris echoed this view when the Advisory Committee on Probation examined the proposal of the Joint University Council for Social Studies for an improved training scheme. Training was important, said Harris, but more crucial was 'the right sort of personality'. He also admonished the leading figure of the Joint University Council, Professor Carr-Saunders, that the Criminal Justice Act was largely a development of an existing system, 'in which the past work of the Missionary Societies was entitled to recognition'.[39] Not for the first time, the ancestry of the probation service proved an effective bulwark against the acceptance by official opinion of the claims of training, claims which were put forward with such cogency by the likes of Elizabeth Macadam:

> Personality, religious conviction, the missionary spirit, are surely not less efficacious when supplemented by scientific education for a service which requires infinitely more than those much-belauded qualities, 'kindness, firmness and tact'.[40]

In view of the administrative and legislative attention which had been given to the probation system between 1920 and 1925, the Departmental Committee on Young Offenders considered it unnecessary to tread all the same ground, confining itself, instead, to particular aspects of the service and to the relationship of probation with the other modes of dealing with young offenders. The report of the committee followed the Criminal Justice Act in the sense of supporting the continuation of the voluntary element, despite the evidence of such witnesses as Clarke Hall and Mrs Rackham (representing the Magistrates Association), deploring the enduring imposition of denominational tests on many prospective probation officers and advocating the ending of dual control.[41] On a more positive note, the report recommended that the term 'probation' should be restricted to the release of an offender under the supervision of a probation officer, in an attempt to avoid the tag of a 'let-off', which had attached itself to the penalties of dismissal and binding over.[42] At the same time, the committee hoped for an extension of the work of supervision to

[38] *Magistrate*, vol. I (Oct. 1927), p. 198.
[39] PRO, HO45/16213/486759/1.
[40] Cited in *Howard Journal*, vol. 2 (July 1926), p. 36.
[41] *Magistrate*, vol. 1 (Dec. 1925), pp. 110–11.
[42] *Report of YOC*, op. cit., pp. 1009–10.

neglected as well as delinquent children. The report also suggested that the reports on home circumstances, which the school attendance officers ought always to provide for the court, might 'usefully be supplemented by special enquiries made by the Court's probation officers'.[43] In order, finally, to bring probation officers and the certified schools closer together, the committee felt that the Cardiff experiment of using probation officers, instead of policemen, to convey children to the schools was worthy of wider application.[44] Such was the catalogue of smaller proposals. Two other issues raised larger implications.

The departmental committee received 'a good deal of evidence' in favour of more central administrative control of the probation service. Mrs Rackham, for example, suggested the establishment of a Probation Commission, with inspectors of probation.[45] An attempt by the Labour MP, Rhys Davies, to secure such a commission by way of an amendment to the Criminal Justice Bill had been blocked by the Home Office in 1925 on the grounds that it would isolate the probation system from the other ways of treating offenders.[46] The departmental committee was similarly convinced of the need for closer co-operation between the various modes of treatment, and thus declined to propose any change in the central administration of the probation service.

Secondly, the committee took up the disquieting issue of associating probation with residence in a home. This, too, had failed to get dealt with in the Criminal Justice Bill. An amendment to allow the inspection of these homes was again blocked by the Home Office on the grounds that it raised the unwieldy question of the inspection of all voluntary institutions.[47] A number of witnesses before the departmental committee—Margery Fry, Rackham, Norris and Clarke Hall—strongly objected to this confusion of probation with institutional treatment.[48] Their misgivings were shared by the committee's report, which condemned the illogical position 'in which a lad or girl can be sent under the probation system to an uninspected Home for (say) two years instead of to the institutions which have been specially provided for the training of these young people with the guarantee of government inspection'.[49]

[43] Ibid., p. 992.
[44] Ibid., p. 1020; *Second Report on the Work of the Children's Branch* (1924), op. cit., p. 19.
[45] *Evidence*, p. 967.
[46] PRO, HO45/11934/427105/157.
[47] Ibid.
[48] *Evidence*, pp. 28 and 115 (Norris); pp. 207–8 (Clarke Hall); p. 546 (Fry).
[49] *Report*, p. 1012.

In 1923 518 probationers, of whom 318 were females, had been sent to homes as a condition of probation—224 for a year, 184 for two years, and 34 for three years.[50] The committee were aware that this practice arose, in part, because the courts knew too little about the offender's circumstances before ordering probation. A home was the probation officer's solution to the subsequent difficulties of 'supervision in the open'. In addition, courts used probation homes both to keep the child away from what were considered to be the evil surroundings of the certified schools and to provide institutional treatment without the stigma of a conviction (the corollary of committal to a certified school). The practice had developed, finally, because it avoided the cost to the local authority of sending an offender to a certified school.[51] None of these considerations was any longer valid, according to the departmental committee. A more widespread resort to preliminary enquiries would relieve the misuse of probation; the improvements effected in recent years in the certified schools should allay any fears about contamination. And the committee intended, of course, to recommend the abolition of the use of the term 'conviction'. These observations justified the committee in declaring that homes should not be used as a condition of probation. Hostels, from which the offender went out to work each day, were exempted from this ban, for the reason that the probation officer could keep the probationer under his close supervision. On the whole, therefore, the departmental committee restricted probation to supervision in the open.

Reformatory and Industrial Schools

When the Children Act was passed in 1908, reformatory and industrial schools formed the keystone in the treatment of neglected and delinquent children, a legacy of the nineteenth-century faith in institutional detention as the panacea for most social evils. The distinction between the schools, of course, went back to their origin in the mid nineteenth century. The industrial schools were the successors of the Ragged Schools founded by Lord Shaftesbury, and intended for the orphan or neglected child. The reformatory school was an institution for reforming young offenders instead of sending them to

[50] Ibid.

[51] Ibid., p. 1013.

prison. To industrial schools were sent children under fourteen whose parents were missing or unfit, together with a few offenders. To reformatory schools went children under sixteen who had committed an offence of violence or dishonesty. By 1908 the crusading spirit of the mid-Victorian founders had evaporated, and often all that remained was the rigid conformity of the nineteenth-century methods. Alexander Maxwell, whose knowledge of the schools dated back to 1911, had this to say of the repressive discipline for 'children in disgrace' of the pre-war schools:

In most of the schools the boys and girls were dressed in uniforms quite unlike the clothing worn by other children. They were usually confined within the school premises by locked doors and gates. Within the school buildings ... they walked in files—at some schools with their hands folded behind their backs. ... The bodily needs of the children were adequately cared for, but their lives were extremely uneventful, and the development of their minds and characters was dwarfed by lack of opportunities for the exercise of responsibility and initiative, by lack of contacts with the outside world, and by a scarcity of interests and activities. Their experience was so closely pent within a narrow enclosure of school walls and school rules that they were liable to be stunted in their mental and moral growth.[52]

Alexander Paterson, writing closer to the time, was of the same opinion. The schools, he felt, varied considerably in their 'efficiency and moral tone'. The financial arrangements of most schools made it necessary to rely on the profits deriving from the boys' industrial work, 'forcing the authorities to view the institution now and then as a manufacturing business rather than an educational and moral agency'. Moreover, the training methods did little to instil habits of self-control, and the after-care of discharged boys was generally lax.[53] By 1911, when Winston Churchill, in his capacity as Home Secretary, appointed a departmental committee to review the management and methods of the schools, they had acquired an awesome reputation for penal regimentation, and had strained the goodwill of the Home Office.

The report of the departmental committee, which appeared in 1913, was extremely critical of the schools, and put forward a valuable set of recommendations for extensive changes in classification, management

[52] Maxwell, *The Institutional Treatment of Delinquents* (1949), 9th Clarke Hall lecture, pp. 21–2.

[53] Paterson, *Across the Bridges* (1912, new edn.), pp. 128–9.

and methods.[54] The implementation of most of these proposals contributed to a fundamental change in the outlook of the schools. Of possibly greater significance was the appointment as chief inspector of reformatory and industrial schools of Charles Russell, a member of the departmental committee and one of the pioneers of the boys' club movement. Russell's efforts to improve the certified schools were badly hindered by the Great War: the rise in committals to, and the war-work of, the schools tended to enhance their bargaining power. Even so, before his sudden death in 1917, Russell conducted, according to Alexander Maxwell, 'an inspiring campaign for the abolition of practices which put a stigma on the children'.[55]

The torch of reform was picked up by Russell's friend and former boys' club colleague in Manchester, Dr Norris. The new chief inspector was actuated by the same principles and the same determination to increase the standard of efficiency of the school system. It was a cruel irony, therefore, that one of the first decisions that Norris had to endorse was the official closure of the experimental farm colony for delinquent children in Dorset, the Little Commonwealth, which Russell had certified as a Home Office school in 1913. Under the superintendence of an enterprising reformer, Homer Lane, methods of training had been devised, including a large measure of self-government, designed to inculcate responsibility and self-control.[56] Of course, the school was at the opposite pole to many of the ordinary certified schools, but it embodied principles and practices which Norris wanted the other schools to emulate. In fact, there seems little doubt that the example of the Little Commonwealth eventually leavened the aims, methods and discipline of the conventional reformatories, but not before a disturbed period in the history of penal policy, characterized by sharp differences of opinion as to the comparative role and efficacy of probation and of committal to certified schools. On one side were reforming magistrates and the

[54] *Report of the Departmental Committee on Reformatories and Industrial Schools*, PP 1913, XXXIX (Cmd. 6838), p. 1. See also Mary Barnett, *Young Delinquents* (1913).

[55] Maxwell, op. cit., p. 22. Maxwell again commended Russell for having effected, in the four years between 1913 and 1917, 'a remarkable transformation in the spirit and methods of the schools, and in the attitude of the managers and staffs to new ideas and improved practices': *The Boy*, vol. XXV (Winter, 1952–3), p. 122. See also J. Carlebach, *Caring for Children in Trouble* (1970).

[56] See E. T. Bazeley, *Homer Lane and the Little Commonwealth* (1928); Burt, *The Young Delinquent*, pp. 237–9; John Lawson and Harold Silver, *A Social History of Education in England* (1973), p. 399.

penal pressure groups: they were for exhausting all other methods before committing a child to a protracted term of detention in a certified school. On the other side were the managers and superintendents of the schools, who complained of the difficulty of dealing with children whose committal had been injuriously delayed by the excessive use of probation. The go-between was the chief inspector, whose approach, however, as we shall see, was far from impartial.

One of the most outspoken critics of the certified schools was the stipendiary magistrate, Clarke Hall. He was particularly disparaging of the private management and training methods of the schools. Private ownership led, in his view, to a lack of classification between the schools and a lack of uniformity in the licensing of children. Only direct state control, he argued, could remedy these deficiencies. This would permit a system of classification according to age (there being no sense in the prevailing separation of delinquent and neglected children) and according to vocation. It would also allow a few of the schools to experiment again with the bold practices of the Little Commonwealth. The training methods of too many schools, according to Clarke Hall, relied on mere tuition in profitable trades of immediate use to the school, trades which were rarely followed in the outside world. It meant that too many lads were ending up in the army or on Welsh farms; too many girls were being consigned to domestic service. The aim of the schools, he insisted, should not be to enforce regulations by pseudo-military discipline, but to strengthen character and self-reliance.[57]

Clarke Hall's staunchest ally was the Howard League for Penal Reform. As ardent proponents of the probation system, the League had for long sought to popularize probation at the expense of the certified schools. But they also realized that the schools would retain some role in the penal armoury, and for that reason they campaigned for their improvement. Grist to the League's mill came in the shape of an unpublished report on the salaries and conditions of service of staff in the certified schools, the product of a departmental committee which had sat in 1919 under Norris's chairmanship. This report, said the *Howard Journal*, formed 'the most damning indictment of the privately-managed, publicly-financed Certified School System we have yet

[57] Clarke Hall, *Children's Courts* (1926), pp. 159–68; *TES*, 5 May 1921, p. 207: address to the annual conference of the National Federation of Christian Workers among Poor Children.

seen'.[58] Quite evidently, in the immediate post-war years, the schools were poorly staffed with ill-qualified 'workmen', as opposed to instructors, who worked their underfed charges 'as little factory hands in inefficient factories'. The moral which the Howard League drew from this evidence was that the mere power of inspection was insufficient, that direct state control had to take the place of voluntary management.

In fact, the powers of inspection in the forceful hands of Norris, backed up by the head of the Children's Branch, proved equal to the task of revamping the certified schools system. Norris had a healthy scepticism of the benefits of institutional training, doubtless deriving from his early social work in the Manchester boys' clubs. His mistrust of institutional life was certainly echoed by other social workers who maintained that a child's individuality was best preserved in the natural context of his or her own home.[59] Significantly, Norris told the Young Offenders Committee in 1925 that his policy as chief inspector had been 'to get a great deal more consideration paid, both in Courts and at schools, to the homes of children'. In line with this, the certified schools had been instructed that 'these boys and girls should renew their family life at the earliest moment'.[60] Such a policy required the schools to develop sufficient strength of character in the children for them to be able to return home. But for this, Norris knew that fundamental improvements to the schools were required.

In the period of reconstruction following the War the schools had hit rock bottom. They were still owned by a variety of voluntary bodies with a variety of ideas about the proper standards of premises, regime, and treatment of young offenders. The voluntary funds, on which they relied almost wholly, began to dry up and many of the schools could afford neither sufficient food nor satisfactory staff. In 1919 the Home Office had stepped in and a new financial scheme had been devised whereby the cost of maintaining the schools was equally divided between the State and the local authorities.[61] These new financial arrangements strengthened the chief inspector's hand in the subsequent negotiations with the managers and superintendents of the certified schools. In his daily administrative work, in the reports of the

[58] *HJ*, vol. 1 (Oct. 1921), p. 49.

[59] Carlebach, op. cit., p. 130; *TES.*, 2 Sep. 1922, p. 397. See also Burt, *The Young Delinquent*, p. 113 n. 2; p. 117.

[60] *Evidence*, p. 117.

[61] Children Act 1921, 11 Geo. V, c. 4; PRO, HO45/10996/173982/28–32.

Children's Branch, and in numerous addresses to conferences of managers and superintendents, Norris directed, cajoled and bullied the schools into new ways.[62] He sought to diminish the 'institutionalism' of previous years by getting the staff to see the children as individuals, by stopping the schools from dressing their boys in 'convict' or 'charity-school' garb, and by reducing the isolation of the schools from the outside world. The gradual collapse of the artificial barrier between the reformatory and industrial school would, Norris hoped, facilitate more classification, with each school specializing in one or two trades, and some schools offering facilities for better education. He wanted all the schools to provide more interesting forms of education which, in line with the trend in modern educational thought, would aim to develop self-awareness in pupils.[63] Norris also encouraged the practice of early licensing, and thus the regular assessment of each child's progress in training (although the difficulty of finding jobs in the early 1920s often jeopardized this practice). For young children at industrial schools, he sought a greater use of boarding out with foster parents, a provision in the Children Act which only the London County Council used with any frequency.[64] At the request of certain London magistrates, Norris experimented with short-term committals, without, it should be said, much success.[65] Finally, the chief inspector looked forward to the appointment of better staff and to an improvement in the composition of the management committees of the schools. Without the latter, Norris believed, the voluntary principle, which he wished to retain, would come under further attack.

All this made for an uneasy dialogue between the chief inspector and the certified schools. Indeed, the various associations and societies of managers and superintendents were firmly convinced that the Home Office were conspiring with the magistrates, local authorities and probation service to disband the schools system. Underlying this anxiety about the survival of the schools was the rapid fall in the number of children committed to them between 1920 and 1924 (far in

[62] See *First Report on the Work of the Children's Branch*, op. cit., pp. 17–54. This was the first official review of the schools since 1916. See also Norris, 'The Certified Reformatory and Industrial Schools', *Seeking and Saving*, vol. 22 (Jan. 1922), pp. 13–22. For Norris's administrative role, see, for example, PRO, HO144/1800/136496 (disturbances at St. John's Reformatory School, Walthamstow).

[63] See Lawson and Silver, op. cit., pp. 398–9; Burt, *The Young Delinquent*, p. 610.

[64] *First Report on the Work of the Children's Branch*, op. cit., p. 46; *Hansard*, vol. 139, 15 Mar. 1921, col. 1224; M. A. Spielman, *The Romance of Child Reclamation* (1920), p. 139.

[65] PRO, HO144/8536/154755/24 and 32.

excess of the drop in the numbers appearing before the juvenile courts) and the subsequent closure of between thirty and forty schools.[66] The fall in committals reflected a general improvement in the social and economic health of the country since 1917, and a consequent decline in cases of neglect and delinquency. But, as the managers and superintendents recognized, the fall also reflected a belief on the part of the public that the schools retained their old penal methods and a reluctance on the part of the magistracy to impose the stigma of conviction and long-term detention on a young person, particularly one nearing a wage-earning age. It was in an attempt to increase the use of the schools in the early stages of delinquency, in fact, that the superintendents supported the abolition of the requirement of a conviction before committal to a reformatory.[67] There were other probable causes, too, of the decline in committals. The wider use of probation, both in the 'open' and with a condition of residence in a hostel, was one factor; the other, and perhaps most potent, factor was the increased cost of the schools to the local authority, which led the latter to press the courts to deal with children in a less expensive way.[68] What most incensed the managers and staff of the schools was that the misrepresentation which commonly sustained the criticisms of their work, was rarely effectively countered by the Home Office. Such was the anguish of the certified schools in the early 1920s, indeed, that they demanded both a fuller system of government inspection, with published reports on individual schools, and a departmental inquiry into the efficiency of the schools.[69] Only in these ways did it seem possible for the schools to break free of the stifling dependency on the Home Office which had arisen under Norris's overbearing leadership. In time, the schools were favoured with a committee of inquiry but not, characteristically, with a representative on that committee.

By 1925, however, the schools were not as far from favour as they probably imagined. Already voices had been heard appealing to

[66] Gordon Rose, *Schools for Young Offenders* (1967), p. 11; *Hansard*, vol. 197, 22 June 1926, col. 253. See Tables 1(a), 1(b), 5, and 6.

[67] J. Campbell, 'The Home Office School Boy and Criminal Conviction', *Child*, vol. X (July 1920), pp. 438–42; *TES*, 20 Aug. 1921, p. 377. This had first been recommended by the Departmental Committee of 1913: PRO, HO45/14714/516360/1A.

[68] See Carlebach, op. cit., p. 90; Norris, *Seeking and Saving*, 22 Jan. 1922, pp. 13–22; I. G. Briggs, *Reformatory Reform* (1924). Joynson-Hicks ascribed the decrease to the gradual improvement in 'the moral tone and social well-being of the country': *Seeking and Saving*, vol. 26 (April 1926), p. 87.

[69] Carlebach, op. cit., pp. 103–4; *TES*, 2 Sept. 1922, p. 397.

magistrates to use the reformatories, particularly when the child's home conditions were poor or when probation had already been tried without success.[70] Magistrates themselves were not averse to singing the praises of the schools.[71] This change of attitude reflected the higher standard of training and the seemingly high success rate of the schools. It was also a response to the growing dissatisfaction with the inadequacies and misuse of probation supervision. In time, even those like Clarke Hall and Cyril Burt, whose inclination was to regard institutional treatment as a last resource in difficult cases, started to accept that the schools supplied a real need, that the decisive factor was to discriminate more carefully between those in need of residential training and those for whom it was undesirable, and that the past competitiveness between the school authorities and probation officers should make way for a closer co-operation between what were two wings of an integrated penal system.[72] One sign of this rapprochement was the joint conferences between representatives of the certified schools, probation officers and the Home Office, which came about through the efforts of Sydney Harris and with the assistance of the Reformatory and Refuge Union.[73] Another sign was the agreement that probation officers should escort children to the certified schools.[74] The seal of approval was applied to this development by the Young Offenders Committee when, in the early sections of its report, it explored 'the problem of probation versus institutional treatment' and commented thus: 'It is now being recognised that these two different systems are not in any sense antagonistic. They are really complementary, and the best results can only be obtained by the closest co-operation between them.'[75]

The evidence which the departmental committee received on the subject of Home Office schools tended to settle around two main issues. The first was the long-standing distinction between reformatory and industrial schools. From the representatives of the Howard League, the Magistrates Association, and the Society of Headmasters of Certified Schools, as well as from Dr Norris, came the unanimous

[70] *The Times*, 20 Dec. 1922, p. 12, letter from E. Troup, formerly Permanent Under-Secretary of State, Home Office.

[71] *Seeking and Saving*, April 1925, p. 92.

[72] Clarke Hall, *Children's Courts* (1926), p. 184; Burt, *The Young Delinquent*, p. 195.

[73] See I. Ellis, 'Some thoughts on the Causes and Treatment of Juvenile Delinquency', *Seeking and Saving*, Mar. 1926, pp. 68–76; PRO, HO45/18442/455959/1.

[74] *Seeking and Saving*, April 1926, pp. 101–6.

[75] *Report of YOC*, op. cit., p. 1006.

demand to abolish the distinction once and for all, in view of the similarity of natures and needs of neglected and delinquent children. A single series of schools, they argued, would open up greater scope for classification by age and by type of training. Only Basil Henriques, a juvenile court magistrate and warden of a boys' club in London, contended that the neglected and delinquent should be treated separately, the former in cottage homes.[76]

The second issue was that of short-term schools. Dr Norris was the first and foremost champion of this proposal, explaining to the Committee, 'I think sometimes a vigorous, healthy training for six months or a year is quite sufficient in the case of the boy of thirteen or fourteen who has got into rather slack ways.'[77] Norris had become convinced that magistrates often baulked at sending a boy who was not markedly criminal to a reformatory for three years, in some cases resorting instead to a farm colony. Moreover, he believed that the present-day child required less time away from home, given that there was not the same abject poverty as in earlier years and that families tended to take greater interest in their children. The recommendation which flowed from these views was for the removal of the three-year minimum on a committal to a reformatory school.[78] Norris's evidence was seconded by that from the representatives of the Magistrates Association, the Labour party and TUC, and the Howard League.[79] Miss Fry, on behalf of the League, felt that short-term schools would be particularly helpful for lads who had good homes but bad companions. 'If you could send them away for a drilling for a few months', she said, 'they could then go back home.'[80] But the committee also heard the opposing views of the superintendents of reformatory and industrial schools. Short terms, they argued, would give insufficient time for vocational training and would arouse jealousies amongst the children, unless the short-termers were to be grouped together in a separate school.[81]

In their report, the departmental committee were full of praise for the Home Office schools. 'From the many visits which members of the Committee have paid to the schools', it was stated, 'we are able to

[76] *Evidence*, p. 11 (Norris); p. 410 (Fry); p. 764 (Mr. W. Craven Jones, President of Society of Headmasters of Certified Schools); p. 347 (Basil Henriques).

[77] *Evidence*, p. 11, q. 72.

[78] *Evidence*, pp. 10–11, 54.

[79] *Magistrate*, vol. 1 (Dec. 1925), p. 110; *Evidence*, p. 2657 (Dr Marion Phillips).

[80] *Evidence*, p. 411, q. 3261.

[81] *Evidence*, p. 678 (I. Ellis); p. 780 (W. H. Banister).

confirm the testimony of the present Chief Inspector that the schools are now generally well-equipped and are carrying on their difficult work with marked success.' Between the enquiry of 1913–14 and the present enquiry the change of outlook and approach was said to have been fundamental:

> The needs of the boys and girls are no longer subordinated to those of the institution, but the scheme of education and training is such as to fit them for useful careers when they leave the school. Discipline, as in the case of all good schools, is being maintained by giving a much greater measure of freedom and responsibility to the pupils . . .[82]

The underlying spirit, in all, was disciplined freedom on public school lines, although the extent to which this was executed differed in line with the ability of the headmaster and staff. Industrial schools, for younger children, were largely educational and could bear comparison with residential elementary schools. In the case of older children, more emphasis was put on vocational training.

The committee accepted that the prevailing distinction between industrial and reformatory schools was unsound, for the reasons advanced by various witnesses. The report itself summed up the arguments in the phrase: 'Neglect leads to delinquency and delinquency is often the direct outcome of neglect'.[83] Secondly, as the schools had already largely abandoned the titles 'reformatory' and 'industrial' (on the advice of the Children's Branch), the report recommended that in future they should be known as approved schools.[84] As to the system of control and management of the schools, the voluntary principle survived; state control, either by the Home Office or, as some witnesses had submitted, by the Board of Education, found no favour with the committee.[85] The remaining recommendations had to do with the length of detention in an approved school. Accepting that the value of extended institutional training was open to question, the report proposed that the maximum period of detention should not exceed three years; yet it also wanted the courts to commit for a period of not less than three years in every case, leaving it to the

[82] *Report of YOC*, op. cit., p. 1027.

[83] Ibid., p. 1029.

[84] Ibid. The abolition of the name 'reformatory' had been recommended by the Departmental Committee of 1913: PRO, HO45/14714/516360/1A.

[85] Ibid., p. 1036. For proposed transfer of the schools to the Board of Education, see *Evidence*, pp. 2651–2.

school authorities and the Home Office to select out those who could be granted early release on licence.[86] On the issue of short-term detention, the committee's opinion had vacillated, judging by what Harris wrote a few years later:

> The Committee started with a strong bias in favour of introducing a system of short-term treatment as an alternative in suitable cases both to reformatory schools as well as to prison and Borstal, but they came to the conclusion that the facilities likely to be offered by any such system were outweighed by the difficulties.[87]

An experiment in short-term training had already been launched by the Home Office at a London industrial school, but the committee held that until conclusive evidence as to the success of this venture emerged, the use of short-term schools 'would in our opinion be open to grave risk'. One such danger was the financial impetus to local authorities to press magistrates to choose the short-term option. In consequence, the report encouraged the use of residence in a hostel as a condition of probation, but echoed the staff of the certified schools in arguing that training and short-term sentences were incompatible.[88]

Short-term detention went against the grain of the committee's entire stance, that for most young offenders the main effect of a custodial sentence ought to be a training experience. This, of course, meant periods of detention which seemed incommensurate with the gravity of the offence, but then the committee made it clear that they came to bury 'just proportions': 'The idea of the tariff for the offence or of making the punishment fit the crime dies hard; but it must be uprooted if reformation rather than punishment is to be—as it should be for young offenders—the guiding principle.'[89] From this conviction other conclusions flowed, such as that sentences which were simply penal had to be discarded.

Punishment

By the Children Act 1908 the committal of children to prison, whether on conviction or remand, was prohibited. More specifically, section 102 stipulated that no child under fourteen years could be either

[86] Ibid., p. 1033.
[87] 2 Jan. 1931, PRO, HO45/14715/516360/68.
[88] *Report*, pp. 1033–4.
[89] Ibid., p. 1006.

sentenced to imprisonment or committed to prison in default of payment of a fine; a young person over fourteen but under sixteen years could be committed to prison only if the court certified that he was of so 'unruly' or 'depraved' a character that he could not be held in a 'place of detention'. The effect of these provisions on the admission of children and young persons to prison had been dramatic. In 1904–5 the number of persons under sixteen sentenced or admitted to prison was 1,151; in 1909–10 it was 143. Thereafter, and throughout the 1920s, it was rare for more than 200 children to be received into prison, and most of these were sent there on remand. The number of persons under sixteen received into prison on conviction was much smaller—572 in 1907; 8 in 1925.[90] Hence, the issue of the imprisonment of young offenders was rather more symbolic than corporeal. Even so, attempts were still made to restrict further the use of imprisonment. Mrs Barrow Cadbury recommended an amendment to Mr Ammon's bill in 1924 to make it impossible to send persons of sixteen to eighteen years of age to prison.[91] Moreover, the strength of opposition to the imprisonment of any young offender under twenty-one led the Departmental Committee on Young Offenders to recommend that the age of prohibition of imprisonment, except where a special certificate was granted by the court, be raised from sixteen to seventeen.[92]

An alternative method of punishing young offenders was provided by section 106 of the Children Act, whereby a child or young person convicted of an offence could be committed to a 'place of detention' for a period not exceeding one month. These places of detention served also, of course, as remand homes. In practice, few children were sentenced to mere detention: 364 in 1910; 36 in 1921.[93] This was due partially to the fact that such a sentence implied a conviction, thereby preventing the use of probation on a subsequent occasion. If a short spell of detention seemed appropriate, magistrates preferred to order a simple remand in custody. It was due, also, to the lack of Home Office enthusiasm for such places of detention. Few could provide regular

[90] *Report of Indian Jails Committee*, op. cit., p. 839; *Hansard*, vol. 135, 24 Nov. 1920, col. 472; PRO, HO45/16515/375684/16. Occasionally a prison sentence was passed on a child suffering from the after-effects of *encephalitis lethargica*. Such cases were not certifiable either as lunatics or as mental defectives, and committal to a reformatory did not seem appropriate: PRO, HO144/22370/487003.

[91] PRO, HO45/14714/516360/1A.

[92] *Evidence*, p. 33 (Norris); *Report*, pp. 1006, 1037–40.

[93] *First Report on the Work of the Children's Branch*, op. cit., p. 65.

instruction and physical exercise; all of them grouped convicted offenders with those on remand.[94] It would have been possible to provide separate accommodation for those in custody, in order to avoid such association, as the Report of the Juvenile Organisations Committee had recommended in 1920.[95] A few years later, both Cyril Burt and Clarke Hall advocated the provision of separate places of detention to which boys could be sent for any period up to six months, for the following purpose: 'The shock of a sharp, short separation will often rouse the casual offender to his senses, and bring his family to a feeling of their own responsibility and blame.'[96]

To have separate places of detention seemed 'hopelessly extravagant' to the Children's Branch, however, in view of the small use made of section 106 and of the penalty's poor record as a temporary deterrent. The JOC had illustrated that, in the town in its enquiry which made most use of this provision, over 70 per cent of the delinquents so dealt with reappeared at the court within six months.[97] Not surprisingly, then, the Young Offenders Committee recommended that such detention should be abandoned, except perhaps in the rare cases of enforcing a fine inflicted on a young offender.[98]

That leaves only the controversial question of the use of corporal punishment in the disposal of young offenders, on which opinion was split throughout the inter-war period. In the 1920s the cleavage of opinion was not always between retributive proponents and reformative opponents of corporal punishment, as it was more clearly to become in the 1930s. This fact can be illustrated by reference to two monographs which appeared during the First World War. In the one, Charles Russell, the chief inspector of reformatory and industrial schools, whose reformist credentials have been noted, expressed the view that flogging, in such cases as gross cruelty to animals, was 'a much kinder and more effectual corrective than the long detention in a school'.[99] Moreover, whilst Russell did not want the recourse to this penalty to count as a conviction, he sympathized with those magistrates who hankered for the power to inflict corporal punishment

[94] Ibid., pp. 66–8.

[95] *Report of JOC*, op. cit., p. 41.

[96] Burt, *The Young Delinquent*, p. 107; Clarke Hall, *Children's Courts*, p. 87.

[97] *Third Report on the Work of the Children's Branch*, op. cit., p. 37; PRO, HO45/16515/375684/42; *Detention in Remand Homes* (1952), English Studies in Criminal Science, vol. VII, p. 4.

[98] *Report of YOC*, pp. 965–6.

[99] Russell, *The Problems of Juvenile Crime*, pp. 15–16.

in respect of *any* serious offence committed by a boy under sixteen. The present law allowed the birching of boys between fourteen and sixteen years of age for specified offences only. In contrast, Clarke Hall was of the opinion by 1917 that birching was 'the least deterrent, as well as the least reformative, method' of dealing with young offenders. Drawing upon the figures of children charged at Old Street police court during 1915 and 1916, Clarke Hall maintained that approximately 35 per cent of boys who were birched committed further offences. The strength of such evidence, and the fact that the incidence of delinquency declined at the age of fourteen although the birch was no longer available for most offences, led Clarke Hall to stop sentencing boys to be birched.[100] So, too, the Birmingham juvenile court, under the influence of Geraldine Cadbury, gave up using the birch from the early 1920s. Yet many courts, as at Leeds and Liverpool, persisted; during 1919, 1,599 boys were sentenced by juvenile courts to be whipped.[101]

As late as 1920 the basis of the irreconcilable viewpoints was more surmise, *a priori* deduction, not to say prejudice, than hard fact. In April 1920, indeed, the secretary of the Howard League called for an impartial investigation of the question, through the columns of the *Daily News*.[102] As it happened, the report of the Juvenile Organisations Committee provided, *inter alia*, a rough estimate of the value of corporal punishment. It suggested that birching had little deterrent efficacy, although the report's findings admittedly made no allowance 'for the fact that it is usually the bad type of boy who is whipped'. Of every four boys birched, one was recharged within a month; and four out of every five were recharged within the two years covered by the inquiry.[103] This evidence was manna to the opponents of whipping, and it was recurrently cited for the attention of magistrates and the Home Office in the *Howard Journal* and in parliamentary speeches.[104] The official attitude at this date is hard to gauge, but the Home Office seemed to be trying, first, to discourage courts from using corporal punishment and second, to ensure that a medical examination of the fitness of the defendant to undergo the punishment always prefaced its

[100] Clarke Hall, *Children's Courts*, pp. 75–82; PRO, HO45/16515/375684/10.

[101] *Hansard*, vol. 129, 20 May 1920, col. 1644. For the wartime increase in the use of whipping, see Table 1(b).

[102] *Daily News*, 21 April 1920.

[103] *Report of JOC*, op. cit., pp. 26–9. cf. Scottish National Council of Juvenile Organisations, op. cit., pp. 11–12.

[104] *HJ*, vol. 1 (Oct. 1921), p. 52; *Hansard*, vol. 142, 31 May 1921, cols. 825–6.

infliction.[105] Whether it was this lack of support in official and reforming circles, or whether it was the lack of deterrent efficacy, the use of corporal punishment began to decline. The proportion of children sentenced to a whipping fell from 10.7 per cent in 1916 to 2.0 per cent in 1923.

Yet the division of opinion remained, as was clear from the evidence to the Departmental Committee on Young Offenders. On one side was the Chief Constables' Association, advocates of a wider use of birching and of its use in association with a probation order.[106] On the other side were social workers like Miss Blyth, probation officer for juveniles at Tower Bridge police court, who called for the penalty's abolition.[107] In between were witnesses like the prison commissioner, Alexander Paterson, who accepted that birching was a lazy and generally ineffective way of dealing with young offenders, but felt that the power ought to be left in the hands of the court.[108] The middle way attracted most members of the committee. Warning against 'any indiscriminate use of whipping', urging full consideration of the character and circumstances of offenders, and opposing the association of whipping with any other form of treatment, the report none the less concluded, 'Subject to these safeguards, courts should be enabled to order a whipping in respect of any serious offence committed by a boy under 17.'[109] A memorandum was attached to the report, however, signed by Mrs Cadbury, Rhys Davies and Wemyss Grant-Wilson, formally dissenting from this recommendation.[110] It was one of the few occasions when the committee failed to reach unanimous agreement, and one of the few occasions when the committee placed the punishment of the offence before the needs of the offender.

Summary

The broad outlines of penal policy for young offenders were set down in the legislation of the reforming Liberal governments between 1906 and 1914. Canvas had barely been thrown over this framework before the Great War distracted the attentions both of government and of the

[105] PRO, PCom 7/242; HO45/10912/A54970.
[106] *Evidence*, p. 1548 (Capt. Moore).
[107] Ibid., p. 311.
[108] Ibid., pp. 164–5. cf. Burt, *The Young Delinquent*, p. 121.
[109] Report, pp. 1025–7.
[110] Ibid., p. 1087.

individuals and groups responsible for child welfare. Yet the war brought in its wake a sudden upward shift in the incidence of juvenile crime, which induced the Home Office to appoint the Juvenile Organisations Committee and which reinvigorated the penal reform 'lobby' in readiness for a post-war era of 'reconstruction' which was expectantly awaited. From 1918 renewed pressure was brought to bear upon the Home Office, both to improve existing procedures for trying and treating young offenders, and to appoint an enquiry which would re-assess the general lines of policy. These pressures, plus the independent endeavours of the Home Office, were the essential stuff of policy-making between 1918 and 1928, as the preceding pages have indicated. It is now necessary to pull together the threads of the previous sections in order to present a more integrated assessment of the different forms the impetus to policy-formation could take.

The general backcloth to the making of penal policy for young offenders was both help and hindrance to the process. A help, in that from 1918 the rate of juvenile crime retreated from its wartime peak, giving little cause for concern at any time before 1928. If government departments are more predisposed to think constructively about existing arrangements and future patterns when their backs are not to the wall, then the decreasing crime rate of the 1920s was a helpful factor. In contrast, the post-war economic recession was an undoubted hindrance, aggravating the task of placing young offenders in jobs, and, via the dictates of the Geddes committee, depriving the spending departments of the wherewithal to finance new nation-wide improvements. One impact of this last factor was probably to reinforce the argument that it made economic sense to retain the contribution to the penal system of the voluntary organizations. The Treasury was certainly resistant to proposals which, by enlarging the role of central or local government, would increase the financial burden of the Exchequer.

For direct influences on policy-making, the essential starting point is what has been termed the social conception of delinquency. The main feature of this was the conviction that an offence was merely a symptom of a delinquent's social and personal condition. Delinquency was seen less as a self-contained phenomenon, and more as but one of a large number of manifestations of social and parental neglect. This outlook on delinquent and neglected youth drew heavily on the experience of social workers in university settlements and boys' clubs. The child-study movement and new ideas about the education of children reinforced the view, as did the casework based investigations of the psychologist, Cyril Burt. This view of delinquency, moreover, incorporated an understanding of the social and economic conditions which led to neglect and crime, and a faith in the contribution of investigation, classification and character-training to the promotion of 'good citizenship'. Accordingly, the judicial disposal of the young offender in ignorance of his social and personal circumstances seemed increasingly short-sighted. The ideological and institutional barriers which segregated the treatment of delinquency from the wider patterns of child care seemed ever more indefensible. If this viewpoint was important in educating public opinion to see the delinquency of youth in a more benevolent light, it became a crucial determinant of penal policy when a number of the activists in voluntary youth work were recruited by the Children's Branch of the Home Office.

Charles Russell and Arthur Norris, not to mention Alexander Paterson, moved from the milieu of voluntary social work directly into positions of influence in central administration. Russell and Norris were extremely energetic in their role as chief inspector of reformatory and industrial schools, the former during the war, the latter in the post-war years. Together they redefined the principles and practices of the certified schools, guided particularly by their work in boys' clubs and by a sceptical outlook on the supposed benefits of institutional training. They worked to transform the highly regimented schools, in which the financial needs of the institution often took precedence over the needs of the children, into places which would bear comparison with normal elementary schools, with schemes of education and training designed to fit the children for working life.

Underpinning the efforts of the inspectorate was the clear-sighted and sympathetic vision of the head of the Children's Branch. He it was who first recognized the need to re-assess the general framework of policy for young offenders; to determine, for example, the relationship between probation and the certified schools, to decide whether juvenile courts should approximate civil or chancery courts. The forcing-house of Harris's conviction was the evidence that by the early 1920s local administration had, in certain respects, overstepped legislative sanction. Magistrates and social workers were resorting frequently to extra-legal initiatives as a way of reducing the penal taint on young offenders. One step was the use of hostels as a condition of probation in preference to a committal to a reformatory school. Alternatively, they were keeping cases away from the courts altogether. The Committee on Young Offenders, which Harris was instrumental in getting appointed, would, it was hoped, resolve these difficulties. Harris was a member of this committee, thus enhancing the influence of the Children's Branch on the recommendations of the committee. As Harris told his departmental superiors in October 1927, 'Dr Norris and I discussed constantly and in detail during the sitting of the Young Offenders Committee all the proposals that came before it.'[111]

Not that the head of the Branch and the chief inspector agreed at every point. For some time they had been at variance concerning the proposed change from criminal to civil procedure in the juvenile courts and concerning the provision of short-term reformatories. These disagreements aside, the Children's Branch was a formative influence in the creation of policy for young offenders. In the reports of 1923 to 1925 the Branch had disseminated the evidence of local deficiencies in juvenile justice. It had directed magistrates and the staff of certified schools to improve their methods; it had encouraged greater co-operation between the probation system and the certified schools. And, lastly, it had received and sifted the proposals which had poured in from the penal reform groups.

Another main stimulus to policy formation came from the individuals and organizations which constituted the penal reform 'lobby'. Two of the most prominent and effective individuals were Clarke Hall, the metropolitan magistrate, and Geraldine Cadbury, the Birmingham juvenile magistrate and member of the Young Offenders Committee. Protagonists on behalf of juvenile courts to which parents and social workers would be eager to bring neglected and delinquent children, critics of long-term committal to reformatory institutions in cases where probation would be more constructive and less stigmatizing, Clarke Hall and Cadbury built up international reputations as practical-minded idealists on behalf of a reformed juvenile justice. Their influence was felt in two main ways. First, they gave advice to departmental officers like Maxwell and Harris, often at the request of the department itself. Secondly, the courts over which they presided were working models of the kind of juvenile justice the Children's Branch and the penal reform societies were championing.

The main organized pressure groups were the Howard League and the Magistrates Association. They were ably assisted in a number of

[111] PRO, HO45/13403/510865/7.

campaigns by such child welfare bodies as the State Children's Association and the Committee on Wage-Earning Children, and by the People's League of Health. These groups did not see eye to eye on all the reform proposals which were under discussion in the 1920s, but there was general agreement on the need for specialist magistrates in special juvenile courts, for a wider use of probation and the ending of the use of corporal punishment, and for better facilities for pre-sentence enquiries, notably in the shape of observation homes. By way of conferences, deputations, and published literature, these organizations were active propagandists. They also worked through the Parliamentary Penal Reform Group, although to no real legislative effect in the 1920s. In addition, there were the organized bodies of practitioners: the National Association of Probation Officers and the societies of managers and staff of the certified schools. The former rallied the opinion of the scattered probation officers in favour of an expanded and improved probation system, and a larger element of central administrative direction. The latter organizations, whilst dissatisfied with the treatment the schools had received at the hands of the Home Office, and critical of such proposals as short-term reformatories, nevertheless gave their blessing to the abolition of the requirement of a conviction before committal to a reformatory, and to the final repudiation of the distinction between reformatory and industrial schools.

These converging streams of opinion fed into the most important official enquiry of the 1920s, the Departmental Committee on the Treatment of Young Offenders. Of course, the outcome of this enquiry did not fulfill everyone's expectations. Whether on the age of criminal responsibility, the issue of corporal punishment, the idea of short-term reformatories, or the legal principle underlying the juvenile court, the committee were criticized for erring on the side of caution. There was criticism, too, of the committee's reluctance to place the guardianship of delinquents more firmly in state hands. Yet most members of the committee were prepared to defend a more cautious approach. Harris, for example, considered the recommendations were

> characteristically British in the sense that they do not involve any revolution in theory and practice but encourage further progress on existing lines. They do not go as far as many social reformers would wish to go but they are probably none the worse for that from the point of view either of legislation or administration.[112]

[112] PRO, HO/45/14801/594745/4A.

Moreover, despite the occasional cry of disappointment, it was widely held that in proposing an extension of the law's jurisdiction, an improvement of its procedure and a more careful selection of its officers, the committee had gone a long way towards ensuring that the young offender would be treated not as an enemy of society but as a citizen *manqué*, to be restored to his proper status. More significantly still, the recommendations of the Young Offenders Committee reflected the wide consensus of opinion which had developed on the subject of the young delinquent by 1925.[113] A formidable alliance had been forged, linking social workers, magistrates, penal reform groups, associations of penal practitioners, and the administrators and inspectors of the Children's Branch. The strength of the alliance lay in a shared experience of voluntary social work amongst school-children and working lads, in an interchange of personnel between the voluntary and official spheres of child welfare, and in a like-minded evaluation of the causes and correctives of juvenile delinquency. The way now seemed clear for a new Children Act, some twenty years after the initiatory statute of 1908.

[113] It was in keeping with this consensus that the Scottish Committee on the Treatment of Young Offenders should endorse most of the recommendations of the English Committee: PRO, HO45/13403/510865/25.

PART II

Creating the Children and Young Persons Act 1933

3

Juvenile Justice, 1927–1932

Chronology

As early as July 1927, Sydney Harris proposed that a parliamentary bill should be drafted in the autumn, with an eye to its introduction in the following year. It was to embody the suggestions of the Child Adoption Committee (Third Report) in regard to the registration and inspection of voluntary homes, most of the proposals of the Young Offenders Committee relating to children and young persons under seventeen years, and the recommendations of the Sexual Offences Committee dealing with child welfare. The time was ripe, he advised the department, for amending the Children Act of 1908:

> A new Children Bill would I believe receive a great deal of support in different quarters of the House and would be welcomed by all those who are concerned in the social welfare of young people. It is not likely to be controversial, and it would enable us to make a considerable advance in giving effect to the recommendations of three Committees in the directions where they are least open to dispute or discussion.[1]

In a number of high-level meetings held within the department, Harris's view prevailed. Hence, in mid November 1927, the Conservative Home Secretary, Sir William Joynson-Hicks, informed the Commons, in reply to a question from Edward Cadogan, that he had given instructions for the drafting of a new Children Bill.[2] This was taken in hand in December. By January 1928, the Home Office was in discussion with the Treasury and the local authorities (including the

[1] 21 July 1927, PRO, HO45/14714/516360/1. Most of the recommendations made by the Sexual Offences Committee which were concerned with the protection of children and young persons, in respect of whom sexual offences had been committed, were dealt with in the new Children Act. Some, for example, were covered by the wider definition of 'neglect' which the statute included. See PRO, HO45/14801/594745/4A; HO45/14716/516360/109; HO144/20112/548577/9.

[2] *Hansard*, vol. 210, 16 Nov. 1927, col. 1052; *The Times*, 2 Dec. 1927, letter from Cadogan; PRO, HO45/13403/510865/12.

London County Council) concerning the financial implications of the bill. Neither the Treasury nor the local authorities were prepared to accept any substantial consequential expenditure, and the Home Office had to allay their fears on this score.[3] In fact, in the ensuing meetings, the local authorities proved extremely supportive of most of the bill's provisions. A month later, however, the Cabinet decided not to adopt the Children Bill for the coming session, in view of the restricted parliamentary time available.[4] Little more was heard of the measure until July 1928 when Joynson-Hicks, on opening the first purpose-built juvenile court in Birmingham (a gift to the city from Barrow and Geraldine Cadbury), stated that he was looking forward to introducing a new Children's Charter. But a week later the Cabinet again barred the way. When they were asked by the Home Secretary to consider the possibility of introducing the bill in the coming parliamentary session, the suggestion was made, and evidently accepted, that it would be wiser to keep this particular measure of social reform until after the next general election.[5] The latter was held on 30 May 1929, but resulted in a victory for Labour.

In June, a Labour government took office with J. R. Clynes as Home Secretary.[6] Judging from a reply to the National Federation of Women's Institutes, in September, the government had every intention of proceeding with a Children Bill. The Cabinet, however, declined to introduce it in the autumn parliamentary session.[7] Nor was a bill introduced in 1930, except, that is, for the one drafted by the Howard League and brought in by Rhys Davies under the ten minutes rule. This was in July, towards the end of the session, and thus there

[3] PRO, HO45/14714/516360/8, 10A and 15–18; HO45/13403/510865/9 and 17. Harris stated on 22 Dec. 1927, for example: 'There are signs that the local authorities may take this opportunity of raising the question of their responsibility for payment in the case of delinquent children and young persons.'

[4] PRO, CAB 23/4 (28), 1 Feb. 1928.

[5] *Magistrate*, vol. 1 (July 1928), pp. 241–2; Janet Whitney, *Geraldine S. Cadbury, 1865–1941* (1948), p. 124; PRO, CAB 23/41 (28), 25 July 1928.

[6] J. R. Clynes, born 1869, a former president of the National Union of General and Municipal Workers, was Labour MP for the Platting division of Manchester, and Deputy Leader of the Labour party, 1923–31. He was Home Secretary from June 1929 until August 1931. Clynes, 'a bristly little ex-weaver', according to Colin Cross—*Philip Snowden* (1966), p. 184—had served in the Coalition government during the war, in the Ministry of Food. He was closely affiliated to the Trade Union world; disliked by the left wing of the Labour party; and unable to develop any real public stature. See *DNB 1941–50*, pp. 161–3.

[7] PRO, HO45/14714/516360/44; CAB 23/30 (29) and 23/36 (29).

was never any likelihood that the bill would make any progress.[8] By October 1930, Clynes was telling the annual meeting of the Magistrates Association that the government had decided to bring in a Children bill.[9] To this end, in the first months of 1931, the department was busy with a detailed draft of a bill, and, as in 1928, was in discussion with the Treasury in order to convince it that 'the new system which the Bill will introduce is not expected to prove much more costly than that which is now in force'.[10] Yet by April the Home Office did not rate highly its chances of finding parliamentary time that session.[11] Shortly afterwards, the bill fell victim to the financial crisis and the parliamentary turmoil of 1931, out of which emerged the National government.

Greater fortune attended the measure when the Liberal leader, Herbert Samuel, was appointed Home Secretary in the National government. Samuel had been Parliamentary Under-Secretary of Home Affairs when the 'Children's Charter' of 1908 was passed, and was doubtless invigorated by the opportunity to sponsor yet another, improved measure of child welfare.[12] At a conference in the Home Office in November 1931, the Home Secretary summed up the discussion between the permanent and parliamentary officials by stating that a Children Bill should be introduced, that it would form a useful part of the government's legislative programme, and that it would most likely be passed by the present House of Commons.[13] In December 1931, the Cabinet agreed to the bill's introduction, subject to further consideration of the proposals for the regulation of employment of persons between fourteen and eighteen years of age in 'unregulated occupations', which, at this stage, formed a controversial part of the measure.[14] This time things went to plan. In the capable hands of the Conservative Under-Secretary, Oliver Stanley, on whom fell practically the whole burden of the ministerial work, the second

[8] 'A bill to Amend the Law relating to Juvenile Offenders', PP 1929–30, I (248), pp. 335–46.

[9] *Magistrate*, vol. 2 (Oct–Nov. 1930), p. 433.

[10] PRO, HO45/14715/516360/71 and 75.

[11] Ibid., 516360/82; PRO, CAB 23/53 (30).

[12] See Viscount Samuel, *Memoirs* (1945), p. 219; John Bowle, *Viscount Samuel. A Biography* (1957), p. 284.

[13] 17 Nov. 1931, PRO, HO45/14716/516360/105.

[14] PRO, CAB 23/87 (31) and 23/93 (31), 16 Dec. 1931; HO45/14801/594745/1. The Cabinet eventually decided to omit from the bill the proposals for the regulation of employment of persons between fourteen and eighteen in 'unregulated occupations': HO45/14716/516360/131.

reading of the Children Bill took place in February 1932.[15] In July the measure was accorded the Royal Assent.[16] It had been drafted with a view to the passing of another bill which would consolidate the first bill with the Children Act of 1908. Thus the operation of most of the 1932 Act was suspended, pending the passage of the Children and Young Persons Act 1933.[17]

Such, in bare outline, is the five-year voyage of the Children Bill through the reaches of the Home Office and of Parliament. The process was long-drawn-out owing to the troubled political situation, and, as we shall see, to the difficulty of getting the agreement of the Treasury and the local authorities to the financial implications of a central remand home. It was certainly not because of a lack of support on the part of the department or of successive home secretaries, judging from the official papers. These latter form the essential basis of the next two chapters, in which the genesis of the Children and Young Persons Act between 1927 and 1932 is examined in the light of both outside influences on the Home Office and internal departmental discussions. For if there was unanimity within the Home Office on the overall design and content of the bill, a number of the specific proposals aroused considerable argument. This had been foreshadowed in October 1927 by Sydney Harris when he spoke of his disagreement with Dr Norris, the chief inspector of Home Office schools, over some of the proposals of the Young Offenders Committee. Harris concluded thus:

> On some of these matters, e.g. short detention and the relation of probation to institutional treatment, the Committee only arrived at its recommendations after prolonged discussion and with much hesitation, and there is ample room for further consideration before a definite policy is adopted.[18]

[15] *Hansard*, vol. 261, 12 Feb. 1932, cols. 1167–1246; Samuel, loc. cit.; PRO, HO45/14804/594745/107. Oliver F. G. Stanley, born 1896, was Conservative MP for Westmorland, and Parliamentary Under-Secretary of State for Home Affairs, Sept. 1931–Feb. 1933. He had been regarded in February 1930, by Thomas Jones and Beatrice Webb, as a future Tory Cabinet Minister: see Thomas Jones, *Whitehall Diary*, ed. Keith Middlemas (1969), vol. II, pp. 244 and 247. In the House of Lords, the Lord Privy Seal, Viscount Snowden, took charge of the Children Bill: C. Cross, op. cit., p. 328; *Hansard*, vol. 84 (Lords), 26 May 1932, col. 447.

[16] Children and Young Persons Act 1932, 22 and 23 Geo. V, c. 46.

[17] 23 Geo. V, c. 12.

[18] 27 Oct. 1927, PRO, HO45/13403/510865/7.

Juvenile Courts

The first step taken by the Home Office, in the aftermath of the Young Offenders Committee, was to issue a circular letter to all magistrates, advising them on the implementation of some of the committee's recommendations which did not require legislation. The circular of 30 September 1927 dealt only with the organization of juvenile courts. Its opening observation was that the importance of the juvenile tribunal was still not always fully recognized and acted upon by magistrates, 'and that adequate steps have not always been taken to discriminate between the treatment of young people and the trial of older offenders, in the manner contemplated by the Children Act, 1908'. Hence, the circular hoped that effect would be given to the committee's proposal of a small panel of specially-qualified justices to serve in each juvenile court according to a rota, with no more than three justices being present at any one time (as was already the case in London). Turning from constitution to procedure, the department hoped that proceedings would be kept as informal and untechnical as possible. As to location, the justices were informed of the committee's firm recommendation that the juvenile court should be held on premises other than those where the ordinary court was held. Lastly, magistrates were encouraged to require the fullest information as to each young offender's antecedents; to prohibit the publication of personal details by the press; and to limit the number of persons present in court to the required minimum.[19]

To press the magistrates to reorganize the juvenile courts was one thing; to obtain marked improvements in juvenile justice was another. Sure enough, the survey of juvenile courts which the Fourth Report of the Children's Branch presented in 1928, disclosed that no real advance had taken place in the methods of many courts since the Third Report of 1925, despite the appearance of official reports and circulars.[20] The exemplary courts of Liverpool and Birmingham remained exceptions to the rule. Thus social workers, magistrates, the police, and the education authorities were often still reluctant to bring children before the courts. Hardly the coveted arrangement, in short, of juvenile courts at the centre of work for delinquent, neglected, and defective children. Non-permissive legislation seemed more essential

[19] For the Circular, see Ibid., 510865/12.

[20] See *TES*, 8 Dec. 1928, p. 533; *Howard Journal*, vol. 2 (June 1929), p. 349.

than ever, as the penal reform societies were wont to tell the Home Office.

The immediate priority of the reform groups was to assess whether the lines laid down by the Young Offenders Committee were the soundest ones on which to run fresh legislation. For this purpose, the Howard League for Penal Reform convened a 'Representative Conference' of over sixty societies, ranging from the London Police Court Mission to the Prison Officers' Representative Board and from the Conservative and Unionist Central Office to the Independent Labour Party. Geraldine Cadbury, a member of the Departmental Committee, was in the chair.[21] At the same time, the report of the YOC came under the independent scrutiny of the Committee of the Howard League, the Council of the Magistrates Association, and the Association of the Probation Officers of the London Juvenile Courts.[22] Common to all these groups was the conviction that if reality was to be given to the committee's valuable proposals, the appointment of younger, specially qualified magistrates of both sexes was fundamental. Where they were most at variance with the YOC was on the issue of chancery procedure. The Howard League condemned the committee's contradictory stance on the general principles which should underlie the law, submitting that 'it might have been more statesmanlike to adopt the principle that children of school age should not be charged as criminals, but dealt with as being under the ultimate guardianship of the State'.[23] This view was seconded by the London probation officers who claimed that the prevailing jurisdiction resulted in children not being brought to court by the public or the police, and to children being discharged by magistrates when they did appear. They felt that the solution to this difficulty was to be found 'in developing juvenile courts along lines analagous to those followed in America'.[24]

The head of the Children's Branch, whilst gratified to see the probation officers examining the report of the Young Offenders Committee so carefully, did not believe that their objection to criminal

[21] *The Treatment of Young Offenders*, Being the Report of a Representative Conference, convened by the Howard League for Penal Reform, 27 Oct. 1927 (1929).

[22] PRO, HO45/13403/510865/2, 5 and 6; *Howard Journal*, vol. 2 (1927), pp. 100ff; *Magistrate*, vol. 1 (Oct. 1927), pp. 193–4 and 196–7; *TES*, 15 Oct. 1927, p. 457.

[23] Ibid., 510865/2.

[24] Ibid., 510865/5; *Magistrate*, vol. 1 (Oct. 1927), p. 196. See also Janet Courtney, 'Children's Courts', *Fortnightly Review*, vol. 127 (May 1927), p. 630; Harry Stephen, 'Young Offenders', *Edinburgh Review*, vol. 246 (Oct. 1927), p. 321; A. Fenner Brockway, *A New Way With Crime* (1928), pp. 39–42.

jurisdiction and preference for civil jurisdiction amounted to much. Harris reasoned thus: 'This is an idea which appeals to many, but it seems to me to involve loose thinking. The Committee sought to arrive at the same result without doing violence to elementary principles.'[25] But the penal reform lobby had an ally of sorts within the Children's Department, in the shape of the chief inspector of reformatories. In October 1927, Norris urged Harris to explore further the fundamental issue of criminal versus civil procedure, given the manifest deficiencies of the status quo:

> I submit that the present practice is unfair to the neglected child, harsh on the young delinquent, is more concerned with the offence than the offender and often leaves the young with a strong sense of injustice. Further, it is certain that so long as the Juvenile Court remains a Criminal Court it will only be as a last resort, if at all, that child welfare workers will use it to secure protection and training for the delinquent child.[26]

Additional consideration was forthcoming both from Harris and from a conference of senior departmental officials held at the beginning of November to consider the full set of proposals of the Young Offenders Committee.

Harris accepted that many of the juvenile courts were 'unsatisfactory', but he still maintained that the required change of outlook and method should be secured, less by a major change of principle than by a development of the existing system. He was confirmed in this opinion by the consideration that the adoption of the 'chancery' principle would necessitate trained and experienced justices to act as the guardians of the children. Yet it seemed out of the question that special juvenile courts presided over by paid magistrates would be established. The administration of 'chancery' courts would, therefore, be in the hands of the existing lay magistrates who, in turn, would have to rely on their clerks and probation officers. But the latter, Harris argued, 'are not really competent to advise them as to institutional treatment'. 'Powers which are now vested in the Home Office and the Managers of Schools', he went on, 'would have to be surrendered to the Juvenile Courts and the results might well prove very embarrassing', particularly since, outside London, the Home Office had little control over probation officers.[27] The fate of the 'chancery' principle was finally

[25] 7 Sept. 1927, Ibid., 510865/5.
[26] 24 Oct. 1927, Ibid., 510865/7.
[27] 27 Oct. 1927, Ibid., 510865/7.

sealed by the Home Office conference, composed of Sir John Anderson (Permanent Under-Secretary of State), Sir Ernley Blackwell (Assistant Legal Under-Secretary of State), Mr Maxwell (an Assistant Secretary), and Sydney Harris, which considered the objection to the adoption of the principle to be conclusive.[28]

Not that the department wished to depreciate the role of the juvenile court in the proposed new Children Bill. For the next few years, indeed, successive drafts of the bill invariably opened with the juvenile court—its powers, constitution and procedure—on the principle that it formed the base of any scheme for dealing scientifically with juvenile crime.[29] This was an improvement on the statute of 1908, in which the juvenile court experiment looked rather like an afterthought. The leading position of the children's court also testified to the department's determination to secure more efficient tribunals throughout the country, in view of the fact that most of the juvenile courts were still little more than police courts for children. The justices, it was said, 'comply with the requirements of the law but the spirit is disregarded'. This remained the official assessment up to 1932, judging from Harris's memorandum in preparation for the second reading of the Children Bill. Drawing upon the evidence available to the Children's Branch, he maintained that

> in the majority of divisions the Juvenile Court is still held in the ordinary Court—juvenile cases being taken on a different date or more commonly before or after the ordinary sittings. It is the exception rather than the rule for Justices to be specially designated and the number of Justices taking part is often excessive. In many cases there is no attempt to discriminate between the trial of a juvenile and the trial of an adult: there is no contact with the education authority, no effective probation system, and indeed none of the valuable methods which now characterize some of the best Juvenile Courts in London, Birmingham and Liverpool.[30]

[28] Ibid., 510865/12. Anderson, born 1882, had entered the Colonial Office in 1905. He rose rapidly to become secretary to the National Insurance Commission before the First World War, and secretary to the Ministry of Shipping during the war. By way of the newly-created Ministry of Health, he became Permanent Under-Secretary of State at the Home Office in 1922. He was regarded as one of the very ablest of civil servants, such were his capacities as an administrator, his sure judgement, and his personal, not to say pontifical, authority: *The Times*, 6 Jan. 1958, p. 14.

[29] See Harris, 22 Dec. 1927, PRO, HO45/14714/516360/8; Harris, 5 Jan. 1931, HO45/14715/516360/71; Feb. 1932, HO45/14801/594745/4A; J. R. Clynes, 'Probation to Preventive Detention: A Survey', *Magistrate*, vol. 2 (Oct.–Nov. 1930), pp. 433–4.

[30] Feb. 1932, PRO, HO45/14801/594745/4A.

For these reasons, the draft bills which were prepared within the Home Office sought legally binding changes in the constitution, procedure and premises of the juvenile courts.

A number of the proposals of the Young Offenders Committee claimed rather more departmental attention owing to the conflicting views they aroused, both inside and outside parliament. A notable victory for the reformers was the abolition of the terms 'conviction' and 'sentence' from juvenile court proceedings, the events surrounding which deserve closer attention. The YOC had made their recommendation in response to the views of witnesses like Sir Harry Stephen, of the London County Council, who pointed to the danger lest young offenders should suffer in after-life by reason of having a conviction recorded against them.[31] To begin with, the Home Office, with Joynson-Hicks's approval, accepted the recommendation only as regards young offenders who were committed to reformatory and industrial schools.[32] Three years later, however, in the Labour government's bill of 1930, the full recommendation was adopted. The provision was defended by Harris on the grounds that it would further mark the difference between the adult and juvenile court, and would 'tend to get rid of the gulf between putting a child on probation and sending him to a school (which is still regarded in many quarters as a severe punishment instead of an alternative method of treatment)'.[33] Even so, the National government's bill of 1932 omitted any such clause.

In April 1932, therefore, pressure was brought to bear upon the Home Office by the Magistrates Association and the Association of Head Masters of Certified Schools, both of which supported Mr. Rhys Davies's amendment in favour of not recording a conviction.[34] Norris sided with the amendment, too, feeling that it accorded with the endeavour on the part of the Children's Branch since 1917 to minimize

[31] See also Education Committee of LCC, Min. of Proceedings, 19 Oct. 1927, in PRO, HO45/13403/510865/9; Lucy Masterman, '["Y.P.s"]', *Contemporary Review*, vol. 135 (May 1929), p. 595. Under the Children Act 1908, a committal to an industrial school could be made without the formality of recording a conviction; in contrast, a committal to a reformatory school had to be preceded by a conviction.

[32] Nov. 1927, PRO, HO45/13403/510865/12.

[33] 5 Jan. 1931, PRO, HO45/14715/516360/71. The court made a probation order 'without proceeding to a conviction'.

[34] PRO, HO45/14801/594745/29 and 45. The amendment read: 'Where a court finds a child or young person guilty of an offence, such finding shall not be recorded or rank as a conviction.'

the penal features of juvenile justice. In a characteristic outburst, Norris minuted thus:

I probably possess a more intimate knowledge than anyone else of the strong feeling held on this question of conviction of children, by workers among children and young people throughout the country, and I press very strongly that the amendment which is being put forward by Mr Rhys Davies should be accepted . . .[35]

But the authorized departmental opinion was that any change in the law in the proposed direction would not have the desired consequences. The bar to emigration or to joining the army and navy, for example, was said to be related to the commission of an offence rather than to the fact of 'conviction'. As to the supposed unfairness between committal to a reformatory and probation, the Home Office argued that the principle of the suspended sentence, which underlay the probation system, and the related right of the court to sentence the offender for the original offence, put probation on a different footing to residential treatment. The strongest argument, finally, was said to be the unintended side-effects which abolishing the fact of conviction could bring. It might, for instance, prevent an offender from being sent to Borstal at a later stage of his criminal career, because under section 10 of the Criminal Justice Administration Act 1914, a summary court could not commit an offender to Quarter Sessions (where a Borstal sentence could be awarded) unless it was proved that he had previously been convicted of an offence.[36]

Even so, in Standing Committee, Oliver Stanley offered, by way of a compromise, that in the regulations stipulating the procedure of the juvenile courts the Lord Chancellor would recommend that 'conviction' and 'sentence' should not be used in the juvenile courts. At this proposal, Rhys Davies withdrew his amendment.[37] At the equivalent stage in the House of Lords, however, the Earl of Feversham, President of the National Association of Probation Officers, successfully carried an amendment, the effect of which was to dispense with the words 'sentence' and 'conviction', without confusing the power to send an offender to Borstal training. Judging from Stanley's grudging

[35] 13 April 1932, Ibid., 594745/45.

[36] Alternatively, an offender could be committed to Quarter Sessions if he had previously failed to comply with the conditions of a probation order: Ibid., 594745/45 and 89.

[37] Ibid., 594745/64.

acceptance of the amendment when the bill returned to the Commons, the department were unconvinced of its merit, but they comforted themselves with the view that the amendment was 'in a form in which it can do no practical harm'.[38] Outside the Home Office, the change was applauded as a further shift from the notion of retributory punishment for offences committed by young delinquents.

Controversy also surrounded the proposals to extend the jurisdiction of the juvenile court, namely the age of criminal responsibility, the age limit for juvenile courts, and the hearing of joint charges in the children's court. On the first point, the Home Office were anxious to fight off those who would extend the age of criminal responsibility beyond what the Young Offenders Committee had recommended and thereby, in the department's judgement, deter moderate opinion from accepting any change at all. The upshot of this approach was a good deal of vacillation as to whether to include the provision in the Children Bill. In July 1930, the bill, which was introduced under the auspices of the Howard League, included the recommendation of the Young Offenders Committee that the age of criminal responsibility should be raised from seven to eight years.[39] In the Labour government's bill, as printed in December 1930, there was no such subsection. Harris explained this by reference to the fact that the original recommendation 'was of the nature of a compromise as several members of the Committee would have preferred 9 or even 10', and that it did not seem worth the effort to raise the age by one year. Home Secretary Clynes decided, therefore, to leave the law on this point undisturbed.[40]

When, in December 1931, the provisions of the National government's bill were under discussion, Home Secretary Samuel was advised that the inclusion of a clause on the age of criminal responsibility would probably lead to pressure to raise the age further and to a controversial parliamentary discussion. Oliver Stanley, however, was prepared to risk this outcome, in order to be able to justify the omission

[38] Ibid., 594745/89 & 106; *Probation*, vol. 1 (Oct. 1932), p. 195; *Hansard*, vol. 84 (Lords), 9 June 1932, col. 740; *Hansard*, vol. 267, 30 June 1932, col. 2095. Feversham was President of the National Association of Probation Officers from 1930. After school at Eton he had gone to Johannesburg where he worked as a probation officer for two years, returning to England in 1927. Finding the probation system in England less well developed than in South Africa, Feversham set to work to improve the English probation service.

[39] PRO, HO45/14714/516360/55.

[40] 5 Jan. 1931, PRO, HO45/14715/516360/71.

of some other reforms by pointing to their omission from the recommendations of the Young Offenders Committee. Unless a provision as to the age of responsibility was included in the bill, this justification could not be employed.[41] At the second reading of the bill in February 1932, Rhys Davies, speaking on behalf of the official Opposition, asked for the age to go up to nine years; and in Standing Committee, Mr Kirkwood unsuccessfully moved for the age to be fourteen years.[42] Eight years, however, stood as part of the bill. Judging from a League of Nations Report on the age of criminal responsibility in various European countries, which appeared shortly after the passage of the Children and Young Persons Act, England was hardly a front runner in relieving its children of responsibility for crime.[43]

The proposal of the Young Offenders Committee that the age limit for juvenile courts should be raised to seventeen years was initially well supported. There was the belief that sixteen did not necessarily represent the onset of maturity and, hence, that many youngsters between sixteen and seventeen would benefit from the procedures and practices of a juvenile court. It was also felt that such a change in the law would give the court a choice between Borstal and a reformatory school for the lad of sixteen. Were the age to be raised, assistance could be given, finally, to parents of uncontrollable children of sixteen years, for the change would apply equally to neglected youth. Yet by February 1932, the provision had aroused rather more disagreement. Some wanted no change in the law, lest the atmosphere of the ordinary police court were imported into the juvenile court. Others wanted an intermediate court, or some kind of concurrent jurisdiction whereby those between sixteen and eighteen years could be sent either to a juvenile or to an adult court.[44] These disagreements surfaced in the Commons at Committee stage, when competing amendments were introduced.

[41] PRO, HO45/14716/516360/107.

[42] *Hansard*, vol. 261, 12 Feb. 1932, col. 1189; *Hansard*, vol. 265, 12 May 1932, col. 2234. Stanley stated that to accept Kirkwood's amendment would be to take away from the State 'any opportunity of dealing in any way, however reformative and however lenient, with the young offender under 14' (col. 2238).

[43] *TES*, 11 June 1932, p. 217. See also League of Nations Advisory Committee on Social Questions, *Principles Applicable to the Functioning of Juvenile Courts* . . . (1937), appendix by Miss Wall, contained in PRO, HO45/17043/652494.

[44] See *Justice of the Peace*, vol. 94 (12 July 1930), pp. 439–40; *Hansard*, vol. 261, 12 Feb. 1932, cols. 1173–4; Oliver Stanley, 'The Children Bill', *Magistrate*, vol. 2 (Feb.–March, 1932), p. 569.

Edward Cadogan wanted young persons between the ages of sixteen and seventeen to be dealt with in the adult courts, and sent to juvenile court only when they seemed suitable cases to be dealt with there. Rhys Davies, in contrast, wanted the age limit for juvenile courts to be raised to eighteen, but he agreed to withdraw his amendment if Cadogan did the same, declaring in committee, 'This is not a Party question; it does not belong to parties at all. The children of all classes of the community commit offences against the law, and I believe the Committee will agree that it is better to come down upon the middle course.'[45] Mrs Tate, National Conservative MP for West Willesden, and JP for Middlesex, supported Cadogan's motion, claiming, in doing so, that the London Police Court Mission were opposed to the bill's proposal to raise the age limit to seventeen. Against this, Stanley arrayed the Magistrates Association, the Incorporated Justices' Clerks' Society and the National Association of Probation Officers, all of which supported the provision in the bill.[46] The defeat of Cadogan's amendment did not, however, settle the issue. At Report stage, the same amendment was moved by Sir Walter Greaves-Lord, Conservative MP for the Norwood division of Lambeth, and Recorder of Manchester, supported by Cadogan and Mrs Tate. On this occasion, the latter asserted that since 1927, when the Young Offenders Committee reported, both the nature and the extent of juvenile crime had become more serious, facts which the impending legislation ought not to ignore:

> Leniency and sentimentality can be carried too far, and, in my opinion, there is to-day not only a lack of discipline but a lack of reverence for the rights and property of other people. Bringing this higher age group into the juvenile courts will not act as a deterrent to the motor bandit and house-breaking type of adolescent who has figured so largely in recent convictions.[47]

Stanley was again able to fight off the amendment, and the age limit of the juvenile court was raised to seventeen. The final word, however, belongs to the extremely inauspicious references to leniency and

[45] PRO, HO45/14803/594745/61–2. Cadogan, born 1880, was Conservative MP for the Finchley division of Middlesex, 1924–35. He was a barrister, a JP for the County of London, and an ardent supporter of boys' club work. He was later to become Chairman of the Borstal Association and of the Departmental Committee on Corporal Punishment: *Who Was Who*, 1961–70; *The Times*, 14 Sep. 1962, p. 13.

[46] *Hansard*, vol. 265, 12 May 1932, col. 2218; PRO, HO45/14801/594745/24 and 29.

[47] *Hansard*, vol. 265, 12 May 1932, col. 2214.

sentimentality, a reproach which was to reach a crescendo in the mid 1930s.

One argument deployed by Oliver Stanley in the above debates was that the purity of the juvenile court had already been violated by the hearing of joint charges. The Young Offenders Committee, anxious to reduce the large number of children and young persons who were being tried before the adult courts as a result of being charged jointly with other offenders, had recommended that all joint charges should be dealt with by the juvenile court (at least where the older person was under twenty-one), unless the older person objected. It was a recommendation based largely on the progressive practice at Liverpool, of which the clerk to the justices, Mr Barton, who sat on the Young Offenders Committee, gave favourable reports.[48] But once more, differing views existed. At the Home Office conference in November 1927, senior departmental officials had agreed in principle to the proposal, but they had also pondered whether the provision should be limited to summary offences, presumably to stop more serious offenders coming before the juvenile courts.[49] Doubts still existed when the Labour government's bill was being prepared in the first months of 1931. Both Sir Ernley Blackwell, the Legal Adviser, and Sir John Anderson, the Permanent Under-Secretary, felt that adults charged jointly with children or young persons should not be dealt with in the juvenile courts. So, too, Harris was sceptical about whether the work of the juvenile courts would not be jeopardized by the effect of bringing lads of nineteen or twenty before them. Thus, even though it was apparent, by this date, that Liverpool was not alone in hearing joint charges, the bill did not seek formally to recognize the practice.[50] Again in 1932, the department was worried about the effect on the character of the juvenile courts which might result from bringing adult, and possibly serious offenders before them. As Harris declared in his notes for the second reading of the bill: 'The raising of the age from 16 to 17 is in itself something of an experiment. It might be dangerous to push too far the principle of widening the scope of the Juvenile Courts.'[51]

Hence, the recommendation was not included in the bill of 1932. Power was simply given to the adult court to remit the young offender

[48] Harris, 25 July 1927, PRO, HO45/14714/516360/1.

[49] PRO, HO45/13403/510865/12.

[50] Harris, 5 Jan. and 30 Mar. 1931, PRO, HO45/14715/516360/71 and 81.

[51] PRO, HO45/14801/594745/4A.

to the juvenile court for treatment, once the case had been formally heard. The Home Office were aware, however, that the bill in no way proscribed the practice of hearing joint charges in juvenile courts, and, further, that Liverpool were anxious to maintain what, for them, was a beneficial arrangement.[52]

Two final points merit attention. First, the National government suffered a small defeat in 1932 on the clause, to which it attached considerable importance, providing for a separation in venue of the juvenile and adult courts. The initial draft of the bill laid down that the children's court had to be held in separate premises from the adult court. The clause as finally adopted, however, represented a compromise between the government and the House of Lords. Encouraged by the County Councils' Association, and abetted in particular by the West Riding of Yorkshire, the Lords convinced the government that most local authorities would simply not provide a separate juvenile court, but would ask the Home Office for exemption, as the clause allowed them to do. The government had no alternative but to back down and allow the existing practice to continue, whereby the juvenile court used the same premises as the adult court, but sat on a separate day.[53]

Secondly, on the recommendation of the Incorporated Justices' Clerks' Society, the Home Office added a clause to the 1932 bill to allow a decision on the method of treatment to be taken by any juvenile court acting for the same place, even though it be constituted differently from the court by which the young offender was found guilty. This was meant to facilitate remands for enquiries after conviction, but before sentence, especially in rural areas where there was greater difficulty in constituting the court in the same way. Interestingly, the Home Office recognized that the issue turned on the question whether the juvenile court should treat the offence as the occasion for assessing the whole character of the delinquent with a view to 'readjusting him to his environment' or, rather, as the opportunity to 'punish for the offence'. The department appreciated, moreover, that the report of the Young Offenders Committee, as indeed the bill of 1932, had endeavoured 'to find some half-way house

[52] PRO, HO45/14716/516360/134.

[53] *Hansard*, vol. 261, 12 Feb. 1932, col. 1172; vol. 84 (Lords), 9 June 1932, col. 685; vol. 267, 30 June 1932, col. 2062; *TES*, 16 July 1932, p. 277; *Howard Journal*, vol. 3 (1932), p. 13.

between the two principles'. Thus, the same departmental minute had concluded:

> It would not perhaps be inconsistent with this compromise to take the line that in offence cases the proceedings up to and including the finding of guilty might be held in one court, while the decision as to method of treatment might be arrived at by another.[54]

An amendment to this effect was carried on the Committee stage in the Lords.

The Children and Young Persons Act 1933, represented considerable progress on lines approved by the Young Offenders Committee and favoured by the child welfare lobby. It provided for panels of specialized justices, more simplified judicial procedures, a more effective separation of juvenile and adult courts, and an extension of the juvenile court's jurisdiction in respect of both young offenders and young persons in need of care or protection. Given how closely the Act followed the proposals of the Young Offenders Committee, it, too, had to be a memorial to limited changes justified by experience, rather than to fundamental innovations inspired by revolutionary principle. But it also has to be said that on most of the major questions of principle which came under discussion, the government stood firm. Thus, for example, they refused to put back to sixteen the upper age limit in the definition of a young person. If they were ultimately obliged to modify the proposals concerning the separation of juvenile from adult courts, yet, as a Home Office review of the enactment of the statute declared, 'the provision finally substituted for them will secure the most important object, viz. the prevention of association between juveniles and adult offenders'.[55] And, finally, the Act gave greater prominence to the position and role of the juvenile court, defined more clearly the distinction between the children's and the adult court, and underlined the principle that the welfare of the child should be the court's uppermost if not exclusive consideration.[56]

[54] 25 May 1932, PRO, HO45/14803/594745/69.

[55] 15 July 1932, PRO, HO45/14804/594745/106; *TES*, 16 July 1932, p. 277.

[56] The Act also abolished the right to trial by jury for children under fourteen, except in cases of homicide. For commentaries on the Children and Young Persons Act, see *Magistrate*, vol. 3 (July-Aug. 1933), pp. 701–2; *Howard Journal*, vol. 3 (1932), p. 14.

Observation Homes

Existing arrangements for remanding young offenders, in order to learn more about them, were, as the Young Offenders Committee demonstrated, extremely unsatisfactory; medical examinations were rare occurrences, and observation no more common a phenomenon. The committee recommended, therefore, that at least three observation centres or central remand homes should be provided by the State, to assist the juvenile courts in deciding on the class of treatment to adopt, especially in relation to difficult children. But if the merit of the recommendation seemed incontestable, the resulting clause proved to be one of the most difficult for the Home Office to incorporate into the Children Bill.

In July 1927 the head of the Children's Branch included a brief discussion of the recommendation of central remand homes in his memorandum on a proposed new Children Bill. For three reasons Harris was in favour of omitting the proposal: the scheme applied to young offenders up to twenty-one years of age (and not just to children and young persons), the required expenditure was likely to be considerable, and the entire plan needed more detailed consideration.[57] Meantime, the penal reform groups displayed an undiminished enthusiasm for the establishment of state observation centres, if they also raised the stakes by demanding more than three such centres, and by insisting that the centres should be supplemental to improved remand homes in each locality. For the Howard League, the observation centres constituted one of the most valuable recommendations of the Young Offenders Committee, and one which they were not averse to taking a good deal of the credit for—'The Howard League once more finds the bread which it cast upon the waters returning to it after many days.'[58] The Education Committee of the London County Council was more concerned to calculate the impact that the proposal might have on metropolitan arrangements for bail and remand. There now seemed little point in the LCC instituting its own central remand home, as it had been planning to do before the

[57] PRO, HO45/14714/516360/1.

[58] *Magistrate*, vol. 1 (Oct. 1927), pp. 194 and 197; *The Treatment of Young Offenders*, op. cit., pp. 29–32; *Howard Journal*, vol. 2 (1927), p. 102. The Howard League described the proposed establishment of observation centres as 'one of the most valuable recommendations made by the Committee, and we strongly support it as a first step towards an adequate system of mental examination prior to treatment': PRO, HO45/13403/510865/2.

appointment of the Young Offenders Committee. But the education committee also felt that the proposed scheme was in a rather ragged state, a view put more forcefully by Sir Harry Stephen, after having given evidence to the YOC on behalf of the London County Council. '[T]he vague and grandiose scheme', he said, referring to the observation homes, 'suggests that medical opinion has so far prevailed over legal opinion as to lead the Committee to yield in this particular to the principle that guilt is a question for a doctor rather than for a magistrate.'[59] The comment not only betrayed Stephen's lack of understanding of the role of observation homes, but epitomized the critical stance which the LCC continued to take towards the scheme in the following years.

The Home Office conference held in November 1927 decided that Maxwell and Harris should examine the administrative and financial details of the plan for observation homes.[60] The recommendation was still under consideration at the end of December, but Sir John Anderson sounded a more constructive note when he directed that a permissive clause should be included in the latest draft of the Children Bill.[61] No further decision was reached until January 1931, when the question of observation homes was the only remaining complication in respect of the Labour government's Children Bill.[62] Harris tried to lend wings to a departmental decision by specifying the weaknesses of existing arrangements for remand and outlining the functions of an observation centre. The London County Council came in for particular criticism in Harris's memorandum. Despite the large number of young offenders in London, which should have been conducive to the provision of adequate remand homes, the 'place of detention' in Ponton Road, Vauxhall, was said to be thoroughly ill-suited for the purpose, added to which, the LCC's management had been 'unprogressive and uninspired': 'There have been a good many complaints of bad handling of children, and as in so much of the work of the London

[59] PRO, HO45/13403/510865/9; Stephen, op. cit., p. 329.

[60] Ibid., 510865/12.

[61] Harris, 22 Dec. 1927, PRO, HO45/14714/516360/8.

[62] In July 1930, however, the bill which Rhys Davies introduced on behalf of the Howard League included a clause which provided for observation centres: PP 1929, vol. I (248), p. 343; *Hansard*, vol. 241, 22 July 1930, col. 1954.

County Council there is a good deal of "red tape".' And finally, the medical reports which were transmitted to the juvenile courts were criticized for being 'formal and scanty and not always reliable'.[63]

Turning to the role of central remand homes, Harris emphasized that they could be seen as the keystone to the legislative attempt to improve the methods of dealing with young delinquents. He went on to argue that something on the lines of the Moll observation centre was required in England, his view having been reinforced by the recent report of Dr Culverwell and Miss Warner, both inspectors in the Children's Branch, on the Belgian institutions. The position in England had improved since 1927, Harris believed, with the establishment of child guidance clinics, which magistrates were increasingly making use of. But he also maintained that clinics were of no great help with the more difficult cases, where remand in custody was needed for close and extended observation, not to mention public security.[64] Norris added at this point that observation centres could also serve the function of assessing how best to deal with the boy or girl of border-line mentality in the reformatory schools (or on licence from such), whether by transfer to another school, or to Borstal, or to an institution for the mentally defective.[65] Any such scheme, of course, raised financial difficulties. Harris thought that the government would have to provide the whole of the initial capital expenditure, estimated at £40,000, and at least a half of the cost of annual upkeep, put at about £3,000. None the less, Harris's overall conclusion was that better facilities for the medical examination and observation of young offenders was a priority.[66] Sir John Anderson agreed 'that without such provision the Bill will be incomplete and amendments are certain to be moved'.[67] The government would, it was thought, find it difficult to rebut the criticism which would be raised by omitting the observation homes, in view of the recommendation of the Young Offenders Committee. Hence, a provision to establish observation homes found

[63] 17 Dec. 1930, PRO, HO45/14715/516360/67. The London County Council were contemplating building a new remand home. A sum of £45,000 was included in the Three-year Programme, 1927–30, but the matter was postponed, pending action by the government.

[64] Ibid.

[65] 17 June 1930, PRO, HO45/14715/516360/67. This was a growing problem, as probation siphoned off the less difficult offender cases.

[66] PRO, HO45/14715/516360/67 and 71.

[67] 17 Dec. 1930, Ibid., 516360/67.

its way into the Labour government's bill, and Home Secretary Clynes looked forward to instituting a home in the London area.[68]

The Treasury soon put paid to this. In June 1931 they scuttled the scheme of observation homes in view of the existing financial circumstances, and because a dangerous precedent would be created by relieving local authorities of their duty of providing a service of this nature. Efforts ought to be made first, the Treasury advised, to persuade the local authorities to establish these places.[69] The Home Office was dissatisfied at the Treasury veto, particularly since the latter's reply had conveniently neglected a number of relevant considerations, such as the fact that in default of State intervention, a central remand home would have to be established by the London County Council and would still thereby be a drain on the exchequer. Anderson decided to meet the Treasury officials in August to see what could be resolved. A compromise proposal was the outcome, whereby the bill would entrust the establishment of an observation home to an independent body, composed of representatives nominated partly by the Home Secretary and partly by the local authorities, which would be empowered to borrow money.[70] Anderson's novel idea of an independent body of managers had now to be sold to the London County Council, a conference being arranged with Mr Gater, the education officer of the LCC, for the autumn. The Home Office hoped that the LCC would be willing to provide the required capital expenditure.[71] By September 1931, however, the Labour government had resigned in the wake of the financial crisis of the summer, and with the National government confining its attention to matters of immediate financial importance, the conference between the Home Office and the LCC was postponed.

Before the year was out the new Home Secretary, Herbert Samuel, had accepted Anderson's scheme of an enabling power providing for the establishment of observation homes by a body of managers. It was

[68] In May 1931, the Howard League forwarded four resolutions which had been passed at a conference on 27 March, one of which was in support of observation centres. A Home Office minute of 6 June 1931 stated that the provisions as to observation centres were at present in the draft of the government bill, 'and, apart from the financial questions involved ... there is no reason to suppose that these provisions will be withdrawn before the Bill goes before Parliament': PRO, HO45/14715/516360/85.

[69] 9 Feb. 1931, Ibid., 516360/75; Treasury reply, 26 June 1931, Ibid., 516360/93; 1 July 1931, Ibid., 516360/85 and 93.

[70] 6 Aug. 1931, Ibid., 516360/93.

[71] 29 July 1931, Ibid.

to be made clear, however, that no steps would be taken to put the powers granted into operation until the country's financial situation improved.[72] But, by now, the financial emergency, and particularly the large cuts made in the LCC's expenditure for education, had turned Gater against the whole scheme. Moreover, Gater was forecasting that, even with an assurance as to the postponement of actual expenditure, the scheme for the institution of observation homes would probably prejudice the LCC and the other local authorities against the whole bill. Harris knew Gater to be a level-headed person who carried considerable weight with the LCC and whose advice, therefore, could not be disregarded. He also doubtless knew that the LCC were more than able to orchestrate effective parliamentary opposition. Short of time to negotiate with the local authorities, Harris could only recommend omitting the provision as to observation homes.[73] Oliver Stanley agreed, not wishing the government to appear as if it were forcing through some new extravagant measure in the face of the economical LCC.[74] The Home Secretary was less willing to abandon the notion of an enabling power, and met Gater and Sir John Gilbert of the LCC.[75] But this came to nothing and when the Children and Young Persons Bill had its second reading in February 1932, there was no reference to observation homes.

Needless to say, the government faced a good deal of parliamentary criticism for this omission, whilst the LCC was rightly implicated in this indictment against false economy. A Commons amendment, introduced by Rhys Davies and Edward Cadogan, sought to rectify the position, but it was ruled out of order for being beyond the scope of the Financial Resolution.[76] The government tried to keep face by trusting that the purpose of observation centres would be met by improved remand homes (the term which was now to be used instead of 'places of detention'). To this end, the responsibility for providing remand homes was transferred from the police authority to the local authorities, and the latter were encouraged to use their medical

[72] 17 Nov. 1931, PRO, HO45/14716/516360/105 and 107.

[73] Harris, 14 Dec. 1931, Ibid., 516360/136; Gater to Harris, 2 Feb. 1932, PRO, HO45/14801/594745/11.

[74] PRO, HO45/14801/594745/1. The reduction in expenditure on education and the social services was made on the recommendation of the May Committee: 'Report of the Committee on National Expenditure', PP 1930–31, XVI (Cmd. 3920), p. 1.

[75] PRO, HO45/14716/516360/136.

[76] PRO, HO45/14802/594745/57: Committee Stage, 6th Day, 16 March 1932, clause 37. See also *Hansard*, vol. 261, 12 Feb. 1932, cols. 1188–9 (Rhys Davies).

services to provide facilities for medical examination.[77] Profound disappointment at the abandonment of the observation homes filled the penal reform lobby. The Magistrates Association had given its backing to the Commons amendment, to no effect.[78] As for the Howard League, the provision of such homes had been the only truly pivotal proposal: 'All other reforms relating to Young Offenders pale into insignificance beside the need for expert observation and diagnosis, after trial and before sentence. The plea that this country cannot afford a single Observation Centre is simply beneath contempt.'[79]

The whole episode suggested that the Children Bill was chosen by the government as a measure which would promote social reform, yet which would be relatively inexpensive and non-controversial. Hence, the scheme of observation homes was sacrificed on the altar of national economy; this was, after all, why a National government had come into being.

[77] See *Hansard*, vol. 84 (Lords), 26 May 1932, cols. 454–5; Home Office Circular, 19 Jan. 1933, in *Magistrate*, vol. 3 (Jan.–Feb. 1933), pp. 655–7; HO Circular, 9 Aug. 1933, in L. Le Mesurier, *A Handbook of Probation and the Social Work of the Courts* (NAPO, 1935), pp. 354–5. Only in 1937 was the first new, purpose-built remand home established, by the Hull Education Committee: *Magistrate*, vol. 4 (Nov.–Dec. 1937), p. 1243.

[78] Letter from Cecil Leeson, 2 March 1932, PRO, HO45/14801/594745/29.

[79] *Howard Journal*, vol. 3 (1932), p. 12; M. Ryan, *The Acceptable Pressure Group* (Farnborough, 1978), p. 33. See also *TES*, 16 July 1932.

4
The Hegemony of Child Welfare

Probation

The Children and Young Persons Act hardly affected the probation system; a few amendments were made to the law on probation, the main one of which is dealt with below. In one other clause—that concerning the provision of information to the juvenile court—the probation service had a stake. The Young Offenders Committee recommended that the juvenile court should be supplied with details of the home surroundings, as well as the school and medical records, of those appearing before it; and that, to this end, there should be closer co-operation between the court and the local education authority. In line with this recommendation the bill of 1932 included a clause to the effect that the police should notify the local authority of all charges or applications in respect of children and young persons, and that the local authority should see that information as to home surroundings and the like was available for the court. This was not to the liking of the National Association of Probation Officers, which enlisted the support of the Howard League, the Magistrates Association, and the Parliamentary Penal Reform Group, in an attempt to amend the bill, by according probation officers a statutory role in the making of reports in all juvenile court cases. Without this, Mr Norman, Secretary of NAPO, argued, the services of the probation officer in ascertaining, for example, whether cases were suitable for probation, would be used even less than they were already. The Home Office were reluctant to compel magistrates to make use of probation officers for preliminary enquiries, but they offered the compromise of a provision enabling courts to relieve the local authority of the duty of making reports and to entrust the task to the probation officer.[1]

The National Association of Probation Officers accepted this compromise amendment, although remaining unconvinced that jus-

[1] See Dorothy Bochel, *Probation and After-Care* (Edinburgh, 1976), p. 116; Harris, 23 April 1932, PRO, HO45/14802/594745/49–50.

tices would voluntarily use probation officers for this purpose. A last attempt was made, therefore, in the House of Lords to secure a clear-cut position for the probation officer. The Earl of Feversham moved an amendment which would have limited the local authority's duty to the supplying of relevant information at the time when it was notified of a case, and would have given probation officers the duty 'to make such further investigation and supply such additional information . . . as the court may require and direct'. But Lord Snowden would not accept the amendment, which was lost, leaving the primary responsibility for furnishing reports in the hands of the local authorities.[2]

The most significant provision in the Children Bill, as far as the probation service was concerned, was the power to insert in probation orders a condition as to residence in an approved home. The Young Offenders Committee had warned against the use of the probation system as a way of compelling probationers to reside in a home, and had recommended that probation be restricted to 'supervision in the open' under a probation officer, or to a condition of residence in a hostel (the latter being intended mainly for those over sixteen years of age). This stand had not found favour with either the Magistrates Association or the Howard League who objected to the possible loss of residence in a training home.[3] Dr Norris was sufficiently swayed by this pressure to advocate non-compliance with the YOC's recommendation.[4] Sydney Harris, despite being a signatory to the report, continued to find the question of the relation of probation to institutional treatment a difficult one. He knew that some 450 young offenders under twenty-one (122 of whom were under sixteen) had in 1926 been sent to homes as a condition of probation, notably to rescue homes for immoral girls; and he was reluctant to bring this useful work to an end.[5] His suggestion, accordingly, 'though it would strain a little

[2] Ibid., p. 117; *Hansard*, vol. 84 (Lords), 9 June 1932, col. 732. Snowden opposed the amendment on the grounds that the education authorities would ask probation officers for their help. Feversham, however, could not see 'in the justices, the local authority and the probation officers the happy trium-virate' which Snowden implicitly depicted: quoted in Bochel, p. 117.

[3] See PRO, HO45/13403/510865/2; *Magistrate*, vol. 1 (Oct. 1927), pp. 193–5. The Council of the Magistrates Association recommended that magistrates should retain the power to insert in probation orders a condition as to residence in an approved home providing that the period did not exceed six months.

[4] 24 Oct. 1927, Ibid., 510865/7.

[5] 27 Oct. 1927, Ibid. It was mainly girls of over sixteen who were sent to homes as a condition of probation, although, Harris noted, 'a few lads are dealt with in this way in

further the meaning of probation', was to allow young offenders under twenty-one to be sent not only to hostels but also to approved and inspected homes for a period not exceeding six months as a condition of probation. He advocated the case thus:

> It could be defended on the ground that if a person is placed on probation for a period of (say) three years he would only be away from the immediate supervision of the probation officer for a limited time; the probation officer could write to and, if necessary, visit him; and the probationer would return to his supervision at the end of the six months—thus providing a convenient and satisfactory form of after care'.[6]

This policy was accepted provisionally by the Home Office conference of November 1927, on the grounds that 'there was need for some form of institutional treatment to serve as an alternative to supervision in the home on the one hand and to long term training on the other'.[7] At the same meeting, Norris and Harris were delegated to see if a Home Office school could be diverted to this work as an experiment; the idea at this stage was to restrict the age limits to between fifteen and eighteen years. The department clearly found it difficult to accept the strictly logical view of the Young Offenders Committee that probation was inconsistent with institutional training, particularly when homes would provide a further alternative to prison for offenders over sixteen. There was more to gain, it was believed, by the compromise of advising courts to combine probation with short-term institutional treatment.

The first official step was a Home Office circular of 20 July 1928 which introduced a scheme for contributing out of government funds to the maintenance of probationers in hostels and homes, a power which the Criminal Justice Act 1925, had conferred on the Home Secretary. This was extended two years later by way of another circular letter. In both cases, however, the scheme applied only to probationers between the ages of sixteen and twenty-one sent to homes for not more

places like Yiewsley and Basingstoke which are under the control of the Police Court Mission'. See also *Fourth Report on the Work of the Children's Branch* (HMSO, 1928), pp. 19–20.

[6] Ibid.

[7] Ibid., 510865/12.

than six months.[8] The question of including such a provision in the Children Bill was next raised in the last months of 1930, when the decision went against inclusion.[9] Shortly afterwards, however, in view of the continued abuse of the residence condition, Harris secured the introduction of a clause whereby a court could send a child or young person to a home as a condition of probation only if the home was 'liable to inspection by the Secretary of State'.[10] An identical clause went into the National government's bill in 1932. But the chief inspector of certified schools now intervened to press the case for restricting the power to homes which were *approved* by the Home Secretary. Norris was clearly impelled by the past abuse of this power. 'One of the worst features at the present time of the use of the Probation Act', he alleged, 'is the sending of girls of 13 and 14 to homes where there are a considerable number of bad rescue cases.' Yet most of these places, he pointed out, would be liable to inspection under the voluntary home provisions of the bill.[11]

Harris accepted that to retain the clause as it stood would oblige the Home Office to rely upon persuasion rather than compulsion, but he feared that Norris's proposal, by mentioning 'approval', would imply Home Office responsibility for the character of the home, and thus open the gate to demands for financial support. The only other course would have been to endorse the recommendation of the Young Offenders Committee and prohibit the use of homes as a condition of probation. Harris leaned towards this option 'if it were considered practical politics', but he doubted that it would be. The reality of judicial practice could not be ignored:

> The Courts have possessed and exercised the power for many years and one of the reasons why they use it is because it does not appear to carry the same stigma as a school 'sentence'. The Bill aims at getting away from this stigma as far as possible but I am not sure that we shall get rid of it altogether—at any rate at first.[12]

[8] For Circular, 20 July 1928, see Ibid., 510865/24. For Circular, 31 July 1930, see Mrs L. Le Mesurier, *A Handbook of Probation*, op. cit., pp. 332–5.

[9] PRO, HO45/14714/516360/1A. Rhys Davies's bill of July 1930 had included a clause providing that residence in a home or hostel, as a condition of probation, should be for a period not exceeding six months, and the home or hostel should be one approved by the Home Secretary.

[10] 26 Nov. 1930, PRO, HO45/14715/516360/62.

[11] 18 Feb. 1932, PRO, HO45/14801/594745/20.

[12] 19 Feb. 1932, Ibid.

The Children and Young Persons Act, therefore, gave juvenile courts the power to send young persons under seventeen to homes, which were subject to Home Office inspection, as a condition of probation, in the knowledge that these homes were being used as a way of avoiding the long terms of detention in reformatory and industrial schools.

Approved Schools

The two main recommendations of the Young Offenders Committee in relation to the Home Office schools were the abolition of the distinction between reformatory and industrial schools, and the period of detention in such institutions. Before dealing with the incorporation of these proposals into the Children Bill, however, it is useful to document the anxiety felt within the Home Office at the excessive use of probation and the limited use of the Home Office schools. It was evident to the Home Office that the two principal methods of dealing with young offenders would continue to be probation and schools. However, the figures showing the use of these two penalties in the post-war period raised the question whether the juvenile courts were making too much use of probation and too little use of residential training. As a proportion of juveniles found guilty in 1913 and 1930 respectively, probation increased from 13.6 to 32 per cent, whilst the use of reformatory and industrial schools fell from 6.9 to 5.5 per cent.[13] These figures convinced the department that there was undoubtedly a tendency towards the excessive use of probation in the juvenile courts, one effect of which was the growth of crime between the ages of sixteen and twenty-one. The problem which the Home Office now faced was how to curtail the mistakes made by the courts when choosing between probation and schools because of either insufficient enquiry, or prejudice, or economy.

In the Home Office circular on juvenile courts (30 September 1927), the Home Secretary urged the magistrates to use the certified schools

[13] The figures were as follows:

Number found Guilty	Recognizances	Probation	Industrial Schools	Reformatory Schools	Year
32,862	2,447	4,465	1,200	1,082	1913
22,019	1,726	7,042	586	618	1930

There was also a marked fall in the use of fines, from 35.9% to 23.5%. See also Table I(b).

where probation had failed or was inappropriate, and not to be influenced 'by considerations of the additional cost, ... it is false economy to postpone institutional treatment where it appears to be necessary'.[14] A month later the chief inspector of certified schools informed the department that local parsimony and the wish to avoid branding offenders with the stigma of a conviction were resulting in the widespread practice of sending children for long periods to uninspected, inefficient and generally unsatisfactory voluntary homes and in the marked decrease in the number of children sent to Home Office schools.[15] Norris also warned that the proposals of the Young Offenders Committee would only aggravate the situation, 'with the ultimate consequence that most of the remaining Schools will be closed'; and this at a time when the schools had reached a post-war peak of efficiency, logging a 90 to 95 per cent success rate,[16] through a good deal of hard work on the part of the Children's Branch. For these reasons, the chief inspector recommended further consideration of two proposals which the departmental committee had discarded: the experiment of short-term schools, of which more later, and the use of probation to secure institutional treatment in a Home Office school. The latter proposal, Norris explained, would both eliminate the stigma of conviction and committal, and allow greater flexibility in treatment:

> It would simplify Court practice if Probation with a condition of residence became the method of securing residential training for all young offenders requiring it; it would entail no committal or appearance of sentence, and if circumstances at any time made it unnecessary for the young person to remain in a Home Office School, the Court could vary the Order and allow a different means of treatment, say, in a Hostel, lodgings or at home.[17]

The less excitable Harris was unable to agree with Norris's proposal to send boys to Home Office schools as a condition of probation, involving as it did 'a misuse of terms which scarcely seems defensible';

[14] For Circular, see PRO, HO45/13403/510865/12.

[15] 24 Oct. 1927, Ibid., 510865/7. The number of committals had decreased by nearly 60 per cent between 1913 and 1927. At this date there were 28 reformatory schools (23 for boys) and 58 industrial schools (38 for boys). The total number of committed children in the reformatories was 2,102; in the industrial schools, 4,424. In addition, there were 21 special schools for those requiring special mental or physical treatment. See also Table 5.

[16] This figure was calculated on the basis of the records of inmates, three years after having been discharged.

[17] 24 Oct. 1927, PRO, HO45/13403/510865/7.

nor could he 'share his [Norris's] fears as to the effect of the recommendations on the schools'. Harris cavilled neither at the evidence of the depopulation of the schools nor at the probable causes, but he considered that the position was reaching stability, and anyway, he preferred 'a smaller number of really efficient schools than a larger number of schools run under the conditions of inefficiency which were common before the new financial scheme was started in 1919'. Of course, the chief inspector's figures implied a need to close even more schools, but, said Harris, a decision on this point had been delayed for two reasons: it was essential to gauge the effect of the recommendations of the Young Offenders Committee, and it was feared that another rash of closures would further discourage headmasters and managers in their work.[18]

But the problem which Norris had brought to light continued to perplex the department. Between 1928 and 1931 the Children's Branch came upon a number of individual cases in which the reluctance of magistrates, local education authorities and watch committees to pay their share of the cost of maintenance had led to a failure to take advantage of Home Office schools.[19] This evidence forced the head of the Branch to consider meeting the difficulty in one of two ways: 'either by saddling the local authorities with a share of the Prison and Borstal services [thus removing the financial incentive to delay treatment] or by the Government taking over the whole or a greater share of the cost of Home Office schools'.[20] When, in May 1931, Harris again pressed these remedies, however, the financial crisis ensured that the government grant in respect of reformatory schools would not be increased.[21] The only alternative ploy was to make the work of the Home Office schools better known; this was done by the Children's Branch in its Fourth Report (1928) and by Norris in the numerous speeches he gave to such bodies as the Magistrates Association.[22] His message was always couched in the same terms: institutional training ought not to be unduly delayed; training was more likely to succeed with the youth of twelve or thirteen than with the lad of seventeen or eighteen; and the aversion to commit children,

[18] 27 Oct. 1927, Ibid.

[19] See PRO, HO144/22572/562557/1; HO144/22370/487003/39.

[20] 16 April 1928, Ibid., 487003/39.

[21] PRO, HO45/22572/562557/3.

[22] See *Fourth Report*, op. cit., Part III; Norris, 'The Young Delinquent', *Magistrate*, vol. 2 (Aug.–Sep. 1930), p. 418.

on grounds of economy, led to older, more recalcitrant cases eventually being sent to the schools. From the touchline came the encouraging pronouncements of the *Times Educational Supplement* to the effect that, in view of the industrial depression and the increase in juvenile crime since 1929, probation ought not to be used at the expense of early residential training.[23]

This was the backcloth, then, to the Home Office's aspiration to develop the work of the certified schools on progressive lines and to encourage their greater use, by putting flesh on the recommendations of the Young Offenders Committee. One proposal was to do away with the distinction between reformatory and industrial schools, on the grounds that the character and needs of the neglected and the delinquent child were very similar, and that a more scientific classification of the schools would facilitate their work. The proposal was warmly supported by the representatives of the schools, themselves, as well as by the local authorities and magistrates.[24] Hence, the 1933 Act swept away the artificial distinction between reformatory and industrial schools and established a single class of 'approved schools', which were to be classified according to the age of the pupils and the nature of the training. This, in turn, made it necessary to take away the right of managers to refuse to receive a particular child or young person, and to confer on the Home Secretary an unfettered power of transfer from one school to another.[25]

The most controversial recommendations, however, related to the period for which persons might be detained in Home Office schools. Under existing law it was the usual practice to commit a child to an industrial school until the age of sixteen; while a young person could be sent to a reformatory school for not less than three or more than five years. The departmental committee recommended that the period of detention be limited to three years dating from the time of committal, except that children of school age should be able to be kept until school leaving age, in order not to interrupt the course of their education, even if this meant detention for more than three years.[26] This recommendation seems to have been induced particularly by Norris, who informed the committee that he was unhappy with the practice of

[23] *TES*, 8 Dec. 1928, p. 533; 9 April 1932, p. 121.

[24] PRO, HO45/13403/510865/9 and 16.

[25] PRO, HO45/14801/594745/4A; O. Stanley, 'The Children Bill', *Magistrate*, vol. 2 (Feb.–Mar. 1932), p. 571.

[26] The maximum age of detention was to remain at nineteen years.

keeping boys until sixteen, but that he was unable to enjoin earlier licensing because of the difficulty of finding work for the boys.

The proposed shortening of the period of detention aroused its share of opposition. The London County Council wanted no three-year limit on detention and recommended, instead, that the courts should have power of committal up to nineteen years of age, determination of the period of detention resting with the court. The headmasters and managers of the schools also had their misgivings; at a meeting of the Home Office Schools Central Advisory Committee, in October 1930, they argued that a system of compulsory placing out as soon as school age was passed was the crudest of discharge procedures. Moreover, they considered that the shorter period of detention would make it impossible for the reformatory schools to give a boy vocational training up to the stage of 'improver'.[27]

But the department stuck to their guns. A tendency existed, they argued, for schools to keep their charges too long, which, in part, underlay judicial reluctance to use them, particularly when the delinquency was none too serious. Confirmation existed in the fact that in the late 1920s more young girls were still being sent to homes as a condition of probation than were going to reformatory schools. For several years now the department had been impressing on managers the need for early licensing. '[W]e have aimed at getting boys from industrial schools at work at 15 or 15½', declared Harris, 'and for Reformatory schools we have endeavoured to secure the completion of training in 2½ or 3 years'.[28] But not all schools were co-operating; managers still often clung on to their charges in order partly to keep the schools going and partly to avoid taking any risks. A reduction in the statutory period seemed the only way, therefore, to ensure that the average period of detention came down, and this was provided for in the 1933 Act. Only in one respect did the Home Office indulge the wishes of the schools. A proviso was added to the appropriate clause of the bill to allow the training to be extended for a further six months; this was meant for boys whose chances of employment on release would be improved if they could complete their vocational tuition up to the stage of improver.[29] But this qualification aside, the department succeeded in limiting the maximum period of detention to three years.

[27] PRO, HO45/13403/510865/9, 15 and 16; HO45/14714/516360/59.

[28] PRO, HO45/14801/594745/4A.

[29] Ibid., 594745/12. The LCC moved the amendment; it was supported by the Association of Managers of Home Office Schools and the Head Masters' Association.

This provision, it was estimated, would reduce the average period of detention by some seven or eight months.[30]

The Young Offenders Committee had also recommended that the court should no longer specify the period of detention, but should in every case commit for a period of not less than three years, leaving it to the school authorities and the Home Office to pick out those who could be released on licence at an earlier stage. This idea of a semi-indeterminate sentence was applauded in many quarters. 'The Committee seem to be on right lines', the *Times Educational Supplement* proclaimed, 'when they suggest that short-term detention can be of little value if training for character and for vocation is the objective'.[31] But the chief inspector of Home Office schools was disappointed that his proposal of a six months school had been turned down in favour of a statutory three-year sentence. Undeterred, Norris told the Children's Branch of his fears that the number of children sent to certified schools would further decline unless his proposal of short-term schools was put into effect. His idea was explained thus: 'to give one period of six months detention for young people who in the opinion of the Magistrates need a sharp "pull up", are not suitable for probation in a Hostel, nor require a long period of training'.

He had marked down for such short-term reformatories, 'those who loaf about the streets, appear before the Courts on such charges as obstructing, gaming, malicious damage'; the aim of detention being 'to make these young persons self-respecting, hardworking, clean-living members of the community'. Norris was conscious of the objection that magistrates might fail to discriminate between those needing a long term of training and those who would be suitable for a short sentence. His riposte was double-edged: the observation centres, when established, would assist the task of allocation; and failure on a six months' sentence would almost always be followed by a long period of training. Finally, Norris dredged his early social work experience for evidence that short-term institutions were of value, and came up with the following:

30 PRO, HO45/14715/516360/75.

31 *TES*, 28 May 1927, p. 245. The Association of Managers of Home Office Schools also told the Home Office that in their view, training and short terms of detention were incompatible, and that courts should always send for the full term allowed. See PRO, HO45/13403/510865/16. The Council of the Magistrates Association, however, recommended that power should be given to justices to commit for a shorter period than was allowed at that time: *Magistrate*, vol. 1. (Oct. 1927), p. 195.

'I was years ago associated with the late Mr. C. E. B. Russell at Heyrod Street Lads Club, Manchester, in a system which, taking some of the worst young offenders released from Manchester Prison, insisting upon residence under close supervision and heavy labouring work in neighbouring iron works, led to the reclamation of a considerable percentage of failures'.[32]

The head of the Children's Branch accepted that there was room for further consideration of short-term detention, if only because the Young Offenders Committee had excluded it from their scheme with some hesitation. Harris, himself, had opposed the idea of short-term schools for those under sixteen in the committee's discussions, for fear that 'if the Courts were given a choice between short and long detention they would be forced by the influence of parents and by reasons of economy to choose in very many cases short detention when training was really required'. He was also worried that the effect of the courts using short-term schools too freely would be to disrupt the long-term schools severely through a shortage of pupils.[33] Part of the difficulty, as so often with inter-war policy-making, was the lack of hard evidence on which to base a reliable conclusion. From 1924 the Field Lane Industrial School in West Hampstead had, at the Home Office's request, received short-term committals; in February 1928 the superintendent was asked to report on the scheme's operation. Only a few boys had been committed for short-term training by the courts; of these, very few had proved satisfactory. Even Norris was obliged to concede that, at least in relation to children of school age, the results of the experiment were poor. His concession went further. 'There is no doubt', he minuted, 'that the Magistrates used this method when a longer training was desirable and I am doubtful whether as a rule it is desirable to commit a boy for a term less than that which would bring him to the end of his school attending age.'[34] For the time being, therefore, the Home Office decided simply to examine the feasibility of using a Home Office school, in order to test the policy of coupling probation with residence in certain approved and inspected institutions for a period not exceeding six months.[35] In fact, this experiment of associating short-term treatment with probation for those under sixteen was never set up.

[32] 24 Oct. 1927, Ibid., 510865/7.
[33] 27 Oct. 1927, Ibid.
[34] Ibid.; PRO, HO144/8536/154755/32 (21 Feb. 1928).
[35] PRO, HO45/13403/510865/7.

Dr Norris next raised the issue of short-term schools before a meeting of the Home Office Schools Central Advisory Committee in October 1930. Harris arrayed the snags with this proposal, and the schools' representatives had no hesitation in opposing a scheme they had never liked.[36] At Harris's request, Norris returned to the fray a month later, this time describing the omission of short-term training from the Labour government's bill as 'a serious defect . . . and one which will probably raise considerable criticism in the House of Commons'. He was as convinced as ever that 'there are many delinquent young people for whom periods of six months would be sufficient to give them a sharp pull up and a fresh start'. Norris also found new arrows in his quiver. Magistrates, he claimed, were in favour of being able to send suitable cases to a school for less than three years, to judge from the applause evoked by an address to the Magistrates Association by Mr Hayward (clerk to the Cardiff justices) when this topic was raised. Secondly, the Children Bill which had been introduced by Rhys Davies at the behest of the Howard League had provided for short-term training.[37] And finally, Norris argued that the Home Office had already accepted the principle of short-term institutional training for those over sixteen—as a condition of probation—and was, indeed, supporting the policy by government grant.[38]

At this point, however, the head of the Children's Branch put forward an alternative approach which was to become the official policy. Harris pointed out that the semi-indeterminate quality of the three-year sentence gave scope for an experiment; a few schools could be classified as short-term institutions which would release the young persons sent to them after a period of six months' detention. If, at this juncture, the conduct of the youngsters was unsatisfactory, they could be transferred to ordinary schools. If, moreover, the whole scheme were to prove unsuccessful, 'the experiment could be brought to an end without any serious dislocation of or disadvantage to the schools provided for long-term training'. Dr Norris accepted that this proposal went a good way to meeting his views, and Sir John Anderson agreed that this was the best way of resolving the matter.[39]

[36] PRO, HO45/14714/516360/59.

[37] Rhys Davies's bill had provided that detention should be for a minimum period of six months or a maximum period of three years.

[38] 24 Dec. 1930, PRO, HO45/14715/516360/68.

[39] 2 Jan. 1931, Ibid., 516360/68 and 75.

The disagreement between the head of the Children's Branch and the chief inspector of reformatories, which had made it so difficult for the department to reach agreement on the policy of short-term reformatories, was not really one of principle. They were both of the opinion that in the treatment of young offenders a gap existed between supervision in the home and long-term training in a school; that some young offenders over school age, whilst not requiring long-term training, would benefit from being taken away from their surroundings, detained for a few months in a disciplined regime, and then placed out in employment. The difference was that Harris could not accept that the power to order short-term detention was one which could safely be entrusted to the courts. For that reason, he devised a scheme which facilitated an experiment with short-term schools, yet which neither breached the statutory three-year sentence nor took away the decision as to length of detention from the executive.[40] But if this compromise proposal made it possible to placate the advocates of short-term training, it depended as much as Norris's original scheme on the facilities of the proposed observation homes, which were omitted from the final statute.

Boarding Out

Such was the belief in the causative effect of the defective family on delinquency and neglect that the removal of children from a poor environment assumed a new significance in the late 1920s. This conviction underlay the advocacy of a more widespread use of Home Office schools where children and young persons would be trained to cope with the stresses of a deficient home setting. It also reinforced the policy of providing substitute family care, outside an institution, by means of boarding out.[41]

The Children Act 1908 contained the power to deal with children committed to industrial schools, if under eight years of age, by finding them foster parents. In this way, the benefits of a normal home life could be provided for children, the majority of whom had been brought before the courts because of unsatisfactory home conditions and not because of delinquent behaviour. Apart from the London County Council, however, few education authorities or school

[40] See *Hansard*, vol. 265, 12 May 1932, cols. 2257–8.

[41] See Jean Heywood, *Children in Care* (1959), p. 130.

managers pursued a regular policy of boarding out, owing largely to the difficulties of finding suitable foster parents. Barely 300 children in all were boarded out in the mid-1920s.[42] Additionally, the Children Act empowered courts to commit young children to the care of 'a relative or fit person'. This provision, intended for those under twelve years of age, was used in fewer than twenty cases a year. Under the promptings of such witnesses as Margery Fry to develop the practice of boarding out, the Young Offenders Committee recommended that courts should have power to transfer to the local education authority the guardianship of a child or young person under seventeen who had to be taken from the control of his parents but who did not need institutional training; the education authority would have the duty to find a new home for him and watch over his future welfare. This method, it was proposed, would replace the system under which children were boarded out from industrial schools.[43]

The only difficulty that the Home Office had to overcome in regard to the inclusion of this recommendation in the new Children Bill was the LCC's demand to be allowed to place a child or young person committed to their care in an institution, or to transfer him to an approved school, without having to apply to a juvenile court. This was resisted by the department on the grounds that it would deprive youngsters of the safeguards which the bill provided with reference to institutional treatment. The enlarged powers of guardianship were thus included in the Children Bill. For children under ten, guardianship was to be the most significant method of treatment since the bill also took away the power to send children below this age to an approved school.[44]

Corporal Punishment

By existing law, boys under fourteen years could be birched up to a limit of six strokes for any indictable offence except homicide;[45] boys of between fourteen and sixteen years could be whipped for a number of

[42] See Cyril Burt, *The Young Delinquent* (1927, 2nd edn.), p. 114; PRO, HO45/14714/516360/1A.

[43] *Report of the Departmental Committee on the Treatment of Young Offenders*, PP 1927, XII, pp. 1021–3; *Evidence*, p. 558 (Miss Fry).

[44] See PRO, HO45/14801/594745/20; *Hansard*, vol. 261, 12 Feb. 1932, col. 1175.

[45] This power was given to courts of summary jurisdiction by section 10 of the Summary Jurisdiction Act, 1879.

offences under various statutes. The recommendation of the Young Offenders Committee was that courts should have the power to order a whipping in respect of any serious (i.e. indictable) offence committed by a boy under seventeen. If anything, this proposed an extension of the existing powers of corporal punishment by abandoning the former discrimination between types of offence. 'The majority of the Young Offenders Committee', according to one of its members, Harris, 'deprecated the indiscriminate use of whipping but thought that if it were retained for exceptional cases it ought not logically to be restricted in its application to certain offences.'[46]

The immediate response to the recommendation was almost uniformly critical. The Magistrates Association and the Education Committee of the LCC followed the minority memorandum of the YOC in believing that whipping served no useful purpose. At the representative conference, convened by the Howard League in 1927, a resolution to the same effect moved by Mr Whiting of the Penal Reform Committee of the Society of Friends, was passed *nem. con.*[47] At this stage, the head of the Children's Branch was unable to recommend its inclusion in a Children Bill, preferring to leave the law as it stood. He minuted thus: '. . . the question is so controversial that it would be unwise to draw any attack. I should be disposed to leave matters as they are'.[48] The same line was taken by the Home Office conference of senior officials in November, although the Home Secretary, Joynson-Hicks, minuted in his distinctive red ink that 'nothing could be better for a lad, if convicted of rape' than corporal punishment.[49] For the next few years the department paid little attention to the issue; the only exception was the Home Office circular on probation (31 July 1930), which advised justices that the practice of combining whipping with probation was 'open to grave objection'.[50]

Meanwhile the focus of attention shifted to the Commons where two attempts were made to get rid of corporal punishment, without success. In July 1930 the bill introduced by the Labour MP, Rhys Davies, with the help of the Howard League, provided for the abolition of birching for those under twenty-one. Davies's introduc-

[46] PRO, HO45/14801/594745/4A.

[47] See *Magistrate*, vol. 1 (Oct. 1927), p. 195; PRO, HO45/13403/510865/9; *The Treatment of Young Offenders*, op. cit., p. 34.

[48] 25 July 1927, PRO, HO45/14714/516360/1.

[49] PRO, HO45/13403/510865/12.

[50] See *Justice of the Peace*, vol. 92 (24 March 1928), p. 204; *Magistrate*, vol. 2 (Oct.–Nov. 1930), p. 434; PRO, HO45/14801/594745/4A.

tory speech argued that birching degraded the child and brutalized the man who had to inflict it, and stressed that the courts were 'gravitating towards the total abolition of whipping'.[51] A few months earlier, in February, George Benson, Labour MP for Chesterfield, and an active campaigner on behalf of penal reform, introduced a bill for the abolition of corporal punishment in respect of male persons convicted on indictment.[52] Presumably, this measure would have removed the power, given by individual statutes, to whip boys under sixteen convicted on indictment of certain serious offences, but would have left untouched the general power to whip children under fourteen convicted summarily of an indictable offence. Benson also pressed Home Secretary Clynes to appoint a departmental committee to examine the whole question of corporal punishment. Clynes agreed that there was a case for an enquiry but declined to institute one, in view of the controversial nature of the subject and the fact that the Children Bill would not be brought in that session.[53] Benson again introduced his bill in January 1931, a measure for which there was evident sympathy in official circles:

> The Government are in general sympathy with the objects desired by the promoters of this Bill. The humanitarian and other grounds which can be argued in support of these proposals have been put with great force, and the general intention of the promoters of the Bill is one which must command a special sympathy of a Labour Government.[54]

But the minute also argued that the acute division of opinion on the subject demanded that a government enquiry should first review the subject.

As to the Labour government's Children Bill, by 1931 Harris was strongly urging a modification of the existing law by repealing the power of summary courts to whip children under fourteen for indictable offences, whilst leaving unchanged the power conferred by various laws to punish certain types of offence by whipping. Home

[51] PRO, HO45/14714/516360/55; *Hansard*, vol. 241, 22 July, 1930, col. 1953.

[52] 'A Bill to provide for the abolition of corporal punishment', PP 1929–30, I (123), p. 77. George Benson, born 1889, was Labour MP for the Chesterfield division of Derbyshire, 1929–31. He was a pacifist—and imprisoned for conscientious objection during the First World War, a prison reformer, and one of the leaders of the campaign against capital punishment. He was the author, with Edward Glover, of *Corporal Punishment: An Indictment* (1931). See *The Times*, 22 Aug. 1973, p. 16.

[53] Clynes to Benson, 25 Feb. 1930, PRO, HO45/14178/436329/59.

[54] Ibid., 436329/86.

Secretary Clynes supported this course in preference either to leaving the law as it stood or to implementing the recommendation of the Young Offenders Committee.[55] This approach was also followed by the National government, Herbert Samuel likewise wishing to restrict rather than enlarge the scope of corporal punishment.[56] The strongest reason for the department's determination to restrict, if not abolish, corporal punishment was said to be the magistrates themselves. Whipping as a penalty was practically moribund, suggesting that 'the general feeling of magistrates is that whipping is ceasing to be a suitable or an effective deterrent'. The number of cases had fallen from 2,079 in 1913 to 130 in 1930; in towns such as Liverpool and Manchester there had been no case of whipping for years. Then why not let the penalty die a natural death? Because, said Oliver Stanley, corporal punishment was 'a fatally easy remedy for the lazy or the reactionary magistrate'. The other reasons for the departmental policy were set out as follows.

> In the case of young people brought before the Courts corporal punishment has usually been tried already at home, and if not the Court can, if it likes, advise the parent to apply it. Corporal punishment by a parent or by a schoolmaster stands on a very different footing from a Police Court whipping. The latter is exposed to the risk of being brutal, but much more often of being too lenient, because the police officer hates to exert any force. This power has certainly been abused by the Courts in the past, and in several cases the Home Secretary has been called upon to intervene.[57]

Finally, to those who thought that whipping was particularly appropriate in the repression of offences against morals, it was submitted that this was to ignore the circumstances which often led to the offence.

These considerations were put before the Commons by Stanley when he opened the second reading debate in February 1932. His speech concluded by saying 'It is because we believe that the interests of the State, at this age of the young offender, lie more in trying to

[55] 5 Jan. 1931, PRO, HO45/14715/516360/71; Clynes, 'Probation to Preventive Detention: A Survey', *Magistrate*, vol. 2 (Oct.–Nov. 1930), p. 434. One advantage of adopting this course was that no explicit mention of whipping would be required in the Children Bill; the repeal of section 10 of the Summary Jurisdiction Act, 1879, would automatically have the desired effect.

[56] PRO, HO45/14716/516360/107; *Hansard*, vol. 259, 20 Nov. 1931, col. 1172.

[57] See Ibid.; PRO, HO45/14801/594745/4.

mend than to govern, that we urge this alteration on the House.'[58] The government's stand on whipping met with very little criticism in the Commons; the problems came with the House of Lords. At the Committee stage in the Lords, Viscount Bertie of Thame moved an amendment which sought to restore section 10 of the Summary Jurisdiction Act 1879. The government declined to accept the amendment, but this only served to multiply its protagonists. Lord Danesfort's forthright intervention, for example, left little to the imagination:

> I do think that this effeminate, over-humanitarian, ultra-sentimental view that to correct a child by reasonable correction is something which is out of date, which is wrong, and which offends the minds of proper thinking people, is a view which we cannot and ought not to adopt.[59]

The amendment was eventually agreed to.

Back in the Commons, the government moved to reject the Lords' amendment. There followed an impassioned speech from David Kirkwood and speeches from Sir Vivian Henderson, former Parliamentary Under-Secretary at the Home Office, and Mr Ramsbotham, Parliamentary Secretary to the Board of Education, in favour of the abolition of whipping.[60] Two points were reiterated: one, that studies like Burt's *The Young Delinquent* proved that flogging was the lazy way out, calling for no consideration of the underlying causes; two, that the abolition of corporal punishment would lead to the earlier use of institutional training. But the Lords insisted upon their amendment, and rather than allow the bill to fall for that session, Stanley gave in.[61] As Clynes said a few years later, the clause abolishing whipping was defeated 'by the savage patricians of the House of Lords'.[62]

The mood in the penal reform camp was again one of intense disappointment. The power to whip, they protested, was inconsistent

[58] *Hansard*, vol 261, 12 Feb. 1932, col. 1178.

[59] *Hansard*, vol. 84 (Lords), 9 June 1932, cols. 721 and 725. The Incorporated Justices' Clerks' Society was also in favour of retaining whipping: PRO, HO45/14801/594745/24.

[60] *Hansard*, vol. 267, 30 June 1932, cols. 2080, 2083–4. Sir Vivian Henderson, b. 1884, was Parliamentary Under-Secretary of State at the Home Office, 1927–29, during which he took a particular interest in the problems of juvenile delinquency. He was Conservative MP for the Chelmsford division of Essex, 1931–35.

[61] *Hansard*, vol. 85 (Lords), 7 July 1932, col. 695; *Hansard*, vol. 268, 11 July 1932, col. 1067. Rhys Davies, col. 1069, declared that the Labour opposition would not give way on this issue.

[62] J. R. Clynes, *Memoirs* (1937), vol. 2, p. 163.

with the entire spirit of the Children Act. According to the *Times Educational Supplement*, it was 'the only serious blot upon the measure' (perhaps forgetting about the omission of observation homes).[63] At the Labour Party Conference, Mrs Clara Rackham regretted the retention of 'that out of date and discredited penalty', which made it more necessary than ever to have Labour magistrates, especially female ones, appointed to serve in the juvenile court.[64] And naturally the Howard League was critical of the government's failure, particularly in the House of Lords where the spokesmen and supporters of the National government had been respectively ineffective and apathetic.[65] The penal reform bodies could only take comfort, as did the Home Office, in the fact that 'if the number of whippings continues to decrease at the present rate the power will soon cease to be used to any considerable extent in practice'.[66]

Summary

The Children and Young Persons Act included more provisions than the ones examined. So, for example, the Act, following the recommendation of the Young Offenders Committee, prohibited the application of capital punishment in the case of young offenders under eighteen. For nigh on half a century no one under the age of eighteen had, in fact, been executed; Home Secretaries had invariably reprieved offenders under that age. The clause in the 1933 Act, in short, gave legislative effect to what was already the administrative practice.[67] Another proposal of the departmental committee which found a place in the statute was the abolition of imprisonment for young persons between sixteen and seventeen, except when a certificate of unruliness or depravity was given.[68] And, lastly, the Act dealt with neglected

[63] 16 July 1932, p. 277.

[64] *Labour Party Conference Report*, 1932, p. 172.

[65] *Howard Journal*, vol. 3 (1932), pp. 12–13.

[66] 15 July 1932, PRO, HO45/14804/594745/106. See also A. Paterson, 'Youth and Crime', *Listener*, vol. VII (13 April 1932), p. 518.

[67] See *Hansard*, vol. 265, 12 May 1932, cols. 2241–50. An unsuccessful attempt was made to get an amendment to the bill which would have prohibited capital punishment for young persons up to the age of twenty-one.

[68] PRO, HO45/13403/510865/12. The Howard League and the Magistrates Association wanted to add the rider that even when a certificate of unruliness was given, imprisonment would be permitted only with the consent of the Home Secretary. The Home Office considered this proposal to be unworkable. See 510865/2 and 6.

children, in addition to the young delinquent. 'It is really in this class of case', claimed Stanley, in an address to the Magistrates Association, 'that we have made the most revolutionary change in the Bill.'[69] He had in mind the general definition of neglect which was substituted for the specific categories of the existing law, experience having shown them to be too limited. Moreover, this power to rescue boys and girls from dangerous home surroundings was to be applied in respect of children and young persons up to the age of seventeen. Hence, where parental control was inadequate, it was more likely than before to lead to the State stepping in.

Without doubt, the most significant contribution to the genesis of the 1933 Act in these years was made by the permanent officials of the Children's Branch. Sydney Harris was largely responsible for arranging the main heads and formulating the detailed provisions of successive drafts of the bill. He was also a key figure, in conjunction with the chief inspector of certified schools, in a series of internal discussions and conferences pertaining to the most controversial clauses of the proposed legislation.

Harris remained as firm an opponent of chancery or civil jurisdiction for the juvenile court as he had been when sitting on the Young Offenders Committee. Accordingly, he advised his superiors that improvements in juvenile justice would be secured more effectively by strengthening existing practice rather than by instituting a new legal principle, particularly since the latter would require better qualified magistrates than could be provided in the near future. Equally, Dr Norris held firmly to his conviction that a change of legal principle was an essential prologue to a more frequent use of the juvenile court by social workers and others. But again, the chief inspector failed to get the department radically to modify the criminal law in the interests of young people. The half-way house of the Young Offenders Committee was endorsed as official policy; a limit was put upon the invasion of the territory of the criminal law by child welfare legislation.

More prolonged discussion was given over to the question of a form of institutional treatment to fill the gap between probationary supervision 'in the open' and long-term residence in a Home Office school. Two complementary schemes were examined by the Children's Branch, neither of which had found favour with the Young Offenders Committee. One was residence in a home as a condition of probation;

[69] *Magistrate*, vol. 2 (Feb.–Mar. 1932).

the other was the short-term reformatory. Norris's suggestion that all forms of institutional training should be secured by way of a residence condition in a probation order was always too radical, although the element of flexibility in treatment which the idea embodied has been viewed more sympathetically in recent times. When the scheme was restricted to homes for probationers, however, Harris generally saw eye to eye with Norris, despite the fact that the former had been party to the departmental committee's disavowal of this practice. Harris simply felt unable to recommend the abolition of a practice which the courts had grown accustomed to using, mainly in order to avoid the stigma associated with committal to a certified school, and a practice which secured for some youngsters, particularly girls, a helpful form of treatment.

Dr Norris was also an energetic proponent of short-term detention, convinced that some lads would benefit by a short, sharp 'pull up' for a period of six months. Harris, in contrast, was worried on a number of counts. The rationale for providing an automatic three-year sentence was two-fold: to ensure that boys would be sent for a long enough stay to turn them into decent citizens, and that the decision as to release would be taken by the school authorities who were in the best position to assess the inmates' response to the training. Short-term detention, as conceived by Norris, would, in Harris's estimation, undermine both these principles. At a more practical level, Harris feared that the magistrates, urged on by the local authorities, would use the short sentence to excess, thereby committing some lads to an inappropriate form of detention and starving the long-term schools of pupils. For these reasons, Harris came up with the scheme of an experiment in short-term training, using the discretion which the semi-indeterminate sentence conferred on the executive.

The discussions which took place on chancery jurisdiction, on a residence condition in probation orders, and on short-term schools, highlighted the strengths and weaknesses of the two main officials of the children's department of the Home Office. Norris was a consistent supporter of the ascendancy of child welfare legislation and of the exclusion of young offenders from the terminology, procedures, and penalties of the criminal law. A vigorous extrovert, he was well equipped to break the hard shell of institutional life in the reformatory schools. As doctor and voluntary social worker turned public servant, Norris was less versed in, and less convinced of, the tradition that government should not educate public opinion or initiate radical social legislation. He displayed a good deal of impatience, therefore, at the cautious and slow-moving ways of the Home Office.[70] Harris, in contrast, was the conciliatory executive officer *par excellence*. Retiring and withdrawn in disposition, the office joke was that if he said 'Good morning', he wondered if he had gone too far. His administrative talents were depicted with some accuracy in a tribute following his death, in which it was submitted that Harris brought to the improvement of the condition of delinquent and neglected children 'not merely profound human sympathy but a clear and logical perception, not only of what needed to be done but of how much could be done at a particular juncture'.[71] It was he who fashioned the experience and reforming ideas of people like Norris into proposals which would claim the support of the department, parliament and the public; and it was he who was substantially responsible for designing a legislative measure which improved on the Children Act of 1908, without subverting the general principles on which the administration of the law relating to young offenders was based. If strongly contrasted in character and capacity, however, Harris and Norris formed a most effective partnership.

When it came to the detailed features of the 1933 Act, the reform bodies, the associations of penal practitioners, and the local authorities played their part, although with variable success. The penal reform lobby seemed reluctant to hail the report of the Young Offenders Committee as a new 'Children's Charter', given the compromising approach to the major issues of principle. Even so, it was recognized that the report was a repository of many valuable reforms which, if fully implemented, would transform the treatment of the young delinquent. Hence, groups like the Howard League and the Magistrates Association urged successive administrations to introduce legislation, using the traditional methods of conferences, resolutions, and parliamentary pressure. On the last score, the most significant move was the bill of July 1930 which the Labour MP, Rhys Davies, introduced on behalf of the League. Yet the reform groups were markedly ineffective when it came to a number of crucial issues—chancery jurisdiction, observation homes, and the abolition of corporal punishment. Without the imprimatur of an official committee of

[70] See the letter from Norris to the *Spectator*, 16 May 1941, in PRO, HO45/20250/838406/6A.

[71] *The Times*, 27 July 1962, p. 16; personal information from Mr C. P. Hill, former assistant secretary in the Home Office.

enquiry (as was the case with the first and last of these issues), and in the face of opposition from the Children's Branch, the London County Council, or the House of Lords, of which more in a moment, the impact of the penal pressure groups was considerably diminished.

The influence of the associations of practitioners was slightly greater. Some success, for example, attended the efforts of the National Association of Probation Officers to establish a more clearly defined role for their members in the making of preliminary enquiries. So, too, the combined efforts of NAPO, the Magistrates Association, and the Association of Headmasters of Certified Schools pulled off a victory over a vacillating Home Office in securing the abolition of the use in the juvenile court of 'conviction' and 'sentence'. Even more effective were the local authorities. Their influence was used in a wholly negative manner to defeat the proposals in the Children's Bill which, in their view, entailed excessive financial expenditure. On the question of the venue of the juvenile courts, the County Councils' Association worked through the House of Lords to uproot the original clause which decreed that children's tribunals should be held in separate premises from adult courts. One of the most important local authorities, the London County Council, was instrumental to the abandonment of the clause which would have made it possible to institute observation centres. The cut-backs in public expenditure, which arose out of the financial crisis of 1931, so reduced the LCC's education budget that they were not prepared to underwrite the capital expenditure needed to establish such centres. The Treasury also contributed to the departmental discussions on this question. Equally governed by the economic crisis, the Treasury were hostile to the idea that observation homes should be financed from central funds, and anxious to prevent the State from taking on board what was seen to be a responsibility of local government. Yet they were prepared to endorse Sir John Anderson's scheme of an enabling power, giving an independent body of managers the authority to establish observation homes when the financial climate was brighter. Even this compromise proposal, however, was unacceptable to the LCC.

As expected of a measure which found favour with successive home secretaries, from the die-hard Conservative, Joynson-Hicks, through the labourite trade unionist, Clynes, to the sentimental Liberal, Samuel, the bill provoked little or no political *parti pris*. Rhys Davies's remark—'This is not a Party question; it does not belong to parties at all'—is worthy of application to the whole bill, as indeed to a good deal of the social legislation between the wars. A cordial welcome was given by all the parties in the Commons to the general principles embodied in the measure. The only truly controversial question was that of corporal punishment, and the animus which this issue aroused owed more to the social composition of the House of Lords than to party rivalry over penal policy.

Although initially steering clear of the controversial issue of corporal punishment, the Home Office ultimately decided to repeal the power of summary courts to whip children under fourteen years. This proposal, which controverted the view of the Young Offenders Committee, was in keeping with both the judicial reluctance to use the penalty and the social conception of delinquency. For a phalanx of 'reactionaries' in the House of Lords, however, the fight to retain corporal punishment as a weapon in the penal armoury represented a last stand against the contagion of leniency and sentimentality which was said to have juvenile justice in its grip. If essentially symbolic, the action of the House of Lords was singularly effective in forcing the government to give way, lest it jeopardized the rest of the Children's Bill. As significantly, the issue of corporal punishment became a standard around which the 'reactionaries' were to rally in the 1930s, providing the first sustained challenge to the child welfare movement.

PART III

Defending the Children and Young Persons Act 1933

5

Reformers and Reactionaries, 1933–1938

Since the Children Act of 1933 has come into force, and juvenile delinquency has apparently increased there has been more talk and argument on birching, as a way out, than at any time I can remember.[1]

As the Children and Young Persons Bill made its way through parliament in 1932, the increase in juvenile crime which had commenced in the late 1920s was already causing anxiety. In the Home Office Supply debate in April, James Lovat-Fraser, a National Labour MP, spoke of the mounting obsession, particularly on the part of the newspaper press, with the need to act firmly against the increase in delinquency:

Some people have lost their heads and become panicky. I have seen it stated in the Press that our policy of reducing the severity of our penal laws during the last century has been a mistake, and that what we ought to do now is to return to severer methods and the methods which we have been steadily discarding for a century.[2]

There was a brief hiatus in the discussion of this issue whilst the Children and Young Persons Act was being implemented, but from 1935 a vigorous controversy burst forth concerning the reasons for the continued upward trend of juvenile crime.[3] On the one hand, magistrates and the police believed that a real increase of lawlessness underlay the statistics, and that this was due, in part, to the leniency of

[1] 'The Departmental Committee on Corporal Punishment, 1938', *Minutes of Evidence* (seen with Home Office permission), C.P. 18, Mrs Elizabeth Andrews, chairman of the Ystrad Juvenile Court, Glamorgan.

[2] *Hansard*, vol. 264, 15 April 1932, col. 1168. Lovat-Fraser was a Labour Member until August 1931, thereafter a National Labour Member; he was also a supporter of the State Children's Association.

[3] In 1933, 14,358 boys and girls under sixteen were found guilty of indictable offences in England and Wales. The corresponding figures for 1934, 1935 and 1936 were, respectively, 17,887; 22,399 and 22,760. Additionally there were the following numbers of those aged sixteen for the same three years: 2,541, 3,043 and 4,161. See *Fifth Report on the Work of the Children's Branch* (1938), p. 8; *Hansard*, vol. 321, 17 March 1937, cols. 2079–80; *Hansard*, vol. 350, 20 July 1939, col. 734.

the methods of dealing with young offenders, which the 1933 Act had promoted, and, in part, to a simultaneous decline in the force of parental discipline. Only a greater resort to tougher sanctions, notably corporal punishment, would, it was thought, turn back the tide of juvenile crime. These people I term 'reactionaries', in that they sought to return to the former system of deterrent treatment. On the other hand, the representatives of the child welfare societies, seconded by the Home Office, postulated that the increase in delinquency was more apparent than real, a statistical artefact of the recent legislation, the latter having encouraged the police and the public to bring more offenders before the juvenile courts to be dealt with as children in need. Nor was this group entirely convinced by the theory of a decay of parental discipline, preferring still to explain delinquency by reference either to larger social and economic factors, such as unemployment, or to defective domestic conditions. Even when the home and parents were accorded causative significance, moreover, the lesson drawn was less that courts should furnish the discipline that parents were failing to mete out, and more that they should help the young offender to grow up in a congenial family setting either in his own home (with the aid of a probation officer) or in a foster home or, if all else failed, in a residential school. During the 1930s, in short, the first sustained attack on the child welfare movement was launched, in the van of which were influential representatives of the magistracy and police. The ensuing struggle deserves extended consideration, if only for the significant fact that the Home Office were required to fight a rearguard action against those who would divert the course of juvenile justice into sterner channels.

Ideology and Crime: 'the Reactionaries'

Some of the first voices to be raised in opposition to 'sentimental justice' and in favour of harsher penalties were those of the lay magistracy. The panel of juvenile justices for Stalybridge pressed the Home Office in 1935 for more approved schools and for greater caution in the release of offenders from the schools in view of the statistics of juvenile crime.[4] At a meeting of the Manchester Rotary Club, a few months later, Mr J. Wellesley Orr, the city stipendiary,

[4] PRO, HO45/16516/375684/72. See Tables 5 and 6 for the population of approved schools. See also Figure 1. The percentage increase in the number of persons under

criticized the excessive use of probation and the procedures of the juvenile court. 'He objected to the system', according to one newspaper report, 'whereby children were brought before "a benevolent lady and gentleman" in a room devoid of all the appearance of a court.'[5] A year later, in October 1936, a conference of representatives of thirty-six Lancashire juvenile panel justices discussed the resolution that panels 'should not shrink from exercising their power to order corporal punishment in suitable cases'; it was withdrawn only after the voting on it had been about equally divided. The conference did recommend for the guidance of all juvenile panels, however, that when a parent was bound over as surety for the good behaviour of a child and there was a breach of the conditions of the child's probation, proceedings should more frequently be instituted against the surety for the enforcement of the recognizance. And, finally, the conference asked the Home Office for more remand homes and approved schools, and for 'the constitution and whole atmosphere of the Juvenile Courts [to] be revised and made more impressive'. In the opinion of Mr. Macbeth, stipendiary magistrate of Salford, the proposal to abolish 'this nice consulting-room idea' was the best resolution before the conference.[6]

The campaign of the 'reactionaries' was braced by the influential lobby of senior police officials. In 1935 and again in 1936, the annual reports of a large number of chief constables expressed the view that juvenile crime had increased to a marked extent in recent years, and that part of the problem was that young offenders were no longer impressed by their appearance before the juvenile court.[7] The most vigorous attack on the problem of juvenile delinquency was launched by the Liverpool chief constable in his report for 1936. He was determined to impress upon the public the gravity of the position, and condemned the fact that more ingenuity had been expended in official

seventeen found guilty of indictable crime, in the wake of the 1933 Act, was largest for breaking and entering, with receiving, frauds, and false pretences taking second place: H. Mannheim in A. M. Carr-Saunders *et al.*, *Young Offenders. An Enquiry into Juvenile Delinquency* (Cambridge, 1942), p. 47.

[5] Cutting, *Manchester Guardian*, 4 Oct. 1935, in PRO, HO144/22634/677145/8.

[6] PRO, HO45/16516/375684/100. See also *Manchester Guardian*, 27 and 28 Oct. 1936.

[7] Ibid., 375684/89–112; HO45/18118/697558/2, 8, 11–16. In Jan. 1936, the Central Conference of Chief Constables, held in the Home Office, drew attention to the problem of finding vacancies in approved schools: 375684/69.

circles 'in trying to explain away the significance of the statistics than in facing the situation'. His main contention was that juvenile lawlessness had increased continuously since 1930, and that it was directly related to the difficulties put in the way of the police and the courts in bringing home to delinquents the seriousness of their offences. Too many of the penalties at the disposal of the courts contained 'nothing tangible in the way of a penalty to impress upon the juvenile a consciousness of wrongdoing'. For this reason, the chief constable suggested giving greater publicity to the names and addresses of young delinquents; this would restrain them from committing offences more effectively than the secret method of trial which the Act of 1933 had ushered in.[8] And, finally, in a prescient suggestion, he advocated strengthening the hands of the magistrates by coupling probation with some form of punishment and discipline:

> If some sort of scheme could be effected whereby offenders of school age, convicted of offences, could be dealt with by the Education Authority and made to attend at certain schools on Saturday afternoons to undergo compulsory physical exercises or drill, according to the number of hours the Justices' Court might inflict, it is possible the deprivation of liberty at a time when weekly games and pleasures are abundant might have a wholesome deterrent effect.[9]

Such was the gravamen of the police chiefs' accusation: the 'Clarke Hall movement' had gone too far, robbing the juvenile courts of a formal impressiveness and the juvenile magistrates of adequate penalties. A middle way was called for, between 'the barbarism of a century ago and the futile sloppishness of today'.[10]

The criticism of the work of the juvenile courts by the police and by some sections of the magistracy was based on a particular conception of the forces which generally led children to break the law. It was well known that a number of explanations were advanced for the increase in juvenile crime, relating usually to one or more of the many post-war changes. Some commentators had stressed a connection with poverty, unemployment and bad housing; others had blamed the absence of

[8] *Annual Report of the Chief Constable of Liverpool for 1936* (1937), pp. 24–34, in PRO, HO45/16516/375684/82; HO45/18118/697558/11; 'Police and Young Offenders', *Police Review*, 23 April 1937.

[9] *Annual Report of the Chief Constable of Liverpool for 1936* (1937), p. 34; *Police Review*, 23 Apr. 1937, p. 393.

[10] See 'Sentimental Justice', *Spectator*, 27 Sep. 1935, p. 458; R. Walling, 'Are Children's Courts Sentimental?', *Spectator*, 4 Oct. 1935, p. 501.

recreational facilities and boys' clubs, especially on the new housing estates, or the baneful influence of the cinema. Still others had pointed to the increased opportunities for theft provided by the open counters of the new multiple stores (Woolworth, Marks and Spencer) and by unlocked cars. But the police vote went increasingly to a decay in parental control and supervision. The chief constable of Bradford, for example, underlined the causative role of inadequate home training in his annual reports of the mid-1930s. In one such report he wrote:

> The fact that approved schools generally are filled to overflowing with juvenile delinquents demonstrates, presumably, that the Courts throughout the country have deemed it necessary to deprive parents of the custody of such children in order to provide them with the training which has been lacking in their homes.[11]

An associated strand to this viewpoint was that the tendency for the State to assume more and more welfare responsibilities only aggravated the emasculation of parental authority.[12] Nor did modern educational practice escape unscathed. To the deficiency of parental discipline the Bradford chief constable combined the growing fashion of schools to encourage self-expression and discourage compulsion, thus encouraging children to give vent to their acquisitive instinct.[13] Little wonder, then, that the police lobby pressed the courts to fill the breach in parental and educational discipline with more awe-inspiring tribunals and tougher penal sanctions.[14]

Ideology and Crime: 'the Reformers'

Before the conference of representatives of Lancashire juvenile panel justices in October 1936, by no means all magistrates accepted that there had been a vast growth in juvenile crime. The justices of Rochdale, Nelson, and Liverpool declared that the changed methods of dealing with young offenders had resulted in a mere increase in the number of cases officially handled.[15] Many other reforming magistrates

[11] PRO, HO45/18118/697558/2; *Police Review*, 30 Apr. 1937, p. 426.

[12] See Vivian Henderson, 'General Survey of Juvenile Delinquency', *The Year Book of Education 1936*, sect. 3, p. 865.

[13] PRO, HO45/18118/697558/2.

[14] cf. City of Birmingham Education Committee, *Report of the Chief Education Officer on an Investigation into the Causes of the Increase of Juvenile Delinquency in the City* (1935), p. 14, in PRO, HO45/16516/375684/91.

[15] PRO, HO45/16516/375684/100.

remained faithful to the principles embodied in the 1933 Act; Miss Madeleine Symons, Leo Page, and Basil Henriques were amongst the most persuasive of advocates. Henriques admonished a conference of women magistrates not to be alarmed by the statistics of juvenile crime 'because the sooner a wayward or unhappy child is brought before us, the greater are the chances of his eventually becoming a first-class citizen'.[16] The Howard League and a sample of education officers seconded the view that the growth in juvenile delinquency owed more to the change in public policy than to a change in the conduct of the young;[17] to which the official seal was attached by way of both the introductions to the annual *Criminal Statistics* and the speeches delivered at a number of conferences by Sydney Harris, Mr J. F. Henderson and Dr J. C. Methven. Harris, an Assistant Under-Secretary of State by this date, told the annual conference of Superintendents of School Attendance Departments that a greater willingness on the part of the public to use the machinery of the law had followed the Children Act of 1908 and the same thing had occurred in the wake of the 1933 Act. Harris's successor as head of the Children's Branch, J. F. Henderson, presented the same argument to the North of England Education Conference and to the conference of representatives of Lancashire juvenile panel justices, adding only that the number of boy delinquents also probably reflected the high birth-rate of the immediate post-war years.[18]

The Home Office was, in fact, less complacent about the rise in juvenile crime than the above remarks would suggest. For a start, the Children's Branch was struggling with the question of providing extra accommodation in the approved schools, although this was due less to the crime rate as such, than to the wider definition in the 1933 Act of those in need of care or protection, and to the raising by one year of

[16] *Magistrate*, vol. 4 (Nov. 1936), p. 1089. See also M. Symons, 'The Children and Young Persons Act, 1933', *Magistrate*, vol. 4 (Nov. 1935), p. 955; Leo Page, 'Juvenile Court Work', *Magistrate*, vol. 4 (Oct. 1937), p. 1223.

[17] See Cicely Craven, 'The Home Office Takes Stock', *Penal Reformer*, vol. 3 (July 1936), pp. 11–12. Craven followed Margery Fry as Secretary of the Howard League. See also LCC, *Report of the Education Officer on Juvenile Delinquency* (1937), pp. 1–7 and 21–2.

[18] See *Education*, 16 Oct. 1936, p. 378; PRO, HO45/16516/375684/99; *Daily Telegraph*, 9 Jan. 1937; Henderson, 'Juvenile Delinquency', *Magistrate*, vol. 4 (Feb.–Mar. 1937), pp. 1116–7; Methven (Assistant Prison Commissioner), 'Is There an Increase in Delinquency', *Probation*, vol. 2 (Jan. 1937), pp. 97–8. See also *Criminal Statistics, 1934*, PP 1935–6, XXV (Cmd. 5185), pp. 485–6.

the age of young persons who might be sent to a school.[19] The department was well aware, moreover, that a good deal of public anxiety had been aroused by the reports of the chief constables, to judge from leading articles and correspondence in the provincial press; and that the apparent increase in juvenile crime had led to demands for sterner measures, including the renewed use of the formerly discredited penalty of whipping. Some magistrates had already acknowledged the criticism of existing methods by putting police officers connected with the juvenile court back into uniform and by replacing the 'drawing room' atmosphere in the court with more formal proceedings.[20] Not wishing to fuel these developments, the department purposely omitted the figures of juvenile crime in 1937, in reply to a parliamentary question, when it became evident that they reversed the hopeful signs of stabilization in the figures for 1936. The hope was that the 1937 figures, showing a 14 per cent increase in indictable crime amongst boys under fourteen, would attract less attention in the annual criminal statistics.[21] The discontent aroused by the increase in the incidence of delinquency prompted Sir Samuel Hoare, on his arrival at the Home Office in May 1937, to ask the department whether a special inquiry ought to be instituted. Harris was initially attracted to an inquiry into the nature and extent of the apparent increase in juvenile crime, if only to disarm the critics. But he later agreed with Sir Russell Scott, Permanent Under-Secretary of State, that sufficient data already existed for the broad conclusion that the moderate but growing rate of increase in the number of convictions between 1921 and 1933 'can be fully explained by general deterioration of the economic situation of the country culminating in the crisis of 1931', and that the far larger increase in 1934 and 1935 'can be fully accounted for by an increased readiness to charge young offenders as a result of the 1933 Act'. The ensuing question, then, according to Samuel Hoare, was 'whether we need any further support to meet the kind of criticisms (e.g. of sentimentality and sloppiness) that will probably be raised during the passage of a Criminal Justice Bill?'[22] The department's answer was

[19] See *Fifth Report*, op. cit., pp. 101 and 140; E. C. Rhodes, 'Juvenile Delinquency', *Journal of the Royal Statistical Society*, vol. 102 (1939), p. 395.

[20] S. W. Harris, 6 July 1937, PRO, HO45/19065/807624/1.

[21] PRO, HO45/18118/697558/37–8 and 74.

[22] PRO, HO45/19065/807624/1. *Robert Russell Scott*, b. 1877, had a long career in the Civil Service, starting in the Admiralty as a Clerk, Class 1, in 1901. He remained in the

evidently in the affirmative, since in October 1937 Hoare announced that 'a scientific investigation of juvenile crime' was to be launched.[23] In fact, the results of this enquiry into the causation of juvenile delinquency, under the direction of Professor Carr-Saunders, Director of the LSE, took longer to appear than the Home Office anticipated, and were not available before the country was in the throes of war and the Criminal Justice Bill abandoned.[24]

Not that during the 1930s the Home Office were unwilling to express a collective view on the causation of delinquency. The parvenu theory of a decay in parental control, for example, found few devotees in the department; such a slackening of discipline, the official line ran, must be gradual and could not, therefore, explain the sharp variation in the delinquency figures between 1933 and 1935. If an explanation was required, other than an increased readiness to bring children to the juvenile courts, the Home Office believed that social and economic factors, notably the effects of unemployment on both children and parents, still counted for something.[25] In this judgement, the department found allies within some sections of the child welfare lobby.

The high level of unemployment in the 1930s, especially amongst young people between fourteen and eighteen years of age, led inevitably to a resurgence of the established view that crime and unemployment ran in double harness. In 1933, Mr C. G. Ammon, former Parliamentary and Financial Secretary to the Admiralty, declared that 'young bandits' first got into trouble as a result of unemployment. 'My experience', which he had acquired as a magistrate at the London Quarter Sessions, 'has taught me that unemployment stands out as the greatest contributing cause to the

Admiralty until 1920, when he joined the Treasury. From 1921 to 1932 he was Controller of Establishments in the Treasury. He was Permanent Under-Secretary of State from 1932 to 1938: *Who Was Who*, 1951–60; *The Times*, 19 Mar. 1960, p. 8.

Samuel John Gurney Hoare, b. 1880, was Conservative MP for Chelsea 1910–44. He was Secretary of State for Air, for India, and for Foreign Affairs before taking charge of the Home Office in May 1937. Of Quaker ancestry, he was brought up and remained an Anglo-Catholic. He was enamoured of the tradition of penal reform which ran in his family: Samuel Hoare was his great-grandfather; Elizabeth Fry, his great-great-aunt. See *DNB, 1951–60*, pp. 487–90.

[23] See Templewood Papers (Cambridge), Box X:7, speech to be delivered by the Home Secretary at the opening of Remand Home, Hull, 23 Oct. 1937.

[24] See PRO, HO45/19064/807624.

[25] *Magistrate*, vol. 4 (Feb.–Mar. 1937), p. 1117.

making of criminals.'[26] The official *Criminal Statistics* for 1934, relating to the first operative year of the Children and Young Persons Act, similarly described a close relationship between the incidence of juvenile crime and the industrial depression in the years 1929–33. A departmental minute annotated the statistics thus: 'As might be expected, juvenile crime is lowest in agricultural parts, and rises through normally employed industrial districts to a sharp peak in the depressed areas of Lancashire, the North-East, and South Wales.'[27]

A number of unofficial studies also laid emphasis on the levels of unemployment. In 1935, Geraldine Cadbury commissioned a chart showing the close relationship between the curve of unemployment and delinquency from 1905 to the mid-1930s in Birmingham, a city not too badly afflicted by the depression.[28] In the cotton textile town of Oldham, unemployment and delinquency were closely associated, according to an unpublished report of 1936 by Albert Royds, Assistant Director of Education.[29] The findings of the renowned social surveys of the inter-war years, moreover, particularly the figures of the number of children to be found in families whose standard of living was below the 'poverty line', suggested that broad socio-economic conditions underlay a good deal of unwanted juvenile behaviour. Tout, for one, exclaimed in his study of Bristol, 'It is an appalling fact that one working-class child in every five comes from a home where income is inadequate to provide a bare minimum standard, according to the austere Survey rules . . . '[30] The moral of such studies was, in effect, pointed by Geoffrey Lloyd, Parliamentary Under-Secretary of State at the Home Office. Speaking during the second reading of the Criminal Justice Bill, he put forward the following explanation of delinquency:

The best opinion seems to be that it is not so much a case of actual physical

[26] 'Young Bandits', *John Bull*, 15 Apr. 1933; PRO, HO45/17928/429843/10. Ammon had introduced a Children's Bill in 1924, for which see above p. 19. See also Viscountess Astor, 'Unemployment and Delinquency', *Probation*, vol. 1 (July 1933), p. 247. The Chief Constable of Birkenhead also subscribed to the view that unemployment and the increase in larcenies were associated: *Birkenhead News*, 17 Feb. 1932.

[27] 13 July 1935, PRO, HO45/18716/385052/28. cf. *Criminal Statistics, 1930*, PP 1931–2, XXVI (Cmd. 4036), pp. 7–11; PRO, HO45/16516/375684/62 and 64A.

[28] *Magistrate*, vol. 3 (Jan.–Feb. 1935), pp. 874–5; Janet Whitney, *Geraldine S. Cadbury 1865–1941* (1948), p. 160.

[29] See A. M. Carr-Saunders *et al., Young Offenders. An Enquiry into Juvenile Delinquency* (Cambridge, 1942), pp. 28–32; Hermann Mannheim, *Social Aspects of Crime in England Between the Wars* (1940), pp. 146–7.

[30] H. Tout, *The Standard of Living in Bristol* (1938), quoted in J. Stevenson (ed.), *Social Conditions in Britain Between the Wars* (Harmondsworth, 1977), pp. 104–5.

want in these days leading to theft as poverty, unemployment, bad housing and overcrowding producing a variety of circumstances and a general environment which leads to the young people committing offences.[31]

As in the 1920s, however, there was considerable support for a modified environmental interpretation, in which juvenile delinquency was adjudged to be the outcome less of broad social and economic factors than of domestic conditions: the material and psychological conditions of the home and family. Increasingly, the view became that the abnormal conditions of the thirties—depression, unemployment and poverty—were mostly important for accentuating defective family life. Sir Vivian Henderson, for example, told the Magistrates Association in 1933: 'When one gets a household where the parents are out-of-work and the children have no work either, naturally there is much less sense of discipline and greater lack of restraint.'[32] But the root of the matter was neither poverty nor unemployment, but defective homes, by which were meant homes where parental strife or tension existed; or which had been broken by divorce, separation, or the death or disability of one or both of the parents; or where religious and moral training was neglected.[33]

Cyril Burt had been one of the earliest proponents of the role of disturbed family relationships in the making of delinquents. In the 1930s his influence was, if anything, magnified, as he began to address a wider audience. In a radio discussion with Henderson in May 1934, for instance, Burt spoke of the effects of inadequate parental control on delinquency:

Parental influence is the most important of all influences. But it is not necessarily *weakness* of discipline that encourages crime. Quite as often it may be excessive severity; and, most frequently of all, a mixture of the two—an irresponsible, alternating, forcible-feeble kind of treatment.[34]

A further study by the American criminologist, William Healy, *New Light on Delinquency and its Treatment*, once again corroborated the

[31] *Hansard*, vol. 342, 1 Dec. 1938, col. 721.

[32] 'Some Causes of Crime', *Magistrate*, vol. 3 (Nov.–Dec. 1933), p. 733. Henderson was Chairman of Lambeth and Hampstead juvenile courts, a member of the Home Office Probation Committee and President of the Home Office Schools Managers Association.

[33] For an investigation which developed Burt's work on the 'broken home', see Dr M. Fortes, 'Notes on Juvenile Delinquency: II. Step-Parenthood and Delinquency', *Sociological Review*, vol. 25 (1933), pp. 153–8.

[34] 'Causes of Crime', *Listener*, 2 May 1934, p. 750 (emphasis in original). See also Burt, *The Subnormal Mind* (1935).

English evidence of emotional tensions arising from the relationship between children and parents.[35] Significantly, the pronouncements of Burt and Healy were quoted time and again as proof of the impact of disturbed home conditions. S. Clement Brown, tutor to the Mental Health course at the LSE, impressed upon the probation officers of the Midlands branch of NAPO that these studies illustrated the value of 'a careful study of each individual law-breaker in relation to his home setting'.[36] Interestingly, too, social workers seem to have responded practically to these influences, to judge from a comparative analysis of case records drawn up in 1924 and 1934. Between these two dates, the sources of the theories which guided the social worker developed from concern with material conditions ('cleanliness' or 'sobriety') to an interest in intimate social relationships, especially between parents and children.[37] Soon the vocabulary of education officers, schoolmasters' associations, and reforming magistrates was laced with references to the lack of parental control and defective family relationships. The genre is displayed in the *Report on Juvenile Delinquency*, put out by the Leicestershire Schoolmasters' Association:

> Family quarrels, lack of supervision by parents, lack of love, neglect of religious and moral training in the home, are factors so common to many cases of Juvenile Delinquency that the failure of parents to accept their responsibilities is agreed to be its chief cause.[38]

Accentuating the lack of parental guidance, according to the Schoolmasters' Association, were the growth in married woman labour (leading to the 'latch-key kid') and the pursuit of pleasure in the shape of clubs, gambling, and greyhound racing.

Most people who dealt with juvenile offenders at first hand were in agreement, then, about the influence of the home and parents on delinquency. Gradually, too, the Home Office came round to this way

[35] W. Healy and Augusta Bronner, *New Light on Delinquency and its Treatment* (New Haven, 1936); Sibyl Clement Brown, Review of Healy and Bronner, *Howard Journal*, vol. 4 (1937), pp. 391–7; Winifred A. Elkin, *English Juvenile Courts* (1938), pp. 26–7.

[36] 'Is Delinquency an Individual or a Family Problem?', *Probation*, vol. 1 (Apr. 1934), p. 299.

[37] See S. Clement Brown, 'The Methods of Social Case Workers', in F. C. Bartlett, *et al.*, *The Study of Society* (1939), pp. 384–5; Ray Lees, 'Social Work, 1925–50: the Case for a Reappraisal', *British Journal of Social Work*, vol. I (1971).

[38] *Juvenile Delinquency* (1938), pp. 4–5, enclosed in PRO, HO45/18118/697558/97. See also 'The Problem of Juvenile Delinquency', *Education*, 16 Oct. 1936, p. 376; LCC, *Report*, op. cit., pp. 8–13; Birmingham Education Committee, op. cit.

of thinking. In April 1937, the records of information of 230 cases of juvenile crime were examined as they came into the department over a period of three weeks. The survey reinforced the difficulty of making any generalization as to whether poverty was or was not the cause of delinquency, and suggested, according to a departmental minute, 'that most young offenders come from what one might describe as poor homes—and many from broken homes'.[39] Further verification came with the reports of the Borstal Association and the Prison Commission which reckoned that the downfall of older lads could often be traced to a want of discipline and training at home, to trouble with step-parents, or to the taint of illegitimacy.[40] And, finally, the long-awaited Report of the Children's Branch, which came out in 1938, carried an analysis of the home conditions of 150 boys who were consecutively admitted to the Philanthropic Society's senior school at Redhill, Surrey. The verdict of this survey was provided by the warden, who was quoted as saying 'I have formed the opinion that the "broken home" is the biggest single factor in juvenile delinquency'.[41] In keeping with this viewpoint, Hoare declared in November 1938 that the young were not more wicked, but less controlled by their parents, more afflicted by broken homes, indulgent mothers, or unkind stepmothers.[42]

It should be evident that the most accepted explanation of delinquency in the 1930s was one which emphasized unsatisfactory home conditions, psychological as well as material. Clearly, too, this explanation attracted the support of the 'reactionaries' as much as the 'reformers'; the defective family, after all, incorporated the absence or laxity of parental discipline which the police and magistracy were wont to stress. The essential difference between the two approaches to the

[39] 22 Apr. 1937, PRO, HO45/18118/697558/9.

[40] *Report of the Borstal Association for 1938*, p. 1; *Report of the Prison Commissioners for 1937*, PP 1937–8, XIV (Cmd. 5868), pp. 870–4.

[41] *Fifth Report*, op. cit., pp. 42–7.

[42] *Hansard*, vol. 342, 29 Nov. 1938, col. 272. It is significant, however, that the inquiry into the causes of juvenile delinquency, undertaken by Professor Carr-Saunders, examined only the *social* factors (unemployment, urban life, family conditions) which were thought to cause delinquency. The Home Office would not let Carr-Saunders include a *psychiatric* examination of delinquents, because of the research problems which it raised. See Carr-Saunders *et al.*, op. cit., pp. 41–2; PRO, HO45/19066/807624/7–33. The department were disappointed with *Young Offenders*, and Sir Alexander Maxwell, the Permanent Under-Secretary of State, at first doubted whether it should be published (29 Nov. 1941): 'It seems to me rather like an attempt to cloak in scientific phraseology the complete failure of the statistical enquiry to reveal anything of value at all, except perhaps to disprove the theory which has been advanced in the past that one of the important factors in delinquency is the "broken" home.'

problem of juvenile crime was in the conclusions drawn from the evidence about unsuitable home environments. Whereas the reformers looked to the provision of improved conditions of family life, whether in the natural, a foster, or a residential home, the reactionaries put their faith in the reanimation of the legal substitutes for parental discipline. This was the setting, then, for the conflict in the 1930s between those who wished to consolidate and extend the principles embodied in the Children and Young Persons Act and those who incited a tougher approach to the problems of juvenile crime.

Corporal Punishment

By the 1930s, few boys of under fourteen were being sentenced to corporal punishment by the juvenile courts; the figures for 1933–1936 were, respectively, 162, 146, 218, and 166.[43] A small number of courts in the smaller towns and in the counties tended to be responsible for these orders, the large majority of the 1,000 juvenile courts in England and Wales making no use of corporal punishment. So despite the increase in the number of young offenders dealt with, the courts were sufficiently convinced of the ineffectiveness or the psychological harmfulness of the penalty not to step up the use of the method. But in time, the increase in juvenile delinquency reinvigorated the adherents of corporal punishment.

During 1936 and 1937, a number of resolutions were forwarded to the Home Office, in which local panels of juvenile justices complained that existing methods of dealing with young offenders were ineffective, and appealed for the age limit for birching to be raised to sixteen and made applicable to all offences of male children and young persons tried summarily. The magistrates of Lincoln coupled the recommendation of a more frequent use of corporal punishment with the criticism that the probation system was over-used:

> Many magistrates are of opinion that while the probationary system should be given a full trial in suitable cases the infliction of corporal punishment for a second or certainly for a third offence instead of a further period of probation

[43] *Criminal Statistics for 1935*, PP 1936–7, XXVI (Cmd. 5520), p. 486. To put these figures into perspective, in 1935 there were 13,248 boys under fourteen found guilty of indictable offences. Thus birching was used by the juvenile courts in less than 2% of the total number of cases.

or of binding over, would in the great majority of cases be fully justified and would have a deterrent effect.[44]

Endorsement came from more influential quarters. Lord Hewart, the Lord Chief Justice, spoke in favour of retaining corporal punishment in the armoury of the juvenile courts, when delivering the second Clarke Hall lecture in 1935. The penalty was rarely imposed, and always, he argued, 'with great discrimination, and certainly as a mode of treatment, never as a vindictive expression of revenge'.[45] Other protagonists, finally, wanted greater discrimination still, by reserving whipping for cases of cruelty to animals or to other children.[46]

A strong body of opinion, however, remained wholly opposed to corporal punishment in any circumstances. In the columns of the *Magistrate*, for example, the association counselled justices to refrain from using a penalty which had no reformative or preventive effect and which, in practice, was not much of a deterrent—at least for the street urchin. 'Is it not obvious', magistrates were asked, 'that a boy of thirteen, of the sort that is whipped, has a tough life at home and in the streets, and the official standardized birching has not much terror for him?'[47] And again, Clarke Hall's evidence was presented as authority for the view that the best method of ensuring that a young offender would again appear in court was to whip him. The Howard League were also as active as ever. Following the suicide in December 1934 of a convict who had been sentenced to twelve strokes with the 'cat' for an act of violence while trying to escape from Dartmoor, the League got Liberal MP, Robert Bernays, to ask the Home Secretary, Sir John Gilmour, for an official enquiry into corporal punishment.[48] This was

[44] PRO, HO45/18815/800967/19.

[45] Lord Hewart of Bury, *The Treatment of the Young Offender* (1935), p. 37. Gordon Hewart, born 1870, was Lord Chief Justice 1922–40. Before that, he was Liberal MP for Leicester, and both Solicitor- and Attorney-General: R. Jackson, *The Chief. The Biography of Gordon Hewart* (1959).

[46] Vivian Henderson in *Year Book of Education 1936*, op. cit., p. 852.

[47] *Magistrate*, vol. 3 (July–Aug. 1934), pp. 801–2; vol. 4 (Jan.–Feb. 1936), p. 981.

[48] *Hansard*, vol. 296, 11 Dec. 1934, cols. 348–50; Howard League Minute Books, MSS 16B/1/2, 21 Dec. 1934. *Robert Hamilton Bernays*, b. 1902, was Liberal MP for Bristol, North from 1931, becoming a Liberal National in 1936: *Who Was Who*, 1941–50, p. 93; *The Times*, 24 March 1945, p. 7. *Sir John Gilmour*, b. 1876, was Conservative MP for Glasgow, Pollok 1918–40. He was Secretary of State for Scotland and Minister of Agriculture and Fisheries before taking charge of the Home Office in Sep. 1932. He was Home Secretary until June 1935; his term of office was undistinguished as far as penal reform was concerned: *Who's Who of British MPs* (1979), vol. 3, p. 128.

followed by an attempt to hold a meeting of the Parliamentary Penal Reform Group, which failed owing to the House rising for the Christmas vacation, and by an impressive memorial to the Secretary of State. Endorsed by over a hundred leading lights in the arts, science, politics, and religion, the memorial appealed to the Home Secretary to institute an impartial enquiry into the question of corporal punishment—'its effects upon the physique, mental and moral condition of those who have been punished in this way, its effectiveness as a deterrent, and its relation to our modern penal system'.[49] Not for the last time, Gilmour turned a deaf ear to the request for an enquiry. The next Home Secretary, Sir John Simon, was initially no more helpful. A bill to abolish the power of a court of summary jurisdiction to order a child to be whipped, introduced by Mr Parker in April 1936, was blocked by the Home Office; when Robert Bernays in the following month pressed the Home Secretary to introduce legislation to make corporal punishment illegal, he was merely referred to the discussion of the question during the passage of the Children Bill in 1932.[50] The abolitionist lobby was joined, finally, by a number of doctors, notably Dr Hamblin Smith, late medical officer of Birmingham prison, who viewed the use of whipping as antithetical to the investigation and constructive treatment of offenders, and particularly where offences of cruelty to children or to animals were involved. The use of the birch by Aldershot juvenile court in early 1937 provoked a critical letter to the press, above the signatures of some eminent doctors and psychologists, a protest subsequently endorsed by the *British Medical Journal*. In all, the retributive theory of punishment was discarded in favour of the 'scientific' approach to the treatment of delinquency: 'to discover what

[49] 25 Feb. 1935, PRO, HO45/17489/589571/57; *Howard Journal*, vol. 4 (1935), p. 126; *Annual Report of the Howard League, 1934–5*, p. 5. See also C. M. Craven, 'Flogging: Truth and Legend', *Penal Reformer*, vol. 1 (Jan. 1935), pp. 2–4.

[50] *Hansard*, vol. 310, 7 April 1936, cols. 2611–14; PRO, HO144/21050/685768/19 and 23. Sir John Simon, b. 1873, was Liberal MP for the West Riding of Yorkshire (Spen Valley) 1922–40, a Liberal National Member from 1931, and leader of the Liberal supporters of the National government in the 1930s. He was Solicitor- and Attorney-General before the First World War, Home Secretary from May 1915 to January 1916, and Secretary of State for Foreign Affairs 1931–35, before returning to the Home Office, June 1935–May 1937. Simon was a rather cold and austere person, but a considerable lawyer and a firm and intelligent Home Secretary, responsible for getting the Public Order Bill through parliament: *Times Obituaries, 1951–60*, p. 645; *Simon Papers* (Bodley), Boxes 1935–6.

social, familial and personal factors are responsible for his anti-social tendencies, and to institute treatment to correct them'.[51]

Official opinion in the 1930s struggled hard to remain neutral on this controversial issue. The aim of the department seems to have been rarely to intervene in any case where the court could convince the Home Secretary of the necessity of the sentence, but at the same time to discourage birching as a general practice, and its use in conjunction with a probation order.[52] Additionally, Alexander Maxwell, Deputy Under-Secretary of State, co-operated as far as possible with the Howard League when in May 1935 they asked to be supplied with information for their speakers about the age and previous history of offenders who had been ordered to be flogged by the courts.[53] No Home Office official, however, was expected to talk publicly on the question of corporal punishment.[54]

The most important Home Office action, coinciding with the arrival of Sir John Simon, came in response to the Howard League memorial of July 1935. A memorandum was drafted for the Cabinet on the possible appointment of a committee on corporal punishment. If the penalty was to remain in use for young offenders, the draft declared,

> some guidance ought to be given to the Justices as to the type of cases in which the infliction of such sentences is appropriate. At present the imposition of corporal punishment is quite fortuitous and depends on whether the boy happens to come before a Bench which believes in the efficacy of this method.

For this reason, the draft concluded, the Home Secretary was proposing to appoint a committee of persons 'who have taken no sides in this controversy', to investigate the subject, 'including sentences on adults, sentences on boys and disciplinary awards in prisons'. Above all, it was intended that the committee should sift all the available evidence 'with a view especially to discovering what are the effects, particularly the deterrent effects, of this form of punishment',[55]

It is unclear why it took until March 1937 for Simon to announce the appointment of the Departmental Committee on Corporal

[51] See M. Hamblin Smith, 'The Case Against Flogging', *Spectator*, 8 Sep. 1933, p. 304; idem, 'Corporal Punishment for Cruelty', *Howard Journal*, vol. 4 (1934), pp. 15–17; *British Medical Journal*, vol. 1 (March 1937), pp. 618–19.

[52] PRO, HO144/21050/685768/16–18; HO45/18760/532113/42.

[53] PRO, HO45/17489/589571/58.

[54] Ibid., 589571/70.

[55] PRO, HO144/22443/801326/4.

Punishment.[56] What is clearer is that the case of two nine-year-old boys birched by South Shields juvenile court in 1936 gave the final push to the campaign to secure an official inquiry. The South Shields Labour party and trades council seems to have broached this topic with the local MP, Mr Chuter Ede, who then furnished the Home Office with the details; the police officer who administered the whipping had stood too close to the boys, thus leaving weal marks on the stomach of one of them. Ede was informed by the department that a constabulary inspector had been to look into the incident, and that, in future, a leather shield was to be worn to protect the front of the body. This did not pacify local sentiment, however, and the whole incident sparked off a series of protest meetings and the like. 'It was on the known facts of this case', according to Councillor Gompertz of the South Shields Labour party, 'that the public outcry throughout the Country was aroused which led to the appointment of the present Committee.'[57]

None of the ten members of the committee had previously been connected with the movement for the abolition of corporal punishment. Five of the members were magistrates, one a doctor. The chairman was Sir Edward Cadogan, formerly Unionist MP for Finchley, who had experience of the problem of juvenile delinquency, both as a magistrate and as a member of the Borstal Association and the Juvenile Organisations Committee. There is little doubt that in 1937 he was open-minded about the value of corporal punishment, although Leo Page claimed that Cadogan, the magistrate, never ordered a sentence of birching.[58] Nor had he reached a firm conclusion as to the main reason or reasons for the development of delinquency. By the fifth meeting of the committee, in the middle of July, however, he was firmly convinced that the recent rise in the statistics represented a genuine increase in the incidence of juvenile crime, so much so that he suggested that the committee's terms of reference should be enlarged to embrace the whole problem of delinquency and the methods of punishment by which it might be reduced. This, the Home Secretary declined to do.[59]

[56] *Hansard*, vol. 321, 18 Mar. 1937, col. 2238.

[57] PRO, HO144/21050/685768/10 and 23; HO144/20711/695839/1–3.

[58] The Departmental Committee on Corporal Punishment, 1938, *Minutes of Evidence* (seen with Home Office permission), *oral evidence* of Leo Page, member of Juvenile Court Panel for Berkshire, p. 736.

[59] 15 July 1937, PRO, HO144/22444/801326/9.

The first witness to appear before the committee was Alexander Maxwell of the Home Office. A few days before this event, Maxwell had outlined the gist of his forthcoming evidence thus:

I propose to refrain from expressing any opinion for or against corporal punishment—my main object being to give the committee a general review of the subject and some guidance as to the lines of enquiry.

But I cannot help indicating that the Home Office knows of no reliable evidence as to the value of corporal punishment—except possibly as regards prison offences.[60]

Subsequent witnesses were a good deal more partisan. Their evidence, as the report itself illustrates, is best dealt with in four main groupings: justices and stipendiary magistrates sitting in juvenile courts; probation officers; the police; and doctors and medical psychologists.

From the mid-1930s, the controversy over corporal punishment had intensified, particularly as the accommodation at approved schools became scarcer and birching was proferred as a functional alternative. Most of the juvenile magistrates who came before the departmental committee, however, had resisted the temptation to make use of the birch, and now recommended its abolition. Miss Madeleine Symons, chairman of a metropolitan juvenile court, and Miss E. H. Kelly, chairman of Portsmouth juvenile court, both contended that whipping was incompatible with the principle, embodied in the 1933 Act, that the court should attend to the welfare of the child; and that only the least progressive courts persisted in using it. 'There is no case known to me', said Miss Kelly, 'where use is made of the provision for whipping by a Juvenile Court which is properly staffed and organised, and equipped with a team of probation officers and social workers.'[61] Leo Page, a member of the juvenile court panel for Berkshire, said much the same, advancing as one of the weightiest arguments against birching 'that the most experienced and wisest Juvenile Courts do not use it'. Conversely, he claimed, birching was generally used by the worst courts in an indiscriminate fashion.[62] Vivian Henderson, chairman of two metropolitan juvenile courts, told the committee that he had never had occasion to order a boy to be birched. He conceded

[60] 17 June 1937, PRO, HO144/22443/801326/4; *oral evidence* of Maxwell, pp. 59–144.

[61] *Evidence*, CP 24, statement of evidence to be given (Miss Kelly); CP 23 (Miss Symons).

[62] *Evidence*, CP 27 (Page); *oral evidence* (Page), pp. 685–7. See also Leo Page, *Crime and the Community* (1937), pp. 385–90.

that the boy who was cruel to animals or to smaller boys might benefit by a birching, but nevertheless concluded that 'if birching, as a penalty which can be inflicted by a Juvenile Court was abolished, it would neither limit the court's usefulness nor jeopardise its authority'.[63] And, lastly, Basil Henriques, chairman of the Toynbee Hall juvenile court, described birching as an unsuitable method of dealing with offences 'committed out of a misguided spirit of adventure'. As a loyal adherent of deterrent punishment, however, Henriques proposed the supplementation of the powers of the juvenile court on the following lines:

> What is needed is some new form of punishment which will be short, sharp and unpleasant, but will leave its spiritual mark on the mind of the offender rather than the physical mark . . . I want to see established a special place of detention to which boys could be sent for a period not exceeding one month . . .[64]

This was to be followed by a term of probationary supervision.

The witnesses who favoured the retention of the power to order birching, like the stipendiary magistrate of Huddersfield, and the late chairman of the Salford juvenile court, saw in corporal punishment a useful and effective penalty for certain types of offender, and, in view of the recent increase in juvenile crime, an important reserve power which ought not lightly to be discarded.[65] These witnesses, indeed, wanted the power to be extended to cases of young persons up to sixteen years of age. It was doubtless like-minded magistrates who, as the report pointed out, had brought the birch into play again in some of the northern towns in 1936: thirteen birchings in Manchester (two in 1935); seven birchings in Liverpool and South Shields (none in 1935).[66]

Probation officers were unanimously abolitionist, according to the witnesses who appeared before the committee on behalf of the National Association of Probation Officers. The slant of the evidence from people like H. E. Norman, secretary of NAPO, was opposition to the amendment of behaviour by the use of fear, and backing for the rehabilitation of offenders by appealing to the better qualities to be found in every adolescent. So many of the offences committed by

[63] *Evidence*, CP 20 (Henderson); *oral evidence*, pp. 336–7.
[64] *Evidence*, CP 15 (Henriques); *oral evidence*, pp. 377–400.
[65] See *Evidence*, CP 17 (Mr W. Briggs); CP 26 (Mr P. Macbeth).
[66] *Report of the Departmental Committee on Corporal Punishment*, PP 1937–8, IX (Cmd. 5684), pp. 492–3.

youngsters were unpremeditated, it was claimed, and hence unlikely to be influenced by deterrent penalties. When courts used the birch, no time was given for an investigation of the offender's previous history and home background on which the sentencing decision ought to be based. The infliction of corporal punishment, the probation officers argued, finally, tended to encourage only greater cunning to hide the offence, when what was needed was 'a more social desire towards good citizenship'.[67]

As unanimously in favour of retaining corporal punishment were the police witnesses. Those who appeared on behalf of the Association of Chief Constables of Cities and Boroughs conceded that birching was unpopular with chairmen of benches, and that many of their colleagues disliked the degrading features of administering corporal punishment. None the less, a substantial majority of chief constables were said to approve of the birching of young offenders, even though some thought it should be restricted to those persisting in crime or committing particular types of offence—for 'public opinion is not so much against corporal punishment *per se*', the committee was told, 'as against its application in unsuitable cases'.[68] Yet the police were not die-hard exponents of corporal punishment. They were perturbed by the increase in juvenile crime, which they ascribed to the leniency of the juvenile courts, and by the shortage of accommodation in remand homes and approved schools. These facts inevitably reinforced the potency of corporal punishment in the eyes of the police, in that it was the only punitive, non-custodial sentence which the courts possessed. It seemed likely, however, that if another punitive sentence were available, to bridge the gap between probation and committal to an approved school, the police would not stand in the way of the abolition of corporal punishment. The departmental committee took heart from this discovery.[69]

Finally, the doctors, psychologists and psychoanalysts advised the committee that whilst from the physical point of view, there was little if any danger in inflicting corporal punishment on young boys, from the psychological and temperamental point of view, there were many boys who were unfit for this form of punishment. This fact, moreover,

[67] See *Evidence*, CP 38 (NAPO); *Report*, op. cit., p. 494.

[68] *Evidence*, CP 14 (Chief Constables of Cities and Boroughs); *oral evidence*, pp. 266–323. The Association derived their information from the replies of sixty-nine chief constables to a questionnaire.

[69] *Report*, op. cit., p. 496.

could not always be elicited by a brief medical examination. The psychologists argued their case thus: 'There are a few motives', said Burt, 'and a few offences and perhaps even a few types of personality for which corporal punishment may perhaps be specially appropriate', but the selection of such cases required lengthy observation and investigation. In contrast, the effectiveness of corporal punishment was in direct proportion to the swiftness of its infliction. Moreover, whipping dealt only with surface symptoms, not underlying causes; yet the latter, Burt reaffirmed, 'are always manifold and subtle, and call, in each specific case, for manifold and subtle methods of investigation and treatment'.[70] When it came to the psychoanalysts, their evidence was rather more abstruse, concentrating on 'the impulses underlying the desire to inflict corporal punishment'. Dr Edward Glover, director of the London Clinic of Psychoanalysis, informed the Committee so: 'Corporal Punishment is a superstitious and archaic form of moral urge belonging to the torture group . . . It is, in most cases, motivated by sexual and hate urges . . . Its psychological effect is bad.'[71] It was an objection which would, of course, apply to other forms of punishment, and the committee were obliged, therefore, to side-step the issue by arguing that psychoanalysis was in too immature a state for its theories to serve as basis 'for a drastic and far-reaching reconstruction of the whole of our penal code'.[72]

A handful of other interested parties, whose evidence merits attention, fell outside the four main groupings described above. In support of abolition were the Child Guidance Council, the Society of Friends, the Women's Co-operative Guild, and the Howard League.[73] The latter, represented by Miss W. A. Elkin and George Benson, insisted that flogging was no more of a deterrent than other penalties and that its abolition would lead to no increase in delinquency. And public opinion, the League claimed, was on their side:

> Unquestionably the use of the lash is repellant to very large numbers of people in this country. We feel that the retention of a punishment which conflicts so fundamentally with widespread and deep-seated moral feelings could only be justified by grave necessity. . . .[74]

[70] *Evidence*, CP 93 (Burt).
[71] *Evidence*, CP 45 (Glover).
[72] *Report*, op. cit., p. 499.
[73] Ibid., pp. 499–500.
[74] *Evidence*, CP 86 (Howard League).

Of course, the Howard League's indictment was framed with special reference to the flogging of adults, as was the evidence of Sir Edward Atkinson, the Director of Public Prosecutions, and of the high court judges. Whilst the DPP reasserted the far-reaching deterrent effect of flogging, the judges recommended retaining all the existing powers of corporal punishment of persons convicted on indictment. The latter also suggested that, if it were considered desirable to extend the list of offences so punishable, the main contenders should be carnal knowledge of a girl under the age of thirteen and possibly the crime of rape.[75]

The weight of evidence was clearly in support of abolition, and the report of the departmental committee reflected this fact. The arguments which had most impressed the committee were arrayed in the report: corporal punishment as a sentence of the court and as administered by a parent or a schoolmaster had different effects on a child and thus could not be compared; as a sentence, whipping rarely attracted parental approval, too often made the boy a hero in the eyes of his companions, and was used largely as a substitute for probation. Additionally, the committee were swayed by the lack of reliable statistical evidence for the deterrent valuè of birching, and by the rejection of the birch on the part of the most experienced juvenile courts.[76] Hence, the report concluded that 'the balance of advantage lies on the side of abolishing the existing powers of summary courts to use corporal punishment as a method of dealing with young offenders'.[77] Instead, for serious offences, more constructive modes of treatment were needed; for minor offences, 'some form of short and sharp punishment which will pull him up and give him the lesson which he needs' was prescribed.[78] The report's main recommendation, accordingly, was the repeal of all the existing powers of summary and superior courts to order young offenders to be birched, with the rider that further consideration be given to the provision of a short, sharp punishment, possibly involving punitive detention and the deprivation of leisure.[79]

[75] *Evidence*, CP 90 (Atkinson); CP 80 (Lord Chief Justice Hewart, on behalf of HM Judges). See also PRO, HO144/22445/801326/16; Templewood Papers, Box X: 8(9), note from Hoare to Maxwell, 18.6.1938, on views of judges.

[76] *Report*, op. cit., pp. 501–7; *Howard Journal*, vol. 5 (1938), pp. 198–201.

[77] Ibid., p. 500.

[78] Ibid., pp. 511–15.

[79] Ibid., p. 590.

'It is too much to expect', the *Daily Telegraph* declared, 'that even the unanimous and clear-cut verdict of the Committee will avail to allay controversy, so acute is the divergence of opinion on the question, but the sternest critics of the verdict no less than its supporters will acknowledge the cogency of the reasoning and the lucidity of thought which the Committee have applied to their task'.[80] Most of the daily press, metropolitan and provincial, were equally well-disposed towards the report of the Cadogan committee; no newspaper dissented from the proposal to abolish the birching of juvenile offenders, some even criticized the retention of flogging for disciplinary offences in prisons, only a handful objected to the abolition of flogging in the case of adults convicted of robbery with violence.[81] Such a favourable reception was the more surprising given the coincidence of the report's publication with the Lord Chief Justice's sentence of corporal punishment on two young men found guilty of a violent robbery in a West End hotel.[82] As to whether the press accurately reflected public opinion in its assessment of the report on corporal punishment, it is difficult to say, but it is possible that it did exaggerate the magnitude of abolitionist support. When the *Daily Mail* polled its readers as to their views on corporal punishment, just prior to the report's publication, nearly 10,000 were against, less than 5,000 were for its abolition.[83]

In the 'legal' and periodical press, opinions differed. A hard-hitting contribution appeared in the *Law Times*, condemning the report of 'this somewhat amateur committee' for being 'neither a practical nor a useful contribution', and for neglecting the views of the King's Bench judges.[84] Sir Robert Armstrong-Jones, MD, was similarly critical of a recommendation which flew in the face of police and judicial opinion, not to mention the increase in the incidence of juvenile crime.[85] In contrast, the *Howard Journal* and the *Penal Reformer* congratulated the committee for upholding the reformers' case, although they regretted that prison offences had been excluded from the recommendation.[86] The Howard League set to work immediately to compel legislative

[80] See PRO, CAB 24/277(38), Appendix, 'Summary of Press Comments', p. 173.
[81] Ibid., pp. 172–8.
[82] PRO, HO45/17667/805270/51A.
[83] *Daily Mail*, 11 Mar. 1938.
[84] *Law Times*, vol. 185 (May 1938), p. 375.
[85] Armstrong-Jones, 'Corporal Punishment', *Nineteenth Century and After*, vol. 124 (Aug. 1938), pp. 212–20.
[86] C. M. Craven, 'Flogging: The Last Chapter but One', *Howard Journal*, vol. V (Autumn 1938), pp. 104–7; George Benson, *Penal Reformer*, vol. 4 (April 1938).

action on the recommendations, getting League members to lobby their MPs, and seeking the unofficial advice of Alexander Maxwell on how best to lobby the Home Secretary. Maxwell's counsel, with which he favoured Benson, was that any attempt to force the Home Secretary's hand through the activities of the Parliamentary Penal Reform Group, might only harden opinion in the Commons against legislation on the lines of the report. The League made do, therefore, with a letter to Sir Samuel Hoare asking for a clause on corporal punishment to be included in the proposed Penal Reform Bill.[87]

On the assumption that some members of the Cadogan committee would report in favour of retaining corporal punishment, Maxwell had advised the department to omit the subject from the penal reform bill. In December 1937, however, the Home Office got wind of the committee's unanimous recommendations; the knowledge that even members who had initially been proponents of corporal punishment had been swayed by the evidence, altered the whole position. Maxwell now advised Home Secretary Hoare that a unanimous report, emanating from such a neutral body, enhanced the probability that the government would be able to carry the proposals in both houses of Parliament. It seemed wisest, Maxwell added, to incorporate the Cadogan proposals into the wider measure of penal reform (which was to be mainly concerned with adolescent offenders aged seventeen to twenty-one) rather than leaving them for a bill confined to the question of corporal punishment:

> There is a much better chance of carrying reform on this subject if it forms part of a big scheme of penal reform.
>
> Moreover, from the point of view of those who really feel strongly about penal reform, the absence of any provisions on the subject is a defect in your Bill, and the insertion of such provisions will strengthen their enthusiasm in the Bill's favour.[88]

Hoare's opinion was also guided by what he took to be the views of experienced social workers, magistrates and penal administrators, as refracted through the deliberations of an impartial committee of enquiry. He later wrote of his view on the subject of corporal punishment in early 1938 as follows:

> I could not regard corporal punishment as morally wrong, but neither could I

[87] Howard League Minute Book, MSS 16B/1/3, 4 Apr. and 2 May 1938.
[88] 11 Dec. 1937, PRO, HO45/17666/805270/8A.

find any evidence to show that it was an effective deterrent as a judicial punishment. I treated the question as I treated the other questions dealt with in the Bill, and as the available evidence was all against this particular kind of punishment, I came down in favour of abolishing it.[89]

At this juncture, finally, Hoare considered that it would be better to ask the Cabinet to approve the inclusion of a clause dealing with corporal punishment after they had seen the departmental committee's report. This was not generally available until March 1938.[90]

By mid-June, the Home Secretary was ready to ask the Cabinet to implement the recommendations of the report on corporal punishment. In a detailed memorandum, submitted jointly by the Home Secretary and the Secretary of State for Scotland, the Cabinet were first informed that the committee had brought to its task no a priori objection to the use of corporal punishment. In fact, as the memorandum explained,

it is understood that at the outset of the inquiry the prevalent view of the Committee tended in the other direction, but, as the inquiry proceeded and the Committee had before them the facts and figures and the evidence of persons with practical experience of methods of dealing with offenders,

the unanimous conclusions which they reached had emerged. But this style of enquiry further validated the judgements of the committee:

The impartial spirit in which the Committee approached the problem, their empirical method of examining it and their insistent attention to the practical question whether the power to impose corporal punishment is desirable for the protection of the public, give great weight to their findings, and their Report must be regarded as an authoritative pronouncement.

The memorandum also underlined the favourable press response to the committee's proposals; and claimed that, despite the opposition of the high court judges, 'the great body of enlightened public opinion endorses the recommendations'. It was reckoned, lastly, 'that a substantial majority in the House of Commons would be in favour of legislation to implement those recommendations'.[91] The Cabinet was

89 Viscount Templewood, *Nine Troubled Years* (1954), pp. 233–4. See also Templewood Papers, Box X: 8(16), notes on interview with Lord Roche.

90 PRO, HO45/17666/805270/8A; HO144/22445/801326/21.

91 Cabinet memo., 16 June 1938, pp. 1–8 in PRO, HO45/17667/805270/51A; CAB 24/277 (38).

asked, therefore, to agree to the inclusion of the necessary provisions in the Criminal Justice Bill.

To judge from the Cabinet papers, there were ministers who doubted the strength of public and parliamentary opinion in favour of abolition. It was recalled that only two years before, the government's supporters had rejected a private bill on the subject. More ominously, Earl Stanhope believed that the second chamber would likely be as hostile as they had been in 1932. Yet, despite these reservations, the Cabinet went along with the Home Secretary, instructing him only 'to hold the position without making any announcement in parliament until the Criminal Justice Bill was ready'[92]

Meanwhile, the Home Office were considering the suggestion made by the Cadogan committee for an alternative penalty to corporal punishment. A number of schemes to bridge the gap between probation and approved schools had been floated in the past few years. The probation officers of the London juvenile courts, for example, had suggested to the Departmental Committee on Social Services in Courts of Summary Jurisdiction, 'some kind of Training Centre where probationers could be sent for short periods for physical training and discipline'.[93] But the department's mind was only fully concentrated by the evidence presented to Cadogan. The first step the department took was to convene a meeting, in April 1938, of selected juvenile court magistrates and justices' clerks, the collective view of which was that an alternative penalty to whipping was needed.[94] By June, the Home Office had decided to make provision in the Criminal Justice Bill for what were to be known as compulsory attendance centres, and to authorize local authorities to provide such centres for offenders between fourteen and seventeen years of age.[95]

This scheme was then submitted to the Board of Education for their consideration. They had no objection to the proposal, but urged further scrutiny of the kind of 'disciplinary instruction and training' which should be provided for young persons.[96] The last point raised its head a few months later when it became clear that a number of education authorities were apprehensive lest the centres should be asked to give

[92] PRO, CAB 25/29 (38), 22 June 1938, Conclusion 8. Stanhope was President of the Board of Education, and, from Oct. 1938, Leader of the House of Lords.

[93] Departmental Committee on Social Services in Courts of Summary Jurisdiction, *Minutes of Evidence* (seen with Home Office permission), no. 26.

[94] PRO, HO144/22447/801326/31–2.

[95] PRO, HO45/17667/805270/52.

[96] Ibid.

education in school subjects under duress, using forcible education as a form of punishment. Additionally, there were objections that this proposed alternative to whipping was unavailable for boys under fourteen.[97] Following a discussion of these difficulties between Harris, Henderson, and Norris, it was proposed, therefore, that the purpose of the centres should be the deprivation of leisure on Saturday afternoons with physical exercise or other occupation to keep the young offender busy, and that the age limits should be from twelve to seventeen. All reference to 'instruction', suggestive of school lessons, was to be omitted.[98] Such was the scheme presented by Maxwell to the Local Authorities Advisory Committee a few days later. There was general agreement amongst the local authorities to a penalty, the core of which was the deprivation of leisure, although the representatives of the Association of Education Committees and of the LCC objected strongly to the use of a school building or any part of the school curriculum or school teachers for this purpose, in order to keep faith with the general trend of educational development of the past twenty years.[99] Thereafter, no further objections were raised against the proposal, if only because the Home Office declared that they intended to proceed experimentally, trusting to the natural development of a method of occupation and training for compulsory attendance centres.[100]

The second reading debate of the Criminal Justice Bill took place on 29 November and 1 December, 1938. A wide measure of support greeted the bill, including clause 32 which abolished judicial flogging. Mr Pethick-Lawrence, for one, applauded the abolition of corporal punishment and hoped that it would soon be quashed for prison offences.[101] One of the few dissentients was Quintin Hogg, who, in his

[97] Ibid., 805270/59.

[98] 6 Oct. 1938, Ibid.

[99] Ibid., 805270/65. See also John David, 'Education and the Criminal Justice Bill', *Journal of Education*, vol. 71 (Feb. 1939), p. 87.

[100] Ibid., 805270/52. The court could order the offender to attend the Centre for a number of hours not exceeding sixty in all; no offender could be required to attend for more than three hours on any day, whilst the total number of hours which an offender was required to attend had to be completed within six months. The scheme of Compulsory Attendance Centres is examined more fully in ch. 9 below.

[101] *Hansard*, vol. 342, 29 Nov. 1938, col. 295. Frederick Pethick-Lawrence, b. 1871, was Labour MP for Leicester, West 1923–31 and Edinburgh, East 1935–45. In the late 1920s he was the Howard League's main contact in the House of Commons. He had been Financial Secretary to the Treasury, June 1929 to August 1931. Early in the century he had been a major figure in the campaign for women's suffrage: *The Times Obituaries, 1961–70*, pp. 628–9.

maiden speech, declared that the evidence of the King's Bench judges, notably in relation to adult offenders charged with robbery with violence, had been discarded too quickly.[102] Storm clouds gathered in the first two months of 1939 as the pundits prepared for the Committee stage of the bill. Again the *Law Journal* reminded its readers of the judicial opposition to complete abolition, much being made of a recent resolution of the Middlesex justices which stated that no good reason had been submitted for the abolition of corporal punishment.[103] The Council of the Magistrates Association had already discussed the issue, and by a two-thirds majority had decided to approve the inclusion of clause 32; but the fact that the decision was not unanimous was used by Sir Robert Armstrong-Jones to suggest that it could not be taken 'as the considered or deliberate and matured opinion of the Magistrates Association'.[104] In contrast, the Home Secretary's stand on corporal punishment was encouraged by the penal reform societies, and by correspondents to the national press and to Hoare personally.[105] Yet, ominously, at a meeting of the 1922 Conservative Private Members Committee, strong opposition was voiced to the complete abrogation of corporal punishment as a sentence, and amendments to clause 32 were being considered in readiness for standing committee.[106] This was how Hoare himself described the situation:

> By the time that the Bill had reached the Committee Stage, a raging agitation against abolition had been started by my old diehard opponents of Indian days, and by large sections of the Press. The front-line troops of the Party passed many resolutions in favour of flogging in the meetings of the National Union of Conservative Associations.[107]

The question of corporal punishment was discussed at four well-attended sessions of standing committee in March 1939, where a succession of amendments which sought to retain the 'cat' for various offences were fought off by the government, with the assistance of George Benson and Godfrey Nicholson. Clause 32 was finally carried by 32 votes to 17, although those in favour of the clause consisted

[102] Ibid., cols. 301–2. Hogg was MP for Oxford.

[103] *Law Journal*, vol. 87 (Jan. 1939), pp. 2 and 22.

[104] *Magistrate*, vol. 5 (Jan.–Feb. 1939), p. 146.

[105] Clara Rackham, *Penal Reformer*, vol. 5 (Jan. 1939), p. 10; Howard League Minute Book, MSS 16B/1/3; *Howard Journal*, vol. 5 (1939), pp. 192–4; *The Times*, 16 Jan. 1939, p. 13 (letters); Templewood Papers, Box X: 9 (5–13).

[106] *The Times*, 28 Feb. 1939, p. 14.

[107] Viscount Templewood, op. cit., p. 234.

largely of members of the opposition parties; only three government supporters, excluding the ministerial representatives, voted to retain the clause.[108] Yet if the first skirmish ended in success for the abolitionists, the war was far from over. Shortly afterwards, according to the Home Secretary's memorandum to the Cabinet, the chief whip supplied him, in confidence, with 'a list of some 203 members of the Conservative party who, during the Report stage, intend to support an amendment to delete the clause', and Hoare went on, 'I understand that there is a considerable number of other members who desire to retain corporal punishment'. Hoare now asked the Cabinet how he should respond to this backbench revolt. His own view was that the matter should not be left to a free vote in the Commons, since the House of Lords would, in consequence, be more likely to reject the clause, particularly if the vote was close and relied heavily on opposition members. Nor could Hoare see any merit in keeping corporal punishment for specified offences; the lack of evidence regarding the deterrent efficacy of the penalty applied to all offences. The Home Secretary's recommendation, therefore, was 'that the abolition of corporal punishment should in the first instance be for an experimental period of, say five years'.[109]

Evidently, the Home Secretary's view did not prevail, since in June it was announced that the government would allow a free vote on the clause dealing with flogging at the Report stage. The government supporters who had tabled a clause for extending corporal punishment to other offences than those to which it then applied, agreed not to proceed further. 'Ministers expect', declared *The Times*, 'that the Government will carry the clause by a comfortable majority.'[110] Be that as it may, the abolitionists saw only a depressing climb-down by the government—'much more like a concession to uninformed prejudice', the *Manchester Guardian* claimed, 'than any appeal to free and enlightened judgement'.[111] For the *Penal Reformer*, a free vote left the fate of an important clause to the likes of the Women Conservatives who had recently shouted Lady Astor down when she tried to speak on behalf of the abolition of corporal punishment.[112]

[108] 'Proceedings of Standing Committee A', PP 1938–9, VII (103), pp. 440–1 (21 Mar. 1939).

[109] Memo., 27 April 1939, PRO, CAB 24/285(39). See also J. A. Cross, *Sir Samuel Hoare. A Political Biography* (1977), p. 282.

[110] *The Times*, 14 June 1939; *Daily Telegraph*, 14 June 1939.

[111] *Manchester Guardian*, 14 June 1939.

[112] *Penal Reformer*, vol. 6 (July 1938), p. 8.

The Report stage in the Commons was never, in fact, taken, the bill being shelved on the outbreak of war. A number of attempts, press and parliamentary, were made to get the government either to explore the possibility of effecting an agreement on the flogging clause or to drop the clause entirely, and then to find time to carry the measure through its remaining stages.[113] They were all to no avail. The question of corporal punishment clearly divided the Conservative party in the Commons, and it might well have divided, as in 1932, the two houses of Parliament. It seems accurate to suggest, however, that the controversy in 1938–9 centred less on the juvenile than on the adult offender. It was the latter whom the High Court judges had in mind when they endeavoured to retain, not to say enlarge, the powers of corporal punishment. It is likely, too, that the distinction between the young delinquent and his adult counterpart would have been the basis of a compromise proposal. As Harris told Arthur Pearson, the Minister of Education, in 1941:

> It was, of course, recognised that there was a considerable difference of opinion about adult corporal punishment and it may be that the Government would have felt obliged to make some concessions in this direction though this is only a guess on my part. But there is no reason I think to believe that the part of the proposal which related to juveniles would not have been retained, as a very clear distinction can be drawn.[114]

[113] *Hansard*, vol. 348, 22 June 1939, col. 2437; vol. 353, 9 Nov. 1939, col. 408; *The Times*, 17 Oct. 1939, p. 9.

[114] 17 June 1941, PRO, HO45/18815/800967/93.

6

Family Life and Delinquency

In conjunction with the child welfare lobby, the Home Office had managed to hold back the pressures for a change of course in juvenile justice. The view that a decline in parental discipline was at the back of an actual increase in delinquency and that a State alternative in the form of judicial whipping was needed, had failed to win the day. One concession was extracted from the Home Office, however, in the shape of the compulsory attendance centre, a punitive, institutional alternative to the birch. For the department, this was an acceptable trade-off, since the notion of a short-term disciplinary sentence, bridging the gap between probation and the approved school, struck the right chord amongst 'reformers' as much as 'reactionaries'.[1]

Otherwise, the 1930s witnessed a consolidation of the principles and practices of the Children and Young Persons Act. The lesson of the view of delinquency which stressed defective family life was taken to be, not tougher penalties, but the provision of a normal home life; the solution to the problem of juvenile crime was sought in the arrangement of a suitable home environment for each offender. In most cases, it was believed, this could be found in the child's natural home, where he could be left under the supervision of a probation officer. Where the youngster was living in undesirable surroundings, he might be sent, by way of a residence condition in a probation order, to a foster home, to approved lodgings, or to an approved hostel or home. Foster-parents and lodgings could also be secured by committing the child to the care of the local authority. If none of these methods

[1] It is equally significant that for all the talk of the need to use severer penalties, there was only a slight increase in the number of committals to remand homes for a sentence of detention, for a period not exceeding one month. See *Fifth Report*, op. cit., p. 16; *Detention in Remand Homes*, English Studies in Criminal Science, vol. VII (1952), pp. 1–3 and 79. Nor was there any opposition to the clause in the Criminal Justice Bill, 1938, which raised from fourteen to sixteen the age below which a Court might not in any circumstances impose imprisonment. For the infrequent use of imprisonment for offenders under seventeen, see *Annual Report of Prison Commissioners for 1936*, PP 1937, XIV (Cmd. 5675), p. 715.

was thought appropriate, there was the power, finally, to send young offenders to an approved school, either for the full term of three years, or for an abbreviated period to one of the short-term schools with which the Home Office were experimenting. The degree to which this emphasis on home surroundings describes Home Office policy in the 1930s was nowhere better illustrated than in Sir Samuel Hoare's broadcast talk on young offenders in the 'Empire Programme' in February 1938. 'Whenever it can safely be done', the Home Secretary explained,

> we try to arrange that children shall grow up in ordinary conditions of family life where they will find sympathy and affection. If they cannot get this in their own home, another home, a real home I mean, not an institution, is found wherever possible... If none of these methods offers a prospect of success where, for example, the child's character is too weak or too set, the boy or girl is usually sent to a Home Office School.[2]

This policy was described in a Children's Branch report as 'a graduated scheme of separation from home to be applied according as the circumstances require a shorter or longer separation'.[3]

Observation Homes

As in the 1920s, so in the 1930s, the success of this policy was thought to depend upon providing the courts with information about the personal and social circumstances of each offender. In 1935, C. P. Hill, an assistant principal in the Home Office, was given the job of encouraging local authorities both to provide and improve remand home accommodation, and of urging magistrates to use them. At this date, remand for enquiries varied from 1 to 25 per cent of those brought before the juvenile courts; many areas with the highest juvenile crime rates, like Lancashire, barely used the power to remand. In addition, the Home Office pressed the better remand homes in London, Liverpool, Bristol, Birmingham, and Leeds to provide a medical examination for cases sent by adjoining local authorities, and so develop along the lines of observation centres or central remand homes. Indeed, the latter remained the emblem of those who insisted upon pre-sentence enquiry for juvenile offenders.

[2] PRO, HO45/18118/697558/68. See also Templewood Papers, Box X: 8 (3).

[3] *Fifth Report*, op. cit., p. 31.

The champions of state observation homes put the disappointment of the 1933 legislation behind them, and strove to keep the issue before the public and the Home Department. One way of doing this was to examine critically the conditions of existing remand homes. Assessing the position in London, two years after the implementation of the 1933 Act, the *Howard Journal* found the LCC's remand home 'in an old elementary school, dingy and overcrowded, badly staffed, with no possibility of sound educational work, reasonable occupation or recreation . . . and no privacy for interviews by Probation Officers or doctors'. A new remand home was nearing completion, but still the *Journal* argued that, before long, observation centres would have to be provided: 'Till we get them the Juvenile Court will continue to do its job by guess work and to guess wrong in many cases.'[4] In fact, the assistant education officer of the LCC, Mr W. J. O. Newton, accepted the need for observation homes, at least for the 5 per cent of 'problem cases' which, in his view, required continuous observation, and which at that time were generally being sent to child guidance clinics.[5] These clinics were handicapped in relation to court cases by the lack of time for the study of the child, but they were shedding important light on the relationship between the delinquent and his environment, and forging a stronger case for observation homes.[6] In short, the provision of observation homes remained a principal aim of educationalists, medical psychologists, and practitioners and pressure groups concerned with juvenile delinquency.

Sometime around July 1938, the Goldsmiths' Company offered £6,000 towards the establishment of an observation home in London.[7] To examine the implications of this offer, the Home Secretary appointed a small committee, two members of which were John Watson, chairman of the Southwark juvenile court, and Geraldine Cadbury. The committee reported in favour of establishing an observation centre for about thirty boys and girls of under fourteen, in

[4] PRO, HO45/17050/657903; *Howard Journal*, vol. 4 (1935), pp. 122–3. See also 'Causes of Crime: a discussion between Sir Vivian Henderson and Dr Cyril Burt', *Listener*, 2 May 1934, p. 750; Mrs L. Le Mesurier, *A Handbook of Probation* (NAPO, 1935), p. 232.

[5] *Magistrate*, vol. 4 (Nov. 1935), p. 952. See also H. E. Field, 'Psychological Aspects of Juvenile Delinquency', *The Year Book of Education 1936*, pp. 868–9.

[6] See Le Mesurier, *Handbook*, pp. 111 and 208–9; Dr R. N. Craig, 'Report on the Work of the Exeter Child Guidance Clinic', in L. Radzinowicz and J. W. C. Turner (eds.), *Mental Abnormality and Crime* (1944), pp. 300–04.

[7] *Fifth Report*, op. cit., p. 19.

or near London, to be under the control of a voluntary body which would include representatives of the London magistrates and the education authorities. Mrs Cadbury, indeed, added £2,000 to the sum from the Goldsmiths' Company.[8] Another £8,000–£10,000 was required, but in October 1938 Henderson minuted that he had applied to the Carnegie Fund, the City Parochial Foundation, and the Pilgrims Trust, and that between them 'we are likely to get enough to make a start'.[9]

By this date, the Home Office were also considering the inclusion in the Criminal Justice Bill of a clause empowering the Home Secretary to provide 'observation centres' for persons between fourteen and twenty three years of age. Discussions within the department revealed Dr Norris's view that juvenile court magistrates and education authorities, not to say parents, would dislike the notion of sending difficult youngsters between fourteen and seventeen years to a state observation centre to associate with men and women aged up to twenty-three. In addition, Henderson perceived that,

> as the local authorities are taking an increasing interest in delinquent children and young persons, it is important to maintain their direct association with observation centres for children and young persons and this interest is likely to be diminished if the observation is carried out in a state school with whose administration the local authorities have no concern.[10]

Hence, the department asked the Local Authorities Advisory Committee, a few days later, to assess the merit of instituting observation centres for boys and girls under seventeen. The Home Office's objective seemed to be to secure local authority agreement to the creation of five centres in the larger cities—possibly Bristol, Birmingham, Liverpool, and Leeds, as well as London. Fortunately, the local authority representatives agreed that specialized observation centres were needed and that it would be best if the Home Office were to establish them.[11] Clause 11 of the Criminal Justice Bill thus empowered the Home Secretary to provide 'state remand homes', as they were now to be called, where the 'problem cases' amongst children and young persons under seventeen could be kept under observation for an adequate period of time. They were to be

8 Whitney, op. cit., p. 154.
9 4 Oct. 1938, PRO, HO45/17667/805270/59.
10 Ibid.
11 Henderson, 6 Oct. 1938, Ibid., 805270/59 and 65.

additional, of course, to the remand homes currently provided by the local authorities; the local authority from whose area a person was sent to a state remand home was to contribute to the cost of detention.[12] At long last, it seemed, the courts were to have the benefit of expert guidance in dealing with the most difficult delinquents, for which many had been calling since the early 1920s and which had been recommended by a departmental committee of enquiry as far back as 1927. Alas! both the experimental scheme for a London observation centre and the bill of 1938 fell foul of the Second World War. The accolade of establishing the first observation home went, characteristically, to Birmingham, which, through the generosity of the Cadburys, opened Fircroft in the village of Bournville in 1941.[13]

Approved Schools

The desire to restrict the application of institutional treatment to the absolute minimum, plus the belief that some offenders required the disciplinary detention of a Home Office school without needing an extended craft training or a long absence from home influence, underlay the experiment, tried by a few local authorities, of a 'short-time' school, followed usually by residence in a hostel. The scheme also had the advantage, presumably, of relieving the dearth of accommodation in the long-term schools.[14] Towards the end of 1934, the Cadburys donated a hostel for use in connection with the Shawbury approved school. Mrs Cadbury had been a staunch proponent of short-term schools for some years, and she now hoped that Birmingham Education Committee would approve a scheme under which Shawbury would become a short-term school for boys of fourteen and fifteen years of age. The boys would be released after some six to nine months' detention, living for not more than six further months in the hostel, from which they would go out to work. This was indeed sanctioned by the education committee, and the Home Office reclassified Shawbury as a short-term school.[15] A number of similar schemes were launched in the next few years, one by the LCC (at

[12] 'Criminal Justice Bill', PP 1938–9, II (4), p. 322; Templewood Papers, Box X: 9, 'Enquiry into the Mental Condition of Persons charged with Offences'.

[13] Whitney, op. cit., pp. 154–5.

[14] See *Magistrate*, vol. 4 (Nov. 1935), p. 956.

[15] *Magistrate*, vol. 3 (Nov. 1934), p. 847; vol. 4 (1934), p. 81; vol. 4 (Dec. 1936–Jan. 1937), pp. 1106–7.

Cumberlow Lodge), another by the Surrey County Council (at Banstead Hall). Magistrates were instructed to exercise great care in selecting young persons for these schools, and to impress upon the youngsters that failure to seize this chance would result in committal to a long-term school. Some unsuitable cases were sent by the courts, but the main problem was to get the courts to use the schemes at all; Shawbury school soon faced the plight of having a considerable number of vacancies.[16]

Boarding Out

The committal of children to the care of a local authority, which was then expected to board them out with foster parents (if necessary, until the age of eighteen), was used more frequently after the implementation of the 1933 Act: the number of such orders increased from 354 in 1934 to 822 in 1936.[17] The boarding out system was considered to be particularly useful for children under ten years of age, and for older children of school age where delinquency was not too developed, who needed a change of home conditions, for an indefinite period, without requiring approved school training.[18] In the later 1930s, the Home Office felt that this system was worthy of extension to working boys and girls over school age, and in 1937 they encouraged local authorities to find more foster homes to this end.[19] For most of the decade, then, boarding out supplied the need of foster homes for young children whose natural home was considered to be unsuitable but who did not stand in need of long-term residential training.

Probation

Of the 20,540 juvenile offenders under seventeen found guilty of indictable offences in 1934, 54 per cent were bound over with

[16] Ibid., vol. 4 (Apr.–May 1937), pp. 1141–2; *Fifth Report*, op. cit., p. 50.

[17] H. Mannheim, *The Dilemma of Penal Reform* (1939), p. 222.

[18] *Magistrate*, vol. 4 (Nov. 1935), pp. 957 and 975; vol. 4 (June–July 1937), p. 1160.

[19] Circular, 16 Dec. 1937, *Magistrate*, vol. 5 (Jan.–Feb. 1938), pp. 18–20; *Fifth Report*, op. cit., pp. 116–18. The pressure on approved school accommodation forced the Home Office to encourage local authorities to use boarding out more widely.

supervision.[20] The fact that over a half of all cases were dealt with by actual probation was proof, for those who traced the increase in juvenile crime to an excessive leniency on the part of the courts, that probation was being run too hard. Mr J. Wellesley Orr, stipendiary magistrate of Manchester, took the view that probation was being strained by ordering it for young offenders on four or five separate occasions.[21] There was criticism, too, of the unwritten rule that institutional treatment should never be given until the young offender had first been tried on probation.[22] Partly as a response to these criticisms, the exponents of probation began to stress the need emphatically to enforce probation orders; breaches of the conditions of an order should be punished, it was urged, either by tightening the conditions of the order, or by fining, or by conviction and sentence for the original offence. Courts were also encouraged to make more use of the requirement that the probationer should make restitution to the victim.[23]

For their part, the advocates of probation accepted that some courts were using probation too freely, especially for second and third offences; but they also believed that some courts were neglecting to make use of probation. First offenders were often simply dismissed or bound over without supervision, when probation might have been more beneficial; corporal punishment or the approved schools were often used in preference to probation. The upshot was a wide divergence of sentencing practice between courts. In some districts, the share of indictable cases placed under supervision was as low as five per cent, suggesting that some courts either were unaware of the advantages of probation or were reluctant to appoint a proper

[20] In addition, 8% were bound over without supervision, and 21% were dismissed after the offence had been proved. See *Criminal Statistics for 1934*, PP 1935–6, XXV (Cmd. 5185), p. 473; *Report of the Departmental Committee on the Social Services of Courts of Summary Jurisdiction*, PP 1935–6, VIII (Cmd. 5122), p. 463 (App.IV); See also Table 4.

[21] *Manchester Guardian*, 4 Oct. 1935; Henderson, 9 Oct. 1935, PRO, HO144/22634/677145/8.

[22] See Le Mesurier, *Handbook*, p. 167.

[23] See Rackham, *Magistrate*, vol. 2 (April–May 1932), p. 577; Sir William Clarke Hall, 'The Extent and Practice of Probation in England', in Sheldon Glueck (ed.), *Probation and Criminal Justice. Essays in Honor of Herbert C. Parsons* (1st pub., 1933; repr. edn., New York, 1974), pp. 292–3; Alexander Paterson, 'Probation and Reformative Treatment', *Probation*, vol. 1 (Oct. 1933), p. 265; B. Henriques, *Probation*, vol. 2 (Apr. 1938), p. 183. Some magistrates were so determined to make lads regard probation seriously that they remanded them for a week for inquiry, even though they intended ultimately to order probation: L. Le Mesurier, *Boys in Trouble* (1931), p. 184.

complement of probation officers.[24] The prevailing limitations of the probation system were further disclosed in 1935 by the *Handbook of Probation*, put out by the National Association of Probation Officers. Many probation committees, notably those in rural areas, were still ignoring the letter and spirit of the probation rules. Staffing arrangements were often still inadequate, with half-time officers carrying case-loads meant for full-time workers. Yet the part-time officer, the *Handbook* maintained, 'means the ill paid officer, and sometimes unskilled and inexperienced officer'.[25] In brief, then, neither the proper selection of suitable cases to be dealt with by probation, nor the subsequent visitation and supervision of probationers had reached the standards which NAPO demanded.

The Home Office readily acknowledged the deficiencies of the probation system, even though they felt that important advances had been made since the Baird committee of 1922. In July 1934 the head of the Children's Branch drafted a detailed memorandum on the subject, in which he stated: 'The probation system has many supporters but it has its critics also, and the whole system with all its merits may fall into grave disrepute unless care is taken to provide against obvious deficiencies.' The success of the system depended largely upon the calibre of probation officers, since it was they who frequently advised magistrates on the disposal of offenders. Yet, said Harris, 'though steps taken by the Home Office in the last ten years have done much to raise the level of these appointments it is clear we are not attracting candidates of the best possible type'.[26] On the advice of the Advisory Committee on Probation and Aftercare, and with the co-operation of the local authorities, a training scheme had been introduced in 1930 whereby a few selected candidates of adequate education and experience were to receive instruction in practical probation work at the same time as studying for a diploma in social science. The main stumbling block to this recruiting scheme had been the low standard of

[24] See 'Is Punishment a Crime? A discussion between Dr Hamblin Smith and Sir Arnold Wilson MP', *Listener*, 4 July 1934; Leo Page, *Justice of the Peace* (1936), p. 153. For the variable use of probation, see *Report of Social Services Committee*, op. cit., p. 466 (Table IV); *Criminal Statistics, 1935*, PP 1936–7, XXVI (Cmd. 5520), pp. 475–6.

[25] Mrs L. Le Mesurier, *Handbook*, pp. 38 and 69. In 1930 the Home Office's *Directory of Probation Officers* listed 769 officers. Of these, 289 were women, 226 were employees of missions or societies, and 501 were part-time. Of the 268 full-time officers, 82 were women. See N. Walker, 'Crime and Penal Measures' in A. H. Halsey (ed.), *Trends in British Society Since 1900* (1972), p. 536.

[26] 9 July 1934, PRO, HO45/17080/678095/1.

male candidates, due probably to the absence of any prospect of earning a decent salary, given that no avenue of promotion existed to higher paid posts.[27]

There were other problems, too, relating to the number and work-load of probation officers. Little wonder, declared Harris, that a substantial proportion of probationers repeated their crimes, when so many officers were too overworked to give adequate supervision.[28] For probation officers were required not only to supervise probationers, but also to make pre-sentence enquiries (for which probation officers were responsible in London and other large towns, as far as children and young persons were concerned), to supervise persons under twenty-one who had been ordered to pay a fine (although only Liverpool tended to follow this practice), to undertake the after-care of boys and girls from approved schools, and to do matrimonial or 'conciliation' work (allocated to probation officers by virtue of their descent from the police court missionary).[29] And, indeed, it was the multiplicity of functions which the probation service was being called upon to undertake that led Harris to accept the need for a full review of the system.

Harris's memorandum was written in the wake of a statement made by the Lord Chancellor, Viscount Sankey, in May 1934, on the occasion of the second reading of the Summary Jurisdiction (Domestic Procedure) Bill, in which it had been announced that the Home Secretary was willing to investigate the procedures for matrimonial conciliation. Interpreting this as a promise to establish a committee of enquiry, Lord Listowel withdrew his bill.[30] According to Harris's memorandum 'it was not intended that the Lord Chancellor should make such a promise', but, fortunately, as Harris went on to say, 'there are strong reasons from the Home Office point of view for setting up at the present moment a committee on the organisation of the probation

[27] See PRO, HO45/16213/486759.

[28] In the inter-war period there was little hard information as to the after-conduct of young offenders put on probation. All that there was came from the probation committees of towns like Cardiff, which merely calculated the percentages of persons on probation who within a period of five years again appeared before the court. The results for 1922 and 1923 were, respectively, 54.66 and 41.78%. These figures suggest lower success rates, however, than were commonly advanced by the champions of probation. See *Fourth Report on the Work of the Children's Branch* (1928), p. 27; Leon Radzinowicz, 'After-Conduct of Convicted Offenders in England', in L. Radzinowicz (ed.), *The Modern Approach to Criminal Law* (1945), pp. 158–9.

[29] See PRO, HO45/17080/678095/1.

[30] *Hansard*, vol. 92 (Lords), 15 May 1934, cols. 380–88.

service which could be made to include practically the whole ground covered by the Lord Chancellor's statement'.[31] A few weeks later, therefore, the Lord Chancellor announced that the Home Secretary was to appoint a departmental committee to examine the social services connected with the administration of justice by courts of summary jurisdiction.[32]

The National Association of Probation Officers claimed subsequently that the decision to look at conciliation in matrimonial cases in the wider context of the social work of the courts had been prompted by the efforts of Lord Feversham and H. E. Norman. Feversham was well placed to exert some influence on government, having been made a Lord in Waiting in January 1934.[33] But the Home Office files suggest that the decisive figure was Harris, who had been convinced for some years that a review of the probation system was wanted, and who now set about drafting the terms of reference for the enquiry and advising on the composition of the committee.

Most of the people who were appointed to serve on the committee had experience of the working of the probation system. Feversham was president of NAPO and a magistrate; Samuel Osborn was a magistrate and chairman of his local probation committee; Miss Madeleine Symons, JP, was a leading authority on delinquency and a member of the executive committee of the Howard League. They were joined by one of the foremost justices' clerks, Mr E. J. Hayward, and by Miss J. I. Wall of the Children's Branch. The head of the branch, Harris, was made chairman, on the say-so of Sir Russell Scott, Permanent Under-Secretary of State.[34] Harris was extremely well fitted to act in this capacity, in view of his long experience of the probation system and his membership of the Baird committee on probation and of the Young Offenders Committee.

The Departmental Committee on the Social Services in Courts of Summary Jurisdiction heard evidence from 126 witnesses, including representatives of NAPO, the Howard League, the Joint University Council for Social Studies, the Police Court Missions, the Incorporated Justices' Clerks' Society, and the Magistrates Association. This body of opinion was further supplemented by information deriving from a

[31] PRO, HO45/17080/678095/1.
[32] *Hansard*, vol. 93 (Lords), 25 July 1934, cols. 1060–61.
[33] Dorothy Bochel, op. cit., p. 123.
[34] Scott, 28 July 1934, PRO, HO45/17080/678095/2.

questionnaire which had been sent out to a number of representative courts. Yet if the evidence was voluminous, it was also unanimous, both on the description of the existing service and on the suggestions for improvements to the system.

Guided by the evidence of individual magistrates like Claud Mullins, the representatives of NAPO, and the inspectors of the Children's Branch, the report of the departmental committee drew attention to the familiar defects in the existing organization of the probation service: too many part-time officers, too few women officers, full-time officers who were overworked, and probation committees not operating as the intended pivot of the system.[35] Of course, the increase in the volume of probation cases and in the range of duties demanded of probation officers would have put pressure on any system; but the main problem was that the probation service seemed unable to respond to new organizational needs. It was evident, then, that one of the committee's main tasks would be to promote 'an improved system of organization', so making it possible for probation officers to perform the various kinds of social work connected with the courts. What the report recommended, however, was not particularly radical, except with regard to the abolition of dual control, of which more later. Firstly, the Home Office were asked to take a larger role in the direction and supervision of the probation service. Until this date, the department had exercised a general supervision through the Probation and After-Care Advisory Committee, and by circulars to magistrates, by the training scheme, and by the visits of the inspectors of the Children's Branch.[36] The report proposed that the Home Secretary should now have a general power of inspection, 'to satisfy himself that a reasonable standard of efficiency is being maintained before Government Grant is paid'.[37] Many witnesses had spoken in favour of inspection, including the representatives of NAPO, the Howard League, and the Magistrates Association, not to mention the inspectors of the Children's Branch, who thought that their visits over the

[35] Departmental Committee on Social Services in Courts of Summary Jurisdiction, *Minutes of Evidence* (seen with Home Office permission), no. 10 (Mullins); no. 70 (NAPO); no. 55 (Inspectors of Children's Branch).

[36] This was an informal mode of inspection, the time of the inspectors being fully taken up with the inspection of approved schools, remand homes and voluntary homes: Le Mesurier, *Handbook*, pp. 36–7.

[37] *Report of the Departmental Committee on the Social Services in Courts of Summary Jurisdiction*, PP 1935–6, VIII (Cmd. 5122), pp. 406–7.

previous years had been of value to local courts and probation officers.[38]

Secondly, the report endorsed the view of the inspectors that probation would receive more attention if it were made independent of the Children's Branch. The association of probation work with the Children's Branch had, it was felt, lent colour to the notion that probation was a system for the young alone.[39] Thirdly, at the local level, the report encouraged petty sessional divisions to combine to form probation areas; this, it was hoped, would enable more full-time officers to be employed. Probation committees were to remain in charge of the local administration of the system, although the respective duties of the probation committee for the petty sessional division and that for the combined area were more clearly defined. The former (or 'case committee') was to assist the probation officer to do his or her job; the latter was to be responsible for the appointment and payment of probation officers and their allocation to the various courts.[40]

The most controversial recommendations concerned the appointment of probation officers, and the related question of the place of the agents of the voluntary societies. For some time, the more advanced reformers had advocated making probation a national service, under which all probation officers would be appointed and trained by the Home Office and paid out of central funds.[41] 'A State service', the *Handbook of Probation* explained, 'would no doubt do much to remove inequalities of administration, and make it easier to obtain a uniform standard of efficiency.'[42] But the proposal went against the grain of an essentially local service, and would have severed the direct link between the court and the probation officer. The report recommended, in consequence, that the appointment of probation officers should be left in the hands of the magistrates, acting through the probation committees.[43]

[38] *Evidence*, nos. 70 and 55; no. 39 (Howard League); no. 48 (Magistrates Association); no. 26 (probation officers of the London juvenile courts).

[39] *Report*, op. cit., p. 406.

[40] Ibid., pp. 432–3.

[41] See *Annual Report of the Howard League, 1929–30*, pp. 5–6; *Howard Journal*, vol. 3 (Sep. 1930), p. 6; PRO, HO45/14714/516360/55.

[42] Le Mesurier, *Handbook*, p. 32. See also Elizabeth Macadam, *The New Philanthropy—a Study in the Relations between the Statutory and Voluntary Social Services* (1934), p. 231.

[43] *Report*, op. cit., p. 432.

But if probation officers were to be appointed locally, were they still to be drawn from voluntary as well as public sources? A large number of witnesses advised the departmental committee that the division of authority between the courts and the voluntary societies led to friction and a lack of proper direction of probation work, and that 'whilst the probation system may be said to be the child of the missions', in the words of the children's inspectors, 'the time has now come when these appointments should be in the full sense of the word public'.[44] In contrast, the representatives of the Society of Clerks of the Peace of Counties, and of the Police Court Mission, as well as the Archbishop of York (who gave evidence on behalf of the mission) insisted that the voluntary societies attracted to their service men and women with 'a sense of vocation based on religious conviction' who might not be attracted by a public authority. Moreover, the funds of the societies afforded some relief to public expenditure.[45]

The report left no doubt that the departmental committee were in favour of a public service, for reasons which were spelt out as follows: 'We have been much impressed by the almost unanimous opinion of the National Association of Probation Officers, which includes the great majority of the missionary officers, that the service should now be divorced from the Mission.'[46] Another reason was that the contribution of voluntary bodies to probation work had been diminishing for some time, as an increasing number of courts appointed full-time, independent officers. In some places the missions had shut up shop entirely; in London and the home counties they survived, but were seen as a drag on the development of the service. A further reason was the failure of the Police Court Mission to divorce itself sufficiently from the work of the Church of England Temperance Society. Finally, the committee felt that the improved system of organization which they hoped for would be jeopardized by a division of responsibility in the control of probation officers. Yet, whilst recommending that probation should be a public service, the departmental committee also declared that they were 'anxious that the religious and voluntary spirit in probation work should not be lost', and that the Police Court

[44] *Evidence*, no. 55 (Inspectors of Children's Branch); no. 10 (Mullins); no. 48 (Magistrates Association) and no. 70 (NAPO).

[45] *Evidence*, no. 53 (Revd Harry Pearson, Secretary to the London Police Court Mission); no. 54 (Society of Clerks of the Peace of Counties).

[46] *Report*, op. cit., p. 395.

Mission could still lend a hand by helping to provide probation homes and hostels.[47]

A number of smaller, yet important, proposals were finally put forward by the Harris committee. First, a sense of vocation and a sympathetic personality were no longer taken to be sufficient to cope with the increased range of duties of a probation officer; trained social workers were called for. The experimental Home Office training scheme had, by this date, reared a few handfuls of trained entrants; some others had come via the university extension courses of the Police Court Mission.[48] An expansion of the Home Office scheme by the appointment of a central training board was recommended by the departmental committee. This board would include representatives of the universities and the local appointing authorities, it would select candidates for the training scheme, and it would send the names of trained candidates to all local appointing authorities.[49] Second, the committee endorsed the view of the Home Office and of NAPO, that 'no person should be placed on probation without full consideration of his previous history and present surroundings', and that the probation officer was the most suitable person to report on the home surroundings. They had been guided on this item by the view of the probation officers that making contact with an offender prior to sentence helped the officer 'to exercise his influence more effectively at a later stage'.[50] Lastly, the Harris committee reported that the arrangement of sending probationers to a voluntary home as a condition of probation had worked well, but that there had been 'a tendency to prolong unduly the period of residence'. It was proposed, therefore, that 'no period longer than six months should be inserted as a condition in a probation order'.[51]

The significance of the Harris committee's review of the probation system, presented to the Home Secretary in March 1936, was, as Dorothy Bochel rightly states, 'its view of the probation service as an entirely public enterprise, and of the probation officer as a full-time,

[47] Ibid., pp. 393–6.

[48] See Le Mesurier, *Handbook*, pp. 66–8; PRO, HO45/16213/486759/8–40; *Evidence*, no. 39a (Howard League).

[49] *Report*, op. cit., p. 435.

[50] *Evidence*, no. 70 (NAPO); *Report*, op. cit., pp. 335–7 and 430.

[51] *Report*, op. cit., pp. 357–8 and 431; *Fifth Report*, op. cit., pp. 35–6. The Report also called for a sharper distinction between the procedure of 'binding over' and placing an offender 'on probation'. See S. W. Harris, *Probation and other Social Work of the Courts* (1937, 3rd Clarke Hall lecture), p. 21.

trained and well-educated social worker of the courts'.[52] To this end, the committee wished to strengthen the administration of the probation service by greater central supervision, by removing the brake to development which the system of dual control applied, and by introducing a senior grade of officer to oversee the daily work at local level. It also looked forward to a more professional body of trained social workers. As Elizabeth Macadam, of the Joint University Council, told NAPO's national conference, the bogey which had haunted the probation service for too long—'that personality or a deep sense of vocation can be regarded as an alternative to training'—was on its way to being exorcized.[53] In its final form, the report gave satisfaction to many of the groups which had given evidence, such as the Magistrates Association, the inspectors of the Children's Branch, and the National Association of Probation Officers.[54] Indeed, the report bore particular testimony to the public standing and publicity work of NAPO. Under the guidance of Feversham and Norman, both of whom were in close touch with Harris at the Home Office, NAPO became in the 1930s a constructive critic of the probation system and one of the most influential proponents of a properly organized and staffed service.[55] In all, then, the report of the departmental committee gave substantial backing to the probation system at the very moment when the reactionaries' campaign for a less sentimental strain of juvenile justice was gathering momentum.

[52] Bochel, op. cit., p. 149. See also Harris, 'Summary Courts (Social Services) Committee Report', *Probation*, vol. 2 (July 1936), pp. 69–72.

[53] Macadam, 'The Intellectual Background of Probation Work', *Probation*, vol. 2 (July 1937), p. 140. Two years later, E. C. Gates, JP, chairman of the Manchester probation committee, could state: 'The whole idea of Probation as an organized service has undergone a great change. We no longer speak of "redemption", we employ instead such terms as "re-education". The evangelical vocabulary of its early days has passed out of recognition': *Magistrate*, vol. V (Sep.–Oct. 1938), p. 93.

[54] H. E. Norman, 'The Probation Officers and Social Services', *Howard Journal*, vol. 4 (1936), pp. 290–4; *Annual Report of the Howard League, 1935–6*, p. 3; Gertrude Tuckwell, 'The Social Services Report', *Penal Reformer*, vol. 3 (July 1936), pp. 2–3.

[55] Feversham, 'The New Scheme for Further Development', *Probation*, vol. 1 (Apr. 1930), p. 37; R. G. Walton, *Women in Social Work* (1975), pp. 110–11. Another important figure was Miss Gertrude Tuckwell, Vice-President of NAPO. Born 1861, she was a lifelong philanthropic worker and supporter of the Labour party. She was also one of the founders of the Magistrates Association and, like that body, she always attached great importance to the development of probation: *DNB, 1951–60*, p. 997. NAPO was helped financially in the 1930s by the Trust Fund of the Clarke Hall Fellowship, set up in 1933 after his death. By 1935, finally, NAPO was claiming that 95% of all full-time officers were members of the Association.

The report of the departmental committee tacitly sanctioned two new legislative measures: a bill to deal with matrimonial jurisdiction, empowering the Home Office to employ probation officers for conciliation and other social work; and a bill to amend the Probation of Offenders Act. But the erstwhile chairman, Harris, saw little need for haste. 'The second is not urgent', he minuted in May 1936; 'indeed we shall be in a better position to introduce a Bill in a year or two when the organisation of the probation service has made further progress'.[56] The main priority was to act upon the proposals which required no legislative sanction. The first step was to strengthen the staff of the department in line with two of the recommendations: one, that the probation service needed 'the direction and guidance of an active central authority to ensure efficiency, to act as a clearing house for new ideas, and to co-ordinate the work of the various authorities'; and, two, that the responsibility for the administration of the probation service should be taken away from the Children's Branch. Effect was given to these proposals by the appointment of a small group of administrative officers and inspectors, to be known as the Probation Branch. This was established in October 1936, with B. J. Reynolds in charge. The branch quickly found its stride, according to Reynolds, who declared in March 1937, that 'both locally and nationally the creation of the new Branch has met a general and an urgent need'.[57]

The existence of the branch seemed to facilitate the implementation of other of the recommendations of the Social Services Committee: an improvement in the salaries of probation officers, the formation of more probation areas and the appointment of full-time officers, and the establishment of supervisory posts.[58] Furthermore, the Probation Advisory Committee was reconstituted, and a Central Training Board was appointed, with the task of developing the training scheme and of instituting means for the training of existing officers.[59]

[56] 20 May 1936, PRO, HO45/17080/678095/55.

[57] R. R. Scott to Treasury, 9 June 1936, PRO, HO144/22657/801480/1; Reynolds, 24 March 1937, 801480/4.

[58] The Home Office led the way in relation to supervisory posts by appointing Mr Clutton-Brock as a principal probation officer in London: *Hansard*, vol. 342, 1 Dec. 1938, col. 724 (Geoffrey Lloyd). By 1938 there were 1,004 probation officers. Of these, 392 were women, and 585 were part-time. Of the 419 full-time officers, 104 were women. See N. Walker, loc. cit.

[59] PRO, HO144/22657/801480/4; Elkin, op. cit., p. 196; Home Office circular, 4 March 1938, 'Training of Probation Officers,' *Magistrate*, vol. 5 (May–June 1938), pp. 55–6.

Meanwhile, the Police Court Mission were deciding how to respond to this re-organization of the probation system on a wholly public basis. Their first inclination was to contest the position; further reflection, however, led them to relinquish responsibility for those of their agents who acted as probation officers, and to obtain Home Office advice on future fields of activity. A discussion took place between the department and representatives of the Police Court Mission in January 1937, when Harris encouraged the latter to develop, *inter alia*, their work of providing hostels and homes.[60] The Home Office were encouraging the greater provision of hostels, so as to extend the use of residential conditions in probation orders. In 1937, indeed, the department informed the courts that exchequer grants would be available for the maintenance in hostels of persons between fourteen and sixteen (as they were for those between sixteen and twenty-one),[61] and for the arrangement of suitable lodgings, to be used in place of hostels for probationers over school age.[62]

Even with all these promising changes, there remained ample room for improvement in probation work, particularly in some of the smaller courts where probation committees were still neglecting their duties and where probation officers were still poorly trained and inadequate in number.[63] Deficiencies in the law of probation seemed less responsible for the failings in the service than the apathy or obstructionism of magistrates, local authorities, and even probation officers. Even so, the opportunity to implement more of the recommendations of the Social Services Committee, or to give legislative backing to the recommendations already realized administratively, was taken when the government started to draft the Criminal Justice Bill in 1938.

The probation clauses were put in the forefront of the Criminal Justice Bill, the Home Affairs Committee of the Cabinet were told, because probation was the method which summary courts ought to keep in view in most cases, before deciding to adopt a severer mode of

[60] PRO, HO45/17080/678095/66 and 73.

[61] Circular, 6 March 1937, *Magistrate*, vol. 4 (Feb.–Mar. 1937), p. 1120.

[62] Circular, 16 Dec. 1937, *Magistrate*, vol. 5 (Jan.–Feb. 1938), pp. 18–19. In all these cases, the Home Office also allowed a residence condition to operate for not more than twelve months, although a six months' condition was still preferred.

[63] See Reynolds, 'The Work of Probation Committees', *Magistrate*, vol. 5 (March–April 1938), pp. 25–6; Alexander Maxwell, *Treatment of Crime* (1938), Barnett House Paper, No. 21, p. 12.

treatment.[64] One clause defined the respective duties of a 'case committee' and a probation committee; another clause required every probation committee to appoint for their probation area an adequate number of probation officers, and to select a woman officer for every petty sessional division. There were provisions, also, to facilitate the central training scheme, to regularize the use of a condition in a probation order that a probationer submit to mental treatment, and to restrict probation to the method of placing the offender under the supervision of a probation officer (no longer confusing it with dismissal and binding over).[65]

The most disappointing omission from the bill, at least as far as NAPO were concerned, was any statement declaring that the duties of a probation officer included the making of social enquiry reports on behalf of the court.[66] At the Committee stage of the bill, therefore, Mr Godfrey Nicholson sought to make it clear, first, that the making of reports should be the duty of probation officers and, second, that before making a probation order, the courts should consider any report about the offender's home surroundings made by a probation officer. On the last point, the Home Secretary preferred merely to advise magistrates to follow this course; but on the first point, NAPO's perseverance paid off, for the Home Secretary agreed to include an amendment, giving probation officers the task of making reports, although the court was to remain the initiating authority.[67]

The Criminal Justice Bill was withdrawn at the outbreak of war. The measure was a further mark, however, of the failure of the campaign to secure a more limited role for the probation service.[68] Throughout the 1930s, in response to the battle cry, 'you are making it too soft for the offender', the defenders of probation had upheld the view that the aim

[64] 22 Dec. 1937, PRO, HO45/17666/805270/10. This was in line with Hoare's statement to the Magistrates Association: 'I can tell you that, so far as the Home Office is concerned, we are doing our utmost to develop and to expand the probation service and the probation machinery. We now recognize the fact that it is one of the social services': *Magistrate*, vol. 5 (Nov.–Dec. 1938), p. 132.

[65] 'Criminal Justice Bill', PP 1938–9, II (4), pp. 319–20, 339–46 and 350–60; 'The English Criminal Justice Bill', *Columbia Law Review*, vol. 40 (1940), pp. 116–19.

[66] See Claud Mullins, 'The Criminal Justice Bill', *Law Journal*, vol. 87 (May 1939), pp. 373–4.

[67] See 'The Criminal Justice Bill', *Probation*, vol. 3 (April 1939), pp. 69–70.

[68] An associated strand to this campaign was to make probation more disciplinary by allowing it to be used in conjunction with other penalties. See W. A. Elkin, op. cit., pp. 177–8; Claud Mullins, 'Probation', *Quarterly Review*, vol. 268 (April 1937), pp. 349–51. The 'reactionaries' had no success here, either.

of penal policy was to prevent and cure delinquency, not to take revenge for it. They had resolutely promoted the policy, moreover, of keeping the young offender within his home, under the supervision of a probation officer, whenever possible, or, where home conditions were less satisfactory, of using approved hostels, homes, or lodgings, as a condition of probation. Only where home conditions were decidedly faulty was long-term institutional treatment recommended. The courts obliged by continuing to use probation more frequently than all other penalties put together, in the treatment of young offenders. In part, this reflected the rooted conviction that probation was particularly appropriate for the young delinquent. But it was also testimony to the belief that keeping the child with his family, or arranging for a substitute family for a brief period, were the methods most likely to win over wayward youth to sound citizenship.

Summary

The Children and Young Persons Act 1933 was almost immediately entangled in a prolonged discussion about the causes of the rise in juvenile crime. The incidence of recorded delinquencies had been increasing from the late 1920s, but the upward trajectory of the figures became steeper in the years promptly following the implementation of the 1933 Act. These statistical facts were subject in the thirties to two main interpretations. For the 'Clarke Hall movement', with which the Children's Branch of the Home Office were still in essential harmony, the increase in delinquency from the late 1920s was related to the country's economic troubles, culminating in the financial crisis of 1931; whilst the larger increases of the mid-1930s simply reflected a greater inclination on the part of the police, the public and social workers to charge delinquents, now that the new legislation had mitigated the stigma attaching to a juvenile court appearance. For the police and some portions of the magistracy, in contrast, the rise in juvenile crime and the associated pressure on accommodation in the approved schools, was no statistical illusion, but an inevitable behavioural response to an excessive leniency in the modes of juvenile justice and a coincidental decay in parental authority in the home.

The main significance of these conflicting explanations of the upturn in delinquency is the degree to which they sired either shifts or continuities in penal policy. There is little doubt as to the direction in which each group wished penal policy to develop. The 'reactionary' lobby wanted a return to more awe-inspiring procedures in the juvenile court, a more restricted application of probation, and a wider use of corporal punishment. Failing the latter, a penal drill sentence (which Winston Churchill first conceived when Home Secretary in 1910) would equally serve the purpose of a deterrent and disciplinary substitute for parental control. The 'reformers' wanted no such reversal of the intentions of the 1933 Act. If they agreed that a dearth of parental training and discipline lay at the root of delinquency (although this was seen as but part of a larger set of material and psychological defects of the delinquent's home life), the lesson drawn was not that the clock should be put back to earlier punitive times, but that renewed efforts should be made, either to improve the young offender's natural home, or to provide him with a surrogate home for a longer or shorter period. There is little doubt, either, about the differing success with which these two lobbyists pressed their views during the thirties.

The main conflict raged around the question of the whipping of young male offenders. In the early 1930s, as fewer and fewer courts made use of corporal punishment, it looked as if the Home Office's ploy of letting the penalty die a natural death, rather than pressing parliament to deliver a controversial *coup de grâce*, was a sensible one. The rise in delinquency changed all that. The upward trend in the crime figures aroused the chief constables of many large cities to question the efficacy of the new legislation, particularly the anodyne procedures of the juvenile court and the shortage of penalties which relied on good, old-fashioned deterrence. A few courts, moreover, were already responding to the situation by reverting to police court trappings and by ordering whipping in a few more cases, thus adding to the variable and inconsistent use of the sentence. This could not but arouse the child welfare groups, ever alert to signs of deviation from the principles of 1933; again they pressed the Home Office to dispossess the courts of the power to order corporal punishment.

In time, the Home Office responded to what they felt might develop into a fundamental challenge to the entire thrust of policy for young offenders, by asking a decidedly impartial body to assess the merits of each standpoint. As it turned out, this was an effective strategy. Before the departmental committee on corporal punishment, the 'reformers' won hands down. An impressive array of magistrates, social workers, and medical representatives, all of whom had long experience in the practices of juvenile justice, gradually convinced the committee that, as a judicial penalty, whipping should be abolished. Reaching a decision was made easier for the Cadogan committee by the fact that the police representatives were anxious only that the courts should not be deprived of the one penalty, bar the fine, which relied on deterrence. It seemed likely, therefore, that the main opponents of the abolition of whipping could be appeased by the provision of an alternative short, sharp punishment.

A unanimous recommendation from a largely 'neutral' committee was justification enough for the Home Office, with Cabinet approval, to add a clause abolishing whipping to the Criminal Justice Bill. In the same measure, the department incorporated a substitute for corporal punishment which, at this stage, took the form of the attendance centre, the disciplinary features of which were heightened by the determination on the part of the local education authorities that these centres should have no essentially educational functions. What the Home Secretary had not allowed for, with regard to birching, was the strength of Conservative party opposition to abolition; this was now deployed both in the country and in parliament. The main achievement of this rearguard action was to force the government to concede a free vote on the issue when the Report stage was taken in the Commons. In fact, the latter never arrived, but even had this hurdle been cleared, further opposition would no doubt have met the clause on corporal punishment in the House of Lords. This is not to suggest, however, that the 'reactionaries' would have secured victory at the eleventh hour, for Sydney Harris was assuredly correct to suggest that some accord would probably have been reached whereby the whipping of young delinquents, if not of adult offenders, would have been terminated.

Alongside the wrangle over corporal punishment, a more far-reaching and less polemical debate took place concerning the tenor of policy for the prevention, diagnosis, and treatment of delinquency. Significantly, the discussion took place within the parameters established by the 1933 Act and echoed, in consequence, much of what was heard in the 1920s. Renewed emphasis was put on the care needed in the selection of magistrates for the juvenile panels, especially in view of the existence of justices who derided the 1933 Act as sentimental and who were incapable of properly administering it. Further endorsement was given to the value of recreational facilities and of boys' clubs and the like in the prevention of offences, particularly on the new housing estates where delinquency was on the increase. And still the view prevailed that it was crucial to assess the causes of a child's 'malady' before prescribing treatment, whilst the state observation home was as high as ever on the reformers' agenda.

With regard to treatment, the emphasis in the 1930s was firmly on the provision of an improved family life for the young offender, reflecting the ruling view of delinquency as a by-product of the 'broken home' and defective family relationships. 'I think a juvenile court starts with the idea', claimed the magistrate and social worker, Basil Henriques, 'that wherever it is possible with safety to leave a boy or girl in his own home, he should be left there'.[69] Judging by the number of young offenders who were discharged, bound over, fined, or put on probation, the courts did indeed pursue this policy. Only probation, however, offered any constructive assistance to the delinquent and his family, as a result of which it was the non-custodial sentence most favoured by the child welfare movement. Yet probation was coming under increasingly heavy fire from the 'reactionary' lobby, on the grounds that it was too often seen as a 'let-off' and too frequently used for offenders who had previously failed on probation. The reformers' lobby acknowledged these deficiencies, and indeed advanced their own criticisms of the service, particularly in relation to the numerical strength and calibre of the probation staff. More practically, they encouraged magistrates to use the powers of the court to make conditions in the probation order (such as attendance at a boys' club, or residence in a voluntary hostel or home); and they urged probation officers to bring their probationers before the court for breaches of the order. In these ways, it was hoped, probation would be no let-off, but a rigorous form of non-institutional training.

A more telling device to improve the probation system (and perhaps disarm the critics) was the appointment of a departmental committee to review the social services in summary courts, the prime mover and chairman of which was Sydney Harris. With the backing of a large number of witnesses, notably those representing the penal reform societies, the inspectors of the Children's Branch and the National Association of Probation Officers, the committee put forward a set of proposals, the aim of which was to put the probation system on the road to becoming a centrally-directed social service, staffed by trained, full-time, and publicly-appointed social workers. The recommendations clearly touched the right chord in the Home Office, due in part,

[69] Henriques, 'The Child in Trouble', *Listener*, 23 May 1934, p. 882.

one suspects, to the contemporaneous arrival of Samuel Hoare, bent on penal reform. Almost immediately, a number of the proposals of the Harris committee were implemented by administrative fiat; others were incorporated into the leading section of the Criminal Justice Bill.

Of particular importance for young offenders were the provisions in the bill to facilitate the further use of hostels, homes, and lodgings as a condition of probation. For some years the courts had used voluntary hostels and homes for young offenders who needed to be removed from their natural home for a few months, but who did not require the long-term training of a residential school; by sharing some of the financial burden, in the late thirties, the Home Office encouraged this practice. So, too, the department promoted the use of foster homes (or boarding out) and short-term approved schools, as additional means of 'in-patient' treatment which avoided protracted institutionalization; and prevailed upon the headmasters of approved schools to release their pupils on licence as soon as they seemed fit to return to their family or to a hostel. The thrust of this whole policy was to provide the courts with a variable range of measures to improve the home life of young delinquents.

The thirties, in all, was a difficult if ultimately rewarding decade for the child welfare movement. At first things had gone well. The post-war campaign to improve the pioneering Children Act of 1908 had reached fruition in the Children and Young Persons Act 1933, a statute which emerged from a conjunction of interests and ideology between the leading officials of the Children's Branch and the headmen of English social work. Unfortunately, the implementation of the 1933 Act coincided with an increase in delinquency. The latter reflected the socio-economic afflictions of the late twenties and early thirties but was doubtless aggravated by the Act itself. It was cruel irony, then, that the crime rate should fuel denunciations of the measure for being overly sentimental and for diminishing the deterrent efficacy of juvenile justice. More specifically, the 'reactionary' groups pressed for juvenile courts which showed their criminal as well as welfare aspect, for a limitation on the use of probation, and for a greater use of whipping or of a new short, sharp penalty. Had there been a sufficient number of juvenile panel magistrates who were disillusioned with the Children and Young Persons Act, and prepared to act upon their conviction, then the lines of penal policy might well have had to be re-drawn. In fact, thanks largely to the publicity work of groups like the Magistrates Association and to the unwavering support of the Home

Office, the lay magistracy remained faithful to the principles and practices of child welfare. They neither grasped at the straw of corporal punishment to reverse the increase in juvenile crime, nor shrank from ordering probation for the majority of more serious offenders who came before them. For the time being, at least, the 'reactionary' counterstrokes had been parried. It required a further upswing in the crime rate, which the Second World War engendered, before the demand for punitive measures was to any degree satisfied.

PART IV

Training for Citizenship: The Inter-War Years

7
Young Prisoners

But prison for adolescents, whether on remand, or in default of a fine, or on conviction, must be cleared away. So long as it looms there in the background, filling up the scene and blocking out the light as it has done for so many ages, the simplest—and stupidest—thing to do to a lad who has broken the law is to send him there . . . (L. Le Mesurier, *Boys in Trouble*, 1931, p. 273.)

The treatment of young adult offenders differed from that of children and young persons. For a start, offenders aged sixteen to twenty-one were dealt with by the ordinary adult courts, not by the juvenile courts.[1] If remanded, they usually ended up in the precincts of a prison. After conviction, unless fined or put on probation, they came under the aegis of the Prison Commission, not the Children's Branch of the Home Office. Moreover, a large number of adolescent offenders were received into prison on conviction, with only a small proportion ever reaching a Borstal institution, the main custodial alternative to imprisonment. Nevertheless, many of the reforms which were recommended for juvenile delinquents were thought to be equally desirable in the treatment of young adult offenders. Most notably, the surroundings, staff, and routine of a prison were said to be hopelessly unfitted to the effective treatment of adolescent offenders. It is this strand of penal policy, the expansion of alternatives to imprisonment, which forms the essential body of the next two chapters on the inter-war changes in the treatment of adolescent offenders.

Once more, what emerges is the creation of policy by administrators who were guided by personal experience of voluntary social work amongst working-class lads and by a related and widely-accepted conception of the causes and correctives of adolescent crime. Perhaps uniquely, one sees those who had earlier written about youthful crime in positions of administrative influence in the inter-war period. They were determined to counteract the deleterious effect of 'street corner

[1] Following the Children and Young Persons Act 1933, offenders aged seventeen to twenty-one were dealt with by adult courts.

society' by training young criminals in the virtues of citizenship within a non-prison environment. Once again, too, the key administrative figures were abreast, if not ahead, of the penal reform lobby, and in close touch with the voluntary and parliamentary representatives of youth welfare. In short, we see a group of policy-makers who were eager to introduce bold measures of social engineering in the cause of criminal youth. Underlying their policy was a humanitarian desire to help underprivileged working-class lads, a faith in the personal influence of those in charge of reformatory institutions, and a Fabian-like readiness to use administrative as well as legislative modes of attaining their ends.

Remand Prisoners

It is essential, first, to examine the use of imprisonment for adolescents, whether on remand, in default of a fine, or on conviction, in order to assess the scope and criticisms of youth imprisonment.

An undoubted weakness of the penal system for young adult offenders was the insight into prison life accorded unconvicted or remand prisoners, familiarizing them with prison conditions, lessening their apprehension of an actual sentence of imprisonment. Numerous young offenders were sent to local prisons on remand, many of whom were not subsequently sentenced to imprisonment. Thus, of 142 unconvicted prisoners received into one prison in the south of England, forty-six, or nearly one-third were under twenty-one years of age.[2] If the evils of prison were to be avoided, remand homes for sixteen to twenty-one-year-olds were urgently required.

The campaign to avoid remands in prison was given some impetus by the death in 1919 of Ellen Sullivan whilst on remand in Holloway. Her death from diabetes was not, according to the prison staff, explained by the conditions on remand. Even so, the incident provoked press articles, parliamentary debates, and resolutions from trades councils and co-operative guilds, all demanding that unconvicted persons should either be granted bail or accommodated in hostels.[3] Further criticism of the conditions at Holloway led Ruggles-Brise, chairman of the Prison Commission, to invite Adeline, Duchess of Bedford, President of the Lady Visitors' Association, to chair a

[2] *Times Educational Supplement*, 12 Nov. 1921, p. 501.
[3] PRO, HO144/4545/375098/1–23.

committee of investigation. The committee reported that 'a strong tide of public opinion is opposed to the inclusion of remands in a Prison . . . especially in the case of first convictions', and then recommended that first offenders on remand should be sent to a remand home, not prison.[4] But no immediate improvement came from this official activity. More constructively, William Clarke Hall began to admit girls under nineteen to bail on condition they reside at a voluntary home provided by an Anglican order. The Home Office hoped that other courts would copy the scheme.[5] A year later, it was the turn of the Penal Reform League to press the Home Office for a remand home for girls aged sixteen to eighteen. Dr Norris, chief inspector of reformatory schools, acted as go-between, advising the department that the League could no longer be regarded as 'a collection of cranks', but as a fair representative of 'the opinion of social workers and those who are making a study of the young criminal'.[6] But again, no official reform was forced. Voluntary homes were left to fill the gap.

More progress was made in relation to male remands, at least in London. Until 1923, male prisoners aged sixteen to twenty-one on remand or awaiting trial in the capital were sent to Brixton prison, where little was done to separate them from the older prisoners. In that year, however, prison commissioner Alec Paterson put forward the idea of using the boys' prison at Wandsworth both as a reception class for boys sentenced to Borstal detention, and as a collecting centre for all boys who were remanded from courts in the London area, the aim of which was to institute a regular system of furnishing reports on the boys to the courts. The chairman of the Prison Commission, M. L. Waller, thought the scheme was sound, as did the medical inspector of prisons, Dr Dyer. In October 1923 Dr J. J. Landers was appointed governor and medical officer of the boys' prison.[7] It was hardly the special remand home that many wanted. The boys' prison was detached from the main building at Wandsworth, but the remands could still gain a detailed impression of prison life and it was never entirely possible to keep the young offenders away from adult

[4] Ibid. For E. Ruggles-Brise, see note 39 below.

[5] Ibid., 375098/5.

[6] Ibid., 375098/26.

[7] PRO, HO45/20947/448767/26; P Com. 7/598. A third function was added later, to act as a prison for boys under twenty-one from the London area sentenced to terms of imprisonment of three months and under. See section 'Young Prisoners' below.

prisoners. Yet the scheme was evidence of the official aspiration to obtain fuller information on the character, home conditions, and mental and physical health of adolescent offenders in surroundings which would facilitate such enquiries. Remand cases were closely investigated by the medical staff of the prison, their work supplemented by enquiries made into the home surroundings of the boys by a group of voluntary women workers under the direction of Mrs Le Mesurier.[8]

In 1924 the Associated Societies for the Care and Maintenance of Infants and the National Association of Prison Visitors pressed the Home Office to get young women remanded to refuges instead of to prison, but the department, on the advice of Sir John Anderson, preferred to gain experience from the scheme, recently approved, providing for a state contribution towards maintenance in a probation home.[9] It was also known by this date that the question would be treated by the Departmental Committee on the Treatment of Young Offenders.

The evidence presented to the departmental committee was reasonably unanimous on the need for a system of remand homes for sixteen- to twenty-one-year-olds. Dr Landers, Alec Paterson and Basil Henriques, magistrate and club leader, all advocated replacing the remand portion of the Wandsworth boys' prison by remand homes which would be places of examination as well as of safe custody. These witnesses were predictably critical of the judicial practice of giving young offenders 'a taste of prison' by remanding them, when there was no intention of imposing a sentence of imprisonment.[10]

The departmental committee accepted that the examination of offenders between seventeen and twenty-one ought not to take place in prison surroundings, whether in London or outside. The proposed remedy was the central remand home or observation centre. This would make it possible 'to secure a fundamental change in the treatment of young offenders who are remanded in custody, especially in avoiding the use of prison for this purpose'.[11] For those offenders

[8] See *Daily News*, 14 July 1925 in PRO, HO45/16515/375684/55A; *Howard Journal*, vol. 2 (1926), p. 4.

[9] PRO, HO144/4545/375098/37.

[10] *Report of Young Offenders Committee*, PP 1927, XII (Cmd. 2831), *Minutes of Evidence*, qq. 20283 (p. 2281), 20308 (p. 2287) (Landers); qq. 818 (p. 128), 1146 (p. 171) (Paterson); qq. 2712 (p. 348), 3155 (p. 396) (Henriques). For further information on Henriques, see note 28 to ch. 9.

[11] *Report of YOC*, p. 1003.

who could not be accommodated in one of the central remand homes, the local authorities were asked to find suitable premises. The committee also encouraged the wider use of voluntary homes for young women.

In the wake of the Young Offenders Committee, the Home Secretary was pressed by Edward Cadogan to institute remand observation centres. The prison commissioners were already investigating the possibility of a building distinct from an adult prison, when funds allowed, in view of the numbers unnecessarily initiated into prison conditions via this route.[12] In 1928, for example, 2,549 males and 348 females under twenty-one were remanded to prison. Of these, only 562 lads and 43 girls were sentenced to terms of imprisonment. Of the rest, some were fined, some discharged, but the large majority, 1,236 lads and 237 girls—or roughly 50 per cent of all those remanded to prison—were dealt with under the Probation Act.[13] The only change that took place, however, at least in London, was the transfer of the boys' prison from Wandsworth to Wormwood Scrubs. Pethick-Lawrence had complained in May 1928 of the use of Wandsworth for executions, when Sir Vivian Henderson, Parliamentary Under-Secretary, promised to review the position. Later in the year, the prison commissioners accepted Henderson's proposal that an empty block at the Scrubs should become the boys' prison, with arrangements made to separate the young prisoners serving short sentences from those on remand or awaiting transfer to a Borstal institution.[14]

Outside London, the position remained unchanged. There was generally still no place other than prison to which persons could be sent for custody and observation while on remand. Hence, a central plank of Mrs Le Mesurier's 1931 catalogue of reforms to avoid the imprisonment of adolescents was the central remand home.[15]

In summary, nothing seemed more counter-productive to the penal reform lobby and the Prison Commission alike than the remanding of unconvicted adolescents to prison, the majority of whom would not be given a sentence of imprisonment. This policy, it was held, diminished

[12] *Hansard*, vol. 209, 28 July 1927, col. 1545; PRO, HO45/16224/512613/1.

[13] *Annual Report of Prison Commissioners for 1928*, PP 1929–30, XVII (Cmd. 3607), p. 299. These figures exclude offenders who were awaiting a Borstal sentence, having been committed to prison under s. 10 of the Criminal Justice Administration Act 1914; and those who received a Borstal sentence following committal to prison to await trial.

[14] HO45/20947/448767/26; *Hansard*, vol. 217, 21 May 1928, col. 1629.

[15] HO144/22354/474377/24 and 28; L. Le Mesurier, *Boys in Trouble* (1931), pp. 77–81 and 267.

the deterrent threat of a prison sentence, and made it harder to deal with those who were subsequently put on probation. Yet no significant advances were made in the avoidance of remand imprisonment. The only development for male adolescents in the London region was the establishment of the boys' prison, a scheme inspired by Alec Paterson as a way of improving the allocation of boys to the Borstal institutions and of furnishing better pre-sentence reports on the remand cases to the metropolitan courts. But if this arrangement improved the examination of young delinquents, it also faced criticism for the continued use of prison buildings. A purpose-built remand home or observation centre was the preferred alternative to prison, a scheme which received the imprimatur of the Young Offenders Committee in the mid-1920s and which formed part of the Children and Young Persons Bill introduced by the Home Office in the early 1930s. As we know, however, the proposal was eventually dropped from the bill when it became impossible to secure Treasury agreement to the required expenditure.[16] To some degree, therefore, the reform of remand imprisonment ran foul of the economic constraints of the inter-war years.

Fine Defaulters

Section 1 of the Criminal Justice Administration Act 1914 required the courts to allow time for the payment of a fine in all cases, unless there was some reason to the contrary, such as the fact that the defendant had no fixed abode. This provision led to a substantial reduction in the number of young and adult offenders imprisoned in default of a fine. But many courts were still sending youths, particularly those working as street traders, to prison for not paying fines, either by failing to give offenders time to pay, or by neglecting to use the section of the 1914 Act which empowered a court to put a young person between sixteen and twenty-one under supervision until the fine was paid. Of the 1,831 lads under twenty-one who were received into prison under sentences of one month or less during the year ended 31 March 1921, 647 or 35 per cent were committed in default of fine. In 455 of these cases, time had not been allowed by the court in which to pay.[17]

[16] See section, 'Observation Homes' in ch. 3.

[17] *Annual Report of Prison Commissioners for year ended 31 March 1921*, PP 1921, XVI (Cmd. 1523), p. 423. See also *TES*, 12 Nov. 1921, p. 501.

Not surprisingly, the advocates of the view that no youth under twenty-one should be in prison at all, plus those who simply objected to short terms of imprisonment, were critical of the imprisonment of fine defaulters. The prison commissioners were in the forefront of the campaign to change court practice, but the most active lobbyist was the council of the Magistrates Association. In 1924 they pressed the Home Secretary to make it compulsory to appoint a person to exercise supervision when a young offender was allowed time to pay a fine (a procedure which had proved effective in Liverpool in reducing the number of persons sent to prison); and to make it necessary for offenders who had been given time and who had still failed to pay, to appear again in court before committal to prison, thereby giving the court an opportunity to review its original decision.[18] Similar proposals were made to the Young Offenders Committee, which went on to recommend the use of supervision. Successive home secretaries in the late 1920s endorsed the same policy, J. R. Clynes urging magistrates to use 'some social worker interested in boys' clubs and welfare work amongst young people' to act as supervisor.[19].

The courts, however, proved remarkably resilient to this pressure to use the powers they already possessed. Of the 937 sentences of one month or less passed on boys under twenty-one during 1928, 394 or 42 per cent were committals in default of fines. Hence, Le Mesurier was still obliged in 1931 to condemn the use of fines, with prison in default, for adolescents, and to recommend as the proper alternative, putting the offender on probation for a few months, with a condition that he pay restitution for his crime. In default, the offender would be liable to detention, but in a Borstal, not a prison.[20]

Young Prisoners

The prison commissioners had decided as early as 1905 that, as far as practicable, the methods followed at Borstal institutions should be extended to all offenders aged sixteen to twenty-one who were

[18] Ann. Rep. of P. Com. for year ended 31 March 1922, PP 1922, II (Cmd. 1761), p. 1015; *Magistrate*, vol. 2 (1930), pp. 373 and 408.

[19] *Report of YOC*, op. cit., pp. 1040–43 and 1084; *Evidence*, q. 20221 (p. 2274) (Landers). The committee concluded, however, that as some ultimate sanction was needed to enforce the payment of fines, no satisfactory alternative to imprisonment existed.

[20] Ann. Rep. of P. Com. for 1928, PP 1929–30, XVII (Cmd. 3607), p. 298; Le Mesurier, op. cit., pp. 155 and 195.

committed to prison. The first prescription of what was termed the 'modified Borstal' system was the segregation of adolescent offenders from adult prisoners. In practice, this could amount to little more than the collection of adolescents at the far end of a workroom in which adult prisoners were also employed, and to their sleeping in a separate wing of the prison (and sometimes only on a different storey) from the rest. The other main prescription of the 'modified Borstal' system was training and discipline by a programme of work, study, physical drill, and aid-on-discharge.[21] In practice, the shortness of sentence undermined any real training scheme, with nigh on three-quarters of the offenders sentenced to less than one month. To improve the provision of training under the modified system, the prison commissioners decided to transfer suitable male offenders with sentences of over three months to 'collecting depots', located in selected local prisons. At the same time, the commissioners encouraged the courts to avoid a succession of extremely short sentences by giving a sentence of over three months, thus making it possible to transfer the offender to a collecting centre. Those given three months or under, however, were kept in the prison of committal.[22]

The upshot of this activity on the part of the Prison Commission was the planting in the public and judicial mind of the belief that 'modified Borstal' was extremely similar to the system of training at Borstal institutions. This confusion led some sentencers to give a long term of imprisonment, in order to secure the benefit of the modified Borstal system. The issue was not finally resolved until 1919 by the case of *Oxlade*. Modified Borstal, the Court of Criminal Appeal declared, should be regarded as imprisonment, and its existence 'must not lead the Court to sentence him to a long term'. But the continued confusion aroused by the similarity of name led the Prison Commission in 1922 to replace the term 'modified Borstal' by that of 'young prisoners' classes'.[23]

[21] Ann. Rep. of P. Com. for year ended 21 March 1918, PP 1918, XII (Cmd. 9174), p. 605; Arthur Paterson, *Our Prisons* (1911), pp. 25–7; E. Ruggles-Brise, *The English Prison System* (1921), p. 96. See also R. G. Hood, *Borstal Re-Assessed* (1965), p. 17.

[22] PRO, P. Com. 7/597; P. Com. 7/525; Ann. Rep. of P. Com. for year ended 31 March 1920, PP 1920, XXIII (Cmd. 972), p. 13. The collecting centres were located in the local prisons of Bedford, Bristol, Durham, and Liverpool, each of which had between thirty and fifty males in the young prisoner classes. There was no centre for young women prisoners since, except at Holloway, the number of such prisoners was small.

[23] *R. v. Oxlade* (1919), 14 Cr. App. R. 65; HO45/11898/332404/16.

Some attention was also paid to the after-care of young prisoners. To this end, a 'Borstal committee' was established at each collecting centre and at all prisons where young adults were held, composed of members of the visiting committee. But the law provided no period of supervision after release, with a power of recall, for young prisoners. In 1920, the Central Discharged Prisoners' Aid Society (CDPAS) urged the Prison Commission to institute a power of supervision over prisoners who had been dealt with under the modified Borstal system. The Home Office decided to refer the question to the Departmental Committee on the Training of Probation Officers, which refrained, however, from making any recommendation on this point, simply declaring that the CDPAS had recommended for young adults sent to prison for three months or more, a system similar to that available in Borstal and certified schools, offenders remaining under supervision for six months, and liable to recall to prison. This did little to persuade the department to introduce reform. As Sydney Harris advised in May 1922, the scheme would require a large Treasury grant and 'a good deal of improvement in the machinery (of probation) before probation officers could usefully be brought into such a scheme'.[24]

It was never likely that the special treatment of young prisoners would appease those who objected to prison for adolescents. The constant increase of male young prisoners received on conviction between 1918 and 1921 and the proportion sentenced to very short terms only aggravated the position. Of 3,638 male offenders aged sixteen to twenty-one sentenced to imprisonment during 1920–21, 1,831 (or 50 per cent) were sentenced to one month or less. Only around 600 males were sentenced to over three months, of whom 524, or just over 14 per cent of the total number of young prisoners, were transferred to collecting centres.[25] In the early twenties, a number of critics made themselves heard. The Howard League complained of the contamination of young offenders by association with hardened criminals in prison workshops; the report of the Prison System Enquiry Committee, *English Prisons To-Day*, pronounced as futile the imposition of short prison sentences on young offenders.[26] But they were

[24] PRO, HO45/20929/432738/1; HO45/11898/332404/20; *Report of the Departmental Committee on the Training... of Probation Officers*, PP 1922, X (Cmd. 1601), p. 439.

[25] Ibid., p. 450.

[26] *Howard Journal*, vol. 1 (1921), p. 71; S. Hobhouse and A. F. Brockway, *English Prisons To-Day* (1922), p. 297. Stephen Hobhouse came from a wealthy Quaker family, renowned for its social service. He was imprisoned for being a conscientious objector during the First World War: *The Times*, 4 Apr. 1961, p. 11.

preaching to the converted. The prison commissioners, notably the new chairman, Maurice Waller, and Alexander Paterson, were equally dissatisfied with the treatment of young prisoners. Prisons were not designed as educational centres; short sentences of imprisonment gave insufficient time for proper re-education. There was also no effective after-care and control. If persons under twenty-one continued to be sentenced to imprisonment, the commissioners declared, 'a different form of training in separate establishments which are not ordinary prisons at all seems to us to be required'.[27]

Such official statements, however, gave rise to calls for the opening of separate prisons for boys. In April 1924, Pethick-Lawrence urged the Labour Home Secretary, Arthur Henderson, to allocate some of the prisons which had been closed in the past few years, to the treatment of young offenders sentenced to imprisonment. The prison commissioners strongly advised the Home Secretary against the notion. 'For one thing', Waller minuted,

> it would only encourage magistrates to send boys to prison, and we think that is wrong. For another, no system of separate boys' prisons could be complete . . . we should find that it would be impracticable to transfer all the boys on remand, or sentenced to a week or a fortnight, from all the local prisons. A certain number of lads would continue to spend short periods in ordinary local prisons, just as they do now.[28]

Paterson's view was more succinct: ' "Prison" and "boy" must come to be regarded as unrelated terms.' There was a more positive aspect to the commissioners' advice, which entailed recasting the entire system of dealing with young adult offenders.

Under this plan, young offenders would not be sent to prison, except in cases of 'very serious crime', but would, if probation had failed, receive a provisional Borstal sentence, being sent to a special Borstal for a few months, from which they would be released on long licence. If they failed on licence, they would be recalled and sent to an ordinary Borstal for the full period of training. The plan of abolishing imprisonment for offenders under twenty-one was undoubtedly Paterson's brain-child. He urged that it be advocated 'in and particularly out of season'; and he disabused Waller of the idea that Home Secretary Henderson disliked the scheme. The inspectors of

[27] Ann. Rep. of P. Com. for 1923–4, PP 1924–5, XV (Cmd. 2307), p. 350.

[28] P. Com. 7/597; HO45/20947/448767/11. Henderson, an elder statesman of the Labour party, was Home Secretary in the first Labour government.

prisons, Lieut.-Col. Knox and Major Lamb, agreed generally with the scheme, but J. R. Farewell doubted whether it would work to plan, as a result of which 'we should find Courts committing too many uncontrolled lads, whose parents & others should control them first before submitting them to the doubtful & drastic step of a long detention in an Institution on Borstal lines'. The project ran into more concerted opposition in the Home Office in the person of H. B. Simpson, an experienced if eccentric assistant secretary. For Simpson, a sentence of imprisonment was not useless merely because it was unlikely to have a good effect on the prisoner. There were offences not amounting to 'very serious crime', such as indecent exposure or indecent assault, which ought to be punished, even when committed by young adults. Simpson argued, finally, that a detailed inquiry of young prisoners should be made before the abolition of imprisonment was accepted.[29]

In fact, Simpson and Knox were delegated to examine all convicted prisoners under twenty-one in Bedford and Wandsworth prisons. Simpson later reported that, in his view, the courts had done as well as anybody could have done; that there were some lads who 'might certainly have been dealt with otherwise than by imprisonment; others who certainly could not'. The courts, moreover, would be 'terribly embarrassed in enforcing the law, if they were not allowed to sentence anyone under twenty-one to prison except for a serious offence'.[30]

Meanwhile, the prison commissioners were assessing two possible improvements. The first concerned an extension of the system of collecting centres. An advance had been made in March 1924 by transferring young prisoners with sentences of three months (in addition to those with *over* three months) to the collecting centres. Could further advance be made by collecting lads with *less* than three months? Waller considered this 'a poor proposal', but at least 'it would be doing something'. His colleagues disagreed. Mr Farewell of the prison inspectorate thought it would be an expensive venture, with little improvement in treatment as discount. He preferred sending youths to a 'place of detention', where the regime would consist of 'one continuous hustle of drill & lessons all day.' Paterson was blunter: 'I fear this wd. result in a coat of whitewash even thinner than that which covers the 4 collecting centres.'

[29] HO45/20947/448767/11; P. Com. 7/597.

[30] Ibid. See also *Report of Young Offenders Committee*, op. cit., *Evidence*, qq. 11349–54 (p. 1294) (Simpson).

The second potential reform had to do with Wandsworth boys' prison, which was used, *inter alia*, for those sentenced to imprisonment in the London area. According to Waller, the boys' prison was 'a gloomy and somewhat undesirable place', in which separation from adult prisoners was by no means complete. Hence Waller wanted another establishment in the London area, although he realized that any building 'which was sufficiently central would probably be both unsuitable and very costly'. Inspectors Knox and Lamb agreed that a separate establishment should be arranged for the London area, if only because of the congestion in Wandsworth and the paucity of useful employment for such large numbers.[31] Again, therefore, no change was forthcoming.

By the mid-1920s, then, some progress had been made in the establishment and extension of young prisoners classes in the collecting depots, in an attempt to provide a special training regime for those offenders who were not sent to Borstal. This was secondary, however, to the main policy aim, championed by penal reformers and the Prison Commission alike, to end the imprisonment of young offenders, except in cases of serious crime. Already, the Prison Commission had the blueprint of an integrated scheme, consisting in the main of an extension of the Borstal system, with a provisional as well as a full sentence of Borstal training. Another sign of advance was the decline since 1914 in the number of young offenders sent to prison, in part because of changes in sentencing practice, in part because of the fall in the incidence of indictable crime. Yet still, in 1926, no fewer than 2,464 lads and 178 girls between sixteen and twenty-one were sent to prison, either on direct committal or in default of paying a fine. Roughly half this number had not been previously convicted. As such, there remained room for improvement.

At this juncture, the Young Offenders Committee began to take evidence. Without question, the reformers expected the final report to endorse the policy of abolishing prison for adolescents. As Henriques wrote in his diary, following a discussion with Paterson and Mrs Le Mesurier: 'Alex thought that the Departmental Committee . . . would propose that there would be no short sentences for people under 21, but that either probation or Borstal should be the only two sentences.'[32]

[31] P. Com. 7/597.
[32] L. L. Loewe, *Basil Henriques. A Portrait* (1976), p. 72.

The departmental committee were impressed by the unanimity with which prison governors, chaplains, medical officers and voluntary prison workers condemned the policy of sending young people to prison. The committee declined, however, to recommend the abolition of imprisonment. They stated that there were 'strong objections to the imprisonment of young offenders between 17 and 21, and it should be replaced as far as possible by probation or Borstal'. Courts which still found it necessary to pass a prison sentence 'should give a certificate that the offender cannot properly be dealt with except by this course'. This put an unjustified faith in the courts.[33]

At a conference to discuss the committee's proposals, convened by the Howard League, a resolution was carried regretting that no alternative method, other than probation or Borstal, had been suggested. Mrs Rackham, in moving the resolution, looked for a greater variety of institutional treatment, especially a short-term institution. Mrs Le Mesurier had her reservations, but she also believed that few prison sentences would be passed if magistrates had to state that a boy 'was unfitted to profit either by probation or Borstal'. The Home Secretary took a similarly optimistic approach, urging all courts in July 1928 to avoid committing young offenders to prison if an alternative method of treatment could properly be adopted.[34]

The subsequent decline in the number of young offenders imprisoned suggested that the courts were responding positively to this executive exhortation. Yet, as the prison commissioners recorded in the late 1920s, courts continued to sentence to imprisonment, lads with numerous previous convictions 'though they seem obviously of the type for whom Parliament intended Borstal Detention'. Some magistrates also still took the view that young prisoners classes 'lessened the objections to prison sentences . . . and that if substantial sentences are imposed young persons will receive some modified form of Borstal treatment'.[35] Such sentencing behaviour (along with the rise in the crime rate from 1929) meant that by 1931 there were still 342 offenders between sixteen and twenty-one serving sentences of imprisonment, 273 of whom were in the seven collecting centres, with

[33] *Report of YOC*, op. cit., pp. 1039 and 1083; *Evidence*, q. 2712 (p. 348) (Henriques); qq. 20212 (p. 2273), 20257 (p. 2278) (Landers); q. 7652 (p. 889) (N. R. Hilton). See also Le Mesurier, op. cit., pp. 261–3; Wallace Blake, *Quod* (1928), p. 81.

[34] *The Treatment of Young Offenders.* Being the Report of a Representative Conference, convened by the Howard League, 27 Oct. 1927 (1928), pp. 11–17.

[35] Ann. Rep. of P. Com. for 1927, PP 1928–29, IX (Cmd. 3292), pp. 329–31; Ann. Rep. for 1928, PP 1929–30, XVII (Cmd. 3607), pp. 296–8.

the remaining sixty-nine scattered amongst nineteen local prisons. The figures indicate that the new spirit embodied in the official circular of 1928 had failed to infuse sufficient of the summary courts.[36] Any decided improvement, it seemed, required legislation prohibiting the imprisonment of all young offenders.

If the number of young offenders sent to prison either on remand, in default of a fine, or on conviction, diminished in comparison with the pre-war years, a sizeable group of adolescents, at a particularly impressionable stage of life, was still becoming familiarized with prison life each year during the 1920s. This occurred despite the fact that a wide cross-section of public, press, parliamentary, and departmental opinion was openly critical of the continued use of imprisonment for young adult offenders. The failure of this broad-based 'campaign' to stem significantly the flow of young criminals into the local prisons seems to have been caused mainly by the unresponsiveness of the courts to executive entreaties to restrict the use of imprisonment. In addition, the view died hard within judicial and departmental circles that some young offenders required punishment, not rehabilitation, as did the judgement that imprisonment was the only effective sanction in cases of fine default. A final reason for the continued resort to imprisonment, however, was the shortage of alternative methods available to the courts. Investigation centres for all remands were not yet instituted. Following conviction, the only custodial alternative to imprisonment was the Borstal training sentence, the length and legal provisions of which kept courts from using it liberally. The Borstal system, however, formed the bedrock of the prison commissioners' plan in the 1920s to restrict the use of imprisonment.

The Borstal System under Ruggles-Brise

The Prevention of Crime Act 1908, sanctioned the establishment of Borstal institutions, to which young offenders, convicted on indictment, could be sent for a term of not less than one year nor more than three years' detention 'under penal discipline'. It had to appear to the court that

[36] *Magistrate*, vol. 2 (1931), p. 503; *TES*, 21 Jan. 1928, p. 31. For the Home Office circular of 20 July 1928, see HO45/13403/510865/23. For the rise in the crime rate, see Table 8 and Fig. 2.

by reason of [the offender's] criminal habits or tendencies, or association with persons of bad character, it is expedient that he should be subject to detention for such term and under such instruction and discipline as appears most conducive to his reformation and the repression of crime.[37]

Length of detention was to depend, within the limits of the Borstal sentence, on the offender's response to training; on release, the offender was to be subject to supervision and, in the event of misbehaviour, liable to recall. Important changes were made by sections 10 and 11 of the Criminal Justice Administration Act 1914.[38] The Act raised the minimum period of detention to two years, and removed the condition that the offence had to be indictable. Now magistrates' courts, instead of passing sentence, could commit offenders to prison until the next quarter sessions, where they were convicted summarily of an offence for which the court had power to impose a prison sentence of one month or more. The court of quarter sessions had the power to sentence to Borstal detention.

The Borstal experiment was an essential part of the policy of introducing special measures for particular classes of offenders as recommended by the Departmental Committee on Prisons (Gladstone Committee) of 1894. Its introduction owed most, however, to Ruggles-Brise, Chairman of the Prison Commission.[39] But if Ruggles-Brise inspired the institution of the Borstal system, equally he resisted its further development. The emphasis of this section, therefore, is on the source and content of the growing indictment of Borstal training under Ruggles-Brise, and on the new lines of policy which were being demanded.

The most important pressure group was the Borstal Association, a quasi-official body with responsibility for supervising persons discharged from Borstals. Its director and treasurer was Wemyss Grant-Wilson, a barrister and director of a boys' club; he was aided by a non-official executive committee. The association was well-informed about

[37] 8 Edw. VII, c. 59, s. 1.

[38] 4 and 5 Geo. V, c. 58.

[39] See R. G. Hood, op. cit., pp. 14–16; Gordon Rose, *The Struggle for Penal Reform* (1961), p. 77; E. Ruggles-Brise, *The English Prison System* (1921), pp. 85–91. Sir Evelyn Ruggles-Brise was Chairman of the Prison Commission from 1895 to 1921. He was educated at Eton and Oxford, where he took a first in *Literae Humaniores*; he entered the Home Office by open competition in 1881. From 1884 to 1892, he was Private Secretary to four successive Home Secretaries: *DNB, 1931–40* (1949), p. 757; *The Times*, 20 Aug. 1935, p. 14.

the administration of the Borstals, since its representatives visited the institutions to interview inmates due for discharge and supervised them on release. During the war and particularly following it, the Borstal Association used this information to force the Prison Commission into developing the institutions.

In July 1917, the Borstal Association sent a resolution to the prison commissioners, stating that the present system of training and education differed radically from the principles laid down for Borstal institutions by Mr McKenna. What the association had in mind, most likely, was McKenna's 1914 statement that Borstals would be 'more and more removed from anything in the nature of a prison and become more and more purely reformative and training institutions'.[40] Shortly afterwards, the association sent a list of suggestions to the Prison Commission, the most important of which were the avoidance of prison methods (such as the use of handcuffs and chains to transport lads by train to the Borstals); a staff with experience of work amongst young people; a full working day to allow inmates to form the habit of industry; and earlier release on licence where appropriate.

Ruggles-Brise was clearly embarrassed that this attack on the administration of the Borstal system came, as he put it, 'from a body for whose policy and action I am, as Vice President of the Association, at least theoretically responsible'.[41] He was also disappointed that the association had chosen the mode of an official communication, instead of by word of mouth. Even so, he tried to respond constructively to the association's proposals. What emerges from Ruggles-Brise's letter, however, is his distinct view of the type of boy for which Borstals were instituted, from which flowed the essential features of the training regime.

Borstal detention, according to the chairman of the Prison Commission, was designed to deal with a difficult class of young criminal, previously dealt with in the convict prisons. As he told the Borstal Association, his championship of the Borstal system had been influenced by what he had seen in the convict prisons:

> I was struck ... by the number of young convicts whom I found there, and my researches into the history of the older convicts revealed the fact that most of

[40] Borstal Association, *Minutes*, 31 July 1917; PRO, P. Com. 7/541; *Hansard*, vol. 61, 15 April 1914, col. 198. McKenna was Liberal Home Secretary prior to the outbreak of war.

[41] P. Com. 7/541; BA, *Minutes*, 17 Jan. 1918. See also J. W. Gordon, *Borstalians* (1932), p. 80.

them owed a life of crime to the fact that they had been sent to penal servitude in their early years. It was to meet this great evil, and to find an alternative to penal servitude for the dangerous criminal between 16 and 21 that we started the Borstal System.[42]

The character and criminal tendency of Borstal lads thus necessitated a primarily penal establishment, one based on strict discipline, obedience, and uniform treatment. By a system of external controls, resembling that which regulated the army, youths would be made to conform to the demands of industrial society. Finally, Ruggles-Brise warned that reforms to the system which reflected the improved inmate population of the war years, could be counter-productive when the severer forms of adolescent crime returned.

The chairman's reply only convinced the Borstal Association of the former's incapacity to take the system on to a new plateau of achievement. Hence, the association renewed their campaign in the post-war years, pressing particularly for two improvements: a better class of men for the positions of officer and instructor, akin more to reformatory school staff than to prison warders; and better industrial training, such as would fit the lads for outside employment. In this they were joined by the visiting committee of the institution at Borstal, which also pressed for the halls to be made into houses, with housemasters, along public school lines. This, it was claimed, 'would make it possible to judge more closely the progress in reformation of every inmate and to give more individual attention to those who needed it'.[43]

At last, the pressure paid off. In 1920 the Prison Commission introduced some changes, particularly to the establishment at Borstal. The governor, Lieut.-Col. Charles Rich, was told that domestic work was to be reduced to a minimum, and that a systematic course of industrial training was to be introduced along the lines of the pre-war plan. In April the institution was organized into wings, with tutors acting as wing commanders: an important stage in the development of the 'house system'. A new system of grades for the boys to progress through was also initiated, with more freedom from supervision for those in the superior grades. These changes were eventually applied to Feltham Borstal.[44]

[42] Ibid. See also Ruggles-Brise, op. cit., p. 92.
[43] BA, *Minutes*, 6 Nov. 1919; P. Com. 7/521.
[44] Ibid; Ruggles-Brise, op. cit., p. 98.

But the improvements did little to still the critical voice of the Borstal Association. Having learnt that Ruggles-Brise proposed discussing Borstal affairs with all the governors, the association offered further suggestions on the subject of work training. Inmates, they declared, 'work shorter hours than their fathers outside and naturally come out slacker in that important habit of work than they went in'. The association wanted an eight-hour working day, on the grounds that '[t]he Institutions must be primarily Industrial Training places and unless they are so we cannot hope for good results'.[45] At the same time, members of the Executive Committee were submitting reports on what they had seen on their visits to the institutions, extracts from which were put before the chairman of the Prison Commission. In March 1921, Mrs Higgs and Mrs Russell visited the institution at Borstal. Both were disappointed at the prison character of the place, with boys massed into prison-like buildings. They were also concerned at the number of mentally defective boys, for whom a special institution was required, and at the deficiencies of work training. As Mrs Higgs reported: 'the workshops seem too much occupied in repairs for the Institution and too ill-equipped to serve the purpose of Trade Schools'. Mrs Russell concluded that McKenna's assurances that Borstals would become purely training institutions had not been conformed to: 'Indeed, the Governor in my presence told Sir Wemyss Grant-Wilson that Dr. Norris and others who expect to find anything in the nature of a Reformatory altogether fail to understand the situation.'[46] The reports were capped by another resolution to the Prison Commission, recommending the appointment of a special Borstal commissioner. This idea came from one member of the executive committee of the Borstal Association, who had declared: 'it is no one's job to think out what a B. I. should be'. His name was Alexander Paterson.

In short, the Borstal Association was a thorn in the side of the Prison Commission during the final years of Ruggles-Brise's chairmanship. During the post-war years, particularly, the association impatiently pressed for the growth of the Borstal training system away from the 'prison' methods of its origin. It drew its inspiration from a view of Borstal boys as spirited lads, not inveterate hooligans, or, more generally, from the principles and practice of the child welfare

[45] BA, *Minutes*, Dec. 1920.

[46] Ibid., 8 Apr. 1921. Mrs Russell was the wife of the late inspector of reformatory schools; Mrs Higgs was an authority on vagrancy.

movement. The association was, after all, one limb of the charitable social work movement, and many of its executive committee were key figures in that movement. For Ruggles-Brise, however, a group who had been essential to the after-care of 'deserving' Borstal boys, had become a collection of hypercritical 'sentimentalists'. They failed, above all, to realize that Borstals were not reformatory schools, but 'places of detention under "penal" discipline of grown lads and young men—many with bad records of crime . . .'[47] Predictably, the long-serving chairman could not see the object of appointing a 'Borstal commissioner'. Instead, Mr Waller, a prison commissioner, took special charge of Borstal institutions.

The Borstal Association was not alone in its critical appraisal of the war and post-war Borstals. In 1919 the Howard Association complained that both offenders whose previous character was 'good' and offenders who were physically and mentally subnormal were, in effect, denied entry to the Borstals. Shortly afterwards, the Indian Jails Committee adjudged the establishment at Borstal to be too akin to a prison and, at 450 inmates, too far above the ideal figure of 200 per institution. The committee concluded that it remained questionable whether the Borstals 'are to be developed on the lines of a reformatory or of a penal institution . . .' In 1921 the chairman of the Portland magistrates told the *Daily News* that Borstals should be educational in purpose, staffed by 'the type of teacher who is called to train lads in the roughest parts of the East End of London'.[48] By the early 1920s, then, a substantial indictment had been drawn against the Borstal system by a number of unofficial and semi-official hands. Ruggles-Brise still countered, in *The English Prison System* (1921)—his assertive appreciation of the advances in penal policy since the report of the Gladstone committee—that the Borstal system achieved, in the majority of cases, 'the conversion of the inveterate gaol-bird of a few years ago to a strong, well-set-up, well-drilled, handy English lad, with respect for authority, with a new birthright, qualifying him to enter the ranks of honest, industrious labour'. Yet even Ruggles-Brise saw the writing on the wall. In June 1921, he wrote to Grant-Wilson, offering his services to the Borstal Association after retirement, not wishing to sever all

[47] HO45/11898/332404/29.

[48] *The Times*, 22 Oct. 1919, p. 8; *Report of the Indian Jails Committee*, PP 1921, X (Cmd. 1303), p. 851, Appendix IX. Mr Mitchell-Innes, an inspector of English prisons, was a committee member. For *Daily News*, 14 Nov. 1921, see Hobhouse and Brockway, op. cit., p. 422.

connection with the Borstal system, concluding: 'I understand that great changes are pending when I go—I do not know who will be my successor.'[49]

The next chairman of the Prison Commission was Maurice Waller, private secretary to the Liberal Home Secretary, Herbert Gladstone, from 1906 to 1910, before joining the Prison Commission. Waller proved to be a gifted administrator with a good eye for detail, yet equally able to retain a sense of what the penal system might become. Above all, he was instrumental in bringing criticism and experiment to bear upon the routine of the existing penal system.[50] Some of these qualities were instantly required, as a result of a rather fiery baptism. In February 1921, Ruggles-Brise had secured Home Office agreement to convert Portland convict prison into a Borstal institution for males, to relieve the congestion in Borstal and Feltham.[51] Transferred to Portland were those difficult lads who had been in the army, at sea, or in a reformatory, and thus away from home influences prior to reception. The Portland buildings were hardly suitable for Borstal purposes; about one-third of the staff was drawn from former warders of the prison, with no experience of Borstal work. Whether for these reasons or for others, within a few months of the opening, one boy committed suicide, another attempted the same, and a succession of escape attempts occurred.[52]

These incidents were seized upon by the *Howard Journal* as indicative of the need for a committee of inquiry into the penal arrangements for young adult prisoners. In parliament and in the press, a full and preferably independent inquiry into the 'Portland scandal' was called for. The Borstal Association complained that press criticism was undermining the confidence of associates and magistrates in the Borstal system, and trusted that 'a plain statement of the case admitting defects and promising more resolute progress' would be issued.[53] Following visits to Portland by the Medical Inspector of Prisons and

[49] BA, *Minutes*, 7 July 1921; Ruggles-Brise, op. cit., p. 99.

[50] Sir Maurice Waller was Chairman of the Prison Commission from 1921 to 1928. He was educated at Rugby and Oxford, where he took a first in Lit. Hum. He was a Prison Commissioner from 1910: *The Times*, 7 July 1928; *Who Was Who 1929–40*, p. 1407; Waller to Ruggles-Brise, 29 July 1928, Borstal Association documents.

[51] The congestion was caused, in part, by boys being kept longer in the institutions. This, in turn, was due to the poor state of the labour market and to the attempt to return to pre-war patterns. Portland was available for conversion because of the fall in the convict population.

[52] HO45/16953/415065/1–2; *Hansard*, vol. 147, 27 Oct. 1921, col. 1070.

[53] *Howard Journal*, vol. 1 (1921), p. 45; BA, *Minutes*, 21 Nov. 1921.

the Home Secretary, the department put a brave face on the affair, insisting that Portland was suitable, despite its prison associations. Waller did, however, announce that more trained Borstal officers were to be sent to Portland. In addition, the Home Secretary asked Clarke Hall to visit the troubled institution and submit a summary of his impressions. Clarke Hall was particularly critical of the boys' dress ('practically that of convicts'), of the work ('essentially penal'), and of the large number of uniformed warders in the workshops. Overall, he felt that conditions were still too close to those of a convict prison. The aim, he said, should be not simply a 'modification' of the penal system, but one designed to effect the object in view: in other words, to establish reformatories for an older age group; not to adapt prisons for a younger age group.[54]

In large part, these suggestions represented what the prison commissioners were starting to aim at. But the Portland incident, by opening up the Borstals to public scrutiny, encouraged the penal reform lobby to press their case again. The Borstal Association appealed for particular improvements such as a 'sorting depot' to do the job of classification, a longer working day, and an 'Advisory Trades' Board' to examine the methods of work instruction. They also sought greater overall direction of the Borstal system, in order to create institutions 'sufficiently different from prisons to render justifiable the long sentences to Borstal Treatment which are given as an alternative to short sentences of imprisonment'. Once more, therefore, they urged that a commissioner with 'experience of work amongst people of the labouring class' ought to devote his entire time to the Borstals.[55]

The Borstal Association was quickly rewarded with a trades advisory board and an increase in the number of tutors. More crucially, moves were afoot around October 1921 to make a temporary appointment to the Prison Commission of a person with experience of adolescents. It did not prove easy to find the right man, but in February 1922 Alexander Paterson, thirty-seven years old, an acknowledged expert on

[54] HO45/16953/415065/18; P. Com. 7/542; *Hansard*, vol. 148, 8 Nov. 1921, col. 200; vol. 150, 14 Feb. 1922, col. 821. Sir Arthur Conan Doyle was also asked to visit Rochester Borstal. He was impressed by what he saw, though he felt that the warders should be joined by young university men 'of the type who man the hostels and settlements in the slums', to whom the boys would respond: HO45/11898/332404/45; *Daily Telegraph*, 27 Dec. 1921.

[55] BA, *Minutes*, 21 Nov. 1921.

youth welfare, was made a prison commissioner for one year.[56] His credentials were impeccable. From 1906 he was a resident of Bermondsey, in charge of boys' and mens' clubs and camps, from which hailed his study, *Across the Bridges, or Life by the South London River-Side* (1911). At the same time, he helped Herbert Samuel with the Children Act of 1908, served as honorary probation officer at Tower Bridge police court, acted as unpaid teacher for a year in a local elementary school, and lectured occasionally at the London School of Economics. For many years he also acted as an associate of the Borstal Association, frequently visiting the institutions, and supervising Borstal boys returning to Bermondsey. Between 1910 and 1914, as assistant director of the Central Association for the Aid of Discharged Prisoners, he visited every convict prison monthly. Alongside all this went a distinguished war record (joining the army as a private, in preference to taking a commission), and the start of a lifelong association with Toc H, the society for Christian fellowship and social service.

In the immediate post-war period, Paterson served as a principal officer at the Ministry of Labour where he worked with the Juvenile Advisory Committees, finding employment for adolescent boys. His chief at the ministry, Sir James Masterman-Smith, later wrote a glowing testimonial on Paterson's behalf 'as a man of exceptional capacity and character': 'He is industrious, he writes excellent memoranda and letters, and he has a peculiarly attractive and lucid exposition of his subject whether on a platform or in the Office.'[57] This administrative experience aside, Paterson was an unconventional candidate for high government office. He offered wide experience of working-class life and a passionate interest in voluntary social work. W. McG. Eagar, a prominent figure in the boys' club movement, has claimed that Paterson was anxious to become a prison commissioner and asked Lloyd-George to use his influence to this end. Be that as it may, the recruitment of someone from outside the Home Office or the

[56] For the following biographical details, see *DNB, 1941–50*, p. 658; *The Times*, 19 Nov. 1947, p. 6; Gordon Hawkins, *Alec Paterson. An Appreciation* (privately published); Barclay Baron, 'Across the Bridges', *Toc H Journal*, Jan. 1948; items from Maxwell collection. See also note 9 to ch. 1. Paterson was born 20 Nov. 1884 at Bowden, Cheshire, the youngest child of a Manchester solicitor. Originally a Unitarian, Paterson joined the Church of England while at Oxford, where he took a third class honours degree in 'Greats'.

[57] HO45/21687/446037/1.

prison service depended on the strong support of Waller himself, eager to breathe new life into the Borstal system. Paterson's appointment was universally well received, the *Manchester Guardian* surmising that the problems at Portland accounted for it.[58]

The new appointment was to prove an inspired choice. From the early days in Bermondsey and from the association with Toc H, Paterson had developed keen human sympathies, spiritual purpose, and a philanthropist's zeal to serve those in need. Alongside this earnest devotion went a puckish humour, a capacity for enjoyment, and an indifference to many conventional values. His greatest talent, perhaps, as Alexander Maxwell declared in 1946, was 'a unique power of getting his ideals translated into practical form'.[59] Paterson was to recruit most of the really effective workers in the prison service during the inter-war years, whom he then inspired with his idealism and his zest for improvement. 'He was the most unorthodox of civil servants,' according to Sir Harold Scott, 'but I found him stimulating and always easy to work with. He had a quick grasp of what was possible and never let the best be the enemy of the good.'[60] However, he had little interest in the mechanics of administration. Paterson relied heavily on colleagues (some of whom had been war-time comrades) both in the Prison Commission and in the actual institutions to translate his creative ideas into the small change of rules, regulations and regimes. No one was more important than the chairman, Waller, who, until his retirement in 1927, gave Paterson almost free rein to develop the Borstal system.

Paterson contributed to the critique of the Borstal system under Ruggles-Brise, in his capacity as member of the executive committee of the Borstal Association. A more exhaustive appraisal appeared in a chapter of Hobhouse and Brockway's report for the Prison System Enquiry Committee, *English Prisons To-Day*, which was written most probably by Paterson, just prior to his appointment to the Prison Commission. At the least, according to Brockway, Paterson 'certainly had long discussions with my joint secretary Stephen Hobhouse, and

[58] For a highly critical appraisal, see W. McG. Eagar to Barclay Baron, 15 Feb. 1957, in Paterson papers. Paterson liked the adulation of young men, and it is generally accepted that he was homosexual.

[59] HO45/21687/446037/8.

[60] Recollections of Harold Scott in Paterson papers.

encouraged the expression of the opinions which were in our book'.[61] The chapter thus represents Paterson's personal indictment of the existing Borstal system, and points the way to the changes in policy which he desired. Heading the list of defects was the statement that the institutions were still too overshadowed by the 'penal element'. More specifically, the establishment at Borstal was too large for 'personal influence and direct human contact' to exist. Institutions ought to be limited to 200 inmates, divided into four 'houses' of fifty inmates each. The industrial training remained inadequate: the period of detention was too short to teach a trade, the machinery, materials, and instructors insufficient to take advantage of the time that was available. Borstal was 'a colony where incompetent young workers supply as best they can, under competent direction, the needs of the institution, largely irrespective of their own needs'. The report was also critical of the progressive grades system, with the special grade the reward for 'exemplary institutional behaviour', not for initiative and self-reliance. Finally, the dominance of the 'military and disciplinary element', with Borstal warders still essentially drawn from the prisons, was anathema to the educative principle of treatment. This was the telling verdict: 'It is self-discipline that the Borstal boy needs most, and the army (and prison) system of mechanical obedience entirely fails to engender it.'[62]

Thus Paterson signposted the way forward before taking charge of the Borstal institutions. Rigid, para-military establishments were to make way for essentially educational institutions. Penal discipline, imposing conformity by external force, was to be replaced by self-discipline and a standard of social behaviour that would endure after release. The route to be taken was deeply influenced by Paterson's long standing connection with the Borstal Association. In his letter of resignation from this body, following his appointment to the Prison Commission, Paterson wrote, 'I shall do my best to fulfil our common aim—and if in any measure I succeed, it will surely be because I have shared so many ideas and experiences with you . . . '[63] The origins and outline of this new policy, how and to what extent the policy was implemented, are the subjects of the next chapter.

[61] Personal communication from Lord Brockway, Jan. 1982. The enquiry committee had been set up in 1919 by the Labour Party Research Department. Members included Sydney Oliver, Sidney and Beatrice Webb, George Bernard Shaw, Margery Fry and Paterson.

[62] Hobhouse and Brockway, op. cit., p. 421.

[63] Paterson to BA, 19 April 1922 in BA, *Minutes*.

8

The Paterson Era

The natural starting-point for a statement of the cardinal aims and ideals of the inter-war Borstal system is the set of three articles which Paterson wrote for *The Times* in August 1925. The substance of these articles went almost verbatim into the initial sections of a booklet, *The Principles of the Borstal System*, which the Prison Commission had printed in 1928.[1] Characteristically, the first article began with a description of 'street-corner society . . . the soil from which spring the great majority of young criminals'. Unemployment, poor housing, bad company, and harmful amusements were singled out for critical reference. Not that Paterson saw delinquency as strictly environmentally-determined. He also stressed the lack of self-control on the part of young offenders.

> Their condition results from a weakness of inhibition arising from lack of early training at home, contrasted with a desire for those things they have neither the patience nor the opportunity to earn, and emphasized by surroundings which do not exercise their vitality or give any scope for their capacity.[2]

In a word, few lads were predestined to a life of crime; rather, they drifted into delinquency for want of any power of self-control or any guiding principle of life. Paterson's approach was based on the liberal doctrine of non-determinism. The delinquent was essentially responsible for his actions; he simply acted irresponsibly through lack of will-power. How then to teach this self-control; to give boys the capacity to withstand the environment to which they were to return?

One thing was clear. Delinquents were to be neither beaten nor moulded into shape, methods that relied on 'the imposition of authority from without, a use of force which may easily provide a reaction more anti-social than the original condition'. Paterson embraced a different mode of training, one which discarded mass

[1] The second revised edition of *The Principles of the Borstal System* (1932) was known as 'The Grey Book': G. Hawkins, op. cit., p. 28; P. Com. 7/523.

[2] *The Principles* (1932), p. 6; *The Times*, 4 Aug. 1925.

treatment of a supposedly uniform criminal type, depending instead on the principle of individualization. The method was explained as follows:

> to treat a lad as a living organism with a life and soul of his own, and to stimulate some power within to regulate conduct aright. It then becomes necessary to study the individual lad, to discover his trend and his possibility, and to infect him with some idea of life which will germinate and produce a character, controlling desire, and shaping conduct to some more glorious end than mere satisfaction or acquisition.[3]

The task of moral training—building on the goodness that resided in each boy—was to be achieved in the Borstal institutions by the daily employment of two main forces: one, 'the personal influence of the members of the staff upon the boys'; and two, 'the public opinion of the lads themselves'. For this, in turn, the setting of the small group or house was required.

The House System

Each of the three boys' institutions was split into houses, four each at Borstal and Feltham and three at Portland. Each house, with its own buildings and staff, ideally held no more than seventy lads, who were, in turn, divided into smaller 'sections' of ten to fourteen boys. The object of the house plan was threefold: to increase the level of individualization in treatment, to make it possible for boys to exercise a small degree of responsibility in the role of house monitor, and to arouse the lads' 'innate corporate spirit which will respond to the appeal made . . . to play the game, to follow the flag, to stand by the old ship'. In short, said Paterson, the division into smaller groups 'releases the two great weapons of moral training—personal influence and the corporate spirit'. The Borstal boy

> becomes proud of his House. He can be induced sometimes so to change his habits as to conform with its traditions. The Housemaster and his staff set a standard, the boys catch the spirit, and on it rolls to successive generations . . .[4]

Not surprisingly, many have considered that the life of the Borstal institutions, with their housemasters and house-matches, was modelled

[3] *Principles*, p. 14; *The Times*, 5 Aug. 1925.

[4] Ibid., pp. 8–9; *The Times*, 4 Aug. 1925. For official circular, 18 Dec. 1922, on the introduction of the house system, see BA, *Minutes*, 18 Jan. 1923.

on the practice of the public schools. Some have gone further, and accused the house system of attempting to transfer public-school values to working-class youth.[5] Of course, there is some validity in all this. But the analogy with public schools should not be pressed too far. Both Waller and Paterson were alive to the differences between these two institutions, and particularly to the difficulties of maintaining a general tone of decency within the Borstals. Paterson also insisted that

> [o]f all the catch-words which have conspired to misconstrue the system of Borstal Institutions, perhaps the suggestion that they are modelled on public schools is one of the most mischievous: it suggests the old delusion that esprit-de-corps was invented by, and in a peculiar sense belongs to, the English Public School.

Corporate spirit, Paterson argued, was not the exclusive property of the public school; there was a proletarian moral equivalent to the public school ethos:

> . . . no Club could keep its doors open for a week, however generous its support or perfect its control, without esprit-de-corps: it is at the basis of factory life and it flourishes even at the street corner: it existed during the War just as much with the Tyneside Irish as in the Public Schools' Battalion.[6]

Thus the house system was no 'slavish copy' of the public school, but a recognition that corporate spirit flourished best in the small unit. 'Just as in an ordinary lads' club', said Paterson before the Young Offenders Committee, 'it is very difficult to deal with a number of lads in a mass, and it is found better to divide them into groups or sets, so we have found at Borstal'.[7]

The Staff

By 1921, when Waller took over from Ruggles-Brise, the six tutors (two per male institution) had extended their sphere of action beyond the schoolroom. In effect, they were deputy governors, in charge of a division of the institution, teaching in class, supervising the industrial work, organizing games, and getting to know every lad in their division. They had become, according to the Home Office, 'the key to

[5] Hood, op. cit., p. 110; Stephen Humphries, *Hooligans or Rebels?* (Oxford, 1981), pp. 223–4.

[6] P. Com. 7/540.

[7] *Evidence*, q. 869 (Paterson).

the success or failure' of the Borstal system.[8] With the introduction of the house system, the influence of the tutors or housemasters reached its apex.

Paterson attached supreme importance to the recruitment of the right kind of staff. As he declared in *The Principles of the Borstal System*, 'The Borstal system has no merit apart from the Borstal staff. It is men and not buildings who will change the hearts and ways of misguided lads.'[9] To this end, he invested a lot of time in finding the men who were to be Borstal housemasters, men like R. L. Bradley, Bill Llewellin or H. J. Taylor, using his contacts with the boys' clubs, the public schools, the universities, and Toc H. Many of the early recruits were university trained, but recent graduates were generally advised to 'knock about the world', as Harold Scott recollected.

> On one occasion he told a young man just down from the University: 'You don't know enough of life to be any use to us at present. Go away and get to know the world for a year or two . . . and when you return, if you still want to enter the Borstal service, come back and tell me.' The young man took him at his word and shipped before the mast. After a year or two he came back, was accepted and made a very useful Housemaster . . . [10]

Recruits were drawn from a wide variety of occupational backgrounds. Of the twelve assistant housemasters in 1928, four were promoted prison officers, two had been elementary school teachers, one had served in the merchant service, one had been on the staff of a reformatory school, and two others had experience of voluntary work with boys' clubs and the Scouts. Six of them were young men between twenty-three and twenty-six years of age. It was rare for housemasters to be trained social workers, but some went off to do the Diploma in Social Work at London University. Above all, however, Paterson looked for breadth of experience, a high standard of honour, an ability to communicate with young people, enthusiasm, and an imaginative individuality (which in some cases verged on idiosyncracy).[11]

This was Paterson's raw material on which he set to work. 'No one could be with him', said Harold Scott, 'and not catch the fire of his

[8] HO45/11898/332404/46.

[9] *Principles*, op. cit., p. 20.

[10] Recollections of Sir Harold Scott, op. cit. Interviews with Tom Hayes and H. J. Taylor. For Llewellin, see section 'Lowdham Grange' in ch. 9; for Scott, see section 'North Sea Camp' in ch. 9.

[11] See HO45/16224/512613/13; *Evidence*, q. 862 (Paterson); *Hansard*, vol. 241, 23 July 1930, col. 2176.

enthusiasm.'[12] He was often to be found in the institutions, encouraging disciplinary officers and housemasters to work together within the house plan. 'We are as one body of colleagues', insisted Paterson, 'intolerant of division by caste or income.' He persuaded the disciplinary staff to throw off their uniforms in favour of *mufti*. For all the staff, he set extremely demanding standards. The Borstal officer was expected to think and act as a man who had found his true vocation. 'He receives a living wage', said Paterson, 'but his real reward is in the nature of his work: promotion may seem desperately remote, but the measure of his success is the progress of his lads.'[13]

The essentials of the housemaster's job were also spelt out by Paterson. First, the staff needed to exercise discipline, not by the weight of authority, but by 'a control, human and full of understanding'. The Borstal officer ought to treat the boys not as young criminals, but 'as he would treat working lads in a rough club outside'. Secondly, the staff had to try 'to arouse the right forces in the lad', bringing out the good in each boy by way of both personal example and the corporate spirit of the other inmates. Creating a good house spirit was the key contribution of the housemaster and his colleagues. This would be achieved 'by the careful selection of leaders, by training them and standing very close to them, by being always in and out of the house, by thinking of it as their family, by being there for meals and recreation because they do not want to leave it'.[14] Demanding standards, indeed, yet Paterson's level of commitment proved infectious. Very soon the new housemasters, and even the chief officers, were suggesting ways of improving the effectiveness of Borstal training.[15]

The Training Scheme

The house system was meant to facilitate individualization, to make it easier for the staff to assess each boy's responsiveness to the training scheme and his fitness for release. A crucial aid to this assessment was the system of progressive grades, the aim of which was 'to confer, in proportion to the lad's progress, increasing trust and freedom of choice

[12] *Magistrate*, vol. 9 (1951), p. 151.

[13] *Principles*, op. cit., pp. 21–3. See also Hawkins, op. cit., pp. 19, 26–7; BA, *Minutes*, 14 Oct. 1924.

[14] Ibid., pp. 23, 63–4. By 1932, each house had the following staff: housemaster, assistant housemaster, principal officer, two house officers, and a matron.

[15] P. Com. 7/542. The chief officer was the head of the entire discipline staff.

and action, increasing responsibility, and increasing privileges'. The danger was that promotion would become mechanical. Hence, Paterson stressed the need to preserve 'the difficulty of ascent, so that the minimum of promotion may reward a maximum of effort'.[16] Lads in the earlier grades wore a brown uniform; promotion in the 'brown' stages conferred such privileges as increased time for games and recreation. By the start of the second year's training, most lads entered the special grade and wore the blue dress. In the 'blue' stage, lads were given greater freedom of movement about the institution, and in line with Paterson's famous epigram, 'it is impossible to train men for freedom in a condition of captivity', the 'blues' were allowed to join technical classes in a nearby town or to go by themselves to the local church. They were also eligible for the summer camp, 'giving their word of honour to play the game in the freedom of hut and tent'. Starting experimentally in 1923, on the model of the boys' clubs, the week's camp soon became an important element in the training programme.[17]

The Borstal programme consisted of an active fifteen-hour day, starting with physical exercise, continuing with eight hours' work, and finishing with two hours of study. Physical training formed an essential part of the daily routine, as did games and sports. Indeed, a former inmate of Portland considered that physical development was the only tangible benefit of his Borstal sentence. Each institution was also expected to provide eight hours' study each week. Discipline officers and voluntary teachers from outside were encouraged to take evening classes, supplementing the work of the housemasters. One evening a week was set aside for vocational subjects, when the boys were arranged in classes for technical instruction according to their work parties. On the other evenings, boys were divided into classes of twenty to twenty-five in number, according to intelligence. For the backward lads there was elementary education, although the teaching staff were hardly trained for this task. For the small minority of intelligent lads, a more advanced education was provided. For the majority, the emphasis was on hobbies and handicrafts, ranging from wireless, rugmaking, and fretwork to the keeping of rabbits and pigeons.[18]

[16] *Principles*, p. 34.

[17] Ibid., p. 12. See also P. Com. 7/544; Ann. Rep. of P. Com. for year ended 31 March 1923, PP 1923, XII (Cmd. 200), p. 409.

[18] See Mark Benney, *Low Company* (1936), p. 236. Borstal educational conferences and individual Borstal staff contributed to the scheme of education: P. Com. 7/555; P. Com. 7/542.

The object of education, therefore, was to improve the boy's power of concentration and to increase his food for thought. Hence, the more orthodox school subjects were discarded. 'The whole purpose of continued education at a Borstal Institution is not to impart information or to make dullards into scholars', said Paterson, 'but to get rusty and ill-controlled brains to work, to enlarge the sphere of interest, and to discover a point of contact with each lad.' Borstal education should make the lad think and should enrich his life.

To discover and develop a love for music or letters, an interest in flowers or animals or stamps, is to foster the growth of something good, which will occupy the stage of interest in a lad's life and oust the idle and unclean things that formerly held possession.[19]

All this was to be imparted, moreover, by enlightened teaching methods which demanded involvement on the part of the pupils.

This evidence has led to the charge that Paterson used education to prise working-class boys from their indigenous values, in favour of the rudiments of middle-class culture. The indictment is not without substance. The Borstal boy was to be weaned off 'the drivel that once enslaved him' and fed on the solid food of 'good English literature'.[20] But the charge can be sustained only by ignoring the determination on the part of the staff to offer subjects for which the lad showed 'taste and capacity'. A concerted assault on proletarian values would hardly have countenanced pigeon-fancying!

The Borstal system was characterized less by an attempt to inculcate middle-class virtues, and more by a realistic acceptance of the limitations of its young charges. Behind the scepticism about high scholastic standards lay a judgement that the Borstal lad 'is not, as a rule, going to be more than an unskilled labourer who can sign his name and read his newspaper . . .'[21] The same conviction lay behind the scheme of work training. About a half of the inmates were employed in trade parties: in carpentry, metalwork, tailoring, shoemaking, and various building trades. For those who would not benefit

[19] *Principles*, p. 51. cf. Erica Stratta, *The Education of Borstal Boys* (1970), p. 9.

[20] Ibid., p. 54. See Hood, op. cit., pp. 110–11.

[21] Ibid., p. 50. Prior to Borstal, 37 per cent of boys were employed in 'blind alley' jobs (van boys, messenger boys), 13 per cent were general labourers, and another 13 per cent were unemployed, according to Hermann Mannheim's study of 606 Borstal boys discharged between 1922 and 1936. Nearly 50 per cent of these boys were from London and other large cities; the majority were committed for property offences. See *Social Aspects of Crime in England Between the Wars* (1940), pp. 253–6.

by workshop training and for those who intended returning to their trade, hard manual labour (on farm, field, garden, or road-work) was arranged. Finally, all inmates began as 'cleaners', engaged on the domestic work of the institution. In the early 1920s, the Borstal Association criticized the gap between judicial statements that lads sent to Borstal were taught a trade and the actual work training facilities.[22] The point was taken by the Prison Commission, who declared in 1922 that they wished to improve the industrial training and to establish an eight-hour day in the workshops. Machinery for the manufacture of wood and iron was subsequently introduced. This, in turn, led the surveyor of prisons, Lieut.-Col. H. S. Rogers, to press Paterson to put the Borstal shops on a proper footing for industrial purposes, both in respect of teaching and manufacture. A chief instructor was appointed and he succeeded in improving the instruction and output of the workshops. A start was also made with the vocational testing of inmates, to improve the allocation of each inmate to the trade for which he was most suited.[23]

Increasingly, however, the Borstal staff underlined the difficulty of teaching lads to become tradesmen in two years, and fell back on the defence of fitting boys to be unskilled labourers. Dr Methven, governor of Borstal, told the Young Offenders Committee that 50 per cent of the inmates were born labourers, incapable of learning a trade. T. Paterson Owens, governor of Portland, insisted that lads were taught no trade, only the value of hard work and of sticking to a job. Even the most promising lads, receiving instruction in the use of tools and machinery, were simply fitted to take up the position of 'improver'. Whether Alec Paterson ever believed that the Borstals could provide trade training for all inmates, by 1925 he, too, was stressing the need to teach the lads to work an industrious eight-hour day. 'Our task is not so much to teach them any particular efficiency in handling tools', he told the Young Offenders Committee, 'as to try to teach them the habits of industry.' Paterson reiterated this theme frequently. He wrote in the *Principles*:

[22] See BA, *Minutes*, 14 Nov. 1919; J. W. Gordon, op. cit., p. 49; *The Times*, 21 Oct. 1919, p. 5. The Prison Commission was also guilty of fostering the belief that Borstal boys learned a trade.

[23] See P. Com. 7/554; HO45/19688/442964/1–5. Most of the work was done under contracts from government departments; contracts for outside work were resisted by the trade unions. Complaints about Borstal employments were still made, however, by members of the Borstal Association: *Minutes*, 29 May 1924, 13 Jan. 1925, 14 Jan. 1926. Nor were the Borstal staff yet satisfied: P. Com. 7/542; *Evidence*, qq. 19149–52 (Dr Methven).

The great majority of the lads are going out to unskilled labour. Many were born to be hewers of wood and drawers of water, and it is idle to spend the money of the State in seeking to change them into incompetent tradesmen. For them, labouring work, arduous and continuous, is the best preparation for the life that ensues.[24]

In short, the Borstal boy had to be ready to earn his living on discharge in whichever monotonous, ill-paid job the Borstal Association found. Habit, not interest, would have to be the main stimulus to industry for most lads. It was thus essential to prepare the boy for the hard facts of the industrial world. 'Directly or indirectly, week after week it must be borne in upon him that the top of the Borstal ladder is the bottom of the industrial ladder.' Accordingly, every Borstal officer was enjoined 'to preach the gospel of work . . . because it is the condition of honest life'.[25] No less than Ruggles-Brise, albeit through different means, Paterson strove to send out honest, steady workmen, satisfied with their lot, willing to 'play the game' without challenging the rules or the referee.

The training programme reserved an important place, additionally, for religious instruction. Religion, according to the *Principles*, 'touches the deepest springs of human conduct, for it can furnish to the weak and unstable the highest ideals and the sternest inhibitions. It should therefore be awarded the first place among all forms of character training'.[26] Instruction was the job of the chaplains, but Borstal officers were expected to show how their lives were influenced by religious faith.

Discipline

'Where necessary no one could be more insistent on discipline or order than Alexander Paterson.'[27] This was Sir Harold Scott's retort to the accusation that Paterson was soft when it came to anti-social behaviour. Borstal officers were expected to control the lads less by the 'weight of authority' and more by personal influence and group opinion, but when such restraints failed, they were to punish

[24] *Principles*, p. 41; *Evidence*, q. 871 (Paterson); q. 19096 (Methven); q. 18750 (T. Paterson Owens).

[25] Ibid., pp. 32 and 43. Trade unions were never mentioned by Paterson. Clearly, individual, not collective, action was uppermost in his mind.

[26] Ibid., p. 48.

[27] *Magistrate*, vol. 9 (1951), p. 151.

defaulters. Shortly before Paterson's appointment, the Prison Commission asked Borstal governors to reserve the use of dietary punishment with solitary confinement for the most serious offences, and to rely instead on loss of privileges.[28] Difficult characters could also be dealt with by demotion to the penal class, where the lad would spend a gruelling day on bone-crushing or stone-pounding. A former inmate of Portland Borstal recalled the quarry, site of the punishment party, 'where we toiled with picks and shovels and monstrous wheel-barrows doing penal servitude in a Borstal, moving thousands of tons of rock and rubble in freezing weather and howling gales'. If a lad still bucked against efforts to train him, he was transferred to the strenuous regime of the Borstal revokee centre of Wormwood Scrubs prison, in order to remind him 'that the reformers are not soft people, but have power behind their patience'.[29]

Classification

The special block at Wormwood Scrubs was only one of the steps taken by the Prison Commission in the direction of classification, in an attempt to individualize treatment. The most significant step was the reception centre at Wandsworth boys' prison, where offenders were examined before admission to the most suitable Borstal. Paterson's aims in implementing the Wandsworth scheme in 1922 were to expedite the diagnosis of the boys sentenced to Borstal, hence reducing the time spent in prison surroundings, and to use the data for a scientific study of the causes and correctives of delinquency. The medical staff at the boys' prison, assisted by a band of women visitors, investigated the social, physical, and medical characteristics of all boys sentenced to Borstal.[30] For some, the routine at Wandsworth was an improvement on that of an ordinary prison. In contrast, a former Borstal inmate objected to the 'draughty stinking yard where the lads . . . spent their weary waiting days—sitting hunched in the dirt in cold miserable rows, breaking stones into acceptable pieces with a brick hammer'. Even Sydney Moseley, whose *The Truth About Borstal* was highly complimentary, objected to 'the association of this most

[28] HO45/11898/332404/55; *Howard Journal*, vol. 1 (1925), p. 209.

[29] Testimony of R.H.H., inmate of Portland Borstal, 1929–32, seen by courtesy of Prison Service Journal; *The Times*, 6 Aug. 1925.

[30] Ann. Rep. of P. Com. for 1923–4, PP 1924–5, XV (Cmd. 2307), p. 357; P. Com. 7/598; P. Com. 7/176; Le Mesurier, op. cit., p. 94.

repelling-looking prison with Borstal'. Many prominent Borstal officers were also critical. Dr Landers, governor of the boys' prison, and Dr Methven, governor of Borstal, told the Young Offenders Committee that remand homes would be better than Wandsworth for the assessment work. But the Prison Commission managed only to transfer the boys' prison to Wormwood Scrubs.[31] By this time, the overcrowding at the Borstals meant lads were waiting even longer in the boys' prison before transfer to an institution.

Wandsworth's diagnostic work, it was claimed, allowed classification in accordance with an individual's training needs. In fact, allocation was a good deal cruder, the object being simply to separate first offenders and cases of 'mild' criminality (in Feltham) from the relatively 'hardened' lads, with criminal records and previous institutional experience (in Portland). Intermediate cases were sent to the establishment at Borstal. Allocation, as Roger Hood rightly concluded, 'rested more on an assessment of the degree of criminality than on personal "treatment needs" . . . [T]he regimes at the borstals at this time did not differ appreciably enough to make classification by training needs the most important consideration.'[32] The training needs of one particular class of offender, however, were given more attention.

Critics of the Borstal system under Ruggles-Brise often referred to the difficulties posed by lads who were physically and mentally handicapped. Such cases had been committed more freely from 1915, when, in response to the wishes of the courts, the commissioners relaxed the conditions of entry to Borstal institutions. The troubles at Portland in 1921, moreover, were due mainly to the 'temperamental' cases, whose mental condition ranged from impulsive and uncontrolled to certifiable mental deficiency. The commissioners responded in 1922 by sending the handicapped to Feltham; by mid-decade, about one-third of Feltham's intake was mentally or physically inferior.[33] Inevitably, the problem group disrupted the training routine for other Feltham inmates. According to the Borstal Association, the success of the entire Borstal system was hindered by the admission of 'mental borderline cases', who constituted some 10 per cent of the total intake.

[31] Testimony of R.H.H., op. cit.; S. Moseley, *The Truth About Borstal* (1926), p. 41; *Evidence*, p. 2290 (Landers), p. 2171 (Methven); P. Com. 7/517; HO45/15649/430246.

[32] Hood, op. cit., p. 113; *Howard Journal*, vol. 2 (1926), p. 4.

[33] See HO45/11898/332404/46; P. Com. 7/539; S. Barman, *The English Borstal System* (1934), p. 172; L. L. Loewe, op. cit., p. 81.

Clearly, the effective treatment of the unfit required a separate Borstal institution, as Dr Methven and Dr Landers told the Young Offenders Committee. The latter recommended a separate institution for the subnormal lads, but the pressure of numbers forced the Prison Commission to earmark any new institution for a less specialized role.[34]

The Borstal Girl

Borstal training for girls had fallen a long way behind that for boys by 1920. The institution for girls, which housed around 200 girls on average, was sited in the former prison at Aylesbury; its training regime was monotonous and repressive, little different from that of a conventional prison, despite the special physical and emotional problems of delinquent girls.[35] In 1923, therefore, Paterson asked a former colleague in the Ministry of Labour, Lilian Barker, to be governor of Aylesbury Borstal. Miss Barker was a small, square-cut woman, nearing fifty years of age, her hair in a close Eton crop under a pork-pie hat, and nearly always dressed in a severely cut tweed suit. As a former elementary school teacher and lady superintendent of the munitions workers at the Woolwich Arsenal, she was an experienced social and educational worker. To begin with, she investigated the general condition of Aylesbury, reporting that it was heading for trouble, with a disaffected staff and a regimented body of inmates. Then, on condition that she was given a free hand for the first twelve months, she agreed to become governor. Immediately Barker tried to change the regime at Aylesbury. She experimented with self-government, giving the girls increasing responsibility; she urged the staff to treat the girls individually rather than make them conform to a rigid type. She improved the cells, the meals, and the uniform, revised the system of education, and introduced organized games. She also

[34] BA, *Report for 1924*; *Evidence*, qq. 20237–48 (Landers); p. 2179 (Methven); A. Fenner Brockway, *A New Way With Crime* (1928), p. 101.

[35] See Mary Gordon, *Penal Discipline* (1922), pp. 158–60; Ann D. Smith, *Women in Prison* (1962), p. 257; Hobhouse and Brockway, op. cit., pp. 435–9. The average number of girls sentenced each year to Borstal for the five years ended March 1924 was 55. The daily average population for 1920–1 was 191, for 1927, 74, and for 1929, 104: L. W. Fox, *The Modern English Prison* (1934), p. 189. In 1920–1 there was a large increase in the number of punishments recorded at Aylesbury Borstal, leading to press criticism. According to the Prison Commission, many of the incidents involved certified girls who were awaiting transfer to institutions for mental defectives: P. Com. 7/542.

began to release some of the girls on licence at the end of a year. Alas, Miss Barker, too, was heading for trouble.[36]

Between 1923 and 1925, reports from representatives of the Borstal Association revealed some of the difficulties the new governor was facing. There was no doubting the vitality, integrity, and deep humanity of Miss Barker; under her influence, said Mrs Le Mesurier, the Borstal 'was alive—moving, not a valley of dead bones as so many girls' institutions, as contrasted with boys', seem to be'. But the reports disclosed a regime unfitted to the needs of female inmates, many of whom, according to Mrs Higgs, 'bore plain signs of less than normal capacity, either in physique, brainpower or will-power'. Higgs also stated: 'One result of the relaxation of *discipline* consequent on the new atmosphere . . . was a sort of slackness, that is in my opinion remediable, but only by new methods.' In the following year, Gilbert Johnstone complained that there was insufficient hard work and discipline to fit the girls to face working life on release. Additionally, many girls responded defiantly to the governor's reforms by an outburst of 'smashing up'.[37] In consequence, Barker was rapidly 'converted' to firmer discipline, especially since the courts tended to reserve committal for the most troublesome cases. Having formed the opinion that girls ended up in borstal due to bad housing, blind-alley jobs, and poor recreational facilities, Barker now saw her task as the infusion of discipline and order. Her approach to training had thus changed, as she informed the Young Offenders Committee, 'When I began there I was far too sentimental and soft; I find now that I get far better results from the girls . . . by having a really strict discipline but with really a very great deal of affection behind it.'

By this date, the girls worked eight hours a day at laundry work, cleaning, cookery, gardening, and needlework. In a word, they were trained for domestic service, whether in the home or in hotels. Barker made no apology for this emphasis; it was the only occupation in which there were vacancies. Dressmaking, millinery, and other such occupations were already overcrowded with skilled female workers. Barker also believed that a sound domestic training prepared the girls to be good wives and mothers. It remained only to persuade

[36] See *DNB 1951–60*, p. 64; Elizabeth Gore, *The Better Fight. The Story of Dame Lilian Barker* (1965), pp. 119–21.

[37] BA, *Minutes*, 17 Jan. and 14 Oct. 1924; Gore, op. cit., p. 128.

magistrates to commit girls to Borstal before they had a string of convictions and prison sentences to their name.[38]

A more disciplined regime did not, in fact, dispel the problems of training delinquent girls. Evidence presented to the Young Offenders Committee suggested that girls were not as successfully dealt with by Borstal detention as boys. Little *esprit de corps*, for example, was aroused amongst the girls at Aylesbury, despite the efforts of the staff. The committee thus concluded that training for girls of this age 'should provide for varied forms of appeal suited to individual temperament', and they went on to advise that some cases might be dealt with by detention in a voluntary home, where the influence of an individual teacher could exert itself.[39] Already, Waller had consulted Miss M. A. Cullis, a teacher in Holloway prison, about the training of girls of Borstal age in voluntary homes. Miss Cullis endorsed the use of homes, on the grounds that training had proved ineffective.

> ... it is clear we have been offering something which the majority of the girls persistently reject. You may of course still 'train' and develop the backward girl and the weak girl, as Borstal has indeed done, but I doubt whether in the case of the others, 2 or 3 years of instruction under institutional conditions ... *can* eradicate and fundamentally alter the warped mind and character that is the result of all the powerful influences of early years.[40]

Cottage homes, small in size, varied in kind, could provide more individualized treatment. Little came of this groundwork, however, in part, no doubt, because after 1928 it was possible to sentence offenders of between sixteen and twenty-one to homes, for not more than six months, as a condition of probation.

The Training Period

The minimum length of a Borstal sentence was two years, the maximum, three years. In the 1920s a number of Borstal staff, the Borstal Association and the psychologist, Cyril Burt, all advised that there should be a three-year minimum sentence. More significantly,

[38] *Evidence*, qq. 19809 and 19833; *Magistrate*, vol. 2 (1929), p. 289. Before Borstal, around 50 per cent of girls were employed in domestic work, 25 per cent in factory work, according to Mannheim's study of 411 Borstal girls. Most of these girls were committed for stealing. See *Social Aspects*, op. cit., p. 263.

[39] *Report of YOC*, op. cit., p. 1085; *Evidence*, pp. 413–25 (Mrs L'Estrange Malone).

[40] P. Com. 7/542.

the Court of Criminal Appeal periodically ruled that the term of detention should be three years, affording offenders 'an opportunity of learning discipline and acquiring a trade'.[41] This was grist to Paterson's mill. 'If Borstal it must be,' he wrote in *The Times*, 'then let the sentence in every case be for the maximum of three years', however minor the culminating offence. The training course was devised on the assumption that most lads needed two years' training; each boy was told on arrival that the normal period of detention would be two years. The merit of the maximum sentence was that each boy could earn a year's remission, an important incentive to effort, and would be on licence for two years—or under control, in all, for four years. A two-year sentence reduced the period under supervision to one year, and took away the incentive of earning release at the end of two years. Paterson's argument, and the unanimous view of the Borstal staff 'that many a lad who has failed might well have succeeded if he had received the full sentence', induced the Young Offenders Committee to recommend that the length of a Borstal sentence should be three years in all cases. No legislation was recommended, however, by the Home Office conference held to consider the committee's proposals.[42]

The prison commissioners could release on licence after six months (or after three months in the case of a girl) if convinced that the offender would lead an honest, industrious life. That they were rarely convinced of this is suggested by the fact that the average period of Borstal detention was, in mid-decade, rather more than two years. The Young Offenders Committee encouraged periodic reviews of the progress of inmates, so that 'those who become fit for freedom at an earlier date may not be longer detained'. In consequence, the commissioners were asked to examine the question of regular review and early licensing. Against a background of overcrowded Borstals, and the related need to hasten the date of release, the commissioners and the Borstal governors agreed upon the following steps: to encourage the visiting committees of the three male Borstals to make more liberal use of the power to release lads on licence after six

[41] W. Blake, op. cit., p. 82; P. Com. 7/542; BA, *Borstal in 1927*, p. 3; *Minutes*, 17 Jan. 1924; C. Burt, *The Young Delinquent* (1927), p. 235; *The Times*, 21 Oct. 1919, p. 5; *R.* v. *Revill* (1925), 19 Cr. App. R. 44; *R.* v. *Frier* (1927), 20 Cr. App. R. 30.

[42] *The Times*, 4 Aug. 1925; S. Barman, op. cit., p. 12; *Report of YOC*, op. cit., p. 1060; HO45/13403/510865/12. See also Table 12: in 1920, over 12% of all Borstal sentences were two years in length.

months, and to review the cases of all inmates at Feltham and Borstal at the end of twelve months.[43] Even so, the attempt to break old habits and fashion new ones put a premium on lengthy detention, and in the Paterson era, the completion of institutional training was given precedence over early release on licence.

After-Care

When the visiting committee of a Borstal institution, having reviewed the progress and prospects of an inmate, decided that he was fit for freedom, a recommendation for release went to the prison commissioners. The latter issued a licence, the main condition of which was that the lad 'must keep in close touch with the associate to whom he is attached, changing neither work nor lodging without his consent'. The second stage of the training process was under way, the responsibility of the Borstal Association and 1,000 voluntary associates, spread across the country. Representatives from the Central Office spoke to many of the lads in the institutions before release, and with the help of the local associates, made arrangements for work and lodgings. If a lad's behaviour deteriorated, or if he was reconvicted, the boy's licence was revoked and he ended up in the special block at Wormwood Scrubs, from which he was again licensed, generally within six months.[44]

The main difficulty confronting the Borstal Association was that of finding work for the discharged boys, particularly in the late 1920s when a rise in the number sentenced to Borstal coincided with a period of high unemployment. The trade conditions of the immediate post-war years first led to such a difficulty, as a result of which the prison commissioners experimented with a system of parole. A lad who was nearing the time for licence was permitted to leave the institution on parole to search for work. The merit of the plan was that at the end of the parole period, if the search for work proved unsuccessful, the lad returned to the Borstal without the disgrace of a revoked licence. No scheme, however, overcame the problems posed by increasing unemployment and by the increased committals to Borstal; in 1928, over 800 lads were discharged to the Association's care. In desperation,

[43] HO45/13403/510865/12; *Report of YOC*, p. 1061; BA, Circular, 24 Feb. 1928.

[44] *Principles*, pp. 16–17; Hobhouse and Brockway, op. cit., p. 430; *Magistrate*, vol. 1 (1924), p. 33.

the BA established more shipping agencies in London and South Wales, and persuaded boys to take service on ship.[45]

In addition to the state of the labour market, the association complained about the attitude of the Borstal inmates. In a letter to the annual conference of housemasters in 1931, the BA presented its case:

> ... we have to place a large number of lads who are without character on a market which is terribly over-crowded, and ... we find a large proportion of them quite unreformed in their attitude towards honesty, lazy in the mornings, insolent and grasping in manner, and with little desire to hold a job.[46]

But the fault was not entirely with the boys. The Borstal Association never insisted on a standard wage, although they tried not to fall below 27 shillings (£1.35) a week for a lad of eighteen or nineteen. Too often the result was that Borstal boys were placed in low-paid, 'blind-alley' occupations, exactly the type of job, ironically, that Paterson and other analysts of boy labour condemned as a staging post to unemployment and delinquency. When lads threw in such jobs and returned to the BA, they were rebuked for wanting a bed of roses, before being found an equally unrewarding job, under the threat of having their licence revoked if they discharged themselves again. This was the assessment, at least, of a former inmate of Feltham, who stated that in the late 1920s he had met dozens of ex-Borstal lads 'and their general bitterness and disgust for the "lodgings, employment and support" given them when they were discharged is readily expressed'. He also had unkind words for the head of the Association. 'He seemed a snob doling out charity with an air of lofty superiority ... here I sensed a feeling of hostility, mechanical advice, stock-phrased warnings, and lack of genuine interest.' Under pressure from Grant-Wilson, the writer subsequently published an apology for these remarks, but they remind us that the Borstal Association began life as a system of 'patronage' or charity. It was, in Roger Hood's phrase, 'a philanthropic body imbued

[45] BA, *Minutes*, 20 Oct. 1926, 13 Feb. 1929; P. Com. 7/559. Brockway, op. cit., p. 101, suggested the opening of hostels for ex-Borstal boys. Although the scheme confronted the widespread problem of homelessness, as well as that of finding work, it did not commend itself to the Prison Commissioners, who feared that hostels would undermine the attempt to segregate the hardened from the less corrupt offender.

[46] Ibid., 8 July 1931. The Borstal Association wondered whether the fact had become obscured that 'the main business of the Institutions is to produce sturdy and honest workers'.

with much of the spirit of the Charity Organisation Society'.[47] The associates tended, therefore, to concentrate on the 'deserving' cases, those with a home to return to and who posed few disciplinary problems. The social standing of the first voluntary associates, who varied in experience and devotion, reinforced the style and content of after-care. But the proportion of probation officers and social workers acting as associates on a voluntary basis did gradually increase from the mid-1920s. Grant-Wilson tried, moreover, to get the after-care of Borstal lads declared a duty of the probation service. Gradually, aid-on-discharge was turning into professional casework.[48]

Results

At first, the success of Borstal training was assessed in relation to the fall in the number of prisoners serving penal servitude. The Borstal system was introduced, after all, to halt recruitment to the ranks of the habitual criminal. '[T]he effect of the Borstal Institutions', declared Paterson in 1923, 'was seen in the halving of the prison population at Dartmoor, and the closing of Portland Convict Prison.' Increasingly, however, success was measured in terms of the percentage of boys who were not subsequently reconvicted. In 1925, Waller asked Grant-Wilson for figures showing the results of the Borstal system since the early days. Sixty-five per cent of the 6,140 lads discharged from the institutions since 1910 had not since been reconvicted; 66 per cent of the 836 girls were likewise classified as successes. If one added those who were reconvicted once only, then, as Paterson claimed, 'three out of every four Borstal boys are reclaimed and live out their lives as honest citizens'.[49]

In fact, Paterson believed that reconviction statistics were open to 'a wide margin of error' and provided no reliable test of the Borstal system. How could one compare the results between different time periods when the type of entrant could differ appreciably under the variable impact of poverty, unemployment, or war? Nevertheless, in

[47] *Evidence*, q. 19997 (J. Cunliffe); Gordon, op. cit., p. 211; Benney, op. cit., p. 246; Hood, op cit., p. 167.

[48] BA, *Minutes*, 8 July 1931. In 1931 the Home Office Advisory Committee on Probation urged probation officers to assist the Borstal Association in their work. In 1932 the Annual Conference of Probation Officers undertook to be officially responsible for the after-care of Borstal boys.

[49] Quoted in Hood, op. cit., note 2, p. 207. See P. Com. 7/540; P. Com. 7/543; *The Times*, 6 Aug. 1925.

an attempt to mould opinion in favour of Borstals, Paterson informed all Borstal governors in 1928, that 'something like 80 per cent of the lads discharged during the year under review are now established in honest life after two years of liberty'. In the face of such promotion, the Young Offenders Committee concluded that 'the system had fully justified itself by its success'.[50]

Reactions

The Prison Commission, with the help of the Borstal Association, also educated press and judicial opinion about the improved methods and results of Borstal training. To start with, however, the popular press was critical, none more so than *John Bull.* Under such titles as 'The Bad Boys' Bastille', with lurid content to match, the paper called for an official enquiry into the Borstal system, provoking the staff of Feltham Borstal to protest to the Prison Commission. By April 1923, after another crop of 'delirious articles denouncing the brutality and failure of the institutions and the unsympathetic treatment meted out by the Borstal Association', the responsibility of the *Evening Standard*, *Daily Express* and *Reynolds News*, Grant-Wilson considered taking legal proceedings. Instead, he persuaded Sydney Moseley, on the staff of *John Bull*, to examine the work of the institutions.

Moseley remained critical of the prison surroundings of Portland Borstal and of some of the 'old guard' amongst the Borstal staff, but in *The Truth about Borstal*, he declared that 'many of the evils against which the Press was moved to protest of late have been ameliorated'. He was particularly impressed by the new regime: 'The old Borstal and the new afford a miraculous comparison. From chains, bread and water, strait-jackets and iron discipline, we come with a jump to university tutors, common rooms, Shakespearean plays, and technical education.' Thereafter, the press had, in general, only kind words for the Borstal system. Former critics were now instrumental in the creation of a favourable public opinion, which,

[50] P. Com. 7/540; P. Com. 7/543; *Report of YOC*, op. cit., p. 1056. Paterson also stated in May 1925: 'Our only method . . . in discriminating between different forms of training and in deciding that some are right and others are wrong, is to employ our experience of human nature, to analyse all the experience we have of the forces that make bad boys into good men, and to say both from our experience and from our faith in first principles "This must be right and that cannot be right".'

in turn, allowed the Prison Commission to extend the Borstal system.[51]

The campaign to influence press opinion ran in harness with an attempt to discourage the judiciary from making critical remarks about Borstal training. In response to Judge Atherley-Jones's remark that Borstals were ineffective, the Prison Commission underlined the proportion of lads restored to citizenship. The recorder of Shrewsbury, J. W. St. Lawrence Leslie, aired his doubts about the milder discipline of the reformed Borstals. Worried that such statements would set the public mind against the institutions, the commissioners brought Leslie to book. The Borstal regime, they said, was no milder than before. 'It is more like a school and less like a battalion, and the inmates are trusted much more and encouraged to show themselves worthy of trust. But their life is harder and more active than it used to be, and they work a longer day.' From the mid-1920s, however, whether in response to such reprimands or to official information about the success rate, the judiciary began to sing the praises of Borstal detention. Young offenders were told by the courts of the advantages of a Borstal sentence, particularly the trade training. Former critics, like Clarke Hall, changed their tune. More favourable statements appeared also in the legal press. The *Justice of the Peace* defined Borstal as 'a valuable and progressing portion of the English penal system'.[52]

The reaction of the Borstal Association, itself, was not uniformly uncritical. At first, the BA worked in close accord with the new Prison Commission, particularly Paterson. The steady improvement of the institutions fired its determination to silence press and judicial denunciation of the Borstal system. Later in the decade, however, relations between the BA and the prison authorities were strained by overcrowding and staffing problems. The receipt of 'an increasing volume of complaints from associates and employers throughout the country' in 1928, led the BA to inform the Home Secretary of the overcrowded condition of the Borstals. Next year, the Association grumbled that many of the lads were unreformed in their attitude to work, owing to 'the frequent changes of Officers, and the atmosphere of unrest and consequent lack of attention to work which prevails at

[51] HO45/11898/332404/65–75; BA, *Minutes*, 12 April 1923, 31 May 1923, 20 April 1926; Moseley, op. cit., p. 164. The bad publicity was made worse by an increase in absconding from Borstals in 1923–4: HO45/11898/332404/77.

[52] HO45/16976/485552. For Clarke Hall's criticism in *Daily Sketch*, 28 Jan. 1922, see P. Com. 7/542. See also BA, *Minutes*, 19 Jan. 1927; *Justice of the Peace*, 17 Dec. 1927, p. 964.

the Institutions'.[53] In this way, the BA exposed the divergent claims within the Borstal idea of character building and industrial training; of public school codes, and preparation for the rigours of industrial life. The association also raised implicitly the larger issue of expanding the Borstal system, without jeopardizing the essential principles of the training or the level of success.

Recapitulation

It is difficult to overestimate the contribution of Paterson in a discussion of the origins and burden of the Borstal idea. Drawing upon extensive experience of the education and welfare of adolescents, Paterson designed a system of institutional training to remove young offenders from what a Home Office circular described as 'the evil environment of their homes and the wicked influences of their associates', and to teach them self-control, self-knowledge, and the qualities of good citizenship.[54] By the latter, Paterson included the willingness to work hard, to 'stick to it' when the going got rough, and a civic, as opposed to a class, awareness. The essential instruments of this process of re-education were the personal influence of the Borstal housemasters and the arousal of a corporate spirit amongst the boys. Throughout the daily programme of exercise, work, and education, both forces would be operative.

Of course, the implementation of this policy left something to be desired. For a measure that sought to keep boys out of prison, it had the unfortunate effect of sending lads to the boys' prison in London as the first step in their Borstal career. The attempt to match the boys' needs to the training regime of particular Borstals was severely limited by the small number and basic similarity of the institutions. The training programme, finally, was often at cross-purposes, encouraging self-discovery and personal development whilst requiring unquestioning acceptance of the work ethic. Yet despite these limitations, the Borstal system attracted almost universal public support by the late 1920s. Such popularity was a firm platform on which to build the inter-war extension of Borstal training. For at the same time as Paterson and the

[53] BA, *Minutes*, 18 Jan. and 12 April 1923, 14 Jan. 1926, 13 Feb. 1929, 22 Jan. 1930, 8 July 1931.

[54] HO45/16224/512613/3A.

Borstal staff were shaping the new Borstal regimes, discussions were held between the prison commissioners about the future of Borstal.

The Future of Borstal

For what sort of person was a Borstal institution meant? There was still no categorical answer to this question at the start of the Paterson era, even though the definition of who was eligible was crucial to the continued expansion of Borstal training. Evidence from the Gladstone committee and from the debates on the Prevention of Crime Act 1908, suggested that Borstal was to receive neither the very depraved nor novices in crime. But uncertainty remained, particularly in the courts. The ex-reformatory boy, for example, was not generally recommended for Borstal, but the courts seemingly disagreed, since one-sixth of boys discharged from Borstal in 1919 had previously spent time in a reformatory.[55] In 1922, therefore, the new chairman of the Prison Commission asked his colleagues for a clearer definition of 'suitable cases' for Borstal treatment.

There was, according to Waller, 'a fairly constant disposition on the part of Courts to commit to B.I.s any persons with whom they do not know what to do. A common case is where there has been a single offence, the life is an aimless and drifting one, and the home and relations are unsatisfactory.'[56] So liberal an interpretation of the law, he argued, would lead to overcrowding and a consequent reduction in the quality of training. It also raised the issue of contamination. The institutions were classified, but 'it is better', declared Waller, 'that nobody who has anything in the way of evil still to learn should be sent to one. If they are to be, we shall require a fourth Male B.I. expressly for "Star" cases.' Of the three inspectors of prisons, Major Lamb and Mr Farewell advised that for lads susceptible to contamination (what Farewell termed the 'waster class in need of discipline'), probation or a prison sentence was preferable to Borstal. Lieut.-Col. Knox simply hoped that some of the ex-reformatory lads would continue to be given another chance. The most significant minute came from Paterson, in which he gave an outline of the future he envisaged for the Borstal system.

[55] HO45/11898/332404/16; P. Com. 7/538. See also Hood, op. cit., pp. 28–31. The 1908 Act stated that the offender must, *inter alia*, be of 'criminal habits or tendencies', or the associate of 'persons of bad character'.

[56] The next four paragraphs are based on P. Com. 7/538.

There were many lads, he said, who were, 'by the idleness of their life and by the natural contamination that ensues from standing at a street corner, deteriorating steadily in the direction of a criminal life'. On first conviction, this type of lad should get probation; in the event of a breach of the probation order, or of a further offence, he should be sentenced to Borstal training. The intervening short sentence of imprisonment was to disappear. 'There should be no power to send him to prison before he is 21. The only alternative to probation should be a Borstal sentence of three years.' Legislation to this end, 'when public opinion is ready for it', continued Paterson, 'will drive a greatly increased number of lads into the Borstal net . . . ' This, in turn, would require greater classification. He then spelt out what would eventually be the Prison Commission's policy for young adult offenders.

Borstal training was to be the only form of custodial sentence. Young offenders would be sent first to a 'reception institution', where they would spend from three to six months. Most would then be released on licence; if they failed on licence, they would serve the rest of their sentence in an ordinary Borstal institution. Besides dispensing with imprisonment, this plan, said Paterson, 'would give us the advantage of a long licence in many cases, and many of these lads require supervision rather than detention. Furthermore, supervision is vastly less expensive than detention.' He also wanted to re-name the institutions, 'Borstal schools', to point up 'the small changes, both in regulation and in spirit, which we are trying to effect'.

Paterson's blueprint was, in part, a product of talks with Grant-Wilson of the Borstal Association and Norris, chief inspector of reformatory schools, both of whom wished to extend the advantages of training beyond young criminals to boys of sixteen and seventeen who, as Norris wrote, 'are living a low, degraded life, becoming more and more intimate with the more criminal portion of our population'. Short of legislation, said Norris, the Home Office should encourage magistrates 'to take a wide view of the possibilities of committal to Borstal'. He also agreed with Paterson that for many of these cases, a shorter training period would suffice, if associated with long licence and power of recall. As yet, however, the objectives of administrators with substantial experience of youth work ran foul of the financial constraints of the period. After only a year in office, Waller minuted that he was directed to reduce his estimate of the number of prisoners and Borstal inmates to be fed and clothed in 1923–4 by no fewer than 1,000. 'It is therefore,' he stated, 'no time to admit any fresh classes of people to B.I.s; and we may have to do what we can to stop so many coming.'

The future of Borstal, however, remained high on the commissioners' agenda. In April 1925, following internal discussions about assembling a larger staff, acquiring new buildings and 'educating the Judiciary'—all with a view to expanding the Borstal system—Waller called upon his colleagues to clear their ideas on the subject once more.[57] The chairman himself had doubts about expansion, given the inherent evils of institutional life. Borstals were not 'public schools in the ordinary sense, nor can they be. They are, at the best, a kind of continuation residential school for young fellows who are no longer boys but men.' To maintain a decent tone required close supervision and energetic leadership; without holidays or home influences, an institutionalized 'barrack life' was inevitable, with all the unhealthy practices that this was heir to. The prison commissioners should be careful, therefore, said Waller, 'not to induce those who have to administer the law to consider [institutional life] the remedy for all social ills'.

Waller's approach was seconded by Lamb and Knox. Lamb was worried that extending the Borstal system to first offenders of good character, including petty offenders, would incite charges of injustice at the period of detention. Knox also doubted the wisdom of inundating the institutions with 'youthful delinquents of every description', but this was supplementary to his desire to avoid all forms of incarceration. 'The hope for the future in this respect', he declared, 'lies with the Probation Acts and the working of them by the right sort of people.' Dr Griffiths and Paterson agreed that non-custodial methods were to be preferred, but they pointed out, first, that the success of these methods depended upon an ample supply of good probation officers, which did not yet exist. Secondly, for lads who 'live at home in overcrowded rooms, and with parents and companions who are either uninterested or actively inimical to their reform', custodial training, for all its drawbacks, was the only alternative. Paterson's memorandum boldly faced the implications of this stance.

During the last twelve months for which figures were available, 2,500 young adults had been sentenced to terms of imprisonment. Even if 2,000 of these were put on probation, 500 extra candidates each year would have to go to Borstal, for imprisonment to be

[57] The next four paragraphs are based on P. Com. 7/540.

abolished, thus doubling the normal Borstal intake. If, in turn, Borstal institutions were not to exceed 250 inmates, new buildings and staff would be needed. This would prove expensive, said Paterson,

> and it is well the Government of the day should realise the fact and should not embark on a shortsighted policy of trying to 'Borstalise' the prisons in a cheap and ineffective manner. Assuming, roughly, that it costs £50 a year to keep a lad in prison and £100 a year to train him in a Borstal Institution, it will cost sixteen times as much to send that lad for two years to a Borstal Institution than it would to send him for three months to prison. Let us, therefore, state the increase of cost boldly, rather than be party to a cheap compromise.

That still left the question of whether the courts would commit 'the average petty thief at the street corner' for three years. Paterson believed this would pose no problem if his plan of a provisional and a full sentence of Borstal was realized. As he explained, 'The fact that a considerable number of lads who are licensed after a short period were not so recalled, would encourage the courts to commit lads for Borstal Training whose offences were few or trivial'.

If nothing else, the departmental discussion suggested that the chairman and some senior members of the Prison Commission considered that social conduct was best learnt in the ordinary conditions of free life. Hence, a more uniform and efficient system of probation was as effective as Borstal detention, especially for the first offender of good character who was currently given a short term of imprisonment. Paterson took the point, but still argued that non-custodial sanctions could not alone provide alternatives to imprisonment; there were offenders, whilst not 'advanced in crime', for whom institutional training was most effective. Paterson now envisioned Borstal not simply as an alternative to lengthy imprisonment for the potential recidivist, but also as a substitute for *short* terms of imprisonment—in all, as the exclusive mode of institutional training for young adult offenders.

Paterson's next task was to convince the departmental committee of the need to re-organize the system of treating young adult offenders. He expected, of course, that the enquiry would recommend that no offender under twenty-one should be sentenced to short-term imprisonment. Paterson's evidence explained that the Prison Commissioners wanted courts to refrain from sending lads under twenty-one to prison, except in the case of murder; instead, to deal with them either by probation or custodial training. If probation failed, the court would put the young offender 'under the protection of the State for a certain period', leaving it to the executive to decide where the institutional treatment, if any, would occur:

> The State would treat him as a ward of the State, and would keep him in an institution just so long as necessary. At the end of that time he would spend the remainder of his period of protection on probation under supervision.

As a safeguard, parents or the lad himself would have a right to appeal against extended incarceration. Paterson's outline, finally, incorporated his earlier idea of 'star' and ordinary Borstals. Before the same committee Miss Fry and Mrs Rackham, representing the Howard League and the Magistrates Association, respectively, and Mrs Le Mesurier, leader of the women visitors at the London boys' prison, endorsed much of Paterson's blueprint.[58]

As we know, the committee failed to recommend that the imprisonment of young offenders between seventeen and twenty-one should be abolished. It did propose, however, on the a priori assumption that criminal habits would be better curbed by constructive training than by imprisonment, that where detention was necessary, it should for the large majority be Borstal training. To this end, the committee suggested that in a new definition of suitability for Borstal, 'prominence should be given rather to the need of training than to the existence of formed criminal habits'. In addition, the committee recommended that courts of summary jurisdiction should be able to commit directly to Borstal. Under existing legislation a Borstal sentence could only be passed by a court of assize or quarter sessions. Magistrates' courts could convict young offenders and commit them to a higher court for sentence to Borstal training, but the procedure led to the detention of young offenders in local prisons for quite a few weeks. In practice, moreover, higher courts simply rubber-stamped the lower court's decision. During the war years and beyond, a number of magistrates, along with the Borstal Association, complained about the unnecessary complication of the procedure, and the time spent in prison surroundings. Before the Young Offenders Committee, many witnesses supported the power of direct committal, including Paterson, who pointed out that nearly one-third of Borstal committals were merely sentenced by the higher courts. In line with its critical view of

[58] L. L. Loewe, op. cit., p. 72; *Evidence*, q. 1101 (Paterson); q. 8352 (Rackham), q. 18494 (Le Mesurier).

imprisonment and its desire to expand Borstal training, the committee put its faith in the magistracy and proposed the power of direct committal.[59]

If the Young Offenders Committee declined to put its imprimatur on Paterson's radical scheme, it showed considerable confidence in the Borstal system. The committee was convinced, indeed, that Borstal training, in tandem with probation, could better deal with the 1,700 young offenders then committed directly to prison each year. It realized that its proposals would double the number of committals to Borstal, necessitating four new Borstals if the system were not to be overloaded. The last condition had to be avoided, since '[m]ass treatment would not afford sufficient justification for asking courts to order prolonged detention'.[60] Here, then, was a major stimulus to Borstal training.

The Home Office response was hardly encouraging, however; the departmental conference appointed to consider the committee's proposals agreed that Borstal deserved further development, but did little to ensure this. Neither the proposal to redraw the definition of Borstal eligibility nor that to empower summary courts to commit directly to Borstal was accepted. Nor was the Home Secretary prepared to make provision for any such increase in the Borstal population as the committee foreshadowed. Financial constraints even precluded a fourth Borstal simply to relieve the pressure on existing institutions. Any substantial increase in Borstal committals would be restrained, the department hoped, by earlier licensing and a wider use of probation, especially in conjunction with probation homes.[61]

The penal reform lobby seconded the Home Office's cautious policy. At the Howard League conference on the young offender, great play was made of the fact that Borstal was a penal institution. Hence, the recommendation to alter the wording of the 1908 statute, replacing 'detention under penal discipline' by 'commitment for training', was, for Cicely Craven, 'mere camouflage'. So, too, the proposal to allow magistrates' courts to commit offenders to Borstal was opposed. 'It was important', Miss Fry submitted, 'that only a very weighty tribunal should decide upon the disposition of a young person's life for three

[59] *Report of YOC*, op. cit., p. 1057; *Evidence*, q. 808 (Paterson); H. T. Waddy, *The Police Court and its Work* (1925), p. 131; C. Chapman, *The Poor Man's Court of Justice* (1925), p. 301; BA, *Minutes*, April 1923.

[60] Ibid., pp. 1044 and 1066.

[61] HO45/13403/510865/12; HO45/16224/512613/2.

years.' The problem of the time in prison awaiting sentence at a higher court could be avoided by the establishment of observation centres. In short, whilst the reformers renounced imprisonment for young offenders, they were doubtful about a more liberal use of Borstal institutions, which, for all their educational ambitions, were essentially penal. For this reason the Howard League worked for a greater variety of institutional treatment, notably for 'some alternative between the leniency of Probation and the severity of the Borstal sentence'.[62]

Miss Fry had suggested a short-term Borstal, in her evidence to the Young Offenders Committee. Other witnesses, however, warned that a short-term institution would undermine the work of the ordinary Borstals. The committee, itself, according to Sydney Harris, 'started with a strong bias in favour of introducing a system of short-term treatment as an alternative . . . to prison and Borstal'. The merit of such a measure, said Harris, was that 'it gives the young offender a necessary "shock" or takes him away from bad associations, and after a short period of active work finds him a suitable job'. In the event, the committee decided that the disadvantages of such a system outweighed the advantages.[63] In 1928, Sir Vivian Henderson instructed the department to discuss again the question of a short-term Borstal. The most penetrating and influential minute came from Paterson.

He emphasized that the core of the Borstal system lay in the attempt 'to treat a certain condition in a delinquent youth', not to mark the tariff for the offence; thus, the early stages of a Borstal sentence were devoted to ascertaining the type and length of training that would most improve the condition. The problems of a short-term Borstal flowed from this basic principle. 'If the sentence were but for 3 or 6 months', said Paterson, 'it is likely that many lads would have to be discharged just at the time when it had been discovered that they required at least two years' training in habits of industry and self-discipline.'

Of course, forty to fifty lads, for whom the full training period was considered unnecessary, were released each year from a borstal sentence at the end of six months. But they were then under supervision for some two and a half years, a virtue that a short Borstal sentence would not have. With short-term Borstals, moreover, 'a series of boys' prisons' would, in effect, be established, 'rather than an

[62] *Howard Journal*, vol. 2 (1927), p. 105; vol. 2 (1928), p. 184; *The Treatment of Young Offenders*, op. cit., pp. 12 and 23–4.

[63] *Evidence*, q. 4132 (Fry), q. 19208 (Methven); HO45/14715/516360/68; HO45/13403/510865/7.

attempt to re-educate by all-round training the lad of bad habits and loose principles'. Observing the offence more than the offender, courts would probably 'commit many scores of lads, who require a long course of training, to the summary punishment of a few months' detention'. In a word, Paterson rebutted the idea of short-term Borstals by reference to the merits of diagnosis, treatment, and indeterminacy.[64]

The Home Office did, however, urge justices to commit young adult offenders to Borstal rather than to prison. Before the Conference of Visiting Justices in July 1928, Joynson-Hicks suggested that the judiciary could force his arm on the provision of a fourth Borstal. 'If the justices . . . would only make a determined use of Borstal and would quite definitely show they were going to send more girls and boys to Borstal than hitherto, then he should have to find the essential accommodation.' Other less explicit official pronouncements in favour of an expanded Borstal system appeared in the late 1920s. The Borstal Association published figures indicating that Borstal training was most effective if tried at an early stage. The Prison Commission maintained that with more effective classification of inmates, few offenders were any longer either 'too bad' or 'too good' for Borstal. Lists of cases were also presented of lads who had been frequently sentenced to prison, who were, to quote the governor of Portland Borstal, 'material ripe for Borstal training'. The Home Office continued, finally, to advise individual judges of the advantages of Borstal training over imprisonment.[65]

These official cues had little impact, however, on the sentencing practice of the courts. In 1928 and 1929, the number of committals to Borstal increased, but this reflected, in large part, the rising crime rate. There was little change in the *proportion* of young offenders sent to Borstal. The Court of Criminal Appeal, moreover, tended to adhere to the statutory requirements for a Borstal sentence, substituting imprisonment for Borstal where there was no evidence of criminal habits or of association with bad characters. The court also excluded from Borstal, youths with bad records who were likely to corrupt others. Only in the 1930s did the courts begin to commit the relatively

[64] HO45/16976/485552/23; *Hansard*, vol. 217, 21 May 1928, cols. 1624–7.

[65] HO45/13403/510865; *Magistrate*, vol. 1 (1928), p. 242; *The Times*, 24 July 1928, p. 10; H. A. Taylor, *Jix: Viscount Brentford* (1933), p. 188; BA, *Borstal in 1927*, p. 3; Ann. Rep. of P. Com. for 1930, PP 1931–2, XII (Cmd. 4151), p. 810. The department was less concerned with legislation for Borstals once it was decided, at the end of 1930, that the Children's Bill would not include young adults.

'uncorrupt' and the relatively 'depraved', as the likelihood of contamination receded before a more effective system of classification, which a larger number of Borstal institutions made possible.[66]

Summary

The key to the Prison Commission's aim of restricting the use of imprisonment in the 1920s was the Borstal training system. In practice, financial constraints and judicial scepticism blocked any sizeable expansion in the number of Borstal committals. Doubts about the blessings of prolonged institutional training, which still afflicted the chairman, Waller, and the penal reform groups, similarly held up the growth of Borstal. Paterson had few such reservations. He allotted an important role to the probation service, but he also wished to colonize for the Borstal system, the spaces left by the intended abolition of imprisonment. For Paterson, Borstal was the seat and symbol of the most hopeful experiment in penal reform; by classification, a flexible training programme, and after-care, young offenders would be given a new start in life. In his blueprint for the treatment of young adult offenders, therefore, Borstal was the exclusive mode of custodial training. The plan included the idea of a provisional as well as a full Borstal sentence: in part, to persuade the judiciary to send minor offenders to Borstal; in part, to keep more offenders under supervision for a protracted period; and, in part, to shift the 'balance of power' from the judiciary to the executive. Paterson's ultimate ambition, indeed, was a penal system in which the judiciary would pass a generic sentence, making the young offender a ward of the State; thereafter, the prison authorities would decide upon the appropriate length and nature of treatment, whether custodial or non-custodial. To gain executive sway over the penal system for adolescent offenders was the logical step for an administrator who was doing so much to fashion that system.

[66] Hood, op. cit., pp. 43–44 and 51. See also R. v. *Stenson and Winterbottom* (1930), 22 Cr. App. R. 18; *Justice of the Peace*, 18 April 1931, p. 250.

9

Borstals and the Criminal Justice Bill 1938

By 1927, the resources of the existing Borstals were strained to the utmost, prompting the opening of a fifth house at Portland to relieve the pressure at Borstal and Feltham. This move, the prison commissioners realized, would only bring temporary relief. The daily average population in the Borstal institutions rose further, from 1,253 in 1927 to 1,401 in 1930, in response to an increase in the crime rate.[1] A more durable solution to the problem of overcrowding required the establishment of a fourth Borstal. As the official papers make clear, however, the Treasury wanted to be sure that the existing institutions were filled to capacity, before putting up the money for a new one. With this requirement in mind, Alec Paterson wrote a forceful note to the acting chairman of the Prison Commission, Alexander Maxwell. The capacity of a Borstal institution, he argued, should be governed by the number of lads who could receive individual training. By this yardstick, no house ought to hold more than sixty lads and no institution contain more than 250 boys. At that date, in contrast,

> the size of the average House is 80, and the Institutions vary from 325 to 425. As a result, we are not doing the work nearly as well as it should be done. Governors, Housemasters, and Visiting Committees have alike noted this defect and brought it at different times to the notice of the Home Secretary. Should we attempt to overcrowd the Houses and Institutions still further, we should be . . . detracting from such reputation as the Borstal system now enjoys.

If the increase of committals continued, warned Paterson, overcrowding would, by the end of 1928, 'render unworkable anything that can rightly be called the Borstal System'.[2]

[1] See PRO, HO45/16224/512613/1; HO45/16953/415065/46; *Hansard*, vol. 209, 28 July 1927, col. 1542; Hood, op. cit., p. 44. See also Tables 8 and 11.

[2] P. Com. 9/55. In 1927 Waller, the Chairman of the Prison Commission, suffered a stroke, which forced him to resign in July 1928.

In December 1927, the Prison Commission informed the Home Office that overcrowding was causing the value of Borstal training to deteriorate, and that the problem could not be surmounted either by providing new houses or by using any of the closed prisons. To build a new institution would be expensive—at least £150,000—but the cost would be spread over six or seven years; no more than £10,000 would be required in the first year. The Permanent Under-Secretary of State, Sir John Anderson, was unsympathetic to any scheme involving new expenditure, but he agreed to send the commissioners' memorandum to the Treasury. Joynson-Hicks reinforced the official communication with a personal note to Winston Churchill, Chancellor of the Exchequer, asking him to look sympathetically at the proposal for a new Borstal, and contending that the scheme would ultimately save money by reducing the number of recidivists requiring prison accommodation. Strangely, Joynson-Hicks pre-empted the Treasury reply by appealing to private charity to donate £100,000 to fund a new institution. Why the Home Secretary took this unprecedented step is unclear. It may have reflected his undoubted commitment to the development of the Borstal system in a building free from 'prison' taint; or it may have been designed to exert pressure on the Treasury. For his pains, the Secretary of State received the censure of the Howard League and opposition spokesmen, Rhys Davies and Pethick-Lawrence, for being 'unnecessarily subservient to the exigencies of the Chancellor of the Exchequer'.[3]

Churchill wrote to the Home Secretary in February 1928; speaking as a former home secretary, he declared:

> I am of course a supporter of the Borstal system, though I think that there is a tendency to impose unduly long sentences in the belief that it is so bracing. The decline in prisons and prison population is a wonderful feature of these post-war years, and certainly justifies further improvements and refinements in our prison system.[4]

£150,000 seemed excessive, however, leading Churchill to recommend the adaptation of a prison, workhouse, or reformatory. The Chancellor's veto did nothing to silence the demand of the House of

[3] Ibid; HO45/16224/512613/2 and 3A; *Hansard*, vol. 217, 21 May 1928, cols. 1585 and 1607.

[4] HO45/16224/512613/7.

Commons, the press and the penal reform groups for a fourth Borstal.[5] The Prison Commission also kept up the fight. Characteristically, Paterson went round the department, 'flourishing large sheets of foolscap, on which were daubed the Latin tag, *Borstalia Quarta Aedificanda Est*'. The commissioners also scotched the idea of adapting an existing establishment and clung to the policy of building a new institution, preferably by the Borstal lads themselves. Again, the gist of the commissioners' argument was conveyed to the Treasury, with the rider that the government would be open to serious criticism if it rejected this widely-supported attempt to improve the treatment of young offenders. The Treasury finally bowed to the strength of public and departmental opinion; Churchill agreed to the inclusion of £13,000 in the estimates, with the proviso that the Treasury would scrutinize the overall outlay on the new institution. 'Get on with it at once', Joynson-Hicks instructed the Prison Commission, to which Knox rejoined, 'Thank goodness at last.'[6]

Lowdham Grange

Paterson had long appreciated the problem of training offenders for freedom in conditions of captivity. Thus, whilst the idea of open institutions pre-dated his appointment to the Prison Commission, it was he who conceived the project of using the fourth Borstal to fashion a new philosophy of training. Camp conditions, giving greater freedom to the inmates, would, he contended, promote the growth of an authentic self-discipline and self-responsibility. The Conservative government's decision to build a new Borstal allowed, in short, a major innovation in English penal policy.

By August 1929, an estate of some 340 acres at Lowdham, near Nottingham, was considered to be the most suitable site. In accordance with prison department policy, the construction of the main buildings was to be carried out by Borstal boys, under the instruction of skilled tradesmen. But as befitted a Labour administration in a period of high unemployment, the Treasury suddenly raised the question of 'the displacement of unemployed building labourers by the forced labour of

[5] Ibid., 512613/13. The Borstal Association complained in November 1928 that working parties at the Borstals were so overcrowded that they were of little use as a training for employment.

[6] Ibid., 512613/14; P. Com. 9/55; information from Methven in Paterson Papers.

the boys', and pressed Maxwell to ask the Ministry of Labour for an opinion. Maxwell took umbrage at this, insisting that it was a question for the Home Secretary, and that there was no better training for Borstal boys than the work associated with the new institution. Home Secretary Clynes agreed, but he also wanted the observations of the Ministry of Labour. Fortunately, Miss Bondfield held that the prison commissioners' arrangements would not raise any political problem. However, for over a year, the National Federation of Building Trades Operatives and a group of Labour MPs, representing the building trade, opposed the employment of Borstal boys.[7]

Either Paterson or Bill Llewellin, the governor, now decided to march the first contingent of lads and staff from Feltham, Middlesex, to Lowdham Grange, a distance of some 130 miles. In the spirit of an ascent on Everest, the staff were interviewed by Paterson, after which a photograph of the forty-three lads and nine staff was taken. The press were not at this stage told of the march. On 4 May 1930, following a short service, the party set off, accompanied on this opening day by Paterson himself. Each night, entertainment and accommodation were provided by the local Toc H group. On 8 May, as the party approached Northampton, they were joined by Harold Scott, a Home Office principal, and soon to be chairman of the Prison Commission. Paterson had urged Scott to do this, on learning that Scott had never seen a Borstal institution. At last, on 13 May, the party entered Lowdham village, where many of the inhabitants turned out to welcome them. 'So ended a wonderful ten days', Llewellin wrote in his journal.

It has been a happy and inspiring experience for all; all have shared a common life, entirely out of the common for Borstal officers and lads; this experience will bind us all together and prepare us, in a way no ordinary start could do . . . Personally the march has been one of the happiest experiences of my life; during the course of it, I felt no misgivings nor anxiety concerning the

[7] The co-operation of the trade unions was eventually secured by agreeing that the unions would supply instructors for every trade group of inmate labourers. See HO45/16224/512613/30–42; P. Com. 9/55; Ann. Rep. of P. Com. for 1929, PP 1930–1, XVI (Cmd. 3868), p. 927. The Borstal Association asked the Prison Commission to remember that, in choosing the site for the new institution, the problem of employment on discharge was industrial rather than agricultural; workshops were more important than farmland: BA, *Minutes*, 13 Feb. 1929. In fact, the commission increasingly took policy in the direction of more land work.

absolute loyalty of Staff and lads. For the vision of the march—start for Lowdham Grange, which He inspired, I thank God.[8]

The march to Lowdham and the Lowdham spirit rapidly entered the folklore of the prison service.

An integral part of this folklore is Llewellin himself. He was a devout practising Christian, in search of a way to apply his religious principles. Following an Eton and Oxford education, and service in the Middle East during the Great War, he went tramping to see the conditions in casual wards for vagrants. He eventually found his vocation in the prison service. Starting as an assistant tutor at Portland Borstal in 1923, where he was considered to be a slow, methodical but reliable worker, Llewellin served as housemaster at Portland and as deputy governor at Feltham, before taking charge of the open experiment. From this time on, at Lowdham, and at the new Borstals of North Sea Camp and Usk, Llewellin revelled in the sacrifices of each new Borstal's foundation. One of the best brief descriptions of this stern and serious-minded public servant came from Harold Scott.

Llewellin was a tall, rather shy man, modest to a degree, and with an old-world courtesy to which everyone responded. A devout Christian, he ruled by sheer force of love and personal influence . . . he shared as far as humanly possible the life of the boys under his charge, putting himself at their service for twenty-four hours a day. There was no privileged treatment for the governor; he ate the same food, endured the same discomfort, helped when he could in the same hard labour; and long after the boys had been snugly housed in hutments, Bill Llewellin continued to live under canvas.[9]

His self-denial, integrity, and deep sense of purpose inevitably evoked the respect and affection of most of the staff and Borstal boys who came into contact with him, despite his difficulty in communicating comfortably with either group.

Llewellin always insisted on religious worship, though he was realistic enough to know that most boys would be inwardly untouched by the Christian religion. As he would say, 'while the first aim must be

[8] Governor's Journal (Lowdham), 13 May 1930; Governor's Order Book (Lowdham), 14 May 1930; *Toc H Journal*, June 1930; *Leicester Mercury*, 12 May 1930. See also J. W. Gordon, *Borstalians* (1932), pp. 267–73.

[9] Harold Scott, *Your Obedient Servant* (1959), p. 76; *The Times*, 18 Nov. 1961, p. 10; *Prison Service Journal*, no. 40, Oct. 1980, pp. 1–7; information from M. Selby, governor of Grendon Underwood. Llewellin never married; he had a substantial private income, and paid for many facilities needed by the Borstal.

to make each boy a good Christian we [shall] usually have to be content with the lesser aim of making him into a good citizen'. One of the few injunctions he held to resolutely was that work should continue, whatever the weather, a particularly harsh commandment for the winter marshes of North Sea Camp. In a typical entry in the Lowdham journal, after a bitterly cold day, Llewellin wrote, 'the lads stuck out until cease labour—a good test of stickability; all went through with it. A good effort; Mr Cape and Mr Child worked with the party in the most exposed place.' Llewellin was convinced that life would seem less difficult if the lesson of coping with adversity was well taught. A former colleague of Llewellin at Usk Borstal recently recalled, 'Though I never heard him say so, he [Llewellin] obviously believed that delinquency was most often an escape from painful, if often unacknowledged, difficulties.' The same informant also stated that Llewellin felt that lads learnt from both experience and example:

Putting boys in the way of experience or experience in their way, and himself prepared to share that experience—not imposing rules and standards which he did not himself observe nor demanding conduct which he did not ask from himself—that was how he operated.

Each lad was asked only to observe the precept of St. Luke: 'Endure hardness as a soldier of Christ.' The Borstal staff were to be judged by results not intentions: 'By their fruits you shall know them.' In all, if Paterson conceived the project of the first open Borstal, its development in practical form relied on the likes of Llewellin. As Harold Scott declared, 'No one can ever estimate the influence and effect of this twentieth century saint over generations of Borstal boys. He was Paterson's outstanding disciple, and played a big part in making Paterson's theories work.'[10]

The pioneers in the establishment of the open Borstal system were confronted by an estate of over 500 acres of farm and park land, set amongst attractive undulating countryside. Taking up quarters in tents, using the Grange for cooking, the party began to construct the first purpose-built Borstal. By August 1932, 120 lads were accommodated in the first completed buildings. The population continued to be carefully chosen and its rate of increase restricted. Lowdham took the 'star' offenders, those who had not been in a Home Office school or

[10] Governor's Journal, 24 Feb. 1933; M. G. Dickson's reminiscences, 1974–5; Scott, loc. cit.

prison, who would respond to trust, and who needed to learn a trade.[11] Two principles were fundamental to the new type of training. The first was the principle of trust. Every lad signed a declaration: 'Because of the Trust put in ME, I promise, on my honour, to do my best to keep up the good name of Lowdham Grange.' If the pledge was broken by absconding, the lad, on recapture, was transferred to another institution. To avoid this, the staff tried to create self-discipline, an internal restraint. The second principle was 'to make conditions as like those of ordinary life as possible'. To this end, there were evening hobby classes held by members of Toc H; a Rover Scout crew; attendance at local churches on Sundays; visits from local sports teams; and the Saturday evening trips to Nottingham by a party of twelve in civilian clothes, selected by a committee of the lads themselves.[12]

Conditions of employment were also made more like those in the outside world by requiring boys to report for work at the correct time, and by a system of payment for work done. The labouring gangs, employed on road-making and excavating work, were paid according to output of work, starting at 4d. (1.66 p) a week. The trades parties, including carpenters, bricklayers, plumbers, painters, cooks, and farmers, were paid between 8d. (3.33 p) and 1s. 2d. (6 p). Out of his weekly wage, the boy paid a subscription to any games club he joined and the fine for any minor offence, and saved 2s. 6d. (12.5 p) to qualify for summer camp. There was, finally, an 'unemployed' party for those guilty of misconduct or laziness at work, which did unpleasant, unpaid, though never unproductive work. In September 1931, Llewellin reported that the payment by results scheme had increased work output and had important training value.

> The Payment Scheme here has effected a revolution; the slacker, not the excessively hard worker, is looked upon as a 'blackleg' by his fellows. The hard worker is proud of his prowess, and takes his place as a leader of his fellows, irrespective of his skill at games.

Hence, the commissioners allowed the scheme to continue, and indeed

[11] See C. T. Cape, 'Administrative and other Experiences of a Borstal Governor', *Public Administration*, vol. 19 (1941), pp. 61–4; W. Healy and B. S. Alper, *Criminal Youth and the Borstal System* (1942), p. 65.

[12] S. Barman, *The English Borstal System* (1934), ch. 9, *passim*; *Howard Journal*, vol. 3 (1933), pp. 36–9; *Toc H Journal*, April 1936.

some form of payment scheme was gradually introduced into all the Borstals.[13]

A final way of linking Lowdham to the outside world, as well as 'educating' public opinion in favour of the institution, were the speeches of governor and staff to local societies, visits by interested parties and the press, and staff participation in the religious and recreational life of county and city. Llewellin addressed local Rotary Clubs and Women's Institutes, Nottingham Business Club and Boots' Progress Club. The institution was visited by prison officials and criminologists from abroad, and by members of the National Association of Boys' Clubs. Concerning recreational links, none was more unlikely than the South Notts. Hunt starting out from Lowdham; 'the first time, probably', recorded Llewellin, 'that a meet has taken place at a penal establishment'.[14]

The opening of Lowdham, to which picked offenders were sent, encouraged the prison commissioners to experiment with early release. In 1933, Llewellin stated that the average period of training at Lowdham was thirteen to fourteen months. Elsewhere boys serving a three-year sentence were rarely released inside two years. By the end of 1936, however, the then governor, C. T. Cape, told the Annual Conference of Visiting Justices that the period of training was about two years. Clearly, the experiment with the time factor in training led the authorities to limit the number of early releases. This could have been due to lads failing on licence after early discharge, although the official evidence hardly confirms this. Up to June 1936, of 307 lads released, twenty-one had been reconvicted and only six had had their licences revoked.[15] The change of policy might also reflect the departure of Llewellin, who was particularly sympathetic to early release, for North Sea Camp.

Of one thing there is no doubt: the problem of accommodation in the Borstal system remained as acute as ever. Due to a sharp rise in crime, the total number sentenced to Borstal detention rose from 774 in 1930 to 1,058 in 1932; the daily average population in the same period rose from 1,401 to 1,895. Yet the daily average population of

[13] P. Com. 9/180; *Howard Journal*, vol. 3 (1933), p. 37; *Report of the Departmental Committee on the Employment of Prisoners*, Part I, PP 1933–4, XV (Cmd. 4462), p. 155; S. Barman, op. cit., p. 202; BA, *Report for 1938*, p. 11.

[14] One such visitor was E. H. Sutherland, Professor of Criminology, Chicago University. See Governor's Journal, 22 July 1930, 22 May 1933, 14 July 1933; Barman, op. cit., p. 208.

[15] HO45/20084/482137/20; *The Times*, 18 July 1932, p. 9.

Lowdham in 1930 was just thirty-four, and not until 1932 did it exceed 100. Hence, even with the addition of Camp Hill and Sherwood, two closed Borstals opened in 1931 and 1932 respectively, congestion was worse than ever, with boys waiting longer at the collecting centre before allocation to a Borstal.[16] By 1934 the prison commissioners pressed for a seventh institution. This took the form of a hutted camp situated on the Lincolnshire coast of the Wash, some six miles from Boston. North Sea Camp was Paterson's main scheme for extending the open Borstal system.

North Sea Camp

The chairman of the Prison Commission, Harold Scott, had asked the Home Office for a minimum security Borstal, providing heavy labouring work, in January 1933. By August, the surveyor of prisons had prepared a project for reclaiming the Freiston outmarshes, which the commissioners commended as the most suitable outdoor work for Borstal boys and of value to the community. The scheme was endorsed by the Departmental Committee on the Employment of Prisoners, and attracted the Home Secretary, Sir John Gilmour, not renowned as a penal reformer. When told of the plan for a Borstal camp, he 'entered into it with gusto', according to Scott, 'and accepted at once the view that [the boys] would be held not by bolts and bars but by the leadership of the governor and his staff'.[17] As with Lowdham, however, the scheme had to satisfy both the Ministry of Labour and the Treasury.

The Ministry of Labour was concerned that the scheme would arouse opposition from critics of the National government's policy to assist the unemployed:

> Substantially our view is this that the more you stress the economic value of the work . . . the greater the risk of some criticism that at a time when the Government is not providing money for reclaiming land with unemployed in response to a demand that has been made in so many quarters for such an addition to the Government's unemployment programme, public money is available for doing it by Borstal labour.

[16] Ann. Rep. of P. Com. for 1934, PP 1935–6, XIV (Cmd. 5153), p. 484. See also Tables 11 and 13.

[17] HO45/20190/658284/1–3; Paterson to Ruggles-Brise, 2 Feb. 1934, BA document 15; *Committee on Employment of Prisoners*, op. cit., p. 171.

The way forward, therefore, was to describe North Sea Camp as a scheme for the employment of Borstal lads on a site unsuitable for paid labour, and not as a land reclamation scheme. This settled, a letter went to the Treasury. With a falling Borstal population, the scheme could not be said to be relieving pressure on existing accommodation. Between 1933 and 1935, the numbers sentenced to Borstal fell by one-third, again due mainly to a variation in the crime rate. The number of youths between sixteen and twenty-one found guilty of indictable crimes fell by 15 per cent between 1932 and 1934. Yet with much less evidence of need than in 1927–8, the Treasury more readily granted the finances for a second experimental institution.[18]

In March 1935, a party of five staff, including Llewellin the governor, and eighteen boys marched the 110 miles from Stafford to the Wash. Until October, the party lived under canvas, when the first of the four huts which would make up the institution was occupied. In the summer of 1936 a start was made on building up a sea wall and reclaiming land from the salt marshes. North Sea Camp received 'good risks' who were likely to earn their living as labourers. The virtue of the gruelling work, each boy digging and shifting some twenty tons of mud each day, was to teach the lads to overcome adversity by determined effort. Scott described a trip that he and Paterson made to the Borstal; a biting wind was blowing in from the sea, 'a wind, we felt, which would search out any weaknesses in those who had to work there but would steel those who stuck it out against any difficulties they might meet in later life'. Llewellin echoed these sentiments: 'any lad who has done a winter's work at the North Sea Camp will, I am confident, be capable of sticking any sort of job that he is likely to get'.[19] Llewellin was even more in his element than at Lowdham, sharing the rigours of climate and hard labour. 'Stickability' was again the camp tradition, although at times it was nearly overthrown. On one blizzard of a day, the boys downed tools and set off back to the camp. Before they got there, they were met by Llewellin and the rest of the staff, who worked alongside the eighty shivering lads for the rest of the day. In all, if land reclamation gave a purpose to the hard work, North Sea

[18] The department did argue, however, that another Borstal was needed to cope with the expected rise in the Borstal population from 1937, due to the increase of the birth-rate in the aftermath of the First World War. See Tables 8 and 10.

[19] H. Scott, op. cit., p. 76; *Howard Journal*, vol. 4 (1936), p. 254; HO45/20084/482137/20; Ann. Rep. of P. Com. for 1934, op. cit., pp. 484–5; Governor's Journal (North Sea Camp).

Camp symbolized a deeper purpose—'also of reclamation, but of human waste,' in Llewellin's late-Victorian imagery.[20]

But North Sea Camp was not all pick and shovel. The marsh work in all weathers was joined to an educational scheme of moral training and 'good citizenship'; to the kindling of individual initiative and self-awareness; and to a friendly communion between staff and lads. Llewellin and Barney Malone, the senior housemaster, persuaded the Prison Commission to accept an intensive twelve-month training programme. The programme, which owed a lot to Kurt Hahn's philosophy of education as practised at Gordonstoun, was divided into three main grades. The Beginners grade, for the first three months, consisted of a refresher education course, talks on moral standards, and instruction in citizenship. Moral training provided a set of minimum standards of right living (including frugality, industry, and resolution) for the lad to aspire to. A series of talks on social history, economics, current affairs, and on more practical topics like marriage, fatherhood, and the health and legal services, was designed to inform citizenship.[21]

For the next six months, in the Training grade, the lad did his daily tasks of laundry and physical exercise without supervision, got to work at the right time, and practised the habits and principles of the moral code—in short, he steered his own course. The underlying premise was that character change was the product of 'positive self-effort' and self-supervision. To this end, every boy was expected to assess in private each day whether his conduct had matched the required qualities. In addition, there were the spartan tests of physical endurance: marsh runs dressed only in bathing trunks; swimming the dykes in any weather.

The last three months, in the Leavers grade, were devoted to more practical issues such as accommodation and work on release. At this stage the boy was given even greater freedom, and expected to live up to the tradition of service that developed amongst the leavers. Overarching all the grades, finally, was the appeal to a lad's sense of

[20] *Howard Journal*, vol. 4 (1936), p. 252. cf. Scott, op. cit., p. 77: by 1939 about 180 acres of farming land had been won back from the sea at North Sea Camp 'and who can tell how many personalities were won back from the wasteland of crime?'

[21] M. G. Dickson's reminiscences, 1974–5; Notes by W. B. Malone for the Housemasters' Conference, 1936 (courtesy of Alan Bainton). Malone, a New Zealander, was the senior housemaster at North Sea Camp; he was killed in the Second World War. For Kurt Hahn, see J. Lawson and H. Silver, *A Social History of Education in England* (1973), p. 400.

honour not to betray the trust invested in him.[22] Self-supervision was likewise the key to discipline in North Sea Camp, since there were no discipline officers as such. Nor was there a house system; instead, each housemaster teamed up with a group of about fifteen lads, through mutual liking. In each of the three grades, however, the boy was under a different set of housemasters, to avoid him becoming dependent on any one man. The housemasters slept in the dormitories, ate the same meals, kept the same hours, the aim being not to enforce discipline, but to set a standard. Inevitably such close and continuous contact with the boys made great demands on the staff. Hugh Kenyon, an assistant housemaster in the early days, believes that the regime would not have lasted, even under Llewellin. In fact, when Llewellin left to take charge of the open Borstal at Usk in 1939, the regime at North Sea Camp moved towards greater privacy for housemasters. Nevertheless, the original staff were obviously wedded to the ideal of social service, confident in the rightness of traditional moral values, and deeply committed to the rehabilitation of the young offender.[23]

North Sea camp was, in many respects, the inter-war summit of Borstal training in open conditions. Here, at its most developed, was Paterson's conception of the likelihood of personal change through alteration in a boy's social environment. M. G. Dickson's description of the early days illustrates what the staff believed the boy encountered during his twelve months' training.

During his time at North Sea Camp a boy was exposed to new ideas and experiences likely to widen and change his outlook on life. He was constantly subject to pressures and influences of different sorts designed to induce him to lead an honest and industrious life when he returned home. There was the constant pressure exercised by the routine of the camp—especially the need to get himself to work punctually, to earn good work reports and to avoid even the smallest lapse into dishonesty. There was the incentive to earn an early discharge by showing that he was likely to be successful when released. There was the personal influence of Llewellin and the boy's wish to gain his approbation and to avoid disappointing him. There was the stimulus provided

[22] As Llewellin stated: 'A high sense of honour is by no means restricted to the Public Schools, but is implanted in every boy . . . to be fanned into flame by trust and confidence.', *Howard Journal*, vol. 4 (1936), p. 254.

[23] P. Com. 9/60; Notes by Malone, op. cit. Kenyon had been brought up in a Yorkshire parsonage; educated at public school and Oxford. He had a strong social conscience, and enjoyed being a leader of men.

by the need to assess himself constantly in the light of the moral standards put before him . . . There was the effect of the work on the marsh.[24]

In a word, each boy would respond, it was thought, to a different element in his new environment. The essential ingredient was to expose young offenders to a variety of influences, inducements, and pressures, designed to encourage honest citizenship in a natural and challenging environment. The paradox was, of course, that delinquents were trained to overcome urban temptations in Arcadian surroundings.

Under the impact of a steady rise in the number of male committals to Borstal from 1935 onwards, the Prison Commission looked to the opening of an eighth institution. This became Hollesley Bay Colony, opened in May 1938, situated on the coast, sixteen miles from Ipswich, providing outdoor work in agriculture and horticulture.[25]

Three new minimum security Borstals were thus established in the 1930s, allowing the prison commissioners to experiment with styles of building, types of staffing and forms of labour. More crucially, the new regimes greatly assisted the commissioners' policy of developing the responsibility, self-discipline, and self-reliance of Borstal lads. The methods of the Borstal system still fell short of inmate self-government or inmate freedom of choice of work and evening classes. The establishment of inmate councils was the preserve, at this date, of voluntary experiments like the 'Q' (for Quest) camp started in 1936 by a Quaker Q Camps Committee, with the help of the Institute for the Scientific Treatment of Delinquency. Moreover, the open Borstals received only those who could be trusted; the boys who most needed to be taught responsibility were excluded because of the security risk and the fear of contamination.[26] The open institutions, nevertheless, guaranteed the transition from the disciplinary detention of the Ruggles-Brise days to the educationally-based training of the Paterson era. Fluctuations in the crime rate were helpful to these policy

[24] Dickson, op. cit. cf. BA, *Report for 1938*, p. 17. For the enthusiastic press response to North Sea Camp, see *Daily Mail*, 1 Sept. 1936; *The Sunday Times*, 7 March 1937; *News of the World*, 15 Aug. 1937.

[25] HO45/21884/806808/1 and 5; Ann. Rep. of P. Com. for 1937, PP 1937–8, XIV (Cmd. 5868), p. 854; *Daily Herald*, 2 Mar. 1938.

[26] See *Magistrate*, vol. 4 (1935), p. 930; (1937), p. 1133; *Penal Reformer*, vol. 3 (1937), p. 11; vol. 5 (1938), p. 6. In 1938 the daily average population of 2,020 males was distributed as follows: 1,567 in closed Borstals, 351 in open Borstals and 102 in the disciplinary block at Wandsworth. Hence, the open system catered for only 17 per cent of the Borstal population.

developments. The rise in crime in the late twenties forced the government to provide Lowdham; the rise in the late thirties resulted in Hollesley Bay Colony and Usk Borstal. In the mid-thirties, the drop in crime gave the scope to experiment with North Sea Camp. But if the context was favourable, the decisive factors of policy-making lay elsewhere, in the original conception of Paterson, the administrative skills and support of Maxwell and Scott, and the leadership of governors like Llewellin. To what extent, however, did administrative experimentation with open institutions react on the closed Borstals in the 1930s?

Classification

The investigation and classification of Borstal boys took place at the collecting centre, transferred in 1931 from Wandsworth to Wormwood Scrubs, where the boys could be better segregated from older prisoners. This did not, however, mute the critics of detention, pending allocation, in prison surroundings. The increase in the early thirties of the number of boys, and the time they spent, in Wormwood Scrubs, caused by a sharp rise in adolescent crime, was critically examined by both parliament and the Salmon Committee on Prison Labour. The Prison Commission could only promise that better accommodation would soon be set aside for the purpose. Fortunately, by the mid thirties, the time spent in the collecting centre came down. The problem was also obscured by official stress on the finer classification which more institutions allowed.[27] In fact, preliminary investigation hardly led to allocation to an institution specifically geared to the particular needs of the youth. 'Classification', Hood concluded, 'consisted of fitting a boy into a broad type, in which the accent was still mainly on avoiding contamination.' By 1938 there were the three open institutions for trustworthy 'stars', two closed institutions for the 'intermediates' (Rochester, Camp Hill), two for the worst boys (Portland, Sherwood), and Feltham for the immature and mentally unstable. There was no classification at all for Borstal girls; all types were dealt with at Aylesbury, including the licence revokees. There were continued limitations, then, with the system of classification. As

[27] HO45/20602/827672/1; HO45/15649/430246/15–19; *Committee on Employment of Prisoners*, op. cit., pp. 186–7; Ann. Rep. of P. Com. for 1938, PP 1939–40, V (Cmd. 6137), p. 283. See also L. W. Fox, *The Modern English Prison* (1934), p. 180.

Henriques complained in 1937, boys still acquired a knowledge of prison life. 'Every single Borstal boy knows well the taste of prison life in Wormwood Scrubs, and if he comes from the provinces, of the life of the provincial prison *as well*.'[28]

Houses and Housemasters

The essential unit of Borstal training was the house, made up of the housemaster, assistant housemaster, and two house or discipline officers. The house officers had become important components of the Borstal system, and Paterson and Methven, the assistant commissioner in charge of co-ordinating Borstal work after 1930, selected men who were likely to exert a beneficial influence on the inmates. So much was the house the centre of institutional life, that in 1929 Paterson pressed for the abolition of principal officers, who were part of the discipline staff, on the grounds that they had no role in educational establishments. The majority of housemasters and assistant housemasters were still recruited by direct entry from a wide range of military and civilian occupations, normally in their late twenties or early thirties. Now that the pioneering days were over, at least in the closed Borstals, one might have expected the search for individuality and breadth of experience to give way to greater emphasis on educational and social work training. This was not the case before the 1940s, to judge from John Vidler's account.

> The housemaster was expected to be a bit of an educationalist with ideals about the training of youth. But he also had to be someone of definite personality; he had not only to be responsible for the smooth running of his house, he had also to enthuse his colleagues and to keep up their morale.

Vidler was a case in point. During his university days he worked with Paterson in Bermondsey boys' clubs; after a spell of tea planting in

[28] Hood, op. cit., p. 128; Fox, op. cit., p. 189; *Magistrate*, vol. 4 (1937), pp. 1144 and 1213; HO45/18498/655767/7; HO45/15649/430246/22; Templewood Papers, Box X:7: Notes on Prisons (Miss Melanby). Basil Henriques was founder and warden of the Bernhard Baron St. George's Jewish Settlement. He was educated at Harrow and Oxford, where he came under the influence of Alec Paterson. He decided to make social work, and notably club work among underprivileged Jewish boys, his profession. In 1925 he was put on the panel of London juvenile court magistrates, where he served under Sir William Clarke Hall; in 1936 he became chairman of the East London Juvenile Court. See *DNB 1961–70*, p.506; *The Times*, 4 Dec. 1961; L. L. Loewe, *Basil Henriques* (1976), *passim*.

Ceylon and leather-making in London, he joined the prison service in 1932 as deputy governor of Feltham. In 1934 he was transferred to Portland, where he became governor two years later. An opinionated, wilful character, Vidler's views were based more upon feeling and intuition than science or statistics. If further proof were needed of the role of quality before qualifications, it exists in a Prison Commission memorandum on the recruitment of housemasters, prepared in 1939:

> The quality in a would-be Housemaster which is first sought is a sense of vocation. Experience in social work is valuable, though not necessarily more valuable than experience won at first hand, in workshop or fo'c'sle . . . A man who has had training in social service has a valuable qualification to offer, but it is the man himself, his outlook, his intelligence, his personality, the faith that is in him, which concern the selectors most of all.[29]

Housemasters were encouraged to work out their own methods of training or controlling delinquents; the housemaster, said Vidler, 'was encouraged to feel that he was king of his castle'. In consequence, housemasters gradually became an independent influence on the modes of training and, to a degree, on the shape of penal policy. The mediating mechanisms were the conferences of governors and housemasters arranged by the Prison Commission, and the annual conferences of housemasters and assistant housemasters, the first of which was financed by the staff themselves. These conferences fostered specific proposals for experiments in training methods, and a general determination to combat any resurgence of negative thinking in this area of penal policy.[30]

The house system and housemasters were not, however, immune from criticism in the 1930s. Mrs Rackham's review of Barman's gushing study of the Borstal system remarked that 'much is made of the individualisation of the House system, but it appears from the statistics that a house may contain as many as 94 boys, which must make individual treatment a difficulty'. Meanwhile, the Borstal Association pursued its campaign to make the staff 'keep in view the fact that inmates had on their discharge, as a rule, to return to a dull and monotonous life and a poor home'. Many officers, it was claimed,

[29] P. Com. 9/74; HO45/23018/659525/9–11; *Hansard*, vol. 274, 15 Feb. 1933, col. 1030; John Vidler, *If Freedom Fail* (1964), pp. 26, 37–9. Vidler was never actually a housemaster, however.

[30] Vidler, op. cit., p. 43; Fox, op. cit., p. 188; interview with Alan Bainton.

unintentionally misled the boys as to their future prospects.[31] Another charge, put more forcefully in the 1940s, was that the application of modern psychiatry was almost entirely neglected.

In their study of the Borstal system the Americans, William Healy and Ben Alper, accepted that the staff : inmate relationship in the institutions 'partakes of the nature of psychotherapy', but they thought the staff were too impressionistic:

Their knowledge of the causations of human behaviour is not that of the psychiatrist who patiently unearths a life story and has the opportunity of fitting it together with what a psychiatric social worker has learned . . . from the stories of the families.

The only systematic attempt at psychiatric treatment began in 1934 at Wormwood Scrubs. Any lad considered by the prison medical staff to be likely to respond to such treatment was retained at the boys' prison; any one in a Borstal who was thought to be in need of treatment was returned to the Scrubs. A report on the results of this experiment appeared in 1939, co-authored by W. N. East and W. H. de B. Hubert. Significantly, the Prison Commission's view of this effort at psychological treatment was that only a limited number of cases required it, and that 'the ordinary conditions of training . . . provide a suitable environment in which lads can readjust themselves to the needs of everyday life'. The moral was clear: the Borstal system aspired less to diagnosis and psychological treatment than to condition boys to live in society by a vigorous programme of re-education. The frame of reference remained environmental. Delinquent lads were 'the product of social impairment', declared Paterson in 1932, 'and Borstal must give them a training that should have been given earlier in home or school, in church and club'.[32]

The Training Scheme

The eight-hour day remained the vital element in the training curriculum, spent ideally in trade parties, otherwise in cleaning, labouring, and laundry work. Bricklaying, painting and decorating,

[31] *Howard Journal*, vol. 4 (1934), p. 85; R. T. Stephens, 'The Borstal System', *Nineteenth Century*, vol. 121 (1937), p. 227; BA, *Minutes*, 12 July 1933, 17 Jan. 1934.

[32] Healy and Alper, op. cit., p. 228; HO45/21884/806808/5; W. N. East and W. H. de B. Hubert, *The Psychological Treatment of Crime* (1939); Paterson, 'Youth and Crime', *Listener*, vol. 7 (1932), p. 518.

shoe repairing, baking, fitting and turning, tailoring, and farm work were the staple trade parties. In the 1930s, trade training came under fire, notably from the Salmon Committee on Prison Labour, which took evidence from Borstal governors, the Prison Commissioners, the Howard League, and from Maxwell, deputy under-secretary at the Home Office. Seemingly the courts still pretended that boys would be taught a trade at Borstal, when, of course, two years did not allow this. The period was further abbreviated by the fact that inmates spent up to nine months in domestic and labouring work before starting industrial training. The delay in placing boys into trade parties arose from the Borstal staff's opinion that a period of acclimatization and assessment was needed, and from the shortage of accommodation and equipment in the workshops. Training was also attenuated by a concern for 'production' in fulfilling orders from government departments; large orders for one kind of product reduced the variety of work and led to a neglect of trade training. Instructors were so anxious not to show a loss on contracts that, as the committee reported, they 'perform themselves much of the skilled work and the trainees' education suffers accordingly'. In addition, housemasters could pull off trade training those boys who were capable, for example, of looking after new receptions, and the boys themselves frequently asked for, and were granted, a change of labour. Overall, inmates with the aptitude for skilled work were taught the rudiments of a trade, the use of tools and of the simpler forms of machinery, and the discipline of regular work. The training, it was claimed, was sufficient to get work as 'improvers'; in fact, improver standard was reached by only '45 per cent of the boys passing through the wood and metal workshops'.[33]

In view of these deficiencies, the Salmon Committee proposed that industrial training, rather than production on an economic scale, should be the primary consideration of employment. To this end, the committee recommended less delay in getting boys into trade parties, which in turn required improvements in the workshops. As part of the modernization of the 'shops', Salmon proposed a greater concentration

[33] *Committee on Employment of Prisoners*, op. cit., pp. 153–4, 160, 186–88. The Committee included Major Isidore Salmon (Chairman), Margery Fry, H. R. Scott and A. E. Watson. See also Ann. Rep. of P. Com. for 1936, PP 1937–8, XIV (Cmd. 5675), p. 719; Fry, 'The Borstal system', in *Penal Reform in England* (1946), vol. 1 of English Studies in Criminal Science, eds. L. Radzinowicz and J. W. C. Turner, pp. 152–3; HO45/16977/485552/65. Lads who were not fit for trade training were given instruction in unskilled manual work and in the habits of steady industry. Heavy land work, for example, was considered to be good training for taking up navvying work outside.

of industries: only two industries per institution. This would, it was hoped, make for greater variety of work in each industry, and allow for both a 'learners' and an 'advanced' party in each trade. Should the craft unions be asked, therefore, to recognize Borstal training as the equivalent of a period in free apprenticeship? The committee was sceptical. Leaving aside the fact that many boys, on release, took work as labourers, forsaking the poor pay of an improver, the committee was informed by three craft unions that persons who were not trained under normal apprenticeship conditions could not be accepted as skilled workers. The unemployment level amongst union members was too high to accept such a scheme, and 'less eligibility' died hard. As the Union of Building Trade Workers declared, 'it is grossly unfair that honest lads and good citizens should be deprived of the opportunity of training and employment, whilst it is proposed that persons who have committed offences against the law and community are assisted in this connection'.[34] The committee proposed, finally, that a prison commissioner should be appointed to reorganize the prison industries.

John Lamb, a tough ex-industrialist, was appointed Director of Prison Industries. Plans were quickly prepared for a new workshop at Rochester and for modernizing the Portland 'shops'. In 1936, an industrial training scheme was launched, under which a syllabus was devised to provide both theoretical and practical instruction in skilled trades. But little effective progress was made in the 1930s; complaints continued to be heard both at official conferences and from former inmates.[35] More improvement occurred regarding payment schemes and vocational guidance.

The Salmon Committee was impressed by the success of the Lowdham graded payment scheme, and recommended its extension to all Borstal institutions. In January 1934 the Prison Commission agreed to extend the earnings scheme to all institutions, including the girls' Borstal at Aylesbury. The aim, of course, was to impose conditions more akin to those under which inmates had to earn their living outside, and to encourage increased output. Borstal governors later reported that pay led to an improvement in output and in work attitudes. Some governors maintained, however, that pay would have

[34] Ibid., pp. 188–191, 195. The Salmon Committee recommended no great change in the scheme of training at Aylesbury girls' Borstal; the majority, it was claimed, 'find no difficulty in obtaining and keeping situations in domestic service' (p. 189).

[35] Ann. Rep. of P. Com. for 1936, op. cit., p. 717; HO45/16953/415065/81; 21855/687218/3; P. Com. 9/60; *Howard Journal*, vol. 4 (1934), p. 86; vol. 5 (1938), p. 55.

to increase if lads were to be taught how to spend money, and if the association between work and an honest life was to be demonstrated.[36]

When it came to allocating boys to the trade parties for which they had most aptitude, the committee wanted one housemaster from each Borstal to be taught by the Institute of Industrial Psychology to conduct vocational tests. In 1934, the institute completed an experiment on 400 Borstal boys at the boys' prison, their results, according to Methven, justifying further efforts to incorporate vocational guidance into the training system. By 1937 eight housemasters had been trained, and the Prison Commission was satisfied with the way the scheme was working. Boys were settling down quickly in their working parties and were less frequently applying for a change of work. As against this, the range of jobs was still too limited to accommodate the diversity of types of boy.[37]

But vocational guidance could not solve the problem of conflicting objectives in the workshops. If those in charge of the 'shops' aimed for technical instruction, production of manufactured goods, and character training, there was no consensus about the priority of these three objectives. Nor could such work allocation overturn the basic principle underlying Borstal work, that boys had to be taught good work habits, and to learn to accept the monotony of work. If the Borstal staff attached too much weight to the idea of simply 'training for work', they were understandably compelled by the years of depression and unemployment, from which many parts of the country were only just beginning to emerge in the late 1930s.[38]

Discipline, finally, was a persistent feature of Borstal training. If a boy misbehaved, he was punished severely: by reduction in grade (involving loss of remission), by dietary punishment, or by the penal class. The latter meant eight hours a day in the 'bone-yard', what a former inmate described as 'a walled-in garden with doorless, concrete cubicles in one of which you stood and pounded rocks, granite or bones in an iron and concrete mortar with a heavy iron pestle'. The

[36] *Committee on Employment of Prisoners*, op. cit., p. 189; HO45/22974/542336/15–16; P. Com. 9/180; Ann. Rep. of P. Com. for 1936, op. cit., pp. 719–720.

[37] Ibid., p. 188; P. Com. 9/183; P. Com. 9/21. See also A. Rodger, 'Vocational Guidance at Borstal', *Howard Journal*, vol. 3 (1932), pp. 51–6; *idem*, *A Borstal Experiment in Vocational Guidance* (1937); *Lancet*, vol. 1 (1937), p. 576; *Magistrate*, vol. 4 (1937), p. 1145.

[38] See Vidler, op. cit., pp. 22–4; Hood, op. cit., p. 125; Leo Page, *Crime and the Community* (1937), p. 285. As for educational work in the Borstals, the staff lacked the necessary training and experience to deal with the Borstal boy who was either illiterate or a poor reader: Ann. Rep. of P. Com. for 1936, op. cit., p. 719.

rigorous discipline led, furthermore, to an inflexibility in the whole scheme of Borstal training. According to Vidler, the basis of the training in Feltham and Portland 'was to dangle the carrot in front of the donkey, the young men earning their grades by good behaviour, the way they lived according to the rules being the yard stick'. Learning the ropes was not, however, the same as learning to live in the outside world; it was a form of institutionalization. As Vidler advised Samuel Hoare in October 1938, 'A rigid discipline tends to make the well behaved institutional lad more than ever reliant on props, and the badly behaved lad more bitter and more dangerous.' Vidler's testimony, plus that of inmates like Brendan Behan, must be put against the official submission that the closed Borstals were unregimented, educational havens.[39]

Discharge

Given the severe break that departing the institution represented for many Borstal boys, preparing them for discharge was given increasing attention. Despite allegations that boys were discharged too early, very few were granted early release. In 1937, of 822 discharges, over a half spent more than two years under training; 702 served over eighteen months. Only fourty-four were discharged within twelve months. In 1934 a discharge house was formed at Camp Hill, with a view both to encouraging lads to stand on their feet after two years of institutional life, and to weaning boys from the supportive relationship with their housemasters. For two or three months before release, lads were expected to get to work and to organize their spare time without the help of a housemaster, and to wear discharge clothes on Sundays. The experiment was not markedly successful, perhaps because outside conditions were hard to simulate, and by 1938 Vidler advised the Home Secretary that a period of camp life for up to six months before discharge was required for 'the Portland and institutionalized types'.[40] Also in 1934, a system of home leave was tried at Feltham Borstal, a practice copied from the Home Office schools. On reaching the special grade, lads were allowed to visit their homes for a weekend on parole.

[39] R. P. Maxwell, *Borstal and Better* (1956), p. 116; P. Com. 9/76; Vidler, op. cit., pp. 14–15, 30–2; Templewood Papers, Box X: 8 (13); Brendan Behan, *Borstal Boy* (New York, 1970, 5th printing), Part 3.

[40] HO45/16976/485552/49; Edward Cadogan, *The Roots of Evil* (1937), p. 277.

The intentions of the scheme were to familiarize lads with outside conditions, afford a test of reliability before full release, and allow probation officers and Borstal associates the chance to discuss the question of employment. Few lads abused the privilege, so the scheme was extended to the other closed Borstals. Interestingly, the Prison Commission worked by stealth; not until 1937 were the press told about the scheme of home leave.[41] The public support for Borstal training was too important to be squandered.

After-Care

In the early thirties the work of the Borstal Association was dogged by worsening trade conditions. A typical complaint, heard at an executive committee meeting in July 1933, stated that 'the North-west coast of England is deluged with cheap Irish labour, and that and the slump in shipping and in cotton and the recent embargo on the export of English coal to Southern Ireland, have produced an unexampled state of depression'. This coincided with a rapid increase in Borstal discharges. The shortage of factory jobs compelled the association to place lads in, for example, kitchen jobs in hotels, which were not, as a rule, of long duration. A brief experiment with 'transplantation' to other parts of the country failed, as most lads soon fled back to their home districts. By the mid thirties, labour conditions were improving and the number of discharges was falling. It became possible for Borstal Association visitors to spend longer with the lads about to be discharged, and to chat with their housemasters and trade instructors. The result was a less formal relationship between the boy and the association, and stronger links between the Association and the institutions.[42]

The two most significant developments in after-care were the employment of more probation officers as after-care agents, and the formation of Borstal voluntary committees. Probation officers played an important part in after-care by 1935; of 294 associates actively supervising lads, 216 were probation officers. Opinions differed, however, about the value of using probation officers in this role. The

[41] Ann. Rep. of P. Com. for 1934, PP 1935–6, XIV (Cmd. 5153), p. 485; Ann. Rep. for 1936, op. cit., p. 718; HO45/17059/666054/1–7.

[42] BA, *Minutes*, 13 Jan. 1932, 12 July 1933, 17 Jan. 1934; Fry, op. cit., p. 162; Report of Work of Borstal Association for 1935, in BA, *Minutes*, Jan. 1936.

local knowledge and experience of probation officers were useful in finding work and lodgings for discharged Borstal boys. But officers generally gave less time to Borstal lads than to probationers; and lads met one another again when they went to the probation office. In 1936 the Departmental Committee on Social Services in Courts of Summary Jurisdiction provisionally recommended that probation officers should be relieved of after-care work, in view of their burgeoning duties. Immediately the new director of the Borstal Association, T. Paterson Owens, asked committee chairman, Sydney Harris, to re-think the issue. A supporting memorandum argued that after-care by probation officers was 'more consistent and unified than it would be by a heterogeneous crowd of untrained and inexperienced workers'. Convinced by the evidence, the Social Services committee agreed that probation officers should be employed on after-care work. This was doubtless a relief for the Borstal Association. By 1937 it was responsible for more than 2,000 licensees; sufficient voluntary workers could not be found to deal with this number of cases.[43]

The original objective of the Borstal Association, of course, was to recruit 'friends' to provide sympathy and spiritual guidance. Lest professional probation officers failed to afford the same, an experiment was begun in 1935 of providing for each boy a sympathetic friend. The task of finding these voluntary workers was given to local Borstal voluntary committees, representing social work organizations such as Rotary Club, Toc H, and the YMCA. By 1938, voluntary committees were active in over forty towns and districts, helping to bring the principle of individualization of treatment into after-care.[44]

Results

The Prison Commissioners were always ready to answer critics, particularly those who claimed that the prisons were full of ex-Borstal boys. As one annual report drove home, in a male prison population of 8,462 on 1 February 1936, only 688, or 8.1 per cent, were ex-Borstal boys; yet the number of lads who had passed through the Borstal system since 1908 was over 13,000. The success rate of Borstal training

[43] BA, *Minutes*, 25 June 1935; *Committee on Employment of Prisoners*, op. cit., pp. 130–1; P. Com. 9/147; Departmental Committee on Social Services in Courts of Summary Jurisdiction, *Evidence* 82(o).

[44] Ibid., *Evidence* 72 (Scott); P. Com. 9/141; P. Com. 9/5; P. Com. 9/147; BA, *Report for 1938*, pp. 22–24.

was thus of obvious concern to the commissioners. For boys discharged in the three years 1932–4, 57.9 per cent had not been reconvicted, and 22.6 per cent had been reconvicted once only, in periods varying from two to five years after discharge. The results were worse than those of the 1920s. This was due, in part, to a more accurate method of data collection and, in part, to the rapid increase in the number of committals to Borstal and the wretched employment conditions in the early 1930s. In subsequent years, however, the figures improved slightly. Not surprisingly, the highest success rates came from the three open Borstals, the lowest rates from Camp Hill and Portland.[45]

To some extent, the gratifying results related to the type of working-class boy entering the institutions in the 1930s. It is unlikely that they rejoiced in the loss of freedom or the rigid discipline; but it is also unlikely that they suffered any material hardship. As one boy said to Tom Hayes, 'Until I was sent to Borstal I was never not hungry.' More importantly, most inter-war lads were reasonably compliant towards persons in authority; and they were probably not accustomed to any sympathetic attention. Little wonder, then, that boys responded positively to housemasters who took a personal interest in their progress. How much more so, when housemasters in North Sea Camp breached the class divide and shared work, food and accommodation with the lads. As Vidler recalled,

> As a whole, they responded to kindness and understanding, and they did not claim privileges as their right. They could be taught to understand that a privilege demanded an obligation.[46]

The public approval which a good success rate induced had made it possible to extend greater freedom to Borstal boys, either via home leave or, more crucially, through training under open conditions. Thus, when in January 1938 Walter Elliott, Secretary of State for Scotland, informed Home Secretary Hoare that Borstal treatment was no more or less successful than imprisonment, the response was swift. Hoare asked Harold Scott if the figures justified Elliott's contention, for if they did not, said Hoare, 'I am anxious to disabuse him from

[45] Ann. Rep. of P. Com. for 1935, PP 1936–7, XV (Cmd. 5430), pp. 24–5; Healy and Alper, op. cit., pp. 216–7; HO45/16977/485552/60; Hood, op. cit., p. 208. The picture in 1940, of discharges during 1934 to 1938, was that 62.4% had not since been reconvicted, whilst 19.3% had been reconvicted once only.

[46] Interviews with Alan Bainton and Tom Hayes; Vidler, op. cit., pp. 145–6. See also D. M. Lowson, *City Lads in Borstal* (Liverpool, 1970), pp. 5–6.

what would appear to be a very dangerous and reactionary view'. Scott accepted that Elliott's figures were correct as regards first offenders but a Borstal boy was generally not a first offender. When Borstal boys were compared with offenders sentenced to imprisonment after one or more previous convictions, the number of failures was greater in the latter category. To have concluded otherwise would have undermined all that the Prison Commission had tried to do in the inter-war years, in a word, to diminish the use of imprisonment and to encourage the use of Borstal training, which, wrote Maxwell, 'though it is deterrent, is nevertheless calculated to have a reformative rather than a deformative effect on the character of the individual sentenced'.[47]

Use of Imprisonment

The number of young persons sent to prison on conviction showed a welcome reduction between 1932 and 1936. Yet in 1934, 1,900 youths (and 128 girls) were imprisoned, and around 50 per cent received short sentences of one month or less. A high proportion, moreover, had either no previous proved offences or three or more previous convictions, for whom probation and Borstal training respectively would have been more appropriate. From the mid thirties Henriques, chairman of the Young Persons Discharged Prisoners Aid Society, campaigned for the abolition of boys' prisons, on the grounds that no decent system of after-care existed. He was joined by Sir Vivian Henderson and John Watson, secretary of the National Association of Prison Visitors. In March 1935 the association investigated the condition of 318 boy prisoners aged seventeen to twenty-one in twenty-one local prisons. In sixteen of the twenty-one prisons, according to Watson, the boys

> were located in the same halls and frequently on the same landings as men prisoners. In many of these prisons the number of young prisoners is usually small . . . so that any proper organisation of work, education, or physical training is practically impossible, and the boys spend long hours alone locked in their cells.

Along with the Howard League, the Association of Prison Visitors called for a statutory prohibition of imprisonment for youths. The Magistrates Association played its part, instructing new justices to

[47] P. Com. 9/89; P. Com. 9/8; A. Maxwell, *Treatment of Crime* (1938), p. 22.

begin their sentencing deliberation with 'an almost desperate anxiety not to commit to prison'.[48]

Pending legislation, the Prison Commission tried to help the imprisoned. From August 1935, young prisoners with sentences of over one month were transferred to 'collecting centres' where they could be better segregated and treated. But a collecting centre was still a prison. Paterson vigorously spelt this out to an annual conference of visiting justices. An adolescent was not reclaimable, said Paterson, 'by cramping him in a cell in a city prison and confining his employment within a prison cell. I refuse to be party to saying that that is the right place for an adolescent offender.' And a stern reprimand followed:

> The fault is not with us. The fault is with you magistrates who sit, week by week, upon the Bench. When you have a young offender before you . . . and you prefer to send him to the local prison for three weeks or three months rather than to the Sessions to be sent to Borstal for three years, you are doing your best to create one more habitual criminal.[49]

This official tenet, that imprisonment was rarely necessary for a young person, had a tenacious hold upon the policy discussions which took place in the lead up to the Criminal Justice Bill of 1938.

The Future of Borstal Training

In the 1920s, the Home Office had appealed to the criminal courts to take a less strict interpretation of the law and thereby lower the barriers to a Borstal sentence. At last, in the 1930s the judiciary began to comply, encouraged by the Court of Criminal Appeal. In 1932, a

[48] HO45/20947/448767/42; Ann. Rep. of P. Com. for 1934, op. cit., p. 482; P. Com. 9/147; *The Times*, 5 June 1935, p. 12; *New Statesman*, 13 Feb. 1937, p. 234; *Magistrate*, vol. 4 (1937), p. 1213; *The Boy*, vol. 8 (1935), p. 218; *Howard Journal*, vol. 4 (1937), p. 398; *The Year Book of Education, 1936*, p. 861. See also Table 13.

[49] HO45/20084/482137/19; Ann. Rep. of P. Com. for 1935, op. cit., p. 19. There was continued regret in the nineteen-thirties at the absence of a central remand home or observation centre for young adults, who were still being remanded to prison. In 1936, however, the Prison Commission arranged for reports on the physical and mental condition of prisoners to be sent to the London stipendiaries in all cases remanded by the metropolitan courts to Wormwood Scrubs boys' prison, in the hope that fewer prison sentences would result. See HO45/20947/448767/34–39; HO45/14941/652087; P. Com. 9/234. As for imprisonment in default of payment of fines, the Money Payments Act 1935, obliged courts to use supervision before imprisoning fine-defaulters under twenty-one. Hence, the number of young adults received into prison on conviction fell in 1936. See HO45/16736/687245/3; Ann. Rep. of P. Com. for 1936, op. cit., p. 697.

batch of appeals led the court to request information of the prison authorities as to the general principles which guided them in recommending Borstal detention. The department's response emphasized that the existence of five Borstals, and the consequent system of classification, so diminished the risk of contamination that no offender was either too bad or too good for Borstal. At the request of the Lord Chief Justice, Paterson gave evidence to the court, along the lines of the departmental note. The court, therefore, substituted Borstal sentences in a number of cases.[50] Would the other courts now take the view that a wider variety of offenders could be sent to Borstal?

The Prison Commission certainly believed that the increase in the number sentenced to Borstal in the early thirties was due, in part, to sentencing practice. However, the statistical evidence suggests that the rise in committals to Borstal between 1927 and 1933 was due more to an increase in crime amongst this age group than to a change in judicial practice. Having said that, the proportion of Borstal boys with no previous convictions (formerly considered 'too good' for Borstal) increased slightly between 1928 and 1935. Moreover, the increase in Borstal committals from 1936 seems partly to reflect a change in sentencing practice. By 1938, one half of all custodial sentences were to Borstal training, a very different picture from the 1920s.[51]

What about a legislative boost to the expansion of the Borstal system? The Prison Commission was still eager for legislation to be introduced on this subject in a short bill. Such a measure, the commissioners advised Home Secretary Simon in February 1936, should amend the statutory provisions relating to Borstal in two key respects. First, courts of summary jurisdiction should be empowered to pass a sentence of Borstal detention. This proposal (which would obviate the need to commit offenders to prison while awaiting sentence at quarter sessions) was nourished in the thirties by reformers like Le Mesurier, leader of the women social workers at the London boys' prison, by individual benches of magistrates, and by Borstal visiting committees. But it was a controversial reform. The Lord Chief

[50] P. Com. 9/88; *R.* v. *William Rankin*, 23 Cr. App. R. (1932), 200; *Magistrate*, vol. 2 (1932), p. 602. Rankin, aged sixteen, had not been previously convicted, and the court felt it would be wrong to send him to prison. See also *Law Times*, vol. 173 (1932), p. 166; *Justice of the Peace*, vol. 95 (1931), p. 146.

[51] Ann. Rep. of P. Com. for 1931, PP 1932–3, XV (Cmd. 4295), p. 432; Hood, op. cit., pp. 49–50, 56–7. The increase in the rate of committal of boys to Borstal in the late thirties was also due to the rise in the age limit for Borstal training to twenty-three. See also Table 13.

Justice, speaking on behalf of the King's Bench judges in November 1932, had objected to the granting of power to commit directly to Borstal. In the early thirties the Home Office feared that summary courts would use Borstal in cases where less restrictive methods could be adopted. In addition, the proposal involved a substantial extension of the powers of summary courts. By 1936, however, the Prison Commission had the support of the former chairman, Maxwell, now Deputy Under-Secretary of State. Maxwell was persuaded most by the fact that existing procedures led to a continued use of short prison sentences. As he explained in an internal memorandum,

> I believe one of the main reasons why sentences of imprisonment are imposed on youths who need training is that Courts of Summary Jurisdiction do not like handing over to another Court cases which they feel they are perfectly competent to deal with themselves. This feeling may be illogical, but I am sure it is wide-spread. I remember talking to a member of the Bench in my own district who is an experienced barrister, and he said 'Of course we are not going to send to Quarter Sessions boys from our own neighbourhood about whom we know much more than Quarter Sessions can ever know.'[52]

In the choice between justices presently misusing imprisonment, on the one hand, and justices misusing a new power to impose Borstal sentence, on the other hand, Maxwell thus concluded that 'the balance of advantage is heavily on the side of the second course'. He predicted some opposition to the proposal, but also 'a very large measure of support from persons who have taken a serious interest in the treatment of youthful offenders'.

The second amendment that the Prison Commission proposed concerned the definition of suitability for Borstal. For some years reformers like Henriques, the Magistrates Association, and the Borstal Association had pressed for an amendment to section 10 of the Criminal Justice Administration Act 1914, whereby the requirement of a *previous* proved offence would be abolished. Although Maxwell in the Home Office accepted that section 10 led to prison sentences for first offenders and for those put on probation by a summary court (where no conviction was recorded against them), he felt that abolishing the requirement would arouse controversy and might put pressure on Borstal accommodation. In contrast, the prison commissioners wished to make Borstal available to a number of currently ineligible offenders.

[52] HO45/21855/687218/2; HO45/16976/485552/53–4.

In addition to the question of previous conviction, finally, the commissioners thought the requirement that the offender must be of 'criminal habits or tendencies' or an associate of 'persons of bad character' was much too restrictive. 'The need for training', they insisted, 'rather than the existence of formed criminal habits should be the criterion . . . '[53] Legislation on both these issues, however, had to await the arrival at the Home Office in May 1937, of Samuel Hoare, who showed an enthusiasm and a depth of personal conviction for penal reform unknown in a Home Secretary since the early twentieth century.

Criminal Justice Bill

'When I became Home Secretary in 1937', Hoare recalled nearly ten years later, 'I was greatly struck by an anomaly. On the one hand penal reform had, compared with other social reforms, made little or no advance in 50 years. On the other, a mass of invaluable material had been accumulated by practical experience and expert inquiries for creating an up-to-date and efficient prison system.' Hoare resolved to remedy this state of affairs by legislation, the central axiom of which would be that the most fundamental prison reform was to keep people out of prison. Between June and August 1937, he spoke with his under-secretaries about instituting an inquiry into the increase in juvenile delinquency. The question at issue, said Hoare, revealingly, 'is whether we need any further support to meet the kind of criticisms (e.g. of sentimentality and sloppiness) that will probably be raised during the passage of a Criminal Justice Bill?' He interviewed 'practitioners' like W. Young, governor of Wormwood Scrubs, and Vivian Henderson, chairman of the Conference of Borstal visiting committees. Whilst Young deplored short prison sentences for the young, Henderson

[53] See HO144/21948/579079/1–3; BA, *Minutes*, 13 July 1932; B. Henriques, 'Boy Prisoners', *New Statesman*, 13 Feb. 1937, p. 235; *Magistrate*, vol. 2 (1932), p. 588. The Prison Commission also proposed activating the power in the 1908 Act to raise the maximum age for Borstal from twenty-one to twenty-three. The experiment at Sherwood Borstal, where the oldest offenders had been collected since 1932, had proved sufficiently successful to warrant the proposal. The Home Office agreed, and in September 1936 the higher courts were informed of the change in the age of Borstal eligibility: HO45/21855/687218/1 and 2; Ann. Rep. of P. Com. for 1935, op. cit., p. 21. Finally, the Prison Commission recommended that the length of a Borstal sentence, then not less than two or more than three years, should be three years in all cases: P. Com. 9/60.

wished to debar magistrates from sentencing anyone under twenty-one years to imprisonment. Hoare also drew on the experience of Maxwell, whom he asked to list the departmental proposals concerning young adults. In reply, Maxwell listed the establishment of observation centres, extending the probation hostel system, empowering courts of summary jurisdiction to pass Borstal sentences, and restricting summary courts from sentencing a person under twenty-one to imprisonment. Firmly rejected was a short-term Borstal sentence which, declared Maxwell, would be imprisonment under another name.[54]

In late 1937 the pace of reform picked up. A paper went to the Cabinet explaining the proposed legislation. Following Cabinet approval, a bill was prepared and submitted for study to the Home Affairs Committee. The main objects of the bill were to carry out the recommendations of the Committee on Persistent Offenders, to effect improvements in the probation system, and to introduce improved methods of dealing with young offenders, with a view to keeping them out of prison. The highest priority was given to adolescent offenders and to remedying the evils of their imprisonment. This was to be achieved, first, by limiting the power of magistrates' courts to use imprisonment. One clause, the very heart of the bill, provided that a court of summary jurisdiction should not sentence a person between seventeen and twenty-one to imprisonment unless it had information on the character and antecedents of the offender, and was of the view that no other method of dealing with him was suitable. It was also proposed that from some future date, to be fixed by Order in Council, summary courts should be prohibited from sending persons under twenty-one to prison.[55] Secondly, the bill sought to diminish the use of imprisonment by strengthening and augmenting alternative methods of treatment.

Some forty or fifty additional probation hostels were envisaged, to ensure that all courts had access to such facilities. The definition of eligibility for Borstal was to be enlarged, and courts of summary jurisdiction were to be given the power to send offenders to Borstal. This latter was likely to be a controversial point, and hence a detailed argument was developed for the Home Affairs Committee. The

[54] *Evening Standard*, 28 Nov. 1946, in Templewood Papers, Pam. 2; HO45/19065/807624/1; Templewood Papers, Box X: 7 (8).

[55] Criminal Justice Bill, PP 1938–39, vol. II (Cmd. 4), c. 27; HO45/17666/805270/3; Templewood Papers, Box X : 7 (9).

summary courts were clearly vital to the task of improving the modes of dealing with offenders. Nearly 90 per cent of those under twenty-one found guilty of indictable offences were dealt with by the magistrates. For many years, of course, the Home Office had pressed the justices to stop imprisoning young people. But how could this policy be implemented when courts which could use imprisonment had no power to pass a Borstal sentence? In a word, by reserving the Borstal sentence for the higher courts, magistrates thought the sentence was for 'those offenders whose offences are so great that they cannot be sufficiently punished by the powers of punishment vested in a Court of Summary Jurisdiction.' As the Home Affairs Committee was informed:

> The Justices naturally ask themselves not 'can we save this young person from imprisonment by sending him to another Court for a Borstal sentence?', but 'need we refer this case to a higher Court or can we adequately deal with the offender by the use of our own powers?'

The imposition of short prison sentences, a weapon in the justices' armoury, was the inevitable outcome. Over and above these practical considerations, the proposal to give magistrates the power to sentence to Borstal was an integral part of the clause to end the imprisonment of persons under twenty-one dealt with summarily. After all, the effect of the clause to abolish imprisonment was 'to require Courts of Summary Jurisdiction to consider every other method, including Borstal training, before considering imprisonment for a young offender . . . Justices could hardly be expected to consider a method of treatment which is outside their jurisdiction before they consider a method which is within their jurisdiction.'[56]

For offenders who could not appropriately be dealt with by probation or Borstal, the Criminal Justice Bill proposed two new alternatives to imprisonment: task centres and Howard houses. The first proposal was for those convicted of minor offences and those who had failed to pay fines, who could be most effectively 'pulled up' by having to chop wood, or do some other punitive task 'at times when [they] would otherwise be going to a football match or to a cinema or enjoying other recreations'. The scheme was to be launched in London

[56] HO45/17666/805270/3 and 10. In addition, the definition of Borstal eligibility emphasized the need for training, not proof of the existence of criminality; and the Borstal sentence was to be three years in all cases.

under the auspices of the Prison Commission; thereafter, the police authorities would be responsible for the scheme's extension. Howard houses, where youths would live under control, but from which they would go out to work in civilian employment, were for offenders who were not in need of Borstal training, yet because of unsuitable homes or poor environments, could not properly be treated under the Probation Act.[57]

Finally, for those offenders over seventeen remanded to prison, the Home Secretary wanted to establish remand centres where pre-sentence reports could be prepared for the information of the courts. A start was to be made in London, with a remand centre to accommodate 500, with the prospect of three more centres in the large provincial towns. In February 1938, the Home Affairs committee and the Cabinet authorized the introduction of the Criminal Justice Bill into parliament.

The press and parliamentary response to the Criminal Justice Bill was generally very favourable. 'A notable, a welcome and an enlightened endeavour', declared the *Spectator*, 'to increase the constructive and reformative element in our penal system at the expense of the purely deterrent'. '[A] great advance towards a more humane and more scientific penal system', claimed the Howard League. Most MPs expressed agreement with the general principles and purpose of the bill, from the Conservative Quintin Hogg, making his maiden speech, to the old Socialist, George Lansbury. The Home Office now entered into discussion with various interested parties (Borstal governors and housemasters, chief constables, the Parliamentary Penal Reform Group), in order to increase public and parliamentary support for the bill. In consequence, the Home Secretary, in his speech on the second reading, could declare that the bill was based on the direct experience of social workers, prison governors, and the prison commissioners, as well as on the conclusions of official reports. As such, the bill was said to be the product of neither unsupported theories nor sentimentalism.[58]

But criticism there was. It centred on the proposal to allow magistrates' courts to commit offenders to Borstal. If criticism of corporal punishment came broadly from the political Right, then criticism of direct committal came largely from the Left.

[57] HO45/17666/805270/10.

[58] *Hansard*, vol. 342, 29 Nov. 1938, cols. 285, 298 and 327; Templewood Papers, Box X: 9 (24).

The Howard League had consistently opposed the power of direct committal to Borstal. In a memorandum prepared by George Benson for the Parliamentary Penal Reform Group, before the Criminal Justice Bill was drafted, it was stated that the power to award a period of detention for three years would be 'an extremely dangerous weapon to place at the disposal of the Summary Courts'. In February 1938, Benson, Paton, and Miss Fry discussed the proposal with Maxwell, to little effect. Again, in November 1938 the League pressed Maxwell on the issue, when he and Paterson met with the executive committee. Maxwell's argument that direct committal was a prerequisite for ultimately abolishing the power of a summary court to impose imprisonment on offenders under twenty-one, cut no ice with the League, which informed all MPs on the eve of the bill's second reading that they had severe doubts about this particular provision.[59]

During the second reading debate, Pethick-Lawrence, Chuter Ede, Stafford Cripps, and Clynes all pronounced the Labour party's objections to direct committal, on the grounds that a Borstal sentence represented a severe loss of liberty. 'I think it would be altogether wrong', said Pethick-Lawrence, 'to assume that Borstal is a kind of admirable boarding school, a sort of college for the children of working people'. Outside Westminster, the penal reform lobby kept up the fight. The Magistrates Association, Margery Fry and Clara Rackham all inveighed against the proposal. Rackham considered it 'the most disastrous feature of the Bill', a change so sweeping that it had to be explained by 'such a belief in the virtues of Borstal on the part of the Home Office, that their desire is both to widen the entrance to the utmost and also to secure that as many offenders as possible shall pass through'. In the face of such criticism, particularly from the Magistrates Association, Samuel Hoare backed down, abandoning the proposal to give summary courts the right of direct committal to Borstal.[60]

With the establishment of remand centres, however, one of the reasons for direct committal, that young offenders awaiting sentence by higher courts would not be kept in prison, would presumably fall. It

[59] Howard League, Minute Book, MSS 16B/1/3, E. C. meeting 7 Feb. and 28 Nov. 1938. cf. M. Ryan, *The Acceptable Pressure Group* (Farnborough, 1978), pp. 34–5.

[60] *Hansard*, vol. 342, 29 Nov. 1938, cols. 291 and 367; 1 Dec. 1938, cols. 636 and 715; *Magistrate*, vol. V (1939), p. 146; M. Fry, 'The Penal Reform Bill', *Fortnightly*, vol. 151 (1939), p. 8; *Probation*, vol. 3 (1939), p. 71; *Penal Reformer*, vol. 5 (1939), p. 11; *Howard Journal*, vol. 5 (1939), p. 151.

was hoped, moreover, that the provision of new alternatives to imprisonment, bridging the gap between probation and Borstal training, which short prison sentences filled, would lead to a substantial reduction in the number of young offenders sent to prison by summary courts. These new alternatives require further consideration, since the discussion that their proposed introduction prompted illustrates the main thrust of official policy towards young adult offenders in the 1930s.

New Alternatives to Imprisonment

It is unclear exactly when and where the idea behind task centres, or compulsory attendance centres, was conceived. Most probably the idea first surfaced before the Young Offenders Committee. The committee examined the possible extension of the system of detention in police cells for not more than four days, as a way of avoiding short prison sentences, and discussed the related suggestion that such detention might be made intermittent, with offenders sent to a cell for several consecutive weekends. The evidence that this is the birthplace of the attendance centre is strengthened by the report of a conference convened to discuss the proposals of the Young Offenders Committee. In response to a resolution opposing detention in police cells, Paterson suggested that the best way to deal with minor offenders whom you did not wish to imprison was to say to them:

> We will take away from you three spare evenings or your weekend. That is the time you really enjoy, but you shall surrender yourself, not to go away to prison but to sacrifice your leisure, as a reminder that you are not going to be allowed to make yourself a nuisance to your neighbours.[61]

Indeed, Paterson deserves a good deal of credit for raising and reiterating this idea for a new penalty. In evidence to the Young Offenders Committee, he spoke of a more rigid probation for the young adult, compelling him to surrender his leisure for four evenings a week and for part of his weekends. In an address to a magistrates' conference in 1930, Paterson again spoke of petty offenders on week-nights being 'made to chop wood until 10 o'clock, or on a Saturday

[61] *The Treatment of Young Offenders*, op. cit., p. 35; *Report of Young Offenders Committee*, op. cit., pp. 1047–49; *British Journal of Delinquency*, vol. 2 (1951–2), p. 242. cf. *Attendance Centres*. An Enquiry by the Cambridge Institute of Criminology on the use of s. 19 of the Criminal Justice Act 1948, by F. H. McClintock (1961), p. 3.

afternoon instead of going to a football match'.[62] For these youngsters, deprivation of leisure attracted Paterson more than deprivation of liberty.

His was not a lone voice. Le Mesurier advocated dealing with minor offenders 'in public-school fashion': a task of work, completed outside working hours, in a room attached to the probation office. In 1935, Manchester stipendiary, J. Wellesley Orr, actually experimented with young offenders convicted of larceny. 'In such cases', according to the head of the Children's Branch, 'he had been remanding them for four days in the police cells, and then remanding them a second time in the same way, the effect being to give them six or seven days . . . solitary confinement; preventing them from going to football matches on Saturday afternoon, etc.' While in custody, the police left them to stew in their own juices. At the end of seven days, the difference in their attitude, claimed Wellesley Orr, was striking, and no lad so dealt with had reappeared before the court over a period of eight months. However, this was more of a 'short and sharp sentence' to teach unruly youths to respect the law, than a disciplinary deprivation of leisure which would not involve a loss of employment.[63]

In the first draft of the Criminal Justice Bill, task centres found a place, designed to 'pull up' the undisciplined boy by depriving him of his leisure and making him do something in the nature of a 'fatigue'. Harold Scott informed Hoare that lads would be employed on heavy work, such as chopping wood, with some 'brisk physical exercise in the open air,' and possibly an 'educational task such as a requirement to write an account of his occupation or his life'. The Conference of Chief Constables, however, protested that the police ought not to have the responsibility of administering a criminal penalty. Furthermore, the Lancashire chief constable complained that the term 'task centre' evoked all the old prejudices attaching to the poor law and the casual ward for vagrants, and he hoped that the regime would consist less of monotonous labour and more of physical or educational training.[64]

To meet these criticisms, the department decided that the centres would also teach offenders to use their leisure, by way of physical training and of elementary instruction in woodwork and metalwork. By February 1938 the name had become 'correction centre', although

[62] *Young Offenders Committee*, op. cit., *Evidence*, q. 1159 (Paterson); *Magistrate*, vol. 2 (1930), p. 407.

[63] Le Mesurier, *Boys in Trouble*, op. cit., pp. 20 and 265; HO144/22634/677145/8.

[64] Templewood Papers, Box X: 7 (11); HO45/17667/805270/22 and 45.

the combination, not to say confusion, of deterrent and training purposes remained. By the time of the second reading of the Criminal Justice Bill in November, the Home Secretary predicted that the atmosphere of what were to be called 'compulsory attendance centres' would be, 'within, of course, more rigid rules, that of a well-run boys' club or similar institution'. All this was settled before the Cadogan Committee on Corporal Punishment proposed for the minor offender 'some form of short and sharp punishment which will pull him up and give him the lesson which he needs . . .'[65] Cadogan, anyway, was probably thinking less of detention during leisure hours, and more of a short-term, punitive detention sentence.

Alongside the discussion about attendance centres ran a protracted debate over a short-term detention scheme. Two items were on the agenda: a punitive detention sentence and a short-term Borstal sentence, neither of which proved acceptable either to the Prison Commission or the Home Office. The idea of a short-term Borstal had been raised by Miss Fry of the Howard League in evidence to the Young Offenders Committee. After an initial predisposition towards a system of short-term treatment, the committee concluded that it would interfere with the work of the ordinary Borstals. Instead, therefore, it recommended both greater use of probation orders, notably with a requirement of hostel residence, and early release on licence from a full Borstal sentence. The Prison Commission willingly followed this policy; a short-term Borstal would have undermined what Paterson took to be the essence of the Borstal sentence: diagnosis, treatment, and extended licence.[66]

In the mid thirties, the Howard League's persistent demand for short-term Borstals was joined by an appeal from the ranks of the magistracy for a sentence of short disciplinary detention. Henriques was prominent in this campaign for 'a place of detention . . . which will not even aim at character training . . . but which would be definitely punitive in purpose'. Young offenders, guilty of crimes of

[65] HO45/17666/805270/29–30, 33 and 36; P. Com. 9/222; *Hansard*, vol. 342, 29 Nov. 1938, col. 275; Crim. Justice Bill, op. cit., clauses 12 and 29. The details were that the offender might spend up to sixty hours of his leisure time in periods of not more than three hours. No obligation to provide centres was imposed on the police authorities; indeed, by 1939, the Prison Commission was thinking of appointing a Borstal housemaster to run each attendance centre. Finally, clause 40 of the bill prescribed a system of intermittent detention in a police station for minor offenders over seventeen years.

[66] *Evidence*, op. cit., p. 411.

adventure like stealing and driving cars, would be made to work so hard that they would never wish to return. Henriques wanted this kind of lad to be put on probation with a condition that the first month or two be spent in the place of detention. In June 1937, the Magistrates Association entered the lists, recommending 'young offenders detention', a sentence of between three and twelve months, followed by a year's supervision. A month later, a deputation to the Home Office from the Conference of Visiting Justices recommended some form of short-term Borstal training.[67]

The magistracy made no impression, however, on the department, where the conviction remained strong that there were grave objections to short-term establishments. 'Disastrous' was Maxwell's view of the proposal of a short-term Borstal. 'It is essential', the Home Secretary advised the Cabinet in December 1937, 'to resist a proposal which means in effect a system of Boys' Prisons.' The objections were essentially threefold. Firstly, magistrates would send to such places large numbers whom they presently either put on probation or sent to Borstal, and thus damage the latter two systems. Secondly, these special places would, like the prison, hold a mixed population of youths of different types, since the shortness of sentence would preclude any classification according to character. Thirdly, the problem of contamination, allied to the brevity of sentence, would impose a rigid system of discipline on these establishments and rule out any scheme of progressive training. In short, a six months' sentence meant to the department, not a modified Borstal system, but a system of boys' prisons, with all the evils that imprisonment was heir to.[68]

In the Criminal Justice Bill, therefore, the department proposed that a Borstal should be set aside for offenders requiring a short training, who would be licensed after six months or so. If early discharge could not be recommended, offenders would be transferred to another Borstal for long-term training.[69] In addition, of course, the department proposed the Howard house, which would be a stricter form of probation hostel. The offender would earn wages at the going rate for

[67] Howard League, Minute Book, MSS 16B/1/2, E.C. meeting, 9 Dec. 1937; *Magistrate*, vol. 4 (1936), p. 1095; HO45/21855/687218/18; HO45/20084/482137/21; *The Times*, 19 Oct. 1937, p. 11; *Probation*, vol. 2 (1938), p. 183; Leo Page, *Crime and the Community* (1937), p. 266. The Conference of Visiting Justices, headed by Sir Vivian Henderson, submitted that, if imprisonment was to be abolished, a short alternative sentence was required; a boy could not always be sent to three years Borstal.

[68] Templewood Papers, Box X: 7 (7); HO45/17666/805270/10.

[69] Ibid.

the district, and pay for his keep in the house, where he would stay for six months, remaining under supervision for a further six months.[70] Learning how to make use of freedom through a disciplined life of regular work and recreation was considered to be a better solution to adolescent crime than a short and largely punitive detention, whether served in a short-term Borstal or a new detention institution.

Thus the effective coalition of Maxwell and Paterson stood firm against the proponents of a short-term detention scheme. It was not even dislodged by the Cadogan committee's suggestion of 'special places of detention', which bore a close resemblance to Basil Henriques' earlier proposal.[71] In whatever form the idea was served up, it was condemned as a challenge to the system of Borstal training. If the training programme were to be abbreviated, it would be done by early discharge on licence from places like North Sea Camp, following an assessment by the Borstal authorities of the offender's response to training and chance of success on release. All discretion was to be kept in the hands of the Prison Commission, none bestowed on the magistracy.

Yet the magistracy had an important role in Sir Samuel Hoare's scheme of things. If the imprisonment of young offenders was to end, the summary courts had to be given the power of committal to Borstal, in the hope that they would use it and trust the Borstal authorities to release the less hardened offenders on licence at an early date. Of course, direct committal to Borstal proved unacceptable to the penal reform lobby, and it was removed from the Criminal Justice Bill, even before the entire measure ran up against the outbreak of war. So after all the well-laid plans to terminate the use of imprisonment for young offenders, the cardinal theme of inter-war penal policy, the official 'reformers' had to fall back on the criminal courts. As Maxwell resignedly minuted in October 1939:

> . . . we can only hope that the Summary Courts may be induced to make still wider use of their power to commit for a Borstal sentence young offenders who

[70] See Crim. Justice Bill, op. cit., c. 13; *Hansard*, vol. 342, 29 Nov. 1938, col. 276. See also H. Mannheim, *The Dilemma of Penal Reform* (1939), p. 92. Mannheim, the criminologist, was struck by the fact that clause 13 required employment outside the Howard house to be arranged 'at a rate of wage not lower, and on conditions not less favourable, than those generally recognised in the district by good employers'. This, he felt, was a renunciation of less eligibility, and thus to be applauded.

[71] cf. Valerie Choppen, 'The Origins of the Philosophy of Detention Centres', *British Journal of Criminology*, vol. 10 (1970), p. 161.

need training... and that Courts of Quarter Sessions may come to recognise that Borstal sentences ought to be imposed on such offenders having regard to their character, even though the specific offence which they have committed may not be very serious.[72]

Summary

The 1930s were the apogee of the Borstal training system. Paterson's educationally-based philosophy of training, with its emphasis on self-discipline, found its most appropriate milieu in the new minimum security institutions. The governors and housemasters of the open Borstals, hand-picked by Paterson, devised training regimes which looked to provide the moral and vocational instruction that home, club, and school had failed to impart. If the disciplinary days of Ruggles-Brise continued to darken the closed Borstals, they overshadowed neither Lowdham Grange nor North Sea Camp. Public and judicial opinion was contemporaneously persuaded, in part by the high success rate of Borstal training, to accept the provision of 'advantages' for young criminals that were not extended to the young unemployed. The public responded by momentarily relaxing the traditional constraints of 'less eligibility'; the judiciary by opening the Borstal gates to larger numbers and more varied types of young adult offender.

Such was the platform on which the prison commissioners began to erect the legislative edifice of the Criminal Justice Bill. At the heart of the new measure was the clause instructing magistrates' courts to stop imprisoning young offenders. Essential adjuncts to this clause were, first, the provision of new alternatives to imprisonment, in the shape of task centres and Howard houses, and, second, the clause empowering summary courts to sentence offenders to Borstal training. The latter provision ran foul of the penal reform lobby, however, who were unable to accept that the magistracy could safely be entrusted with this large power. Borstals, they argued, were not improving boarding-schools for working-class lads; they were penal institutions that took away an offender's liberty for a considerable period. Confronted by these objections, the Home Secretary backed down, even though 'direct committal' was seen as a vital strand in the new policy for young offenders. When it came to a short detention scheme, however, the official view reigned supreme. Neither short-term

[72] HO144/21228/664824/23.

Borstals nor disciplinary detention were acceptable to the likes of Paterson and Maxwell, who had laboured for years to make the full Borstal sentence the exclusive custodial measure for young adult offenders. The administrators were not in the mood, in the late thirties, to endorse a scheme of punitive, prison-like institutions.

According to its promoters, the Borstal system reoriented the behaviour of delinquent youth and eased their return to society as lawful citizens. Little regard was paid to the stigmatizing effects of a custodial sentence. Whilst Paterson, for one, acknowledged the crucial role of a well-staffed probation service, and promoted the task or attendance centre as another alternative to imprisonment, his concern for individual treatment made him eager to bring offenders into the arms of the reformatories.[73] He seems rarely to have seen any conflict between incarcerating and reforming young offenders, except inside the prisons. This interventionist attitude led gradually to a significant increase in the mechanics of state control of delinquency, and notably in the discretionary authority of penal administrators. One explanation of this development is that Borstal reformatories had a class mission to perform; they were the ultimate weapon deployed by the State to inculcate obedience in working-class children. Such a view, however, forecloses, rather than unlocks, historical debate. More revealing is a detailed assessment of the distinctive approach to penal policy formulated by the 'liberal progressives', humanistic administrators in the Fabian and positivist tradition of social enquiry and planning. They crucially laid a framework of principle, policy, and practice in the inter-war years, which survived the wartime flux of the early forties, and was available to the post-war Labour government, eager to inaugurate a universal welfare state.

[73] Probation was more widely used, of course, than Borstal or imprisonment. In 1938, 43% of offenders aged seventeen to twenty-one found guilty of indictable offences were put on probation, in comparison with 8.6% sentenced to Borstal and 7.4% to imprisonment: see Table 9. Note also that 20% of *all* probation orders were given to offenders aged seventeen to twenty-one: Table 7.

PART V

Delinquency and the Welfare State

10

War and the Criminal Justice Act 1948

In February 1940, the Home Secretary, Sir John Anderson, reassured the House of Commons that delinquency gave no real cause for concern, 'in spite of the conditions arising out of the war which might encourage youthful misbehaviour, including evacuation and the consequent disturbance of school life'. Hermann Mannheim, the German criminologist based at the London School of Economics, was better informed on the likely effect of war on crime. In 1941, Mannheim predicted that 'crime, and in particular juvenile delinquency, will increase even more than it did during the previous war'.[1] The actual amount and supposed causes of wartime delinquency are the subject of the present chapter, as is the response of the Home Office to the movement in crime. From October, 1940, the Home Office was directed by Herbert Morrison, the unassuming cockney boss of London Labour politics, a man of immense organizational and administrative skills.[2] This final chapter is also concerned with the damaging impact of war on the penal system, and, in particular, with the plans for its future reconstruction, culminating in the Criminal Justice Act of 1948. Unlike the previous chapters, it deals with all young offenders under twenty-one years of age.

Statistics

The long-term trend in officially-recorded delinquency was as follows. The number of persons under seventeen found guilty of indictable offences rose rapidly to a peak in 1941, fell noticeably in 1942 and

[1] *Hansard*, vol. 356, 1 Feb. 1940, col. 1308; H. Mannheim, *War and Crime* (1941), p. 142. See also Mannheim, 'Some Reflections on Crime in War-Time', *Fortnightly*, vol. 157 (1942), p. 42.

[2] For Morrison, see *DNB*, *1961–70*, pp. 769–73; Bernard Donoughue and G. W. Jones, *Herbert Morrison. Portrait of a Politician* (1973), pp. 182, 237, 310 and 340.

1943, climbing to a second peak in 1945.[3] For young adults aged seventeen to twenty-one, the long-term trend was almost identical.[4] In the short term, the volume of delinquency rose rapidly in the early months of war, between September 1939 and August 1940. The increase in the number of children under fourteen found guilty of indictable offences during the first year of war, as compared with the previous year of peace, was 41 per cent. In the age group fourteen to seventeen, the increase for the same period was 22 per cent; in the age group seventeen to twenty-one, the increase was 5 per cent.[5] As for the distribution of delinquency, evacuation areas, reception areas and areas not directly involved in such population shifts, all registered increases in juvenile crime. London, Liverpool and other large cities were particularly affected.[6]

Causes

The increase in delinquency among young people was generally attributed to war conditions: evacuation, the black-out, shelter life, the ease of looting, high wages for boy and girl labour, and the closing of schools and youth clubs. However, the commonest explanation, echoing the orthodox view of the 1930s, was that the primary cause was to be found in the home, particularly the broken home. The circumstances of war severely aggravated the lack of home life and parental control. In September 1939, under threat of air raids, a million schoolchildren and nearly 400,000 mothers and infants were evacuated from London and other large industrial centres to billets in safer areas. This enforced migration disrupted the family and the educational system. Evacuated children experienced the emotional stresses and insecurities of being billeted in new homes. In evacuation

[3] See Tables 3 and 14, and Figure 1. There was no fall in 1942, however, in the number of *girls* under seventeen found guilty of indictable offences. The trend in persons under seventeen found guilty of *all* offences (indictable and non-indictable) was identical: Mannheim, *Juvenile Delinquency in an English Middletown* (1948), p. 13.

[4] See Tables 8 and 10 and Figure 2.

[5] See 'Juvenile Offences: A Joint Memorandum of the Home Office and the Board of Education', in PRO, HO45/20250/838406/12. For the age group twenty-one and over, there was a *decrease*, in the number found guilty of indictable offences for the same period, of 12%.

[6] See *Probation*, vol. 3 (1942), p. 234; *Justice of the Peace*, vol. 107 (1943), p. 243; Department of Social Science of Liverpool University, *Youthful Lawbreakers* (Liverpool, 1948), pp. 13–19; Richard M. Titmuss, *Problems of Social Policy* (1950), p. 148.

areas, shelter life weakened parental control, particularly at night, since juveniles often went to different shelters than their families. Finally, the increased employment of married women on war work, allied to the absence of fathers in the armed forces, led to much less supervision of children and adolescents.[7]

Probation officers, the police, penal experts, and the Home Office all endorsed this standard interpretation of delinquency. T. Paterson Owens, chief inspector of approved schools, declared that 'the absence of one and in many cases both parents' was a major cause of delinquency. Chief constables in their annual reports stressed the lack of parental control and guidance; probation officers underlined the role of evacuation in shattering home life for younger children. Clara Rackham, Hermann Mannheim and John Watson likewise pointed to the disruption of family life. The vast majority of young offenders in the juvenile court, according to Watson, came from broken homes, a judgement confirmed by the findings of both Carr-Saunders' enquiry into delinquency and Norwood East's examination of adolescent crime.[8]

Responses

There was little the Home Office could do to remedy the defects of home life. The department had its work cut out simply patching up the badly buffeted penal system. The rise in delinquency quickly overwhelmed the remand homes and approved schools. Remand homes became mere clearing-houses for the schools. At the close of 1941 there were 1,300 children in remand homes awaiting vacancies; several months elapsed, in many cases, before the child was transferred to a school. The closure of a number of approved schools in dangerous

[7] See Susan Isaacs, 'Cambridge Evacuation Survey', *Fortnightly*, vol. 153 (1940), p. 619; Mannheim, *War and Crime* (1941), p. 142; Eileen Younghusband, JP, in *Howard Journal*, vol. 6 (1941), pp. 20–1; *TES*, 4 Oct. 1941, p. 478; John A. F. Watson, 'The War and the Young Offender', *Fortnightly*, vol. 157 (1942), pp. 90–4; Mannheim, *Group Problems in Crime and Punishment* (1955), pp. 87–96.

[8] T. Paterson Owens, 'Approved Schools and Remand Homes', *Medico-Legal and Criminological Review*, vol. XIV (1946), p. 103; 'Juvenile Offences: A Joint Memorandum', op. cit.; *Police Chronicle*, 4 April 1941, p. 5; Rackham in *Eugenics Review*, vol. XXXIV (1942), p. 66; Mannheim, 'Some Reflections', op. cit., p. 44; Watson in *Magistrate*, vol. 7 (1944), p. 38; *TES*, 17 Jan. 1942, p. 32 (review of Carr-Saunders); W. Norwood East (in collaboration with P. Stocks and H. T. P. Young), *The Adolescent Criminal* (1942), p. 304. T. Paterson Owens succeeded A. H. Norris as Chief Inspector of Approved Schools in 1941. John Watson was Chairman of Tower Bridge juvenile court.

areas aggravated the accommodation problem, as a result of which the period of training had to be shortened. Faced with these problems, courts undoubtedly placed more children on probation, even though the probation service was depleted in terms of staff and disorganized by the evacuation of children to reception areas.[9] By March 1941, therefore, the Home Office was receiving complaints from all sides of the increase of juvenile crime and of the inadequacies of the judicial system to deal with children in trouble. C. P. Hill, an assistant secretary attached to the Children's Branch, decided that it was time to examine the position, especially since talk of post-war reconstruction prompted an assessment of the future treatment of delinquency.

The main failure, according to Hill, lay with the local authorities, who had excessive freedom to pursue their own policies. The Children's Branch had to resort to long-winded tactics of persuasion and pressure to get additional accommodation in remand homes and approved schools. Crown control of the schools was the answer. Hill also recommended the earlier treatment of delinquency, with greater restrictions on the practice of police cautioning, which was being used increasingly during the war. Sydney Harris, Assistant Under-Secretary of State, and former head of the Children's Branch, denied that relations between voluntary or local authority managers and central government were consistently bad. He accepted, however, that there was a strong case for a general inquiry into delinquency once the war was over. In the meantime, a conference of experts would suffice.[10]

A Home Office conference was convened in April 1941, between representatives of the central departments and of voluntary organizations, chief education officers, and magistrates, to consider both how to improve the methods of dealing with delinquency and how social and educational agencies could develop to keep juveniles from coming before the courts. The conference resulted in a joint memorandum by the Home Secretary and the President of the Board of Education, which laid stress on the role of prevention, notably by enforcing school attendance and by encouraging better use of leisure. The youth committees of local education authorities were asked 'to strengthen

[9] See Watson, 'The War', op. cit., p. 96; *Hansard*, vol. 370, 18 Mar. 1941, col. 29; Home Office, *Sixth Report on the Work of the Children's Department* (1951), p. 48.

[10] PRO, HO45/20250/838406/1. cf. *TES*, 16 Aug. 1941, p. 386. The Children's Branch had no real head between 1940, when J. F. Henderson retired, and 1942, when Blake Odgers was appointed. For the increase in the use of police cautioning, see *Magistrate*, vol. 6 (1943), pp. 206–7; E. Smithies, *Crime in Wartime* (1982), p. 180.

existing youth organisations and to develop new types', such as the Youth Service Corps. The concluding section of the memorandum dealt with the treatment of offenders along familiar lines: the need for younger juvenile court justices, the value of the probation system, the urgent need for remand home and approved school accommodation.[11]

A number of local conferences were subsequently held to consider the joint memorandum. The one convened by Middlesex County Council, for example, recommended the establishment of a service of child guidance clinics, and discussed the contentious idea that the supervision of juveniles on probation should be transferred to the education authority. Other local conferences considered the new crop of truancy, the need for closer co-operation between home, school, court, and probation service, and how parents could be made more responsible for the child's delinquency.[12] In practice, nothing spectacular resulted, which is hardly surprising in a country embroiled in a major war. A further reaction to the official memorandum, however, was to complain that by depicting delinquency as a war-created problem and by speaking mainly of leisure facilities, the Home Office was distracting attention from long-term planning. The discussion, grumbled Mannheim, had not yet led to 'anything like a comprehensive and constructive programme of reform . . . '[13] Not until mid-1942, in fact, did the department begin to explore the outlines of post-war penal reform. Before tackling the theme of reconstruction, however, it is necessary to examine the impact of war on specific parts of the criminal justice system.

The Juvenile Court

A recurrent demand in the war years was for the appointment of younger magistrates to the juvenile court panels, preferably those in close touch with local youth committees. In 1943 the Lord Chancellor, Lord Simon, asked all justices of seventy-five years and over to retire from membership of juvenile court panels, an action which affected

[11] For the Joint Memorandum of June 1941, see PRO, HO45/20250/838406/6A and 12; *TES*, 12 April 1941, p. 172.

[12] See *Hansard*, vol. 374, 11 Sept. 1941, col. 303 and vol. 378, 5 Mar. 1942, col. 813; *Police Review*, 27 June 1941, p. 401; *TES*, 2 Aug. 1941, p. 365, 11 April 1942, p. 176, 25 April 1942, p. 200, 3 Oct. 1942, p. 485; *Howard Journal*, vol. 6 (1942), pp. 93–4.

[13] Mannheim in *TES*, 30 Aug. 1941, p. 409. See also *Probation*, vol. 3 (1941), p. 221; *TES*, 21 June 1941, p. 291.

some 400 magistrates. This at least established the principle of an age limit, but seventy-five was still too high for people like Leo Page. The circumstances of war, he argued, required energetic and sympathetic young justices.[14]

Another demand was for magistrates sufficiently trained to solicit and interpret a thorough investigation of the child and his home background. This, in turn, required more child guidance clinics and, ideally, state observation centres. Two reports which appeared during the war strengthened this case for the examination of juveniles charged with an offence. In Sheffield, one half of the school and medical reports submitted to the courts revealed that the offender was 'backward', 'subnormal' or a poor school attender. In Bristol, the child guidance clinic reported that the main increase in wartime delinquency, especially of recidivism, came from juveniles of subnormal intelligence. The Home Office also urged courts to use medical reports, in view of the increasing number of cases sent to approved schools who were subsequently found to be mentally defective. Gradually, courts remanded an increasing number of children for examination by a psychologist or psychiatrist before passing sentence.[15]

The war years, finally, heard a more radical critique of the entire juvenile court system, orchestrated by the *emigré* criminologist, Mannheim. Drawing upon his European experience, and his knowledge of American example, Mannheim proposed the 'individualization' of courts for young persons under twenty-one. For those up to thirteen or fourteen years of age, the machinery and stigma of the juvenile court would be replaced by a Child Welfare Council on Scandinavian lines, an administrative tribunal, that is, not a court of law. The existing juvenile court arrangements would remain intact for those aged from thirteen to seventeen; for young adults, there would be adolescent courts on the lines of some American states. Mannheim's scheme attracted some support. His proposals were incorporated into a leaflet published by the Friends' Penal Reform Committee and into the National Union of Teachers' idea of youth welfare councils. More

[14] *Magistrate*, vol. 6 (1943), p. 206; *TES*, 12 Oct. 1940, p. 389; Howard League, *Annual Report for 1943–4*. In London the panel was revised every three years, and justices reaching the age of seventy were not re-appointed: *Justice of the Peace*, vol. 107, 22 May 1943, p. 242. Mannheim recommended trained, full-time *chairmen* for all juvenile courts, to give guidance to the lay justices, as Clarke Hall had done.

[15] Watson in *Magistrate*, vol. 7 (1944), pp. 38–40; *Probation*, vol. 3 (1942), p. 238; *Lancet*, 8 Nov. 1941, p. 572; *Howard Journal*, vol. 6 (1943), p. 144; *TES*, 18 May 1940, p. 188, 6 Sep. 1941, p. 421, 19 Sep. 1942, p. 460.

worrying for magistrates and probation officers was the fact that Mannheim's proposals seemed to strengthen the policy of giving the local education authorities the responsibility for delinquent youth, of which more later.[16]

Remand Homes

Pre-trial reports were usually completed in remand homes, places which the local authorities were obliged to provide. Prior to the war, remand home accommodation was inadequate; the war made the position much worse. Existing homes could barely cope with the detention of approved school committals, let alone with those remanded by a court for inquiries or those brought to the home as in need of care or protection, for whom the homes were originally intended. Courts responded by allowing approved school committals to remain with their parents or by sending children to temporary remand homes. Courts also more readily remanded boys and girls to prison, on the grounds that they were too unruly or depraved to be sent to a remand home. In 1938, 110 cases were so remanded; the figures for 1940 to 1942 were 395, 674, and 557 respectively.[17]

The entire question came to a head in 1944 over conditions at remand homes run by the London County Council. In November, the chairman of Tower Bridge juvenile court, John Watson, publicly criticized Marlesford Lodge remand home for girls. The treatment of a girl of seven, taken to Marlesford Lodge by the police as in need of care or protection, called forth this public attack on the LCC. The case was a mere pretext, however, for Watson and Henriques, chairman of Toynbee Hall juvenile court, having visited the home, to censure the lack of segregation between different categories of girl. Henriques

[16] For Mannheim's scheme, see *Juvenile Delinquency*, op. cit., p. 118; *TES*, 30 Aug. 1941, p. 409, 6 Sep. 1941, p. 421; *Probation*, vol. 4 (1942), p. 6. See also League of Nations, *Child Welfare Councils* (1937); Judge Gamon in *TES*, 16 Aug. 1941, p. 386; Cicely Craven in *Howard Journal*, vol. 7 (1945–6), p. 26; HO45/21804/591529/7. For details of Mannheim's career, see note 43 of this chapter.

[17] See J. Watson, *The Child and the Magistrate* (1945, 5th impression; first pub. 1942), p. 162; Ann. Rep. of P. Com. for 1942–44, PP 1946–7, XIV (Cmd. 7010), p. 31. For the reluctance of local authorities to provide remand homes in the 1930s, see section, 'Observation Homes' in ch. 6. In 1940 and again in 1941 the Home Office urged the local authorities to provide more remand home accommodation, to little effect: F. C. Foster in *Probation*, vol. 3 (1941), p. 197.

described this herding together as 'a public scandal'. Reluctantly, Morrison conceded an independent inquiry into the complaints.[18]

The ensuing report, written by Myra Curtis and G. Russell Vick, KC, accepted that the remand home had been occupied before it was ready and that it was under-staffed and poorly supplied with educational and recreational equipment. The girl of seven had indeed been allowed to associate with older girls, although the committee heard no evidence to suggest that the child suffered any harm in consequence. Moreover, the committee declared that,

> in representing the London County Council to the public as guilty of a grave dereliction of duty because they have not achieved a standard of segregation which has . . . never been authoritatively laid down . . . the Magistrates . . . showed a lack of that moderation of statement and of steadiness of judgment which might have been expected of persons in their position.

Watson and Henriques did, none the less, draw public attention to the discontent of justices and probation officers at the deficient administration of the LCC remand homes. The committee spoke of 'strained relations' and of 'something amounting almost to a state of warfare' between the LCC and the London magistrates. Hence, the report recommended machinery for better collaboration between the various parties concerned with remand homes.[19]

No attempt was made by the committee, however, to place the London incident in the context of national policy. The LCC was not alone in failing to provide places for the different types of girls sent to remand homes, and its task was made no easier by the State's continued failure to establish observation centres for the more difficult cases. A more comprehensive indictment of remand homes was laid by the Curtis committee on the care of children deprived of a normal home life. Children were kept waiting in homes for far too long, said Curtis. Homes were seldom educative and rarely staffed for diagnostic purposes; few were in touch, for example, with child guidance clinics. Nor was there sufficient segregation of different classes of inmate. Curtis recommended, therefore, that homes should be used as short-

[18] cf. R. A. Parker, 'The Gestation of Reform: The Children Act 1948', in P. Bean and S. MacPherson (eds.), *Approaches to Welfare* (1983), p. 203. See also CAB 65/44, W. M. 153(4); Donoughue and Jones, op. cit., p. 308. For Henriques, see note 28, Chap. 9.

[19] *London County Council Remand Homes. Report of Committee of Inquiry*, PP 1944–5, V (Cmd. 6594), pp. 259–81 (quotation is at p. 272.) Shortly afterwards, Myra Curtis was appointed chairman of the Committee of Inquiry into Child Care.

stay places of assessment; special remand centres should be provided for more prolonged observation.[20]

Punitive Detention

Under section 54 of the Children and Young Persons Act 1933, a juvenile court could order detention in a remand home for up to a month, when it wanted to give a boy a short, sharp lesson. The provision was little used during the war, owing to the lack of space in remand homes. Even so, the number of children and young persons committed to detention in a remand home rose from 179 in 1939 to 432 in 1940. Liverpool juvenile court was largely responsible for this increase, sending more cases under section 54 than the rest of the country put together. Liverpool had, in fact, set aside a special remand home for these detention cases. The joint memorandum of June, 1941, held that section 54 was a valuable provision, particularly where such cases could be separated from other remands. However, both the committee of inquiry into Marlesford Lodge and the Curtis committee on child care were more critical of admitting section 54 cases to the ordinary remand home. So, too, was Watson, who argued thus: 'The first essential to a short sharp punishment is that it shall be unpleasant, and a remand home is not—or should not be—an unpleasant place.' Yet Watson, along with some other justices and their clerks, sought a punitive detention sentence 'of short duration but thoroughly unpleasant', apart from the remand home.[21] As we shall see, this demand, voiced loudly in the thirties, was eventually met in the 1948 Act.

Birching

For many courts, especially where there was no adequate remand home accommodation, a birching was the only means of actually punishing a child. The number of birchings inflicted on boys under fourteen certainly rose during the war, from fifty-eight birchings in 1939 to 302 in 1940 and 531 in 1941. This took place against the

[20] See *Howard Journal*, vol. 7 (1946–7), p. 117; *Economist*, 26 Oct. 1946, p. 654; *Magistrate*, vol. 7 (1946), p. 235. See also Jean Packman, *The Child's Generation* (1975), ch. 1.

[21] See P. Hall *et al., Change, Choice and Conflict in Social Policy* (1975), pp. 318–9; Paterson Owens, op. cit., p. 112; Watson, *The Child*, op. cit., p. 144; *L.C.C. Remand Homes*, op. cit., p. 274. In Liverpool, punitive detention was used for more serious cases of breaking and entering and gang offences.

wishes of the Home Office, which continued to remind justices of the Cadogan committee's conclusion that corporal punishment was an ineffective remedy for delinquency, and even against the advice of the main police journals.[22]

Once again the issue was brought into sharp focus by a controversial incident. In January 1943, Hereford juvenile court sentenced two lads, aged eleven and thirteen, each to four strokes of the birch for malicious damage. Despite the fact that the boys' parents wished to appeal against the sentence, the boys were taken to the police station and birched. The appeal to the High Court for an order of *certiorari* to quash the conviction proved successful. Indeed, the Lord Chief Justice forcefully declared that fundamental principles of justice had been ignored by the Hereford court. The public outcry that arose from these remarks was stilled only by Morrison's appointment of a tribunal of inquiry, in the sole charge of Lord Justice Goddard.

The inquiry absolved the magistrates and the local police of misconduct, thus giving centre stage to the birching sentence. Hereford, said the *Howard Journal*, taught 'that birching and the right of appeal are incompatible'; since the right of appeal was sacrosanct, whipping would have to go. In addition, the case revealed how an average bench, without the assistance of clinic, remand home, or probation officer's report on the home conditions, could genuinely look to the welfare of offenders and yet order birching. From this point on, the *Howard Journal* warned, 'any Juvenile Court which now orders birching will do so at its peril'. In fact, the number of birchings fell during the second part of the war. However, the decline started in 1942, before the Hereford case, although the latter probably helped push the figure of birchings to below the pre-war level.[23]

Probation

Not only did the increase in birchings quickly fade during the war, but no excessive decline in the use of probation took place. Probation

[22] HO45/21951/884452/87; Mannheim, *Juvenile Delinquency*, op. cit., p. 70; Titmuss, op. cit., p. 340; *Police Chronicle*, 4 April 1941, p. 11; *Hansard*, vol. 393, 4 Nov. 1943, col. 846. For the Cadogan Committee, see section, 'Corporal Punishment' in ch. 5 above.

[23] Fenton Bresler, *Lord Goddard* (1977), pp. 95–9; *Howard Journal*, vol. 6 (1943), pp. 131–5. Rayner Goddard was Lord Justice of Appeal, 1938–44; then Lord Chief Justice, 1946–58. The birching statistics for under-fourteens for the final years of the war were as follows: 1942 : 314; 1943 : 165; 1944 : 37; 1945 : 25.

remained by far the most important method of treatment used by juvenile courts. In 1938, 51 per cent of all juveniles charged with indictable offences were dealt with by probation; by 1941 the figure was down to 44.5 per cent, where it remained for the rest of the war.[24] Of course, the war placed considerable strain upon the probation service. All full-time, male probation officers under thirty were called to the colours; thereby, some 30 per cent of all male officers were lost. War conditions also made supervision work much harder. It was difficult, for example, to trace probationers who were evacuated. Parents were not eager for it to be known in the reception area that their children were on probation, even threatening to bring their offspring home if it became known. Probation committees in reception areas would not always allow their officers to supervise evacuees, lest they were swamped by the extra work. Eventually, the Home Office was forced to despatch a handful of probation officers from the London courts to help the reception areas. In the war-torn cities, meanwhile, air raid shelter life and daylight bombing made home visiting and reporting by probationers difficult, not to say dangerous. Even so, development of the probation service along the lines laid down by the departmental committee of 1936 continued. The number of full-time and female officers increased, as did the number of principal and senior posts. The official training scheme continued to train prospective officers.[25]

Indeed, the determined way in which the Probation Branch of the Home Office went about implementing the 1936 recommendations during the war, led to accusations that the branch were riding roughshod over local probation committees. The feeling of insecurity which thus afflicted the service was heightened by public discussion of the transfer of all services concerned with children to the education authorities. In mid-1942, the National Association of Probation Officers had to contest the views of the National Union of Teachers and of education directors that either probation officers should become employees of the education authority, or probation work should be done by school attendance officers. But the issue died hard. In April 1945, the Association of Education Directors submitted a memorandum to the Advisory Council on the Treatment of Offenders, proposing the transfer of the probation of offenders under eighteen to

[24] See Table 15.

[25] See Norman in *Probation*, vol. 3 (1939), pp. 113–14; *Probation*, vol. 3 (1940), p. 146, (1941), pp. 194–6, 206; vol. 4 (1942), pp. 17–18; HO45/21874/699846/93.

the local education authority. On this occasion, Harris leapt to the defence of the probation officers, insisting that such a transfer would seriously damage the co-operation between juvenile justices and probation officers, which kept the juvenile court involved in the probation system. Thus, the education authorities were repulsed, and probation officers felt rather more wanted by the Home department.[26]

Approved Schools

If magistrates placed more delinquent children on probation because of lack of space in approved schools, alternatively, they sometimes chose committal over a probation order, because of absent fathers or working mothers. By so controverting the usual penological rhythm of probation, stringent probation, and then approved school, the courts ran the risk of worsening the schools' accommodation problem. In fact, there was a slight decline in the proportion of offenders committed to approved schools during the war, from around 10 per cent to 9 per cent of offenders charged with indictable offences. In absolute terms, however, this represented an increase in the numbers admitted to approved schools (from 3,913 in 1938 to 5,973 in 1942) and in the numbers resident in the schools (from 8,764 to 10,257).[27] These figures underlay the accommodation crisis, which the Home Office met by various emergency measures: the immediate licensing of an extra 5 per cent of inmates; later, the reduction of all terms of training to about half the usual training period in the case of senior schools, and three-quarters or more in the case of intermediate and junior schools. The reforming bodies predictably lamented this interference with the training schedule. In addition, the Home Office induced the voluntary societies, like Dr Barnardo's homes, to establish approved schools, including 'short-term' institutions.[28]

In 1938 there were 104 schools; by 1946 there were 145. Of the 145 schools, 34 were managed by local authorities, the other 111 were the

[26] *Howard Journal*, vol. VI (1941), p. 33; *Probation*, vol. 3 (1942), p. 248; Bochel, op. cit., p. 162; HO45/21804/591529/24. For the establishment of the Advisory Council on the Treatment of Offenders, see pp. 287–9.

[27] See Tables 5, 6 and 15; Mannheim, *War and Crime* (1941), p. 144; *TES*, 27 July 1940, p. 295. The large majority of persons in approved schools had been guilty of offences: *Hansard*, vol. 385, 17 Dec. 1942, col. 1096.

[28] *TES*, 10 Aug. 1940, p. 313; *Probation*, vol. 3 (1941), p. 198; *Magistrate*, vol. 5 (1940), p. 309; *Hansard*, vol. 379, 23 April 1942, col. 731.

responsibility of voluntary managers. There was immense variety among the institutions, with nautical schools, schools for farming, and schools for teaching building construction. Some institutions adopted a house system, some schools for girls were of a hostel type.[29] Three classifying schools were also opened, the product of the most important wartime development in the sphere of reformatories. The first classifying institution was opened at Aycliffe, near Darlington, in 1943. Two senior girls' schools followed in 1944. For two months, educational psychologists and teachers examined the abilities, temperament, and character of each inmate. The assessment, according to the Home Office, improved the allocation of children to approved schools. Not true, said the Curtis committee on child care. The classifying system sought to fit the child to the correct type of training; 'all that was done in effect', said Curtis, 'was to change the character of the schools from being mixed schools taking all types of children within an age group to schools specialising in a certain type of boy, e.g. the bright boy or the backward boy.'[30] Hence, a number of groups and individuals called for more specialized approved schools to deal with subnormal children, persistent absconders and children requiring psychotherapeutic treatment.[31]

The most controversial policy discussion during the war concerned the transfer of the administration of approved schools from the Home Office to the Board of Education. A movement of opinion towards the transfer was evident as early as 1941, when Clara Rackham contended in the *Magistrate* that 'delinquent or neglected children who need education and re-training should be the responsibility of the Board'. Rackham's case inspired rejoinders, notably in the *Approved Schools Gazette*, which maintained that taking the schools away from the Children's Branch would be detrimental to their welfare. There the matter rested until January 1943, when the board reviewed the issue in the course of drafting a new Education Bill. As the board saw it, the

[29] Home Office, *Sixth Report*, op. cit., pp. 79–82; *Making Citizens* (1946), pp. 9–10, 18–19. Fifty-six of the 145 schools were for girls.

[30] *Sixth Report*, op. cit., pp. 68–9; *Making Citizens*, p. 17; John Gittins in *Howard Journal*, vol. 7 (1945–6), p. 35. Gittins was an inspector of approved schools, who volunteered to realize and run Aycliffe classifying school: see Gittins, *Approved School Boys* (1952). The two girls' classifying schools were the Shaw, near Warrington, and the Magdalen Hospital in London. The quotation from the report of the Curtis Committee is from *Magistrate*, vol. VII (1946), p. 235.

[31] See Rackham in *Eugenics Review*, vol. XXXIV (1942), p. 67; Mannheim in *TES*, 6 Sep. 1941, p. 421. See also *Lancet*, 8 Nov. 1941, p. 573; *Magistrate*, vol. 6 (1942), p. 101.

arguments in favour of transfer were that the object of approved schools was to educate, not punish, inmates, that the schools would better keep abreast of educational developments within the sphere of the board, and that the rehabilitation of the children was hindered by their association with the department dealing with police, courts, and the punishment of crime.[32]

Harris could hardly contain himself. 'The way in which this case for transfer is trumped up', he fumed, 'indicates the growing spirit of dictatorship in the Board. It is evident that no dog is to bark (educationally) in the future without their permission.' Under Morrison's calming influence, however, Harris dissected the Board of Education's argument point by point, adding the general defence that the approved schools were an integral part of the department's responsibility for juvenile offenders, and that work amongst children gave the Home Office staff a forward-looking and constructive approach to the treatment of offenders of all ages. The counter-offensive worked. Neither the Machinery of Government Committee nor the Advisory Council proposed that the control of approved schools be assigned to the Ministry of Education. Without question, the contribution of the Children's Department to the improvement of juvenile justice weighed heavily in the scale, as did the fact that few probation officers, juvenile court justices or approved school headmasters sought a new governmental master.[33]

Prisons and Borstals

The war had a larger impact on the modes of treating young adult offenders. The number of offenders aged sixteen to twenty-one received into prison on conviction rose from 1,483 in 1939 to 3,992 in 1942. Thus, while the number of indictable offences committed by males aged sixteen to twenty-one increased by 34 per cent between 1938 and 1942, the number of committals to prison increased by over

[32] *Magistrate*, vol. 6 (1941), pp. 27–9 and 60; *Approved Schools Gazette*, vol. 35 (1941), p. 91; HO45/21804/591529/9.

[33] HO45/21804/591529/9,12,21,24 and 31. The Curtis Committee failed to clarify the question, even though it recommended that child care be made the responsibility of one government department: *Howard Journal*, vol. 7 (1946–7), p. 119.

200 per cent.[34] For the prison commissioners and the penal reform bodies, these were depressing figures. From 1943, the collecting centres, which received young prisoners with sentences of over one month, were told to enliven the training regime: 'a brisk tempo in every form of activity, hard and interesting work, and a sharp but not repressive discipline'. Actual changes included the appointment of housemasters and the introduction of vocational training classes. But overall, the war years only underlined the limitations of prison for young offenders. More valuably, the Home Office tried to reduce the number of young persons imprisoned for breaches of wartime employment orders (absenteeism, persistent lateness), by asking courts to adjourn the case and so allow the defendant a chance to comply with the law.[35] In the long term, however, the prison commissioners awaited legislation to abolish imprisonment for persons under twenty-one.

Meanwhile, the Borstal system was virtually dismantled. On the outbreak of war, some 1,677 boys and 118 girls, or two-thirds of the Borstal population, were discharged. With them, in effect, went the traditions that Paterson had laboriously constructed. Only those inmates who had not served six months were left in the depleted number of institutions. The system sustained another serious blow when almost half the housemasters left the service.[36] The September exodus and the subsequent early release of inmates were emergency

[34] See Tables 10 and 13. cf. Smithies, op. cit., pp. 199–200. For girls aged sixteen to twenty-one, while the number of indictable offences increased by 108% between 1938 and 1942, the number of committals to prison increased by almost 400%: Ann. Rep. of P. Com. for 1939–41, PP 1945–6, XIV (Cmd. 6820), p. 316. In addition, 3,000–4,000 youths were remanded to prison and not subsequently dealt with by imprisonment.

[35] Ann. Rep. of P. Com. for 1945, PP 1946–7, XIV (Cmd. 7146), p. 177 and 228 (Appendix 2A); *Magistrate*, vol. 7 (1944), p. 25. The chairman of the Prison Commission from 1942 onwards was Lionel Fox. A Quaker from Halifax, Fox was educated at Hertford College, Oxford; he fought in the Great War, before joining the Home Office in 1919 as an assistant principal. From 1925–34, he was secretary to the Prison Commission. A quiet and reserved person, Fox was an efficient administrator, a liberal influence on prison administration, and supportive of Alec Paterson and the Howard League: *The Times*, 9 Oct. 1961; *DNB, 1961–70*, p. 386; conversations with Tom Hayes, H. J. Taylor and Alan Bainton.

[36] Mannheim, *War and Crime*, pp. 134–5; D. M. Lowson, *City Lads in Borstal* (Liverpool, 1970), p. 2; Hood, *Borstal Re-Assessed* (1965), p. 63; Ann. Rep. of P. Com. for 1939–41, op. cit., p. 330. By March 1940, 221 males and 23 females of the discharged group were again in custody on reconviction or on revocation of their licences; of the boys still on licence, 481 were known to have joined up: *Hansard*, vol. 358, 14 Mar. 1940, col. 1377. By September 1946, 50% of the males discharged in 1939 and more than 50% of the females had been reconvicted: H. D. Willcock, *Report on Juvenile Delinquency* (1949), p. 129.

measures. Thereafter, lads were told that they would be kept in training until fit for discharge. In fact, as the number of committals to Borstal began to rise, reflecting the increased crime rate, an acute accommodation problem developed, which early licensing could at least contain. Hence, the average period of detention only gradually increased from ten months in 1940 to sixteen months in 1944. The shorter training period undoubtedly led the judiciary to question the deterrent value of Borstal training. Watson only heightened their fears when he stated: 'it is not unknown for young offenders of sixteen, because of the prospect of an earlier release, to ask to be sent to Borstal rather than to an approved school.' The courts gradually responded by a more frequent use of imprisonment, both numerically and proportionately, and a slightly less frequent use of Borstal, proportionately.[37]

Borstal in wartime was thus a shadow of its former self. The institutions were understaffed, the houses overcrowded. In the workshops, production for the war effort took precedence over work training. Nor was there much need to prepare for release, or need of after-care, when three-quarters of the boys were released directly into the forces. This weakened system, however, had to cope with more intractable boys, according to the Prison Commission. 'With no settled purpose, since enlistment in a short time was inevitable, the Borstal youth of 1940–41 was restless, elusive, and uncooperative.' One sign of this was the vastly increased rate of absconding from the institutions. Yet the results of Borstal training were not much worse than before the war. The proportion avoiding reconviction in the two years from discharge fell to around 50 per cent, but the wartime training conditions and type of inmate seemed to explain the deterioration.[38]

On the credit side the war, with its large demand for unskilled labour, led to more outside and often unsupervised work, particularly on farms, for inmates of closed as well as open Borstals. In addition, open institutions began to take more than simply the 'best risks'; Lowdham coped well with the dull and backward boys from Feltham. The end of the war, moreover, saw an increase in the proportion found guilty sentenced to Borstal, from 7.2 per cent in 1944 to 10.7 per cent in 1946. If the judiciary adopted the wartime expedient of imprisoning

[37] See Table 10. See also Ann. Rep. of P. Com. for 1942–44, PP 1946–7, XIV (Cmd. 7010), p. 58; *Prisons and Borstals* (1945), p. 35; Watson, *The Child*, op. cit., p. 160.

[38] See Ann. Rep. of P. Com. for 1939–41, op. cit., p. 332; Ann. Rep. of P. Com. for 1942–44, op. cit., pp. 56–63; Ann Smith, *Women in Prison* (1962), pp. 262–3; A. G. Rose, *Five Hundred Borstal Boys* (Oxford, 1954), ch. 3, *passim*, for Borstal during the war; *Prisons and Borstals* (1945), p. 37. cf. Hood, op. cit., pp. 134 and 212.

more adolescent offenders, they quickly regained faith in long-term reformatory training. Indeed, the courts used Borstal more widely in the post-war years than they had done in the 1930s. Nor had the prison commissioners lost any of their pre-war enthusiasm for the Borstal system. In the last years of war, both Lionel Fox, chairman of the Prison Commission, and Paterson urged housemasters to rediscover that 'imperishable and incurable optimism' which had underpinned the Borstal system in the inter-war period.[39]

In all, the social and physical turmoil of war severely disrupted the penal system. A substantial increase in juvenile crime in the space of a few years revealed the difficulty of responding quickly to an urgent problem when the provision of remand homes and approved schools lay with charitable bodies and local authorities. For some, the only solution was for central government to claim the power to provide and control such accommodation itself. In the meantime, the Home Office simply encouraged improved provision of leisure facilities, echoing the official response to the crime wave of the 1914–18 war. The courts, in contrast, tended to revert to more punitive sanctions, particularly in dealing with the young adult offender. It was as if the years of agitation by the Prison Commission to get courts to prefer Borstal to imprisonment had been for nothing.

Yet the war was not all loss. Within reforming circles, debate continued regarding child welfare councils and the transfer of probation and approved schools to the Board of Education. Informed opinion still hoped to shift the treatment of delinquency into the orbit of civil or educational jurisdiction. More significantly, the war forced public attention on to the condition of children and adolescents. Evacuation first turned the spotlight on to the plight of the urban child. The Hereford birching inquiry and the London remand home investigation followed, the latter wrested from the Home Secretary by the opportunism of magistrates Watson and Henriques. The agitation over the treatment of children deprived of a normal home life likewise resulted in an official inquiry, the Curtis committee on child care.[40] War conditions were not alone responsible, however, for the heightened public sensitivity to children. Also crucial was the war-

[39] See Table 10; Rose, op. cit., pp. 40 and 50; Hood, op. cit., pp. 65–6; Minutes of Conferences of Borstal Housemasters, 30 June 1944 and 1 June 1944, courtesy of H. J. Taylor.

[40] See Watson, 'The Child and the Aftermath of War', *Fortnightly*, vol. 167 (1947), pp. 254–60.

inspired determination of sections of the political leadership to create greater security and well-being for all families in the post-war world. It is to these plans that we now turn.

Plans for Post-War Reform

In May 1942, Herbert Morrison, Home Secretary in Churchill's Coalition government, raised the question of the appointment of a committee on prison reform. Maxwell, Permanent Under-Secretary, advised his chief that the backing of a report from an authoritative committee would certainly clear the path for a resuscitated Criminal Justice Bill: firstly, by convincing the judiciary of the doctrine that the executive should release offenders at the peak of their training; secondly, by meeting criticisms that prisoners were 'pampered'; and thirdly, by winning support for the proposed Howard houses and compulsory attendance centres. Since the department generally preferred inquiries into specific areas, however, as opposed to wide-ranging committees on prison methods, Maxwell recommended the continuation of Lord Roche's committee on courts of summary jurisdiction.[41]

Morrison was not so easily deflected from planning the post-war world. He had already persuaded the national executive committee of the Labour party to establish a body to plan the social and economic policies of a future Labour government. The secretary of this Central Committee on Reconstruction Problems was Harold Laski. He too became a key figure in Labour's attempt to exploit what R. A. Butler termed 'the wartime urge for social reform and greater equality'.[42] Laski told Morrison that he was eager to get a Royal Commission 'which will create the expectation of post-war innovation now while the public mind is attuned to the idea of innovation'. He suggested a commission, not too official or legal in composition, possibly with Carr-Saunders, director of the LSE, as chairman, and with the power to employ experts like Mannheim, Laski's friend and colleague, for special inquiries. The commission's task would be 'to create the opinion which will lead to the establishment of the scientific study of crime in Britain'. Laski added that 'a rightly-composed body might do a job as important in the twentieth century as Beccaria and John

[41] HO45/21948/884452/1.

[42] For Morrison's wartime speeches on reconstruction, see *The Times*, 7 June 1941, p. 2, 15 Feb. 1943, p. 2; Donoughue and Jones, op. cit., pp. 323–29. See also R. A. Butler, *The Art of the Possible. The Memoirs of Lord Butler* (1971), p. 86; Granville Eastwood, *Harold Laski* (1977), pp. 45 and 70.

Howard did in the 18th ... and I should like to think that my friend H. M. made this possible during his tenure of office'.[43]

The idea of a Royal Commission, however, was gradually superseded by the scheme of an Advisory Council on the Treatment of Offenders (ACTO). Towards the end of 1943, Maxwell asked the department to start thinking again about the Criminal Justice Bill. The initial response of both Harris and Fox was to suggest the creation of a council representing all Home Office branches concerned with the treatment of crime, which would meet to discuss policy questions. One such question was the shape of a revived Criminal Justice Bill. In time, the idea of a departmental body grew to include the notion of an advisory council of those with expert knowledge or experience of criminal justice, to advise the Home Secretary on particular proposals, and to form and educate public opinion.[44]

The decision to establish an advisory council did nothing to diminish Morrison's desire to secure legislation. In April 1944, Morrison informed Churchill that the interest shown in the advisory council 'leads me to hope that it may be possible to legislate without undue delay'. Although the Prime Minister opposed any domestic legislation that might impede the war effort, Morrison refused to back

[43] HO45/21948/884452/1. For Sir Alexander Carr-Saunders, see *DNB, 1961–70*, pp. 175–6. Hermann Mannheim fled Nazi Germany in 1934, abandoning high judicial and academic office in Berlin. A year later, through the good offices of Sir William Beveridge, he was appointed at the London School of Economics, where he was involved in the training of probation officers and in teaching criminology. His early research and lectures were eventually published as *The Dilemma of Penal Reform* (1939), *Social Aspects of Crime in England between the Wars* (1940) and *War and Crime* (1941). Mannheim quickly made contact with Basil Henriques, H. E. Norman (secretary of the National Association of Probation Officers) and Dr J. J. Mallon (Warden of Toynbee Hall in the East End) and joined the Executive Committee of the Howard League in 1940. He also became associated with the Institute for the Scientific Treatment of Delinquency, founded in 1932 to further the medico-psychological approach to the study and treatment of delinquency. In association with Carr-Saunders and Dr E. C. Rhodes, and on behalf of the Home Office, Mannheim investigated the subject of delinquency, resulting in the publication of *Young Offenders* (1944). In 1946 he completed his influential book, *Criminal Justice and Social Reconstruction*, and was appointed Reader in Criminology at the LSE. Mannheim's outlook on the subject of crime was practical and positivist, empirical and scientific. He was a lawyer with psychiatric interests and a deep understanding of the social aspects of delinquency. Hence, his contribution to criminology was, as John Croft concluded, an 'understanding of the relationships of sociology to criminal science and penology in its legal setting ... ' See Lord Chorley in *British Journal of Criminology*, vol. 10 (1970), pp. 329–38; Croft in T. Grygier *et al.* (eds.), *Criminology in Transition* (1965), pp. xiii–xix; Edward Glover in L. Radzinowicz and J. W. C. Turner (eds.), *Mental Abnormality and Crime* (1944), ch. 12.

[44] HO45/21948/884452/2,3,3B,3C and 15.

down. He persisted in staking out 'a claim for a Penal Reform Bill in our legislative programme of social reconstruction after the war'. As he explained to Churchill, 'This is not a sentimental journey in quest of ways and means of making life easier for the offender but a realistic attempt to tackle the economic problem of saving the community from the losses and suffering caused by the anti-social activities of criminals.' The issue could not be postponed, the Home Secretary concluded, since the penal reform groups would, at war's end, surely press the government to reintroduce the Criminal Justice Bill. A compromise of sorts was finally reached when Morrison resolved to put a paper before the Cabinet, once the department's ideas had been 'broadened, humanised and improved' by the Advisory Council.[45]

The council was set up in August 1944. It was received as evidence of Morrison's determination to press on with the job of penal reform. Not even the Howard League found much to complain about. The council contained no medical psychologist, which the League regretted, but it included the League's chairman, George Benson, MP, and two vice-presidents, Margery Fry and Laski. A former officer of the Howard League, Hartley Shawcross, KC, was also a member.[46] The chairman of the council was Mr Justice Birkett, the vice-chairman was Maxwell. Behind the council, preparing the agenda of topics for consideration, was the Administration of Justice Standing Committee, made up of Maxwell, Harris, Fox, T. Paterson Owens, and Frank Newsam. The early meetings of this departmental committee concluded that the advisory council should examine juvenile delinquency (since Morrison had already promised the Commons that it would be given priority) and those parts of the Criminal Justice Bill which sought to keep persons under twenty-one out of prison.[47] The advisory

[45] Ibid., 884452/6. Morrison was also gratified by the public response to his speech, given at the opening of a probation hostel in Birmingham, which, in language made familiar by Paterson, sketched out the line of post-war penal reform: 884452/7.

[46] *The Times*, 4 Aug. 1944, p. 5; *Howard Journal*, vol. 6 (1944–5), pp. 179–80. Fry's recent article, 'The Future Treatment of the Adult Offender', had much impressed Herbert Morrison: HO45/21948/884452/2. Hartley Shawcross, Recorder of Salford, from a radical Liberal background, was assistant secretary to the Howard League in 1925–6. He entered parliament in 1945 and served as Attorney-General, 1945–51: *New Statesman*, 21 Feb. 1975, p. 234.

[47] HO45/21948/884452/3A and 15; 20729/893948/1. Frank Newsam was Deputy Under-Secretary of State, 1941–48, when he succeeded Maxwell as Permanent Under-Secretary of State. He had been Private Secretary to John Anderson, 1924–27, and Principal Private Secretary to successive Home Secretaries between 1928 and 1933, as a result of which he acquired considerable political as well as administrative acumen: *DNB, 1961–70*, p. 791.

council set to work, but within a year the war was over, the Coalition government was dismantled, and after an interim Conservative administration, a majority Labour government took office.

Labour Government and Penal Reform

Riding on the wave of public support for post-war reconstruction, Labour embarked upon the most extensive programme of economic and social legislation since the Liberal government of 1906. The aim was a planned economy oriented to social need, not private profit. State management of the country's productive resources was one arm of this project; the other arm was the distribution of these resources to people and communities in need. The socially-divisive class society of the thirties was thus to make way for a community based on economic and social justice. In this 'new Jerusalem', social order would be based less upon the traditional supremacy of law than upon reducing the sources of disorder. The government's economic policy would put down the crimes of property that arose from poverty and unemployment. Social reconstruction would uproot the problem of inadequate family control which was thought to be responsible for so much wartime delinquency. As a 1947 report on *Lawless Youth* declared, the juvenile courts faced the problem 'of winning back for society the children and young men and women whom war had made rebels and outlaws . . . ' Broken or weakened families would be strengthened *pari passu* with the success of social and penal reform. In a word, the condition of criminal justice was an integral part of the post-war Labour government's programme of reform.[48]

The Prime Minister, Clement Attlee, put James Chuter Ede in charge of the Home Office, where he stayed until 1951. Ede was a tolerant yet unsentimental Labour moderate, who, as Parliamentary Secretary to the Ministry of Education during the wartime Coalition,

[48] Margery Fry *et al*, *Lawless Youth. A Challenge to New Europe* (1947), p. 5. The International Committee of the Howard League, which prepared *Lawless Youth*, included Clara Rackham, Mannheim, Max Grunhut and Leon Radzinowicz. See also Ian Taylor, *Law and Order. Arguments for Socialism* (1981), ch. 2, *passim*; Paul Addison, *The Road to 1945* (1982), ch. 10. Given the significance of the nuclear family to the whole project of social reconstruction, it is unsurprising that greater interest was shown in psychoanalytically-inclined research work. A case in point was the work on the relationship to delinquency of prolonged separation of the child from its parents at an early age, by John Bowlby, psychiatrist in charge of the Child Guidance Unit of Tavistock Clinic, London: 'Childhood Origins of Recidivism', *Howard Journal*, vol. 7 (1945–6), p. 30; *Fourty-Four Juvenile Thieves: Their Characters and Home-Life* (1946).

helped to pilot the 1944 Education Act through the House.[49] His task now was to win a place for penal reform in the proposed programme of reconstruction. In April 1946, he decided to introduce the Criminal Justice Bill of 1938, subject to a few alterations. Before the legislation committee in early July, however, Ede was asked by Morrison, now Lord President of the Council, to withdraw the Criminal Justice Bill until the next session. Ede refused, reminding the committee that Cabinet had approved the bill's inclusion in the current programme, concluding 'that the Government would be exposed to criticism if they concentrated entirely on economic measures and did not include among the legislation in the 1946–7 Programme some social and humanitarian measures'. Two days later, Ede informed Maxwell that the bill was safe.[50]

At this juncture a Conservative party report on the treatment of young offenders was published. *Youth Astray* symbolized the post-war consensus on juvenile crime. Delinquency, the report contended, 'is mainly the outcome of conditions, social, economic, and to some extent hereditary, for which they themselves cannot be blamed. The blame . . . rests largely upon society.' With so many of the specific recommendations corresponding with the reforms that Ede was considering, the report augured well for a smooth passage for the Home Secretary's proposed bill.[51] Unfortunately, in October 1946, the legislation committee decided that the Criminal Justice Bill would be omitted from the 1946–7 programme. 'The nationalisation measures are the VIBs of Westminster', the *Observer* complained, 'these bulky Bills sail up the gangway with political priority passports, while

[49] For Chuter Ede, see *DNB, 1961–70*, pp. 216–7; *The Times*, 12 Nov. 1965; Butler, op. cit., p. 93. The early history of the Prime Minister, Clem Attlee, bears a striking resemblance to that of Alec Paterson. Attlee was a manager of Stepney boys' club from 1907 and Secretary of Toynbee Hall from 1910, living in East London for fourteen years in all. He came into contact with Paterson at Oxford and at the Bermondsey Mission. In 1912 he was a lecturer at the LSE: C. R. Attlee, *As It Happened* (New York, 1954), pp. 28–35; Kenneth Harris, *Attlee* (1982), p. 17.

[50] HO45/21950/884452/75 and 77. The press and the penal reform lobby felt that a scheme of penal reform deserved a place in the Labour programme: *The Times*, 12 Mar. 1946, p. 5.

[51] See *TES*, 14 Sept. 1946, p. 438; *Medico-Legal and Criminological Review*, vol. XIV (1946), p. 84. *Youth Astray* was produced by a committee over which the magistrate, John Watson, presided. A foreword to it was written by R. A. Butler, the chairman of the Conservative Party Committee on Policy and Political Education. The report recommended the abolition of whipping for boys under fourteen and of imprisonment for persons under seventeen, and more and better classified accommodation in remand homes and approved schools.

criminals flourish and the children wait'. Further criticism was heard in the House of Lords, when Viscount Templewood, who, as Sir Samuel Hoare, had introduced the 1938 bill, successfully moved a measure of penal reform. The motion was seconded by Viscounts Samuel and Simon, both former home secretaries, who pressed the government to include the Criminal Justice Bill in its current legislative programme.[52]

In March 1947, the long haul began again. Ede submitted a memorandum on the main lines of the Criminal Justice Bill to the Lord President's committee. Once more the bill broadly followed the 1938 bill. There followed a good-tempered wrangle between Ede and Jowitt, the Lord Chancellor, who strongly opposed the abolition of corporal punishment and the leniency of many of the proposals, of which more later. In mid-May, however, the Cabinet agreed that the bill should be included in the legislative programme for 1947–8. In October, the legislation committee authorized the Home Secretary to arrange for the bill's introduction in the Commons.[53]

The Criminal Justice Bill

The proposals relating to young offenders in the Criminal Justice Bill of 1947 were similar to those in the 1938 bill, which, in turn, were based on the 1927 Young Offenders Report. That report, Ede told the Commons, 'strongly emphasised the unwisdom of sending young persons to prison', whether on remand or on sentence. One of the main objects of the new bill, therefore, was to achieve an immediate reduction in the number of young persons received into prison, and to provide for the eventual abolition of imprisonment as a method of treatment for young offenders convicted by a magistrates' court.[54]

[52] See HO45/21951/884452/73, 87 and 116; *Observer*, 24 Nov. 1946; *Sunday Times*, 1 Dec. 1946; *Hansard* (Lords), vol. 114, 27 Nov. 1946, cols. 415–52. Templewood was Chairman of the Council of the Magistrates Association. See also note 22 to ch. 5.

[53] CAB 132/6, L.P. (47) 8th meeting; HO45/21951/884452/99 and 116, 21952/884452/102B, 104 and 124, 21953/884452/127A. William Jowitt was a moderate and undoctrinaire Labour politician, befitting a former Liberal. He had been Solicitor-General and Minister for Social Insurance during the wartime Coalition, and responsible for announcing the Coalition's progress on post-war planning; *Dictionary of Labour Biography*, edited by J. Bellamy and J. Saville, vol. VII (1984), pp. 130–33.

[54] *Hansard*, vol. 444, 27 Nov. 1947, col. 2135. My concern is with the clauses dealing with young offenders. The Criminal Justice Bill also dealt with prison administration and with the treatment of persistent offenders.

Avoiding Committal to Prison on Remand

Under the existing law, a person remanded or committed for trial in custody, if under fourteen, had to be sent to a remand home. If between fourteen and seventeen, he had to be sent to a remand home, unless the court certified that he was too unruly or too depraved to be kept in a remand home, in which case he could be committed to prison. If over seventeen, he could only be sent to prison. During 1945, nearly 5,000 persons under twenty-one were sent to prison on remand or awaiting trial and were not subsequently committed to prison. Such figures disturbed the penal reform bodies and the advisory council. Accordingly, the new bill proposed *remand centres* for persons between seventeen and twenty-one and for those between fourteen and seventeen who were too unruly to be kept in a remand home. Moreover, offenders under seventeen who were remanded for a medical examination could, if there were no facilities for observation in the remand home, be sent to a remand centre. Finally, the 1938 bill had included state remand homes for persons under seventeen on whose mental condition a report was required. On Harris's advice, this proposal was dropped from the 1947 bill. State remand homes with special facilities would, Harris argued, only discourage the local authorities from providing medical observation in their remand homes.[55]

Restrictions on the Use of Imprisonment

Under the existing law, no one under fourteen could be sentenced to imprisonment, and no one between fourteen and seventeen could be imprisoned unless he was too unruly to be sentenced to punitive detention in a remand home. During 1945 over 4,000 young offenders between sixteen and twenty-one were received into prison on conviction. Many of these offenders, the Prison Commission had long argued, could have been sentenced to probation or Borstal training. The new bill tried to improve the position by raising the minimum age for imprisonment to fifteen in the case of courts of assize and quarter sessions, and to seventeen in the case of summary courts. The higher courts were less restricted in their use of imprisonment because the judges, worried by the wartime crime rate, argued successfully that

[55] Ibid., cols. 2136–7; HO45/21987/903499/14; 21949/884452/39; 21950/884452/72 and 75.

youths of sixteen could commit extremely serious crimes. In addition, the bill provided that both higher and lower courts should not impose imprisonment on a person under twenty-one unless, after considering information on the offender, they believed that no other method was appropriate; magistrates were required to give written reasons for their decision. The Home Secretary was empowered, finally, to abolish the use of imprisonment by summary courts, when alternative methods of treatment became available.[56]

Alternatives to Imprisonment

An essential preface to the discussion of alternatives to imprisonment is the proposal in the new bill to abolish corporal punishment, in accordance with the Cadogan committee's recommendation. Jowitt, the Lord Chancellor, with the backing of the Lord Chief Justice and other senior judges, argued forcibly that it was inopportune, when the country was confronted by a serious wave of juvenile crime, to 'proclaim the new experiment that under no conditions would any young person be whipped...' The Attorney-General, Hartley Shawcross, and the Solicitor-General, Sir Frank Soskice, gave him no support, however. They maintained that the great majority of the Labour movement believed that corporal punishment was 'barbarous and degrading to society'. Judicial opinion was not reliable, they concluded, since judges divorced the question of punishment from its wider social setting: 'In the long run', said Shawcross, 'the only way to reduce and eliminate crime is by a drastic improvement of social conditions and the spread of education.' Hence, in June 1947, once Jowitt had accepted that 'for political reasons, it would be very difficult to do less than had been proposed in the Bill introduced in 1938', the Cabinet agreed to abolish corporal punishment as a sentence of the court.[57] This decision put pressure on the department to come up with alternatives to imprisonment which were acceptable to both supporters and opponents of whipping.

One of the new alternatives to imprisonment in the 1938 bill was the state provision and state control of residential hostels, called

[56] See Table 13; HO45/21950/884452/75 and 77; 21952/884452/124; 20729/893948/3; CAB 129/19, L.P.C. 2 Mar. 1947. There seems little doubt that both Paterson and Henriques pressed for a more drastic legislative restriction on imprisonment.

[57] CAB 132/6, L.P. (47) 8th meeting; HO45/21951/884452/86, 99 and 116; HO45/21952/884452/102B and 104.

Howard houses, to which young offenders might be committed by court order. In the early months of the Labour government the proposal was re-examined. On one side was Paterson, who argued the case for Howard houses. He considered it essential that the centres should be state-run, in view of the failure of voluntary effort in the provision of probation homes and hostels, and because good staff could only be obtained as members of a State service. On the other side was Harris, who contended that hostels managed by voluntary bodies were greatly to be preferred to Howard houses, because 'the former were more likely to provide the homely atmosphere essential to the success of this form of treatment'. Harris added that 'the term Howard houses would soon become a music hall joke'. He recognized the deficiencies in the number, condition, and staffing of existing probation hostels, but felt this was mainly a financial problem. With financial inducement, many organizations would be willing to provide hostels.

Harris won the day, and in April 1946, Maxwell told the Home Secretary that the balance of advantage lay with probation homes and hostels, and that the Howard house proposals would be dropped. The new bill, therefore, included capital grants for the provision of more probation homes and hostels, and empowered the Home Secretary to approve such premises and to make rules for their management and inspection. Probation hostels under voluntary management were thus preferred to the potentially stricter regime of state-run Howard houses.[58]

In the 1938 bill, another method of punishing young offenders without removing them from their homes, their schools, or their work, was the compulsory attendance centre. Attendance centres were meant to deprive lads of their leisure, particularly on weekends, thus acting as an alternative to short terms of imprisonment for minor offences or default in payment of fines. In October 1945, a subcommittee of the Administration of Justice Standing Committee, with Harris in the chair, examined the problems of giving effect to the proposal. Finding suitable premises was a difficulty, as was the securing of appropriate occupation and instruction. The aim of the measure was also uncertain: was it wholly punitive, or was reformative treatment to be

[58] HO45/20729/893948/1–3; 21950/884452/75–6; 21987/903499/14. In December 1947, there were thirty-four hostels (twenty-two boys, twelve girls) and eighteen homes (four boys, fourteen girls). In hostels, the probationer went out to daily work from them; in homes, inmates received a short period of training. For the original Howard House proposal in the 1938 Bill, see pp. 257–8.

attempted? Such centres, finally, could become centres of contamination, collecting in one place all the 'bad lads' of the district. The subcommittee decided to get the views of the principal probation officers. The latter unanimously declared that attendance centres were wrong in principle, and recommended, instead, detention in remand homes for the twelve to seventeen age group, and approved homes and hostels for seventeen- to twenty-one-year-olds. Frank Newsam still considered that the rejection of attendance centres would be criticized, but the opposition of the standing committee and of ACTO ensured that the provision was dropped. As Maxwell explained to Ede: 'There will be no possibility of establishing at such centres the tradition of discipline and good order which can be built up in an institution or a club: consequently anything in the nature of reformative training will be impossible . . .'[59]

Where a strictly punitive measure was needed, detention in a remand home, under section 54 of the 1933 Children Act, seemed to be the front runner. In early 1944, Harris had reminded Maxwell that the Cadogan committee recommended a form of sharp punishment to replace the birching of boys under fourteen. This could be met, said Harris, 'by some effective way of enabling the Court to order up to a month's detention in a Remand Home'. Strong objection was taken by some, however, to the association of those in custody on remand with those undergoing a form of punishment; for that reason John Watson, for example, advocated the setting up of separate detention homes where the treatment would be short but sharp. In April 1946, the department examined the issue in the context of devising alternatives to imprisonment. Harris met with two heads of remand homes, two heads of short-term approved schools, the Middlesex principal probation officer, and Henriques. The conclusions of this meeting prompted the department to replace compulsory attendance centres with detention for not more than three months in a remand home for persons under seventeen, or in a remand centre for persons between seventeen and twenty-one.[60]

In the same month, however, the advisory council agreed that a short-term system of training under detention was required for those

[59] Ibid., 893948/1–3; 21950/884452/59, 75 and 76. For the original compulsory attendance centre proposal in the 1938 Bill, see pp. 260–2. The Magistrates Association was particularly concerned about the contamination effect of attendance centres: HO45/21949/884452/58.

[60] HO45/21948/884452/3; 21950/884452/59, 75 and 76; 20729/893948/3; A. E. Jones, *Juvenile Delinquency and the Law* (Harmondsworth, 1945), pp. 164–5.

boys who needed a brief period of strict discipline. The council proposed a sentence of three months' disciplinary detention, spent 'under conditions different from those which obtain in a remand home'. Now it was up to the Home Office to devise an acceptable scheme. The department eventually recommended, for persons between fourteen and twenty-one, detention for up to three months or, exceptionally, up to six months. The primary purpose of the detention was 'to bring [young offenders] up with a jerk and make them realise that they cannot flout the law with impunity'. The new bill thus provided for detention centres; they were clearly not intended for the more persistent offender, since a person could not be sent to a detention centre if he had previously been to prison or in Borstal or, since the age of seventeen, to a detention centre. Where a detention centre was available, finally, courts were deprived of their power to order a month's detention in a remand home.[61]

The proposal ran into opposition in 1947 in the shape of the Lord Chancellor, who considered that while a detention centre would be useful for children up to seventeen, it would be inadequate for young men aged eighteen to twenty-one who had committed serious crimes. For them, Jowitt wanted a prison ('No doubt the Prison Commissioners would want to call it a "Rest Home"', he quipped) which would so drill and discipline the boys that they would never wish to return, and to which they would be sent for sentences appropriate to their crimes. In response, the Home Secretary accepted that the detention centre ought not to be used for the more serious class of crime. For that reason, the bill prescribed few limitations on the powers of judges to impose imprisonment upon young people in serious cases. With this, Jowitt became reconciled to the detention centre principle.[62]

How, then, should we summarize the introduction of the detention centre? The proposal was a development of the existing power of detention for one month in a remand home. The context in which the detention centre superseded remand home detention was the proposed abolition of corporal punishment, the perceived need to bridge the gap between probation and Borstal or approved school training, and the

[61] HO45/21950/884452/75 and 77. The Howard League representatives on the Advisory Council, no less than those representing the judiciary and magistracy, supported the introduction of detention centres. The chairmen of the London Juvenile Courts also recommended 'short and sharp detention': 21987/903499/14.

[62] HO45/21951/884452/99.

disclosed inadequacies of the compulsory attendance centre for this purpose. The wider context was the wartime rise and current level of juvenile crime, and the consequent need on the government's part to replace corporal punishment with a tough and deterrent alternative, one which incorporated features of the military detention camps of the war years. To talk of a 'moral panic' over hooligan elements seems extreme, but public anxiety about juvenile crime certainly contributed to the process of replacing corporal punishment by the detention centre, and not, as looked likely in 1938, by the compulsory attendance centre.[63] A cardinal principle of the inter-war years, that the full Borstal sentence was preferable to short-term punitive detention, was thus abandoned.

Borstal Training

One of the most controversial clauses in the 1938 bill was that which gave magistrates the power to sentence directly to Borstal training (without committing the offender to quarter sessions or assizes for this purpose). In April 1946, Maxwell told the Home Secretary that the department believed the proposal was right; it would lead to more offenders being sent to Borstal instead of to prison. He realized, of course, that the proposal would be controversial; it had been withdrawn from the 1938 bill as a result of objections by the Howard League, the Magistrates Association and the Labour opposition. The Home Secretary, however, informed Maxwell that he did not feel he could defend direct committal. When the issue went before the advisory council, members expressed divergent views. Leo Page defended the proposal on the grounds that quarter sessions almost invariably rubber-stamped the lower court's recommendation, and that magistrates already had the power to sentence to Borstal in the difficult cases of youths who absconded from, or misbehaved in, approved schools. Opposed to direct committal were Margery Fry and George Benson, although the latter stated that he might think differently if the lower courts were required first to try a detention centre. Without advisory council endorsement, and in view of the fact that more remand homes and remand centres would be available for young

[63] Hall *et al*, *Change, Choice*, op. cit., ch. 12, *passim; Hansard*, vol. 444, 27 Nov. 1947, cols. 2131–2. Public anxiety was possibly stoked by the views of those who had to deal with offenders, one of whom was murdered in Standon Farm Approved School in February 1947: Hall, op. cit., p. 320; *Sixth Report*, op. cit., pp. 72–3.

offenders committed for Borstal sentence, the proposal for direct committal was withdrawn from the new bill.[64]

Other important changes went into the new bill. The maximum age for a Borstal sentence was lowered from twenty-three to twenty-one, because of the problems encountered since 1936 in dealing with the older offenders in a separate institution. In contrast, the bill increased the types of offenders eligible for Borstal by allowing the sentence to be imposed where the offender had no previous convictions or other known offences. On the advisory council, Miss Fry opposed this widening of the qualification for Borstal sentence, arguing that 'the guilty person should be proved to be dangerous to society before his liberty was restricted for so long'. But the bill made it easier to impose Borstal for a first offence, and directed the judiciary to base the sentence, in effect, upon the need for training.[65]

Probation

Finally, the proposals in the new bill relating to probation sought, as in 1938, to consolidate the existing law and to change it in line with some of the recommendations of the 1936 Committee on Social Services. The advisory council helped to frame the provisions, taking evidence from the National Association of Probation Officers and from the Probation Branch of the Home Office. For a start, the term 'probation' was confined to supervision by a probation officer. Dismissal and binding over, to which 'probation' was also applied by the 1907 Act, were replaced by absolute and conditional discharge. One year was to be the minimum period for which an offender could be put on probation and the maximum for which a probationer could be kept in an approved probation home or hostel. Furthermore, the making of social enquiry reports for the courts was included in the definition of a probation officer's duties. One proposal, however, was likely to provoke as much controversy as it had done in 1939.

Under the 1907 Act, a court of summary jurisdiction could make a probation order 'without proceeding to a conviction'. The 1938 bill

[64] HO45/21950/884452/75–6; 21987/903499/6 and 14. In May 1946, Lionel Fox declared that the Prison Commission favoured direct committal, to expedite the start of a boy's Borstal training. The Conservative party report, *Youth Astray*, also recommended direct committal.

[65] Ibid./76; Hood, op. cit., pp. 70–1. The Magistrates Association and the senior judges supported the widening of the qualification for Borstal sentence: 21951/884452/86; 21954/884452/159; CAB 129/19, L.P.C., 2 Mar. 1947.

abolished this provision, and the new bill similarly prescribed that a probation order could be made only upon conviction of the offender. Any disqualification attaching to a conviction was not, however, to affect those placed on probation. The department knew it could expect a rough ride in parliament on this proposal. Before turning to the parliamentary stages of the Criminal Justice Bill, it is useful to assess the overall response to the bill's publication in November 1947.[66]

Reviews

The new bill followed the 1938 bill so closely that it was difficult for commentators to wax lyrical about the measure. None the less, Rolph in the *New Statesman* spoke of 'this great Bill', and Viscount Templewood in the *Observer* described the proposals as 'a very notable advance in our penal methods'. In parliament, there was universal praise for the policy of keeping young offenders out of prison. Individual proposals were treated more critically. Clynes, the former Labour home secretary, opposed the abolition of corporal punishment. Templewood doubted 'the wisdom of so extending the definition of the classes that can be sent to Borstal as to make it possible to send to Borstal boys and girls who are not really criminals at all'. Henriques regretted that, without after-care supervision, detention centres could 'prove to be as futile as the short prison sentences have been'. Mannheim, expressing, to some degree, the views of the Howard League and the Institute for the Scientific Treatment of Delinquency, was uneasy about the detention centre. '[T]he danger cannot be entirely ruled out', he warned, 'that these centres may be established in wings of prisons and therefore hardly superior to the existing "Young Prisoners' Centres".' Nor was he convinced about the abolition of the system of making probation orders without a formal 'conviction.'[67] It was soon evident, therefore, that the government could expect amendments to the more controversial clauses.

[66] Ibid./76A; 21987/903499/14; *Hansard*, vol. 444, 27 Nov. 1947, cols. 2141–44; *Probation*, vol. 4 (1945), p. 126; Bochel, op. cit., pp. 166–8. The bill, finally, included a requirement of supervision, with liability to recall, for prisoners under twenty-one sentenced to twelve months or more imprisonment.

[67] See *New Statesman*, 15 Nov. 1947, p. 388; *Observer*, 9 Nov. 1947. cf. *The Times*, 5 Nov. 1947, p. 5; *Economist*, 8 Nov. 1947, p. 750. See also Clynes in *Evening Standard*, 5 Nov. 1947, p. 6; Templewood in *Howard Journal*, vol. 7 (1947–8), p. 166; Henriques in *TES*, 15 Nov. 1947, p. 615; Mannheim in 'The Criminal Justice Bill', *Fortnightly*, vol. 163 (1948), pp. 40 and 45.

The Bill in Parliament

The department was quickly confronted by a phalanx of groups—the Howard League, the British Medical Association, and the chairman of Metropolitan Juvenile Courts—demanding state remand homes, as envisaged in the 1938 bill, for difficult cases requiring skilled observation. Remand centres would not suffice, it was said, since they would deal with adolescents from seventeen to twenty-one and 'unruly' and 'depraved' youths of fourteen to seventeen years. If state remand homes were excluded from the bill, declared the *Howard Journal*, 'it will be a great betrayal of penal reform on a matter high above controversy'. George Benson, Labour MP for Chesterfield, and a member of the advisory council, moved an amendment to the bill, empowering the State to set up observation homes. The government successfully resisted the amendment, however, on the grounds that local authority remand homes were improving and would continue to do so in the absence of state competition. Yet again, the state observation home failed to secure government backing; it had been the same story for over twenty years.[68]

The same outside bodies, with the inclusion of the Haldane Society, also pressed the government to make seventeen the minimum age for imprisonment for all courts. What applied to a summary court under the bill would, thereby, apply to courts of assize and quarter sessions. Charles Royle, Labour MP for Salford, West, moved an amendment along these lines. Ede defended the original provision from the 'sad conclusion' that there were offenders between fifteen and seventeen who committed offences of such seriousness that imprisonment was the only course. The amendment was defeated in committee.[69]

The emotions aroused by the abolition of corporal punishment in 1939 seemed to have been extinguished. No one in the Commons in 1948, for example, sought a division against the government proposal. The spirit of Lord Ellenborough resurfaced, unfortunately, in the House of Lords. The Lord Chief Justice, Lord Goddard, with the support of Lord Roche, moved to preserve whipping by the birch but not by the 'cat-o-nine-tails'. Not even the combined efforts of Lords du Parcq, Samuel and Chorley, spokesman for the Home Office, could

[68] HO45/21988/903499/16 and 26; 21954/884452/159; 21956/884452/181C; *Magistrate*, vol. 8 (1948), p. 88; Fry in *Political Quarterly*, vol. XIX (1948), pp. 111–17.

[69] HO45/21954/884452/134A, 135, 144 and 159; *Howard Journal*, vol. 7 (1947–8), p. 156; *Hansard*, vol. 449, 15 Apr. 1948, cols. 1235–40.

defeat Lord Goddard's amendment. In the Commons, Ede and his under-secretary, Kenneth Younger, defended the view that there should be no judicial whipping, and with this, the Lords did not insist upon their amendment. Perhaps the proposal for detention centres weakened the resolve of this last stand against the abolition of corporal punishment.[70]

Henry Hynd, Labour MP for Hackney, Central, and Conservative MP, Manningham-Buller, were particularly energetic in the cause of amending the clause on detention centres. They tried unsuccessfully on three occasions: first, to set the minimum age for detention centres at the school-leaving age of fifteen; second, to make education and training a main object of the regime; and third, to follow detention by a period of after-care. The Home Office were attracted to the idea of compulsory after-care, but the advisory council had found it impossible to devise a suitable sanction for failure to comply with the licence conditions. The magistrates of the London juvenile courts were more successful. At their behest, the Lord Chancellor secured an amendment to the clause, which allowed the court to send schoolchildren of fourteen to fifteen years to a detention centre for as short a time as one month.[71] The clause also prompted a wider discussion in parliament. Members were concerned that the bill gave 'a very large blank cheque to the Home Office', as Benson put it. A number of lords complained that little or nothing was known of the aims, regime or location of the detention centre. But the government declined to put any more flesh round the skeleton; the detention centre remained experimental. This not only gave the executive a good deal of discretion in implementing the policy; it also made it difficult for an effective opposition to be mounted against the policy.[72]

The most important amendment, probably, was that of Templewood to reinstate the scheme of attendance centres. Whilst the Lord Chancellor opposed the amendment, and Templewood withdrew it, a re-jigged amendment was accepted by the government 'on the basis that this would be an experiment of a limited character'. The maximum number of hours for which an offender could be ordered to

[70] *Hansard* (Lords), vol. 156, 2 June 1948, cols. 191–210; vol. 157, 29 June 1948, cols. 30–6; vol. 157, 20 July 1948, cols. 1073–86. *Hansard*, vol. 453, 15 July 1948, cols. 1546–70.

[71] HO45/21988/903499/16 and 33; 21955/884452/171A; *Hansard*, vol. 449, 15 Apr. 1948, cols. 1244–7; *Hansard* (Lords), vol. 157, 5 July 1948, cols. 360–2.

[72] *Hansard*, vol. 444, 28 Nov. 1947, col. 2286; *Hansard* (Lords), vol. 155, 28 Apr. 1948, col. 495; vol. 156, 15 June 1948, cols. 780–6. cf. Hall *et al.*, op. cit., pp. 322–25, 368–9.

attend was reduced from sixty (in the 1938 bill) to twelve. Moreover, to limit the possibility of offenders contaminating each other, those who had been previously sentenced to imprisonment, Borstal, a detention centre, or an approved school, could not be sent to an attendance centre. Clearly, the government wished to proceed cautiously, and to 'locate' the measure between probation and the detention centre in the tariff of punishment.[73]

There were only two amendments of any consequence, finally, in relation to Borstal training. Lord Raglan, chairman of the visiting committee of Usk Borstal, moved to empower courts of summary jurisdiction to pass a Borstal sentence, but the amendment was defeated. An amendment to do with the minimum sentence fared better. The bill raised the minimum sentence for boys from six months to a year, in order to assure the judges that a Borstal sentence was a stern alternative to a long prison sentence, and would not be undermined by early release. There were cases, however, which benefited from early release, and the Howard League, for one, wanted the existing minimum to be kept. Lord Llewellin, brother of the Borstal governor, Bill Llewellin, thus moved an amendment to restore six months as the minimum sentence for boys. The government really had no case for the twelve-month minimum, other than judicial anxiety, and accordingly they accepted a compromise of a nine months minimum sentence.[74]

Summary

The Criminal Justice Act became law on 30 July 1948. It introduced remand centres, attendance centres, and detention centres; it gave financial backing to the provision of probation homes and hostels; it further encouraged the use of probation and Borstal training; it abolished corporal punishment; and, the cord which pulled the Act together, it placed restrictions on the use of imprisonment. 'The guiding principle of the Act', declared *The Times*, 'is that there must be

[73] HO45/21988/903499/33; *Hansard* (Lords), vol. 156, 3 June 1948, cols. 295–303; *Hansard*, vol. 453, 15 July 1948, cols. 1575–7.

[74] Ibid./48; *Hansard* (Lords), vol. 156, 3 June 1948, cols. 307–13; 15 June 1948, cols. 841–8; vol. 157, 1 July 1948, cols. 241–8. Ede inserted into the bill the power to prohibit the practice of sending absconders, whether 'care and protection' cases or not, from approved schools to Borstal. It should be noted, finally, that the parliamentary stages of the Criminal Justice Bill were dominated by discussion of the death penalty, for which see J. Christophe, *Capital Punishment and British Politics* (1962).

no despair of humanity.'[75] Unconstructive penal measures, like imprisonment, lost further ground to probation and residential training sentences.

There were proposals in the Act, of course, which deviated from this policy. The detention centre marked a shift in policy from the one advocated by Maxwell and Paterson in the 1930s: that Borstal training was preferable to a system of boys' prisons, which short-stay punitive institutions would surely become. Moreover, for all the Act's allegiance to the rehabilitative ideal, it was largely unresponsive to the declared need for medical and psychological observation and treatment. The Henderson home aside, the Home Office did little in the 1940s to treat the 'emotional maladjustment' which caused some delinquent behaviour. Bodies like the Institute for the Scientific Treatment of Delinquency were kept at arm's length by the department. The Criminal Justice Act made it possible to require a probationer to submit to mental treatment, but overall, the Act was a testimony to the social conception of delinquency. The individual shortcomings of the Act aside, it brought an instant and striking reduction in the numbers of young offenders sentenced to imprisonment, from nearly 14 per cent of all those found guilty of indictable offences to only 7.8 per cent.[76]

Who, then, deserves most credit for the Act? *The Times* proclaimed that it derived from 'a common stock of liberal thought to which men of all parties and of none have contributed'. Templewood ascribed both the 1938 and 1948 measures to the long experience and experimentation of social workers and 'expert inquirers'.[77] Can we be more specific? Some credit belongs to the Advisory Council on the Treatment of Offenders, which contributed to the changes which marked the 1948 bill off from the 1938 measure. To some extent, the Council 'institutionalized' the advice offered by the penal reform lobby, although the Howard League and the Magistrates Association retained an independent voice. In addition, in an era of Labour party ascendancy, political theorists like Laski, and reform-minded criminologists like Mannheim, both based at the LSE, had a good deal more influence on the trajectory of penal change than, say, the police and judiciary.

[75] *The Times*, 31 July 1948, p. 5.

[76] See Table 9. For the Henderson home for the psychiatric treatment of maladjusted offenders, see HO45/20729/893948/2. The Home Office did show some interest in John Bowlby's psychological studies of separation experiences in infancy: see note 48, this chapter.

[77] *The Times*, 5 Nov. 1947, p. 5; *Hansard* (Lords), vol. 155, 28 Apr. 1948, col. 466.

At the departmental level, Harris's writ ran large. Skills that had been honed on the Children Act of 1933 were applied to the Criminal Justice Act. It was his final significant contribution to modern criminal policy, since he retired shortly afterwards. The Act was also the climax to Maxwell's long administrative career. His liberal principles and humane influence were at the peak of their power in the 1940s, and they unquestionably guided both Morrison and Ede in their plans for post-war penal reform. In this litany of administrative influence, however, pride of place belongs to Paterson. His detailed contribution to the Act was insignificant; he lost more arguments to Harris over particular clauses than he won. But, as Sir Cyril Osborne, Conservative MP for Louth, told the Commons, the Criminal Justice Act was 'a true memorial to his work'. Paterson died shortly before the measure was debated in parliament, hence the Home Secretary immediately paid tribute to Paterson's vision and persistent optimism in the realm of penal reform.[78]

The vision and the detailed policies of these liberal professionals were available to the Labour party in the 1940s as it set out to establish the 'welfare state'. The Criminal Justice Act was now part and parcel of the party's programme to reconstruct the social and economic framework of the country, as Barnett Janner, Labour MP for Leicester, informed the Commons:

> While this Bill did not owe its original idea to the Government the timing of its introduction is considered necessary in order to make the picture complete of the changing of the general social circumstances of the people, thus enabling the nation as a whole to live on the basis of a family life where even those who have transgressed against the law are taken into consideration in the same way as the lowliest and poorest member of the community.[79]

One way of viewing the social legislation of the Labour government, indeed, is to see the insurance, health, and children's legislation as the preliminary manœuvres in an attack on juvenile crime, to be followed up by those parts of the Criminal Justice Act concerned with young offenders. By the late 1940s, however, this larger attempt to diminish

[78] *Hansard*, vol. 444, 27 Nov. 1947, cols. 2130 and 2323. See also *TES*, 15 Nov. 1947, p. 609. Given the contribution of people like Paterson, the penal reform bodies were critical of the clause in the Criminal Justice Bill which gave power for the abolition of the office of the prison commissioners. In fact, the Prison Commission was not dissolved until 1963, when its staff and functions were transferred to the Home Office.

[79] *Hansard*, vol. 444, 28 Nov. 1947, col. 2335.

the supply of crime in the future claimed the allegiance of Conservative as well as Labour politicians. The injustices of the pre-war era and the wartime struggle for national survival had shaped a political consensus about the needs of a full social democracy, needs which were defined, in large part, by the 'liberal progressives'.

11

Postscript: The End of Consensus

In the 1940s, Fabian welfarism joined with positivism to create the Criminal Justice Act 1948. Fabianism created within the context of the Labour party the belief that it was possible to improve man's moral state by improving his material welfare; positivism produced within the ranks of penal reformers and liberal professionals the belief that a welfare-oriented system of justice would best reclaim delinquents for citizenship. A similar conjunction of forces led to the next major step in juvenile justice, the Children and Young Persons Act 1969. A detailed analysis of the 1969 Act is beyond the scope of this book, but a brief assessment of the genesis and significance of the statute adds further credence, I would submit, to the argument within.

In the 1960s, influential Fabian voices, particularly those of Lord Longford and Barbara Wootton, called for the continued transformation of the juvenile court into a treatment tribunal, where the needs of the child would have primacy over the finding of guilt. They also called for a 'family service' to deal with parental inadequacy, on the grounds that delinquency arose from family incapacity and breakdown. The Fabian conception of parental inadequacy was still primarily 'sociological', focusing on the social skills required for rearing children and coping with modern life, and not much influenced by psychiatry and psychology. None the less, it linked easily with the psychoanalytically-based notions of family maladjustment put forward by professional social workers and by key representatives of the Children's Department of the Home Office. Once again, the combined forces of Fabian welfarists, professional social workers, and liberal administrators carried the day. If the advocates of family casework failed to get rid of the juvenile court and the stigma of a court appearance, they secured legislation which heralded a substantial shift away from courtroom appearances on a criminal prosecution, towards either voluntary agreements (between parents and social workers) or non-criminal 'care proceedings'.

The implementation of the 1969 Act took place, however, as the post-war consensus on delinquency and its treatment reached the point of disintegration. Social positivists like Hermann Mannheim expected the advent of the welfare state to lead to a decline in crime rates; poverty and deprivation were, after all, important causes of delinquency. Yet despite the benefits of the welfare state, crime not only persisted but flourished in the post-war period. The Labour party fell back on the comfortless argument that increases in crime were a feature of all modern industrial societies. In contrast, the Conservative party attacked the failure of social democratic criminal policy as a keeper of social order. Conservative voices were already to be heard in the 1950s berating the welfare state, along with parental neglect and sentimental courts, for encouraging a wave of serious and inexcusable delinquency. Inexcusable, because these youths were the supposed heirs of affluence, not the victims of mass unemployment. At the end of the decade, Tory Home Secretary R. A. Butler just managed to ward off pressure from grass-roots supporters to re-introduce corporal punishment for juvenile delinquents. By 1969, crime was well and truly in the forefront of the Conservative party programme.[1]

Conservative opposition to the Children and Young Persons Act initiated a full-blooded critique of the inadequacies of liberal welfare. Many of the key sections of the 1969 Act, for example, were never implemented. From 1978 the offensive was stepped up. The architects of the 1969 Act hoped to remove the punitive detention centre; instead, the Conservative government introduced experimental regimes at two existing detention centres to put the bite back into the 'short, sharp shock'. More recently, this regime has been extended to all detention centres. Furthermore, as faith in the curative effects of long-term incarceration dwindled, the Borstal training system was replaced by 'youth custody', to be imposed by the courts in proportion to the gravity of the crime committed.

Gone, then, is the unique era of the first half of the century, when leading opinion-formers held a consistent blend of moral and social views, which shaped the main administrative and legislative alterations in the sphere of juvenile justice. No one interest grouping now speaks with the same convincing moral force and legitimacy as the reformers of this study. We are said to have entered an era of

[1] See A. E. Bottoms, 'On the Decriminalization of English Juvenile Courts', in R. Hood (ed.), *Crime, Criminology and Public Policy* (1974); John Clarke, 'Social Democratic Delinquents and Fabian Families', in National Deviancy Conference (ed.), *Permissiveness and Control* (1980); G. Pearson, *Hooligan: A History of Respectable Fears* (1983), ch. 2.

'penological pessimism', very different from the years of moral optimism between the wars. Where optimists saw the delinquent as more offended against than offending, present-day pessimists stress the moral responsibility of offenders. Where optimists proclaimed that the time and technique required to rehabilitate the offender should determine the court's sentence, pessimists simply seek the punishment that fits the crime. In truth, however, the two camps—reformist and retributivist—are now contesting the shape of modern criminal policy. The pessimists have not yet demolished the system of criminal justice erected by the liberal progressives between 1914 and 1948.

APPENDIX

Statistical Tables and Figures

Table 1(a). Persons proceeded against in juvenile courts, 1913–1927

Year	Number proceeded against
1913	37,520
1914	36,929
1915	43,981
1916	47,342
1917	51,323
1918	49,915
1919	40,473
1920	36,064
1921	30,253
1922	31,056
1923	28,769
1924	29,621
1925	27,801
1926	25,600
1927	25,478

Data taken from the *Fourth Report of the Children's Branch*, p. 108.

Table 1(b). Persons dealt with in juvenile courts who were found guilty, with manner of disposal, 1913–27

Year	Number found guilty	Charge proved—Order made *without* conviction							Convicted								
		Total charge proved *without* conviction	Dismissed	Recognizances	Probation	Committed to industrial school	Committed to custody of relative, &c	Sent to institution for defectives, &c	Total convicted	Imprisonment	Police cells	Reformatory school	Whipping	Fine	Recognizances	Otherwise disposed of
Number:																
1913	32,862	17,648	9,529	2,447	4,465	1,200	7	—	15,214	52	—	1,082	2,079	11,805	74	122
1914	32,230	17,256	9,167	2,370	4,496	1,209	13	1	14,974	30	—	1,178	2,244	11,293	108	121
1915	39,164	19,188	8,417	3,011	5,719	2,003	24	14	19,976	4	16	1,508	3,297	14,990	86	75
1916	43,138	19,050	7,532	2,764	6,781	1,939	16	18	24,088	9	10	1,783	4,611	17,444	119	112
1917	46,980	19,690	7,974	3,339	6,548	1,801	12	16	27,290	40	7	1,626	4,951	20,393	130	143
1918	44,976	17,579	7,101	2,971	5,868	1,593	16	30	27,397	25	18	1,510	3,593	21,997	105	149
1919	36,188	13,906	6,482	2,353	4,188	842	22	19	22,282	13	11	937	1,599	19,475	139	108
1920	32,104	14,229	6,355	2,339	4,691	812	16	16	17,875	12	2	824	1,285	15,591	86	75
1921	26,349	12,680	6,078	1,931	4,147	493	4	27	13,669	7	2	608	623	12,288	102	39
1922	27,171	14,643	7,162	2,236	4,715	484	25	21	12,528	3	3	564	508	11,402	17	31
1923	25,279	14,631	6,357	2,316	5,448	463	18	29	10,648	1	2	629	514	9,409	22	71
1924	25,804	15,397	6,569	2,258	5,972	526	33	39	10,407	3	3	530	607	9,178	30	56
1925	24,286	15,633	6,715	1,972	6,357	552	6	31	8,653	5	—	578	452	7,578	8	32
1926	22,822	15,789	6,720	2,124	6,417	487	5	36	7,033	1	3	549	335	6,076	10	59
1927	22,448	15,659	6,729	2,139	6,302	447	8	34	6,789	1	—	525	230	5,971	23	39

Year	Number found guilty	Charge proved—Order made *without* conviction: Total charge proved *without* conviction	Dismissed	Recognizances	Probation	Committed to industrial school	Committed to custody of relative, &c	Sent to institution for defectives, &c	Convicted: Total convicted	Imprisonment	Police cells	Reformatory school	Whipping	Fine	Recognizances	Otherwise disposed of
Percentage:																
1913	100	53.70	29.00	7.44	13.59	3.65	.02	—	46.30	.16	—	3.29	6.33	35.92	.23	.37
1914	100	53.54	28.44	7.36	13.95	3.75	.04	—	46.46	.09	—	3.65	6.96	35.04	.34	.38
1915	100	48.99	21.49	7.69	14.60	5.11	.06	.04	51.01	.01	.04	3.85	8.42	38.28	.22	.19
1916	100	44.16	17.46	6.41	15.72	4.49	.04	.04	55.84	.02	.02	4.13	10.69	40.44	.28	.26
1917	100	41.91	16.97	7.11	13.94	3.83	.03	.03	58.09	.09	.01	3.46	10.54	43.41	.28	.30
1918	100	39.09	15.79	6.61	13.05	3.54	.03	.07	69.91	.05	.04	3.36	7.99	48.91	.23	.33
1919	100	38.43	17.92	6.50	11.57	2.33	.06	.05	61.57	.03	.03	2.59	4.42	53.82	.38	.30
1920	100	44.32	19.80	7.28	14.61	2.53	.05	.05	55.68	.04	.01	2.57	4.00	48.56	.27	.23
1921	100	48.12	23.07	7.33	15.74	1.87	.01	.10	51.88	.03	.01	2.31	2.36	46.63	.39	.15
1922	100	53.89	26.36	8.23	17.35	1.78	.09	.08	46.11	.01	.01	2.08	1.87	41.96	.06	.12
1923	100	57.88	25.15	9.16	21.55	1.83	.07	.12	42.12	—	.01	2.49	2.03	37.22	.09	.28
1924	100	59.67	25.46	8.75	23.14	2.04	.13	.15	40.33	.01	.01	2.05	2.35	35.57	.12	.22
1925	100	64.37	27.65	8.12	26.18	2.27	.02	.13	35.63	.02	—	2.38	1.86	31.21	.03	.13
1926	100	69.18	29.44	9.31	28.12	2.13	.02	.16	30.82	.01	.01	2.41	1.47	26.62	.04	.26
1927	100	69.76	29.98	9.53	28.07	1.99	.04	.15	30.24	—	—	2.34	1.03	26.60	.10	.17

Data taken from the *Fourth Report of the Children's Branch*, p. 109.

Table 2. Number of persons proceeded against for indictable offences in juvenile courts, 1913–1948

Year	Persons under 16	Year	Persons under 17
1913	14,325	1934	22,440
1914	14,845	1935	27,358
1915	20,418	1936	28,723
1916	23,735	1937	30,733
1917	24,407	1938	29,388
1918	21,061	1939–45	n.a.
1919	13,999	1946	38,384
1920	14,380	1947	37,086
1921	11,688	1948	45,973
1922	11,937		
1923	12,170		
1924	12,884		
1925	12,666		
1926	13,115		
1927	12,254		
1928	11,247		
1929	11,361		
1930	12,198		
1931	12,895		
1932	13,978		
1933	14,848		

Data taken from the relevant volumes of *Criminal Statistics, England and Wales.*

Table 3. Number of young persons found guilty of indictable offences, 1913–1948

Year	Persons under 16	Year	Persons under 16	Year	Persons under 17
1913	12,915	1928	10,225[a]	1934	20,540
1914	13,400	1929	11,151	1935	25,543
1915	n.a.	1930	11,995	1936	27,126
1916	n.a.	1931	12,556	1937	29,201
1917	22,670	1932	13,778	1938	28,116
1918	19,397	1933	14,412	1939	30,835
1919	12,684			1940	42,187
1920	12,919			1941	43,594
1921	10,386			1942	38,549
1922	10,644			1943	38,763
1923	10,962			1944	40,554
1924	11,581			1945	43,503
1925	11,410			1946	37,088
1926	12,040			1947	35,694
1927	11,037			1948	44,434

[a] Until 1928 the figures included those found guilty at juvenile courts only; thereafter, at all courts (i.e., juvenile courts, ordinary courts of summary jurisdiction, and higher courts). The figures for every year include those against whom charges were proved and orders made *without* conviction.

Data taken from the relevant volumes of *Criminal Statistics, England and Wales*.

Table 4. Methods by which young offenders[a] found guilty of indictable offences were dealt with by juvenile courts, for selected years, 1913–1948

		Sentences as a percentage of those found guilty													
	Nos. found guilty or	Custodial measure[b]		Probation		Fine		Whipping		Nominal penalties[c]		Fit person order		Otherwise dealt with[d]	
Year	charge proved	No.	%	No.	%	No.	%	No.	%	No.	%	No.	%	No.	%
1913	12,915	1,880	14.6	3,541	27.4	1,287	10	2,072	16	4,121	31.9	—	—	14	0.1
1917	22,670	3,032	13.4	5,587	24.7	3,452	15.2	4,875	21.5	5,605	24.7	—	—	119	0.5
1920	12,919	1,414	10.9	4,041	31.3	2,218	17.2	1,273	9.9	3,890	30.1	—	—	83	0.6
1928	10,225	971	9.5	5,461	53.4	456	4.4	171	1.7	3,107	30.4	—	—	59	0.6
1930	11,137	1,114	10	6,159	55.3	423	3.8	134	1.2	3,263	29.3	—	—	44	0.4
1934[a]	20,428	2,062	10.1	11,158	54.6	871	4.3	130	0.6	6,027	29.5	65	0.3	115	0.6
1938[e]	27,875	2,884	10.3	14,175	50.9	1,678	6	43	0.2	8,613	30.9	198	0.7	284	1.0
1948[e]	43,706	4,437	10.1	18,221	41.7	6,037	13.8	—	—	14,021	32.1	418	1.0	572	1.3

[a] Until 1930, the figures refer to persons of under 16 years; from 1934 onwards, to persons of under 17 years.
[b] Including committal to a reformatory, approved school, or remand home, or imprisonment.
[c] Includes dismissal and binding over with recognizances.
[d] Includes admission to institutions for the mentally disordered, days in police cells, and other miscellaneous methods of disposal.
[e] For 1938 and 1948 it is possible to provide figures of persons under 17 found guilty of indictable offences at Higher Courts:

Year	Committed or returned to approved school	Borstal training (those over 16)	Probation	Conditional discharge	Otherwise dealt with	Total
1938	34	49	116	39	3	241
1948	147	173	328	73	7	728

Data taken from the relevant volumes of *Criminal Statistics, England and Wales.*

Table 5. Number of children and young persons sent by the courts annually to Home Office schools[a], 1913–1948

Year	Boys	Girls	Total	Year	Boys	Girls	Total
1913	4,632	1,112	5,744	1931	1,611	216	1,827
1914	4,678	975	5,653	1932	1,617	233	1,850
1915	5,448	959	6,407	1933	1,723	215	1,938
1916	5,738	864	6,602	1934	2,374	454	2,828
1917	5,236	827	6,063	1935	2,659	482	3,141
1918	4,633	576	5,209	1936	3,188	571	3,759
1919	3,134	412	3,546	1937	n.a.	n.a.	n.a.
1920	2,704	487	3,191	1938	3,256	657	3,913
1921	1,799	389	2,188	1939	3,322	683	4,005
1922	1,545	289	1,834	1940	4,799	821	5,620
1923	1,677	276	1,953	1941	4,566	945	5,511
1924	1,581	310	1,891	1942	4,930	1,043	5,973
1925	1,690	259	1,949	1943[b]	4,612	982	5,594
1926	1,501	290	1,791	1944	4,177	1,196	5,373
1927	1,414	238	1,652	1945	4,464	1,194	5,658
1928	1,424	242	1,666	1946	4,044	950	4,994
1929	1,371	240	1,611	1947	3,494	772	4,266
1930	1,565	243	1,808	1948	3,857	807	4,664

[a] Including reformatories, industrial schools and day industrial schools until 1933. From 1934, the figures refer to senior, intermediate and junior approved schools.

[b] From 1943 the figures include classifying schools.

Data taken from the *Fourth Report of the Children's Branch*, p. 119 and the *Sixth Report of the Children's Department*, p. 149.

Table 6. Number of children and young persons in the Home Office schools on 31 December in each year[a], 1913–1948

Year	Number	Year	Number
1913	18,916	1931	6,287
1914	18,976	1932	6,391
1915	19,103	1933	6,357
1916	19,472	1934	6,905
1917	19,403	1935	7,389
1918	18,743	1936	8,056
1919	17,270	1937	n.a.
1920	15,203	1938	8,764
1921	12,491	1939	8,860
1922	9,886	1940	8,901
1923	8,434	1941	9,538
1924	7,463	1942	10,257
1925	7,069	1943[b]	10,678
1926	6,871	1944	11,150
1927	6,550	1945	11,052
1928	6,307	1946	10,544
1929	6,180	1947	9,198
1930	6,115	1948	9,201

[a] Including reformatories, industrial schools and day industrial schools until 1933. From 1934, the figures refer to senior, intermediate and junior approved schools.

[b] From 1943 the figures include classifying schools.

Data taken from same source as Table 5.

Table 7. Probation orders—all courts, for selected years, 1913–1948

Year	Persons under 16				Persons under 17				Persons 16–21			
	Indictable offences		Indictable and non-indictable offences		Indictable offences		Indictable and non-indictable offences		Indictable offences		Indictable and non-indictable offences	
	No.	%[a]	No.	%	No.	%	No.	%	%		%	
1913	3,643	44.3	4,568	41.3					2,376	28.9	3,177	28.7
1920	4,322	51.7	5,020	46.8					2,442	29.2	3,255	30.3
1925	5,809	48.0	6,827	45.2					3,524	29.1	4,397	29.1
1930	6,583	43.5	7,555	42.1					4,941	32.7	5,876	32.7
1938					14,350	56.7	16,024	54.8				
1948					18,844	64.2	20,238	62.3				

Year	Persons 17–21				Persons under 21	
	Indictable offences		Indictable and non-indictable offences		Indictable offences	Indictable and non-indictable offences
	No.	%	No.	%	%	%
1913					73.2	70.0
1920					80.9	77.1
1925					77.2	74.4
1930					76.2	74.8
1938	5,053	20.0	6,097	20.8	76.7	75.6
1948	4144	14.1	4668	14.4	78.3	76.6

[a] This is the percentage of the total number of probation orders given to offenders of all ages.

Data taken from the *Fourth Report of the Children's Branch*, p. 114, and from the relevant volumes of *Criminal Statistics, England and Wales.*

Table 8. Number of adolescents found guilty of indictable offences at all courts, 1929–1948

Year	Persons aged 16 and under 21	Persons aged 17 and under 21
1929	10,455	
1930	11,929	
1931	12,417	
1932	14,111	
1933	12,507	
1934	12,146	9,508
1935	12,085	8,967
1936	13,331	9,014
1937	14,590	10,292
1938	15,788	11,451
1939	15,435	11,219
1940	18,530	13,039
1941	23,341	17,121
1942	22,377	16,553
1943	20,002	14,422
1944	20,438	14,740
1945	24,052	17,442
1946	20,430	14,908
1947	19,331	14,177
1948	20,268	15,073

Data taken from the relevant volumes of *Criminal Statistics, England and Wales.*

Table 9. Methods by which persons aged 17 and under 21 found guilty of indictable offences were dealt with by all courts in selected years, 1938–1949

Year	No. found guilty	Absolute and conditional discharge No.	%	Probation No.	%	Fine No.	%	Borstal No.	%	Imprisonment No.	%	Otherwise dealt with No.	%
1938	11,451	2,638	23.1	4,995	43.6	1,652	14.4	988[a]	8.6	850	7.4	328	2.9
1948	15,073	3,123	20.7	4,096	27.2	3,720	24.7	1,716	11.4	2,104	13.9	314	2.1
1949	12,576	2,495	19.8	3,532	28.1	3,501	27.8	1,799[b]	14.3	980	7.8	269	2.2

[a] Includes section 10 cases (Criminal Justice Administration Act 1914) from the lower courts.
[b] Includes committal to quarter sessions under sections 20 and 29 of the Criminal Justice Act 1948.

Data taken from the relevant volumes of *Criminal Statistics, England and Wales.*

Table 10. The crime rate among adolescent male offenders and its relation to the use made of imprisonment and Borstal training, 1929–1948

Year	Number of males 16–21 found guilty of indictable offences	Number of crimes per 100,000 boys in the age group 16–21[a]	Number of males 16–21 sentenced to imprisonment for indictable offences	Proportion of total number found guilty imprisoned	Number of males 16–21 sentenced to Borstal for indictable offences[b]	Proportion of total number found guilty sent to Borstal
1929	9,209	536	950	10.3	635	6.9
1930	10,700	622	1,122	10.5	679	6.3
1931	11,130	647	1,100	9.9	812	7.3
1932	12,663	748	1,582	12.5	952	7.5
1933	11,165	678	1,284	11.5	802	7.2
1934	10,757	686	1,131	10.5	742	6.9
1935	10,712	720	998	9.3	620	5.8
1936	11,907	767	818	6.9	742	6.2
1937	12,988	800	845	6.5	996	7.7
1938	14,147	841	807	5.7	1,194	8.4
		17–21				
1939	13,655	643	897	6.6	1,207	8.8
1940	16,031	783	1,567	9.8	1,057	6.6
1941	19,707	1,056	2,379	12.1	1,357	6.9
1942	18,949	1,060	2,527	13.3	1,320	7.0
1943	16,601	921	2,143	12.9	1,197	7.2
1944	17,165	964	1,924	11.2	1,230	7.2
1945	21,133	1,246	2,195	10.4	1,973	9.3
1946	17,891	1,076	2,013	11.2	1,925	10.7
1947	16,679	1,023	2,010	12.0	1,808	10.8
1948	17,485	1,084	1,873	10.7	1,848	10.6

[a] Crimes per 100,000 refer to the age group 17–21 after 1938.
[b] In the years 1936–1948, youths aged 21–23 were also sentenced to Borstal.

Data taken from the relevant volumes of *Criminal Statistics* and the *Annual Reports of the Prison Commissioners.*

Table 11. The daily average population of Borstal institutions, 1926–1948

Year	Males	Females	Total
1926	1,119	67	1,186
1927	1,179	74	1,253
1928	1,203	85	1,288
1929	1,232	104	1,336
1930	1,285	116	1,401
1931	1,488	113	1,601
1932	1,781	114	1,895
1933	1,931	123	2,054
1934	1,887	112	1,999
1935	1,694	114	1,808
1936	1,608	113	1,721
1937	1,732	128	1,860
1938	2,020	140	2,160
1939	n.a.	n.a.	n.a.
1940	1,044	n.a.	1,044[a]
1941	1,212	160	1,372
1942	1,494	n.a.	1,494[a]
1943	1,643	246	1,889
1944	1,623	265	1,888
1945	1,788	298	2,086
1946	2,228	253	2,481
1947	2,626	185	2,811
1948	2,885	221	3,106

[a] Figures available for males only.

Data taken from the *Annual Reports of the Prison Commissioners.*

Table 12. Borstal sentences in selected years, 1920–1938

		Age on conviction						Previous convictions							
		16 and 17 years		18 and 19 years		20 years and over[a]		None		One		2–5		6 and over	
Year	Total no. admitted on conviction	No.	%	No.	%	No.	%	No.	%	No.	%	No.	%	No.	%
1920	774	357	46.1	348	45.0	69	8.9	66	8.5	260	33.6	429	55.4	19	2.5
1930	774	317	41.0	346	44.7	111	14.3	65	8.4	230	29.7	437	56.5	42	5.4
1938	1,347	440	32.6	545	40.5	362	26.9	112	8.3	328	24.3	812	60.3	95	7.1

		Period of Detention					
		3 years		Under 3 years and over 2		2 years	
Year	Total no. admitted on conviction	No.	%	No.	%	No.	%
1920	774	670	86.7	7	0.9	96	12.4
1930	774	746	96.4	1	0.1	27	3.5
1938	1,347	1,213	90.1	2	0.1	132	9.8

[a] Borstal training was made applicable to the age group, 21–23 years, in 1936. The first time this change affected the figures above was in 1938.

Data taken from the relevant volumes of the *Annual Reports of the Prison Commissioners.*

Table 13. Number of persons aged 16–21 sentenced to Borstal and imprisonment for indictable and non-indictable offences, 1926–1948

	Total receptions into Borstal[a]			Total receptions into prison		
Year	Male	Female	Total	Male	Female	Total
1926	561	40	601	2,464	178	2,642
1927	568	34	602	2,221	147	2,368
1928	635	48	683	1,721	128	1,849
1929	679	51	730	1,559	93	1,652
1930	725	49	774	1,872	86	1,958
1931	873	47	920	1,883	119	2,002
1932	1,011	47	1,058	2,653	128	2,781
1933	854	44	898	2,253	127	2,380
1934	793	54	847	1,894	128	2,022
1935	686	35	721	1,608	99	1,707
1936	823	45	868	1,237	77	1,314
1937	1,053	62	1,115	1,275	80	1,355
1938	1,276	71	1,347	1,226	88	1,314
1939	1,327	91	1,418	1,389	94	1,483
1940	1,173	116	1,289	2,149	227	2,376
1941	1,521	218	1,739	3,128	333	3,461
1942	1,475	198	1,673	3,555	437	3,992
1943	1,324	240	1,564	3,223	578	3,801
1944	1,386	274	1,660	3,021	904	3,925
1945	2,166	276	2,442	3,390	792	4,182
1946	2,109	151	2,260	2,726	391	3,117
1947	1,933	144	2,077	2,589	323	2,912
1948	1,975	140	2,115	2,479	277	2,756

[a] From 1936 to 1948, youths aged 21–23 were sentenced to Borstal.

Data taken from the *Annual Reports of the Prison Commissioners.*

Table 14. Index figures (1938 = 100) for the numbers in different age groups (male and female) found guilty of indictable offences for every 100,000 population in the age group, 1938–1948

Year	Age group			
	Under 14	14–17	(Under 17)	17–21
1938	100	100	100	100
1939	116	109	113	88
1940	164	149	157	107
1941	167	166	166	145
1942	151	149	150	145
1943	158	146	152	128
1944	169	152	161	132
1945	173	177	174	162
1946	150	147	148	143
1947	147	138	142	138
1948	185	174	178	147

Data taken from the *Sixth Report of the Children's Department*, p. 46.

Table 15. Methods by which persons under 17 found guilty of indictable offences were dealt with by juvenile courts, for selected years, 1938–1945

Year	Sentences as a percentage of those found guilty					
	Approved school	Probation	Dismissed under Probation Act	Fined[a]	Bound over	Otherwise dealt with[a]
1938	10	51	24	5.9	7.4	1.7
1941						
Boys	11.1	43	20.8	14.8	7	—
Girls	12.4	53	18.4	7.8	6.4	—
1943						
Boys	10.3	44.5	22.8	14.6	6.3	—
Girls	10	55.8	19.1	7.5	5	—
1945						
Boys	8.5	40.6	26.3	16.6	6.6	—
Girls	9.7	48.2	23.4	9.6	7	—

[a] 'Otherwise dealt with' includes Fit Persons orders, Supervision orders, Birchings, Committals to Institutions for Mentally Defectives. The wartime figures of fines include cases 'otherwise dealt with', including birchings.

Data taken from *Hansard*, vol. 428, 5 Nov. 1946, cols. 231–2.

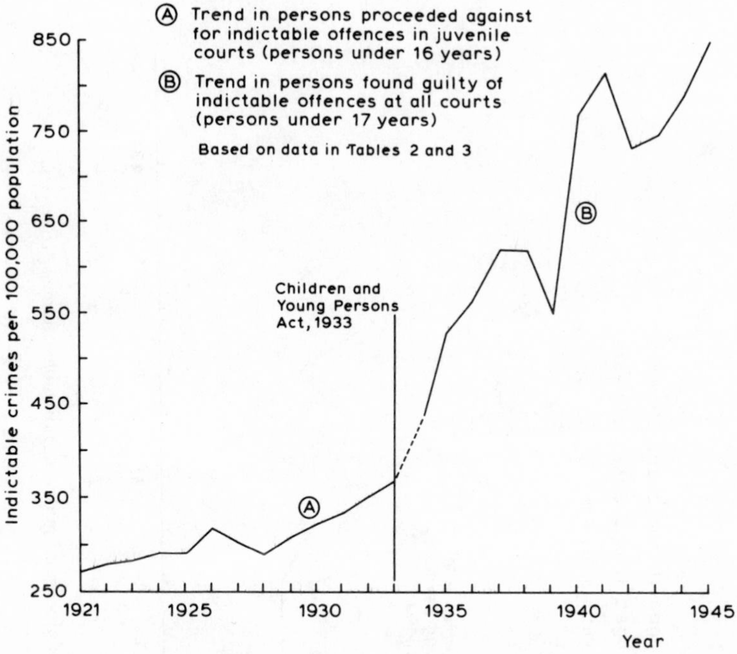

Fig. 1. Trend in children and young persons dealt with by the courts, 1921–1945.

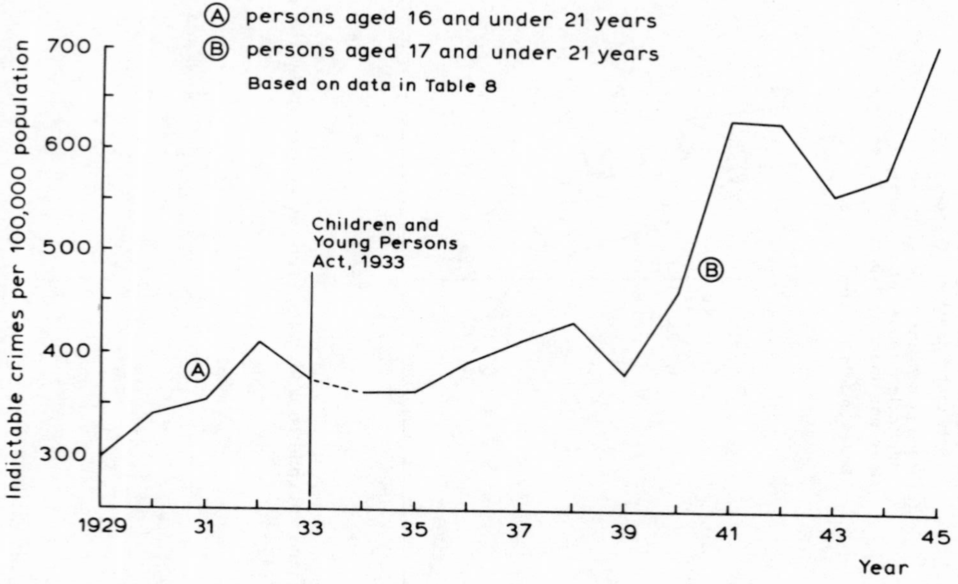

Fig. 2. Trend in young adults found guilty of indictable offences, 1929–1945.

Chronological Chart

1907	Probation of Offenders Act
1908	Children Act
	Prevention of Crime Act
1912	National Association of Probation Officers founded
1913	Charles Russell appointed Chief Inspector of Reformatory and Industrial Schools
	William Clarke Hall made a Metropolitan Police Magistrate
1914	Criminal Justice Administration Act
	Children's Branch of Home Office set up
1916	Juvenile Organisations Committee appointed
1917	A. H. Norris appointed Chief Inspector of Reformatory and Industrial Schools
1919	Sydney Harris appointed Assistant Secretary in charge of the Children's Branch
	Edward Shortt (Coalition) appointed Home Secretary
1920	Magistrates Association founded
1921	Howard League founded
	Portland Borstal opened
1922	Maurice Waller appointed Chairman of Prison Commissioners
	Alexander Paterson made a Prison Commissioner
	Sir John Anderson appointed Permanent Under-Secretary of State
	Departmental Committee on the Training, Appointment and Payment of Probation Officers appointed (Baird Committee)
1923	Wandsworth boys' prison opened
1924	Arthur Henderson (Labour) appointed Home Secretary
	Sir William Joynson-Hicks (Conservative) appointed Home Secretary
1925	Criminal Justice Act
	Cyril Burt's *The Young Delinquent* published
1927	Departmental Committee on the Treatment of Young Offenders reported (Molony Committee)

1928	Alexander Maxwell appointed Chairman of Prison Commissioners
1929	J. R. Clynes (Labour) appointed Home Secretary
1930	4–13 May, March to Lowdham Grange Borstal, led by W. Llewellin
1931	Sir Herbert Samuel (Coalition) appointed Home Secretary
	Boys' prison transferred from Wandsworth to Wormwood Scrubs
1932	Harold Scott appointed Chairman of Prison Commissioners
	Alexander Maxwell appointed Deputy Under-Secretary of State
	Sir Robert Russell Scott appointed Permanent Under-Secretary of State
1933	Children and Young Persons Act
1934	Departmental Committee on the Employment of Prisoners (Salmon Committee)
1935	North Sea Camp Borstal opened
	Sir John Simon (Coalition) appointed Home Secretary
1936	Departmental Committee on the Social Services in Courts of Summary Jurisdiction reported (Harris Committee)
	Age limit for Borstal increased from twenty-one to twenty-three years
1937	Sir Samuel Hoare (Coalition) appointed Home Secretary
1938	Criminal Justice Bill
	Departmental Committee on Corporal Punishment reported (Cadogan Committee)
	Sir Alexander Maxwell appointed Permanent Under-Secretary of State
	Hollesley Bay Colony (Borstal) opened
1939	Usk Borstal opened
	Mass discharge of all Borstal boys who had served six months
1940	Herbert Morrison (Coalition) appointed Home Secretary
1942	Lionel Fox appointed Chairman of Prison Commissioners
1944	Advisory Council on the Treatment of Offenders set up
1945	James Chuter Ede (Labour) appointed Home Secretary
1947	Alexander Paterson died
1948	Criminal Justice Act

Select Bibliography

Note: All references cited were published in London unless otherwise stated.

ARCHIVE COLLECTIONS

Bodleian Library, Oxford

Papers of Sir John Simon.

Cambridge University Library

Papers of Viscount Templewood (Sir Samuel Hoare).

Home Office Library, London

Minutes of Evidence to the Departmental Committee on the Treatment of Young Offenders, 1925–6.

Minutes of Evidence to the Departmental Committee on the Social Services of Courts of Summary Jurisdiction, 1935–6.

Minutes of Evidence to the Departmental Committee on Corporal Punishment, 1938.

First Report on the Work of the Children's Branch (1923).

Second Report on the Work of the Children's Branch (1924).

Third Report on the Work of the Children's Branch (1925).

Fourth Report on the Work of the Children's Branch (1928).

Fifth Report on the Work of the Children's Branch (1938).

Sixth Report on the Work of the Children's Department (1951).

The Principles of the Borstal System (1932).

Prisons and Borstals (1945).

Making Citizens. A review of the Aims, Methods, and Achievements of the Approved Schools in England and Wales (1946).

Borstal Association, *Minutes of Executive Committee Meetings*, 1914–39.

Annual Reports of the Borstal Association, 1924–39.

Annual Reports of the Howard League, 1924–39.

Lowdham Grange Borstal Institution

Governor's Journal.
Governor's Order Book.

Revd R. R. Maxwell, Canterbury, Kent

Papers of Sir Alexander Maxwell.

Modern Records Centre, University of Warwick

Howard League Minute Books.

North Sea Camp Detention Centre

Governor's Journal.

K. J. Neale, Home Office, London

Papers of Sir Alexander Paterson.

Public Record Office, London

CAB 23, 24, 25, 65, 129 and 132
Ed. 24
HO 45
HO 144 (seen with Home Office permission)
LCO 2
P. Com. 7 and 9

PARLIAMENTARY PAPERS

Annual Reports of the Prison Commissioners, 1908–48.
Annual Criminal Statistics, 1914–48.
PP 1913, XXXIX (Cmd. 6838): *Report of the Departmental Committee on Reformatories and Industrial Schools.*
PP 1921, X: *Report of the Indian Jails Committee, 1919–20.*
PP 1922, X (Cmd. 1601): *Report of the Departmental Committee on the Training, Appointment and Payment of Probation Officers.*
PP 1924–5, XV (Cmd. 2561): *Report of the Departmental Committee on Sexual Offences against Young Persons.*
PP 1927, XII (Cmd. 2831): *Report of the Departmental Committee on the Treatment of Young Offenders.*
PP 1933–4, XV (Cmd. 4462): *Report of the Departmental Committee on the Employment of Prisoners.*
PP 1935–6, VIII (Cmd. 5122): *Report of the Departmental Committee on the Social Services of Courts of Summary Jurisdiction.*

PP 1937–8, IX (Cmd. 5684): *Report of the Departmental Committee on Corporal Punishment.*

PP 1944–5, V (Cmd. 6594): *Report of the Committee of Inquiry on the London County Council Remand Homes.*

NEWSPAPERS AND SPECIALIZED PERIODICALS

Approved Schools Gazette
The Boy
British Medical Journal
Child
Daily Express
Daily Herald
Daily Mail
Daily News
Daily Telegraph
Economist
Education
Eugenics Review
Evening Standard
Friends' Quarterly Examiner
Hansard Parliamentary Debates
Howard Journal
Humanist
John Bull
Journal of Education
Justice of the Peace
Lancet
Law Journal
Law Times
Listener
Magistrate
Manchester Guardian
Nature
New Statesman
News of the World
Observer
Penal Reformer
Police Chronicle
Police Review
Prison Service Journal
Probation
Reynolds News
Seeking and Saving
Spectator
Sunday Times
The Times
Times Educational Supplement
Year Book of Education

CONTEMPORARY BOOKS, REPORTS, ARTICLES AND PAMPHLETS

Adler, N., 'Probation in the Courts', *Journal of Comparative Legislation and International Law*, vol. 17 (1935).

Bagot, J. H., *Juvenile Delinquency: A Comparative Study of the Position in Liverpool and England and Wales* (1941).

Barman, S., *The English Borstal System* (1934).

Barnett House Study Group, *London Children in War-Time Oxford* (Oxford, 1947).

Barnett, M., *Young Delinquents* (1913).

Baron, B., *The Growing Generation, a Study of Working Boys and Girls in our Cities* (Edinburgh, 1912).

Bazeley, E. T., *Homer Lane and the Little Commonwealth* (1928).

Benney, M., *Low Company* (1936).

Benson, G. and Glover, E., *Corporal Punishment: An Indictment* (1931).

Blake, W., *Quod* (1928).

Board of Education, *Report by the Juvenile Organisations Committee on Juvenile Delinquency* (1920).

Bowlby, J., *Forty-Four Juvenile Thieves: Their Characters and Home-Life* (1946).

Bray, R. A., *The Town Child* (1907).

—, *Boy Labour and Apprenticeship* (1911).

Briggs, I. G., *Reformatory Reform* (1924).

Brockway, F., *A New Way with Crime* (1928).

Brown, S. C., 'The Methods of Social Case Workers', in F. C. Bartlett *et al., The Study of Society* (1939).

Burt, C., 'The Causal Factors of Juvenile Crime', *British Journal of Medical Psychology*, vol. III (1923).

—, *Psychology of the Young Criminal*, Howard League Pamphlet, 4 (1924).

—, 'The Delinquent Child', *Child*, vol. XVI (1926).

—, *The Young Delinquent*, 2nd edn. (1927); first printed 1925.

—, 'The Psychology of the Bad Child', *Listener* 6 Feb. (1929).

—, *The Subnormal Mind* (1935).

—, 'An Autobiographical Sketch', *Occupational Psychology*, vol. XXIII (1949).

Cadbury, G., *Young Offenders Yesterday and To-Day* (1938).

Cadogan, E., *The Roots of Evil* (1937).

Cape, C. T., 'Administrative and other Experiences of a Borstal Governor', *Public Administration*, vol. 19 (1941).

Carr-Saunders, A. M., 'Crime and Unemployment', *Political Quarterly*, vol. V (1934).

Carr-Saunders, A. M., *et al., Young Offenders. An Enquiry into Juvenile Delinquency* (Cambridge, 1942).

Chapman, C., *The Poor Man's Court of Justice* (1925).

Chinn, W. L., 'A Brief Survey of Nearly One Thousand Juvenile Delinquents', *British Journal of Educational Psychology*, vol. VIII (1938).

City of Birmingham Education Committee, *Report of the Chief Education Officer on an Investigation into the Causes of the Increase of Juvenile Delinquency in the City* (1935).

Clynes, J. R., *Memoirs*, two volumes (1937).

Conservative Party, *Youth Astray* (1946).

Courtney, J., 'Children's Courts', *Fortnightly Review*, vol. 127 (1927).

D'Aeth, F., *The Juvenile Adult Problem* (1916).

David, J., 'Education and the Criminal Justice Bill', *Journal of Education*, vol. 71 (1939).

Dent, H. C., ' "Deprived Children" and the Curtis Report', *Fortnightly Review*, vol. 166 (1946).

Department of Social Science, Liverpool University, *Youthful Lawbreakers. A study of juvenile delinquency in Liverpool* (Liverpool, 1948).

East, W. N. and Hubert, W. H. de B., *The Psychological Treatment of Crime* (1939).

East, W. N., *The Adolescent Criminal*, in collaboration with P. Stocks and H. T. P. Young (1942).

Ehrenwald, H. J., 'Delinquent Defectives', *Journal of Mental Science*, vol. XCI (1945).

Elkin, W. A., *English Juvenile Courts* (1938).

English Studies in Criminal Science, *Conviction and Probation* (1941).

Fortes, M., 'Notes on Juvenile Delinquency: II. Step-parenthood and Delinquency', *Sociological Review*, vol. 25 (1933).

Foulds, Graham, 'The Child–Family Relationship and the Frustration Types among Mental Defective Juvenile Delinquents', *British Journal of Medical Psychology*, vol. XX (1945).

Freeman, A., *Boy Life and Labour* (1914).

Fry, M., 'The Penal Reform Bill', *Fortnightly Review*, vol. 151 (1939).

—, 'The Borstal System', in L. Radzinowicz and J. W. C. Turner (eds.), *Penal Reform in England*, English Studies in Criminal Science, vol. 1 (1946).

—, *Lawless Youth. A Challenge to the New Europe*, International Committee of Howard League for Penal Reform (1947).

—, 'The Criminal Justice Bill', *Political Quarterly*, vol. XIX (1948).

Glover, E., *Diagnosis and Treatment of Delinquency* (1944).

Godwin, G., 'War and Juvenile Delinquency', *Contemporary Review*, vol. 160 (1941).

Gordon, J. W., *Borstalians* (1932).

Gordon, M., *Penal Discipline* (1922).

Gordon, R. G., *Autolycus or the Future for Miscreant Youth* (1928).

Hall, G. S., *Adolescence*, two volumes (1908, first published 1904).

Hall, W. Clarke, 'The Aims and Work of the Children's Courts', *Child*, vol. XI (1921).

—, *Children's Courts* (1926).

—, 'The Extent and Practice of Probation in England', in Sheldon Glueck (ed.), *Probation and Criminal Justice. Essays in Honor of Herbert C. Parsons* (New York, 1974, first pub. 1933).

Harris, S. W., *Probation and other Social Work of the Courts* (1937).

Hatton, S. F., *London's Bad Boys* (1931).

Healy, W., *The Individual Delinquent* (1915).

Healy, W., and Alper, B. S., *Criminal Youth and the Borstal System* (1942).

Healy, W., and Bronner, A., *Delinquents and Criminals. Their Making and Unmaking* (New Jersey, 1969, first edn. 1926).

—, *New Light on Delinquency and its Treatment* (New Haven, 1936).

Henderson, Vivian, 'General Survey of Juvenile Delinquency', *The Year Book of Education 1936* (1936).

Henriques, B., 'The Child in Trouble', *Listener* (23 May 1934).

—, 'Boy Prisoners', *New Statesman* (13 Feb. 1937).

Hewart, G., *The Treatment of the Young Offender* (1935).

Hey, S., *Juvenile Crime* (1916).

Hobhouse, S., and Brockway, F., *English Prisons To-Day* (1922).

Howard League, *The Treatment of Young Offenders, Being the Report of a Representative Conference* (1929).

Isaacs, S., 'Cambridge Evacuation Survey', *Fortnightly Review*, vol. 153 (1940).

Jones, A. E., *Juvenile Delinquency and the Law* (Harmondsworth, 1945).

Leeson, C., *The Probation System* (1914).

—, *The Child and the War* (1917).

Le Mesurier, L., *Boys in Trouble* (1931).

—, *A Handbook of Probation and the Social Work of the Courts* (NAPO, 1935).

London County Council, *Report of the Education Officer on Juvenile Delinquency* (1937).

Lou, H., *Juvenile Courts in the United States* (Oxford, 1927).

Maberly, A., and Sturge, B., 'After-Results of Child Guidance. A Follow-Up of 500 Children Treated at the Tavistock Clinic, 1921–1934', *British Medical Journal* (3 June 1939).

Macadam, E., *The Equipment of the Social Worker* (1925).

—, *The New Philanthropy—A Study in the Relations between the Statutory and Voluntary Social Services* (1934).

MacCalman, D., 'The Present Status and Functions of the Child-Guidance Movement in Great Britain, and its Possible Future Developments', *Journal of Mental Science*, vol. LXXXV (1939).

Mannheim, H., *The Dilemma of Penal Reform* (1939).

—, *Social Aspects of Crime in England Between the Wars* (1940).

—, *War and Crime* (1941).

—, 'Some Reflections on Crime in War-Time', *Fortnightly Review*, vol. 157 (1942).

—, 'The Criminal Justice Bill', *Fortnightly Review*, vol. 163 (1948).

—, *Juvenile Delinquency in an English Middletown* (1948).

—, *Criminal Justice and Social Reconstruction* (1949, 2nd impression).

Masterman, L., 'Y.P.s', *Contemporary Review*, vol. 135 (1929).

Maxwell, A., *Treatment of Crime* (1938).

Morgan, A. E., *The Needs of Youth* (Oxford, 1939).

Moseley, S., *The Truth About Borstal* (1926).

Mullins, C., 'Probation', *Quarterly Review*, vol. 268 (1937).

Owens, T. Paterson, 'Approved Schools and Remand Homes', *Medico-Legal and Criminological Review*, vol. XIV (1946).

Page, L., 'The Child and the Law', *Contemporary Review*, vol. 149 (1936).

Page, L., *Justice of the Peace* (1936).
—, *Crime and the Community* (1937).
Paterson, Alexander, 'Children and the Child', *Fratres*, vol. VII (Dec. 1907).
—, 'The Mission and its Work', *Annual Report of the Oxford Medical Mission* (1908).
—, *Across the Bridges or Life by the South London River-Side* (1911, new edn. 1912).
—, 'Youth and Crime', *Listener* (13 April 1932).
Paterson, Arthur, *Our Prisons* (1911).
Penal Reform League, *A National Minimum for Youth* (1917).
Potts, W. A., 'The Treatment of Delinquents', *Child Study Society Journal*, vol. 1 (1921–2).
Rhodes, E. C., 'Juvenile Delinquency', *Journal of the Royal Statistical Society*, vol. 102 (1939).
Rodger, A., *A Borstal Experiment in Vocational Guidance* (1937).
Ruck, S. K., 'The Increase of Crime in England', *Political Quarterly*, vol. III (1932).
—, 'The Need for the Criminal Justice Bill. A Factual Study', *Political Quarterly*, vol. X (1939).
Ruggles-Brise, E., *The English Prison System* (1921).
Russell, C. E. B., *Young Gaol-Birds* (1910).
—, *Manchester Boys* (1913, 2nd edn.).
—, *Social Problems of the North* (1913).
—, *The Problem of Juvenile Crime* (Oxford, 1917).
Russell, C. E. B., and Rigby, L. M., *The Making of the Criminal* (1906).
—, *Working Lads' Clubs* (1908).
Scottish National Council of Juvenile Organisations, *Report of an Enquiry into Juvenile Delinquency* (Edinburgh, 1923).
Smith, M. H., *The Psychology of the Criminal* (1922).
Spielman, M. A., *The Romance of Child Reclamation* (1920).
Stephen, H., 'Young Offenders', *Edinburgh Review*, vol. 246 (1927).
Stephens, R. T., 'The Borstal System', *Nineteenth Century*, vol. 121 (1937).
Titmuss, Richard, M., *Problems of Social Policy*, W. K. Hancock (ed.), History of the Second World War; United Kingdom Civil Series (1950).
Urwick, E. J. (ed.), *Studies of Boy Life in Our Cities* (1904).
Waddy, H. T., *The Police Court and its Work* (1925).
Watson, J. A. F., 'The War and the Young Offender', *Fortnightly Review*, vol. 157 (1942).
—, *The Child and the Magistrate* (1945, 5th impression).
—, 'The Child and the Aftermath of War', *Fortnightly Review*, vol. 167 (1947).
Weatherly, L. A., 'Juvenile Psychological Delinquents', *Transactions of the Medico-Legal Society*, vol. XXIII (1928–29).
Willcock, H. D., *Mass Observation Report on Juvenile Delinquency* (1949).

Williamson, C., 'The Origin and Cure of "The Bad Boy"', *Sociological Review*, vol. XII (1920).

SECONDARY SOURCES

Abel-Smith, B., and Stevens, R., *Lawyers and the Courts* (1967).
Addison, P., *The Road to 1945* (1982, reprinted).
Advisory Council on the Penal System, *Young Adult Offenders* (1974).
Ashdown, M., and Brown, S. C., *Social Service and Mental Health* (1953).
Attlee, C. R., *As It Happened* (New York, 1954).
Bailey, V., 'Scouting for Empire', *History Today* (July 1982).
—, 'Bibles and Dummy Rifles: The Boys' Brigade', *History Today* (Oct. 1983).
—, 'Churchill as Home Secretary: Prison Reform', *History Today* (Mar. 1985).
Baron, B., 'Across the Bridges. In Memory of Alec Paterson', *Toc H Journal*, vol. XXVI (Jan. 1948).
—, *The Doctor: The Story of John Stansfeld of Oxford and Bermondsey* (1952).
Behan, B., *Borstal Boy* (New York, 1970, 5th printing).
Bellamy, J., and Saville, J., *Dictionary of Labour Biography*, Vol. VII (1984).
Bochel, D., *Probation and After-Care. Its Development in England and Wales* (Edinburgh, 1976).
Bottoms, A. E., 'On the Decriminalization of English Juvenile Courts', in R. G. Hood (ed.), *Crime, Criminology and Public Policy* (1974).
Bowle, J., *Viscount Samuel. A Biography* (1957).
Bresler, F., *Lord Goddard* (1977).
Brown, S. C., 'Looking Backwards. Reminiscences: 1922–1946', *British Journal of Psychiatric Social Work*, vol. 10 (1970).
Butler, R. A., *The Art of the Possible. The Memoirs of Lord Butler* (1971).
Cambridge Department of Criminal Science, *The Results of Probation* (1958).
Cambridge Institute of Criminology, *Attendance Centres*, F. H. McClintock (1961).
Carlebach, J., *Caring for Children in Trouble* (1970).
Choppen, V., 'The Origins of the Philosophy of Detention Centres', *British Journal of Criminology*, vol. 10 (1970).
Chorley, Lord, 'Hermann Mannheim', *British Journal of Criminology*, vol. 10 (1970).
Christophe, J., *Capital Punishment and British Politics* (1962).
Clarke, J., 'Social Democratic Delinquents and Fabian Families' in J. Clarke (ed.) *Permissiveness and Control* (National Deviancy Conference) (1980).
—, 'Managing the Delinquent: The Children's Branch of the Home Office, 1913–30,' in M. Langan and B. Schwarz (eds.), *Crises in the British State 1880–1930* (1985).
Clarke, P., *Liberals and Social Democrats* (Cambridge, 1978).
Croft, J., 'Hermann Mannheim—A Biographical Note', in T. Grygier *et al.*, (eds.), *Criminology in Transition. Essays in Honour of Hermann Mannheim* (1965).

Cross, C., *Philip Snowden* (1966).

Cross, J. A., *Sir Samuel Hoare. A Political Biography* (1977).

Cross, R., *Punishment, Prison and the Public* (1971).

Donoughue, B. and Jones, G. W., *Herbert Morrison. Portrait of a Politician* (1973).

Eagar, W. Mc G., *Making Men: The History of Boys' Clubs and Related Movements in Great Britain (1953)*.

Eastwood, G., *Harold Laski* (1977).

English Studies in Criminal Science, *Detention in Remand Homes* (1952).

Fox, L. W., *The Modern English Prison* (1934).

Fraser, D., *The Evolution of the British Welfare State* (1981).

Freeden, M., *The New Liberalism, an Ideology of Social Reform* (Oxford, 1978).

Garland, D., *Punishment and Welfare. A history of penal strategies* (Aldershot, 1985).

Gilbert, B., *The Evolution of National Insurance in Great Britain. The Origins of the Welfare State* (1966).

——, *British Social Policy 1914–1939* (1970).

Gillis, J. R., *Youth and History* (New York, 1974).

——, 'The Evolution of Juvenile Delinquency in England, 1890–1914', *Past and Present*, 67 (1975).

Gittins, J., *Approved School Boys* (1952).

Gore, E., *The Better Fight. The Story of Dame Lilian Barker* (1965).

Grunhut, M., *Penal Reform* (Oxford, 1948).

Hall, P., Land, H., Parker, R., and Webb, A., *Change, Choice and Conflict in Social Policy* (1975).

Hamilton, M. A., *Arthur Henderson* (1938).

Harris, J., *William Beveridge. A Biography* (Oxford, 1977).

Harris, K., *Attlee* (1982).

Hawkins, G., *Alec Paterson. An Appreciation* (privately printed).

Hay, J. R., *The Development of the British Welfare State 1880–1975* (1978).

Hearnshaw, L. S., *Cyril Burt. Psychologist* (1979).

Heywood, J. S., *Children in Care* (1959).

Hood, R. G., *Borstal Re-Assessed* (1965).

Humphries, S., *Hooligans or Rebels? An Oral History of Working-Class Childhood and Youth 1889–1939* (Oxford, 1981).

Jones, E. H., *Margery Fry* (1966).

Lawson, J., and Silver, H., *A Social History of Education in England* (1973).

Lees, R., 'Social Work, 1925–50: The Case for a Reappraisal', *British Journal of Social Work*, vol. 1 (1971).

Loewe, L. L., *Basil Henriques. A Portrait* (1976).

Lowson, D. M., *City Lads in Borstal* (Liverpool, 1970).

McClintock, F. H. and Avison, N. H., *Crime in England and Wales* (1968).

McWilliams, W., 'The Mission Transformed: Professionalism of Probation Between the Wars', *Howard Journal*, vol. 24 (1985).

Mangan, J. A., *Athleticism in the Victorian and Edwardian Public School* (Cambridge, 1981).
Mannheim, H., *Group Problems in Crime and Punishment* (1955).
Maxwell, A., *The Institutional Treatment of Delinquents* (1949).
—, 'Charles Russell', *The Boy*, vol. XXV (1952–3).
Maxwell, R. P., *Borstal and Better* (1956).
Mennel, R. A., *Thorns and Thistles. Juvenile Delinquents in the United States 1825–1940* (Hanover, New Hampshire, 1973).
Middleton, N., *When Family Failed: the Treatment of the Child in the Care of the Community in the First Half of the Twentieth Century* (1971).
Morgan, K. O., *Labour in Power, 1945–1951* (Oxford, 1984).
Morris, A., and McIsaac, M., *Juvenile Justice? The Practice of Social Welfare* (1978).
Newsam, F., *The Home Office* (1955).
Packman, J., *The Child's Generation. Child Care Policy from Curtis to Houghton* (Oxford, 1975).
Parker, R. A., 'The Gestation of Reform: The Children Act 1948', in P. Bean and S. MacPherson (eds.), *Approaches to Welfare* (1983).
Pearson, G., *Hooligan: A History of Respectable Fears* (1983).
Pellew, J., *The Home Office 1848–1914* (1982).
Pelling, H., *The Labour Governments, 1945–51* (1984).
Platt, A., *The Child Savers: The Invention of Delinquency* (Chicago, 1969).
Radzinowicz, L., 'After-Conduct of Convicted Offenders in England', L. Radzinowicz (ed.), *The Modern Approach to Criminal Law* (1945).
—, *Ideology and Crime* (1966).
Radzinowicz, L., and Turner, J. W. C. (eds.), *Mental Abnormality and Crime* (1944).
Reeder, D. A., 'Predicaments of City Children: Late Victorian and Edwardian Perspectives on Education and Urban Society', in D. A. Reeder (ed.), *Urban Education in the Nineteenth Century* (1977).
Richter, M., *The Politics of Conscience. T. H. Green and his Age* (1964).
Rose, G., *Five Hundred Borstal Boys* (Oxford, 1954).
—, 'Trends in the Development of Criminology in Britain', *British Journal of Sociology*, vol. 9 (1958).
—, *The Struggle for Penal Reform* (1961).
—, *Schools for Young Offenders* (1967).
Ruck, S. K. (ed.), *Paterson on Prisons* (1951).
Rutter, M., and Giller, H., *Juvenile Delinquency. Trends and Perspectives* (Harmondsworth, 1983).
Ryan, M., *The Acceptable Pressure Group* (Farnborough, 1978).
Samuel, H., *Memoirs* (1945).
Schlossman, S., 'G. Stanley Hall and the Boys' Club: Conservative Applications of Recapitulation Theory', *Journal of the History of the Behavioural Sciences*, vol. IX, (1973).

Scott, H., *Your Obedient Servant* (1959).
Simon, B., *Education and the Labour Movement, 1870–1920* (1965).
Smith, Ann D., *Women in Prison* (1962).
Smithies, E., *Crime in Wartime* (1982).
Springhall, J., *Youth, Empire and Society. British Youth Movements 1883–1940* (1977).
—, 'The Origins of Adolescence', *Youth and Policy*, vol. 2 (1983–4).
Stevenson, J. (ed.), *Social Conditions in Britain between the Wars* (Harmondsworth, 1977).
Stratta, E., *The Education of Borstal Boys* (1970).
Taylor, H. A., *Jix: Viscount Brentford* (1933).
Taylor, I., *Law and Order. Arguments for Socialism* (1981).
—, 'Social Democracy and the Crime Question in Britain, 1945 to 1980' (Ph.D. Thesis, University of Sheffield, 1981).
Templewood, Viscount, *Nine Troubled Years* (1954).
Vidler, J., *If Freedom Fail* (1964).
Walker, N., 'Crime and Penal Measures', A. H. Halsey (ed.), *Trends in British Society since 1900* (1972).
—, (ed.), *Penal Policy-Making in England* (Cambridge, 1977).
Walker, N., and McCabe, S., *Crime and Insanity in England*, vol. 2 (Edinburgh, 1973).
Walton, R. G., *Women in Social Work* (1975).
Wheeler-Bennett, J., *John Anderson. Viscount Waverley* (1962).
Whitney, J., *Geraldine S. Cadbury 1865–1941* (1948).
Woodroofe, K., *From Charity to Social Work in England and the United States* (1968; first published 1962).
Wootton, B., *Social Science and Social Pathology* (1967).

Index